The Green Economy in t...

Filling a void in academic and policy-relevant literature on the topic of the green economy in the Arabian Gulf, this edited volume provides a multidisciplinary analysis of the key themes and challenges relating to the green economy in the region, including in the energy and water sectors and the urban environment, as well as with respect to cross-cutting issues, such as labour, intellectual property and South-South cooperation.

Over the course of the book, academics and practitioners from various fields demonstrate why transitioning into a 'green economy' – a future economy based on environmental sustainability, social equity and improved well-being – is not an option but a necessity for the Gulf Cooperation Council (GCC) states. Through chapters covering key economic sectors and cross-cutting issues, the book examines the GCC states' quest to align their economies and economic development with the imperatives of environmental sustainability and social welfare, and proposes a way forward, based on lessons learned from experiences in the region and beyond.

This volume will be of great relevance to scholars and policymakers with an interest in environmental economies and policy.

Mohamed Abdel Raouf is Research Fellow of the Environmental Research Programme at the Gulf Research Center, Saudi Arabia/Egypt.

Mari Luomi is Research Associate at the Oxford Institute for Energy Studies, UK.

Routledge Explorations in Environmental Studies

The Green Economy in the Gulf

Edited by
Mohamed Abdel Raouf and Mari Luomi

Routledge
Taylor & Francis Group

LONDON AND NEW YORK

from Routledge

Gulf Research Centre Cambridge
Knowledge for All

First published 2016 by Routledge

2 Park Square, Milton Park, Abingdon, Oxon OX14 4RN
711 Third Avenue, New York, NY 10017, USA

Routledge is an imprint of the Taylor & Francis Group, an informa business

First issued in paperback 2017

British Library Cataloguing in Publication Data
A catalogue record for this book is available from the British Library

Library of Congress Cataloguing in Publication data
A catalog record has been requested for this book.

ISBN: 978-1-138-92742-1 (hbk)
ISBN: 978-1-138-89475-4 (pbk)

Typeset in Goudy
by Out of House Publishing

Contents

Figures

Tables

Contributors

Ibrahim Abdel Gelil is Professor Emeritus of Sheikh Zayed Bin Sultan Al Nahyan Chair in Environmental Management at the Arabian Gulf University (AGU) in Bahrain. His professional experience has involved work in government, industry and academia. Prior to his appointment at AGU, Dr Abdel Gelil served as the Chief Executive Officer of the Egyptian Environmental Affairs Agency (EEAA) from 1997 until 2002; and the Chairman of Board of the Organization for Energy Conservation and Planning (OECP) from 1994 to 1997. He also served as a Research Fellow at the Natural Resources Department of Cornell University, and Visiting Researcher at the Lawrence Berkeley Laboratory (LBL), CA, United States (US), in 1994.

Mohamed Abdel Raouf is Research Fellow at the Environment Research Program of the Gulf Research Center, and the Global Focal Point of the Science and Technology Major Group of the United Nations Environment Programme (UNEP). Dr Raouf holds a doctorate in Environmental Sciences (Environmental Economics) from the Ain-Shams University, Egypt, and has undergone advanced training in Environmental Management at the Augsburg University, Germany. Dr Raouf was the lead author for the Environmental Governance section of the West Asia chapter of UNEP's GEO-5 and 6 Reports. He is also a part-time lecturer in Environmental Accounting and Economics. He has published various policy papers on environmental issues in the MENA Region and authored three books: *Environment in the Age of Revolution* (Dar El-Maaref: 2014, Arabic); *Green Policy to Balance Energy and Environment Needs – the Case of the UAE* (The Emirates Center for Strategic Studies and Research: 2014, Arabic); and *Economic Instruments and Environmental Policy in the GCC Countries* (Gulf Research Center: 2007).

Ghada Abdulla is an Assistant Researcher at the Bahrain Center for Strategic International and Energy Studies. Her research focus is on the economics of the Gulf Cooperation Council countries. She holds a First Class Honours degree with distinction in Economics and Finance from the University of York, United Kingdom (UK).

Mushtaque Ahmed has a PhD degree in Water Resources from the Iowa State University, US. He joined Sultan Qaboos University (SQU), Oman in 1996 and has more than 30 years of experience in teaching and research at various levels. Presently, he is working as Associate Professor of the College of Agricultural and Marine Sciences at SQU. Prior to that, he worked for various organisations in Australia. His current research interests are biosaline agriculture, managed aquifer research, climate change and adaptability, etc. He has published more than 150 scientific papers in peer reviewed refereed journals, book chapters, conference proceedings and technical reports, as well as serving as editor of various publications.

Bandar Alhoweish[1] is an Energy Specialist in the Islamic Development Bank. He has held a PhD degree in Engineering and Applied Science from Aston University, Birmingham, UK, since March 2012. His research interests relate to the design of a sustainable electricity market in Saudi Arabia, design of government subsidy reform programmes, especially in the energy sector, and design of incentive programmes to promote an energy efficiency culture. He is also a member of the Consultative Group at the Saudi Arabian Energy Efficiency Center.

Salem Ali Al-Jabri is an Assistant Professor of Soil Physics in the Department of Soils, Water and Agricultural Engineering at Sultan Qaboos University, Oman. Dr Al-Jabri earned his PhD degree in Water Resources Management (specialisation in soil physics) in 2001 from the Iowa State University, US. Dr Al-Jabri's research interests comprise physical characterisation of field soils, numerical modelling of water movement and contaminants transport in soils, vadose zone hydrology and management of salt affected soils.

Arnd Bätzner has an educational background in piano, physics and railway engineering. He has held positions at Credit Suisse and Swiss International Air Lines. A Swiss Federal Institute of Technology Zurich (ETH) graduate with a passion for interdisciplinary questions in urbanism, he currently researches for his PhD thesis at the Institute for Systemic Management and Urban Governance of the University of St Gallen, Switzerland on the last-mile linkage role of elevated connectors in dense urban environments. Bätzner is a non-executive director at the nationwide Swiss car-sharing operator Mobility and a member of the Rail Transit Systems Committee of the Transportation Research Board (TRB), Washington D.C.

B. S. Choudri holds a PhD in Environmental Management and his special interests have been environmental management issues related to developmental activities, including global climate change. He is presently working as Senior Researcher with the Center for Environmental Studies and Research (CESAR) at Sultan Qaboos University, Oman. Dr Choudri has more than 15 years of experience in leading research projects and capacity-building activities in the area of environmental management at the national and international level.

---

[1] The views and opinions presented by the author in this volume are solely those of the author and do not necessarily reflect the view of the Islamic Development Bank.

Nihaya Khalaf has a Bachelor of Arts and a Master of Arts in Law from Mosul University in Iraq. She is a PhD candidate at Bangor University Law School and Lecturer in Law at Kirkuk University, Iraq, and an Associate Fellow of the Centre for Sustainable Development Law in Canada. Her academic research interests include international law of biodiversity, agricultural diversity, sustainable development, with special focus on the transition to a green economy.

Kishan Khoday[2] has been with the United Nations Development Programme (UNDP) for 15 years, as UNDP Sustainable Development Advisor and Deputy Coordinator for Natural Resources and Environment in Indonesia (1997–2005), UNDP Assistant Resident Representative and Team Leader for Energy & Environment in China (2005–2009) and UNDP Deputy Resident Representative in Saudi Arabia (2009–2013). Since 2013, he has served as UNDP Practice Leader for Environment & Energy and Team Leader for Climate Change, Energy and Disaster Risk Reduction in the Arab Region. Khoday has been a global CNN Principal Voice on climate change and energy, and has published widely on various aspects of the sustainable development agenda.

Mari Luomi specialises in the politics and political economy of natural resources and the environment. Currently, she is Research Associate at the Oxford Institute for Energy Studies, UK, and Writer and Thematic Expert on Climate Change and Sustainable Energy with the International Institute for Sustainable Development Reporting Services. She holds a PhD in Middle Eastern Studies from the School of Government and International Affairs from Durham University, UK. Dr Luomi's book *The Gulf Monarchies and Climate Change: Abu Dhabi and Qatar in an Era of Natural Unsustainability* (London: Hurst) came out in 2012, and she has published in numerous academic and peer-reviewed publications, including the *Journal of Arabian Studies* and *Middle East Policy*. Her previous positions include Post-Doctoral Fellow at Georgetown University, Researcher at the Finnish Institute of International Affairs, and Senior Researcher and Independent Advisor for the Qatari Government on international climate politics and environmental policy.

Tom S. H. Moerenhout is affiliated to the Geneva Graduate Institute of International and Development Studies and is Associate at the International Institute for Sustainable Development. Moerenhout is a political economy scholar working on the valuation of common goods and resources, in particular energy and water subsidies. He also specialises in international economic law. Besides research, he consults on specific country subsidy-reform strategies.

Chingiz Orujov[3] has, with over ten years of experience in the energy sector, diverse experience earned both in the private and the public sector. Before

[2] The opinions expressed are those solely of the author and do not necessarily represent those of the UNDP, the RIO+ Centre, the UN or its Member States.

[3] The views and opinions presented by the author in this volume are solely those of the author and do not necessarily reflect the view of the Islamic Development Bank.

joining the Islamic Development Bank in 2011, he served as Adviser at British Petroleum. Based in Jeddah, Saudi Arabia, he currently serves as Senior Energy Economist at the Islamic Development Bank where he has contributed to the development of the Bank's energy policy. Orujov has also contributed to the design and preparation of the Bank's Renewable Energy for Poverty Reduction (REPOR) initiative. He holds a Master of Science in Environmental Economics from the University of York, UK.

Amit A. Pandya is a lawyer in private practice who was until 2014 Chief of Staff at the US Department of Labor's International Labor Affairs Bureau. He has previously held positions as Counsel to Committees of the US House of Representatives, at the US Department of Defense, the US Agency for International Development and the US Department of State. His work has focused on the Arab region and Asia. He is the author of studies on Islam and on maritime commerce and security, co-author of studies on environmental change and scientific cooperation, and editor of collections of essays on climate change, water, coastal zones, Islam and politics, migration and natural resource exploitation. He holds degrees from Oxford, Yale and the University of Pennsylvania.

Leisa Perch[4] is a Policy Specialist for the UNDP at the World Centre for Sustainable Development (RIO+ Centre) in Rio de Janeiro, Brazil, where she leads applied research on climate change, natural resource management and sustainable development. A development specialist for more than 15 years, she has set up and led the Rural and Sustainable Development Cluster at the International Policy Centre for Inclusive Growth in Brasília, Brazil, and contributed to the Barbados Sustainable Development Policy. She is a Lead Author for Chapter 13 (Poverty and Livelihoods) of the Working Group II contribution to the Fifth Assessment Report of the Intergovernmental Panel on Climate Change.

Tim Scott[5] serves with the UNDP in New York as a Policy Advisor on environment and as Green Economy Programme Manager of the Bureau of Development Policy's Environmental Mainstreaming Team. He has worked for more than 15 years with the United Nations, as well as with the public sector and civil society on issues of sustainable development and the intersection between environmental sustainability, economic growth and social progress. Scott's previous United Nations assignments have included a focus on green economy (2012–2014), climate change (2011–2012), human development reports (2004–2011), the Millennium Development Goals and economic management (2001–2004).

---

[4] The opinions expressed are those solely of the author and do not necessarily represent those of the UNDP, the RIO+ Centre, the UN or its Member States.

[5] The opinions expressed are those solely of the author and do not necessarily represent those of the UNDP, the RIO+ Centre, the UN or its Member States.

Christopher Silva is the Assistant Director of Housing Services at Qatar Foundation's Hamad bin Khalifa University, Qatar, where his team operates 12 Leadership in Energy and Environmental Design (LEED) Platinum buildings in Doha, Qatar. He previously served as the Sustainability Education Coordinator for Qatar Foundation. Silva earned a Master's degree in Sustainability & Environmental Management from Harvard University, US, and is a LEED Accredited Professional.

Kristin Sparding[6] is a civil servant with the US Department of Labor, where she currently works at the Office of International Relations of the International Labor Affairs Bureau. Her portfolio includes labour and employment issues in Europe and Eurasia, the International Labour Organization, and addressing sustainable development and social protection issues in multilateral fora. A native of Wisconsin, Sparding received a Bachelor of Arts in international affairs and German from Marquette University in Milwaukee, US, and a Master of Arts in International Relations from the Maxwell School of Syracuse University, US.

---

[6] The author writes in her personal capacity only, and the views expressed do not necessarily reflect the views of the United States Department of Labor or the International Labor Affairs Bureau.

Foreword

I am truly delighted to see that Dr Mohamed Abdel Raouf and Dr Mari Luomi have authored this extremely important volume entitled *The Green Economy in the Gulf*. There are a large number of reasons why this book can have a profound impact on thinking by policy makers in the Gulf region itself as well as others round the world in relation to their research on the nations of the Gulf. The entire Gulf region is extremely vulnerable to the impacts of climate change, particularly in respect of sea level rise, increase in the intensity and frequency of heat waves and extreme precipitation events, impacts on food production and marine resources as well as marine ecosystems. It is, therefore, essential that the unchecked increase in consumption of fossil fuels in the Gulf region be moderated through a set of policies that recognise the scarcity of these resources and reflect their real value. There are projections for oil consumption, for instance, which show some of the current exporters of hydrocarbons possibly becoming importers over a period of time. Rational pricing of petroleum products in these countries would extend the life of their recoverable reserves and thereby provide significant economic benefits. Also, given the vulnerability of the region to the impacts of climate change the leaders of the nations in the Gulf would undoubtedly want to be a part of the solution when it comes to dealing with the challenge of climate change.

In my discussions with the leadership of several countries in the region I have always emphasised two important issues. First, those countries which are currently major exporters of hydrocarbons have the benefit of large-scale revenues which need not be frittered away in current consumption, but which, for the benefit of the societies involved in the region, should be invested in creating options by which the region can remain a major exporter of energy. As it happens, the Gulf region has a vast area of land and abundant sunshine, with insolation levels that would make the development and use of solar energy technologies particularly attractive. It is, therefore, entirely feasible to see that over a period of time export of hydrocarbons would give way to export of renewable energy. There is, for instance, the vision of the Desertec project in North Africa where it is conceptualised that solar energy would be produced and supplied to Southern Europe from the states of North Africa. Such a concept should be explored in the Gulf region as well, because that would make it possible not only to export energy to neighbouring regions but also for attracting energy-intensive industries to locate in these countries with the prospect of assured supply of renewable energy well into the future.

The second point that I always make to policy makers in the region is for them to develop a vision by which agriculture and plant based products can be promoted over time. This, of course, would require a sustained effort to improve soil quality through a progressive programme of plantation by which, through successive phases, the topsoil quality can be enriched with dropping of leaves from successive types of plants into the soil, thus using nature to bring about an enrichment of the soil in these nations. Such a programme would have to be a central part of development policy and investment planning. In fact, I have been exhorting the oil exporting nations to 'convert your oil wealth into soil wealth'. Essentially, this would require a vision that looks into the decades ahead, which is what this book is all about.

What is particularly noteworthy about this publication is its down to earth practical orientation which takes into account barriers to greening the energy sector, the needs for pricing reform and strategies for improving energy efficiency and promoting renewable energy on a large scale. The emphasis on green buildings is also particularly relevant. With the massive construction which has taken place in the region and prospects for growth in the future, buildings cannot be locked into an energy-intensive pattern and design. Experience elsewhere has clearly shown that green buildings which demonstrated high efficiency in the use of energy, water and other resources can be an economically viable proposition. My institute, TERI, has been a pioneer in this field in India, and is a humble reflection of Gandhiji's advice to 'be the change you want to see in the world'. The buildings that TERI constructs for itself set a benchmark in energy efficiency. Our major training complex RETREAT, which is on the outskirts of Delhi, uses no power from the grid, and yet we actually save money on this complex, because the additional initial investment has been recovered in a very short period of time providing an extremely attractive payback period.

This scholarly yet practical book by the authors really needs to be disseminated on a wide scale in the Gulf region, and I would go to the extent of suggesting that very simple outreach programmes on its major findings and directions should become an essential part of outreach that the authors may plan through films, TV and the print media. It is essential that through this valuable piece of work we bring about a change in mindsets and open the eyes of policy makers and decision makers on how it is totally possible for the economy of the region to become green and for prosperity to increase at the same time. The average reader would find this book a refreshing piece of knowledge which can bring about a change in the pattern of development in the Gulf for the benefit of not only the people of the region but the world as a whole.

Dr Rajendra K. Pachauri
Director-General of The Energy Resources Institute,
and former Chairman of the Intergovernmental
Panel on Climate Change

Acknowledgements

This volume is based on a selection of papers presented at the Green Economy in the Gulf Region workshop, which was held on 25–28 August 2014 at the University of Cambridge in the United Kingdom. The co-editors would like to extend a warm thank you to all participants of the workshop, totalling 19 scholars and practitioners specialising on the Gulf, who convened over three days to present academic papers and discuss the prospects of a green economy in the six Gulf Cooperation Council member states. The discussions held during the event greatly enriched the chapters of this volume, and also helped the co-editors and authors together define a number of overarching themes and challenges relating to the topic.

The co-editors are also deeply grateful to the organisers of the 2014 Gulf Research Meeting of the Gulf Research Centre Cambridge (GRCC), under the umbrella of which the workshop took place. In particular, we would like to thank Dr Abdulaziz Sager, Chairman and Founder of the Gulf Research Center (GRC), and Dr Christian Koch, Director of the GRC Foundation in Geneva, as well as Elsa Courdier at the GRC Foundation, Dr Oskar Ziemelis, Interim Director of the GRCC, and Sanya Kapasi at the GRC, for their tireless work and support.

It is our sincere wish that this volume will contribute to advancing a purposeful, facts-based and positively oriented debate on the future of the green economy in the fast-transforming Gulf states, which are increasingly exploring the opportunities and prerequisites for success and prosperity beyond the brown economy.

Dr Mohamed Abdel Raouf
Dr Mari Luomi
Cairo and Curitiba
January 2015

Abbreviations

ADNOC	Abu Dhabi National Oil Company
ATV	average thermal value
AUD	Australian dollar
AVF	average value of fuel input for generation of unit of electricity
BAU	business as usual
BREEAM	Building Research Establishment Environmental Assessment Methodology
BRICS	Brazil, Russia, India, China and South Africa
CAGR	compound annual growth rate
CBD	Convention on Biological Diversity
CCS	carbon capture and storage
CDM	Clean Development Mechanism of the Kyoto Protocol
CDR	carbon dioxide recovery
CFL	compact fluorescent lamp/light
$CO_2(e)$	carbon dioxide (equivalent)
CSP	concentrated solar power
DAC	Development Assistance Committee (OECD)
DMP	domestic market price
DSM	demand-side management
DWC	Dubai World Central – Al Maktoum International Airport
DXB	Dubai International Airport
ECF	energy contents of each fuel type
ECRA	Electricity and Co-Generation Regulatory Authority (Saudi Arabia)
ECSUE	economic cost of saved unit of electricity
EIA	United States Energy Information Administration
EOR	enhanced oil recovery
EPF	power generation by each fuel type
ESCO	energy service company
ESG	environmental, social, governance
EST	environmentally sound technology
EU	European Union

EUR	euro
EWA	Electricity and Water Authority (Bahrain)
FIT	feed-in tariff
GCC	Gulf Cooperation Council
GCCIA	Gulf Cooperation Council Interconnection Authority
GCF	Green Climate Fund
GDP	gross domestic product
GEF	Global Environment Facility (The)
GGFR	Global Gas Flaring Reduction Partnership
GGGI	Global Green Growth Institute
GHG	greenhouse gas
GHI	global horizontal irradiance
GNI	gross national income
GORD	Gulf Organization for Research and Development
GPIC	Gulf Petrochemical Industries Company
GRs	genetic resources
GSAS	Global Sustainability Assessment System
GW(h)	gigawatt (hour)
HFO	heavy fuel oil
IDAE	Instituto para la Diversificación y Ahorro de la Energía (Spanish Institute for Energy Diversification)
IEA	International Energy Agency
IFC	International Finance Corporation
ILC	International Labour Conference
ILO	International Labour Organization
IMF	International Monetary Fund
IPP	independent power producer
IPRs	intellectual property rights
IRENA	International Renewable Energy Agency
IsDB	Islamic Development Bank
ITPGR	International Treaty on Plant Genetic Resources for Food and Agriculture
IWRM	integrated water resources management
K.A.CARE	King Abdullah City for Atomic and Renewable Energy
KAHRAMAA	Qatar General Electricity and Water Corporation
KAUST	King Abdullah University of Science and Technology
KISR	Kuwait Institute for Scientific Research
kW(h)	kilowatt (hour)
LAS	League of Arab States
LDC	least developed country
LED	light-emitting diode
LEED	Leadership in Energy and Environmental Design
LNG	liquefied natural gas
MAR	managed aquifer recharge
(m)bpd	(million) barrels per day

MDGs	Millennium Development Goals
MENA	Middle East and North Africa
MEPS	Minimum Efficiency Performance Standard
(MM)Btu	(million) British thermal units
Mtoe	million tonne of oil equivalent
MW(h)	megawatt (hour)
NAMA	Nationally Appropriate Mitigation Action
NOC	national oil company
NOGA	National Oil and Gas Authority (Bahrain)
ODA	official development assistance
ODI	outward direct investment
OECD	Organisation for Economic Co-operation and Development
OFID	OPEC Fund for International Development
OPEC	Organization of the Petroleum Exporting Countries
PAEW	Public Authority for Electricity and Water (Oman)
PAGE	Partnership for Action on Green Economy
PGRFA	plant genetic resources for food and agriculture
PPP	public-private partnership
PRS	Pearl Rating System
PV	photovoltaic
QSAS	Qatar Sustainability Assessment System
R&D	research and development
Rio+20	United Nations Conference on Sustainable Development (UNCSD)
RRC	resource-rich country
RTA	Dubai Roads and Transport Authority
SCP	sustainable consumption and production
SDGs	Sustainable Development Goals
SEC	Saudi Electricity Company
SEEC	Saudi Energy Efficiency Center
SFD	Saudi Fund for Development
SOC	savings on capital investment
SR	Saudi riyal
SSC	South-South cooperation
TEEB	The Economics of Ecosystems and Biodiversity initiative
TK	traditional knowledge
toe	tonne of oil equivalent
TRIPs	Agreement on Trade-Related Aspects of Intellectual Property Rights
TW(h)	terawatt (hour)
TWW	treated wastewater
UAE	United Arab Emirates
UK	United Kingdom
UN	United Nations
UNDESA	United Nations Department of Economic and Social Affairs

UNDP	United Nations Development Programme
UNEP	United Nations Environment Programme
UNESCWA	United Nations Economic and Social Commission for Western Asia
UNFCCC	United Nations Framework Convention on Climate Change
UPOV	International Union for the Protection of New Varieties of Plants
US	United States of America
US(D)	United States dollar
VSFU	value of saved fuel per unit in power generation
WMP	world market price
WTO	World Trade Organization

Part I

Green economy and the Gulf

1 Introduction

Mohamed Abdel Raouf and Mari Luomi

For several decades now, the six member states of the Gulf Cooperation Council (GCC) – Bahrain, Kuwait, Saudi Arabia, Oman, Qatar and the United Arab Emirates (UAE) – have been financing their socioeconomic development with hydrocarbon exports. While their high reliance on external oil and natural gas revenues has exposed these countries to economic vulnerabilities, the revenues have also enabled the GCC states to build modern infrastructure, sustain high levels of welfare for their nationals, and exert regional and global influence through sovereign wealth and investments. Given their hydrocarbon wealth, the GCC states have built economies that are energy-intensive and rely on a comparative advantage of cheap energy. Similarly, they have allowed domestic energy prices to remain low, creating hard-to-rid patterns of overconsumption of fuels and utilities and locking in energy-intensive infrastructure and industries.

Over the past decades, with populations, economies and energy demand growing at fast rates, the GCC states have become increasingly aware of the need to work on the domestic side of the resource equation, in other words, improve energy efficiency and invest in cleaner and more sustainable sources of energy. At the same time, on the international side, they have felt threatened by the intensifying global efforts to shift from fossil fuels to a clean energy economy, which could have negative impacts on the mainstay of the GCC economies, oil exports (Luomi 2012a). The magnitude of these pressures and the sense of urgency created by them arguably constitute the clarion call for the Gulf decision-makers to finally make the difficult decisions required for transitioning to the much-spoken-of, but still elusive, post-oil era. At the same time, deep political economy and cultural challenges, namely the persistent rentier state structures and ruling bargains between governments and citizens that are based on a combination of fossil fuel revenue and post-traditional forms of government, still constitute enormous barriers for transitioning to an alternative, more sustainable system.

Taking bold and prompt measures to tackle the domestic resource use challenges and external oil export revenue dependence may constitute the GCC states' last chance to sustain their prosperity into the future. The time of 'brown' economies may be over much sooner than the world's top oil exporters are willing to admit. Amidst the ongoing global economic and environmental crises, an increasing number of citizens around the world in both developed and developing countries are reaching the conclusion that the current global economic development model has failed both people and nature. Since the financial crisis in 2008, discontent and demonstrations demanding a better quality of life, more social equity and environmental justice have taken place all around the world, from Occupy Wall Street in 2011 to the Arab uprisings, and from the Brazilian street protests in 2013 to the People's Climate March in New York in 2014. Much beyond merely a temporary complication, the entire 'system' – whether related to finance, climate, food, biodiversity or energy – seems to be in a crisis.

Increasing scientific evidence is emerging on the need to change course. In the case of climate change alone, if we are to stay below 2°C of global warming, at current rates of greenhouse gas (GHG) emissions humanity's remaining carbon budget might be exhausted in less than three decades (Levin 2013). This means that global emissions should start peaking soon – something current policies and targets globally do not yet reflect. At an accelerating pace, humans are crossing the 'planetary boundaries' that define our safe global operating space. According to scientists, we have already crossed these boundaries for climate change, biodiversity loss and interference with the nitrogen cycle, and are heading towards the Earth's limits for ocean acidification, freshwater use, changes in land use, and interference with the phosphorus cycle (Rockström et al. 2009).

These crises and the mounting scientific evidence have also had an impact on the global development agenda. At all levels, organisations involved in international development are engaging in a global rethink on the current models of development and doing business. One of the key concepts framing this debate has been the 'green economy'. Emerging from the 2008 economic crisis, the green economy, in the context of sustainable development and poverty eradication, has been actively promoted by a number of United Nations (UN) agencies, as well as governments around the world, and has figured among the central themes in discussions around the post-2015 development agenda, stirring a lot of debate but also a rapidly increasing amount of plans and actions.

Reflecting the diversity of the world we live in, and the uniqueness of each country's national circumstances and development priorities, there is no single model or a pathway to the green economy. However, for all countries, shifting to a green economy – one that sets the economy at the centre of generating sustainable development – will require major economy-wide structural and technological changes, or at least the 'greening' of key sectors, such as energy, urban infrastructure, transportation, industry and agriculture. It will also include 'greening' investments nationally and globally, generating 'green' jobs through new 'green' sectors, and supporting and facilitating 'green' trade internationally through national and international policies.

From a Gulf perspective, the key question that begs answering is: why should the GCC states embark on a transition to the green economy – and why should they do so at this point in time? More specifically: how could the GCC states benefit from the green economy, and what would the key cornerstones of such an economy be in a region that has a harsh climate, few other natural endowments than fossil fuels, and still struggles with numerous sustainable development challenges? Of course, there are a number of barriers and obstacles that need to be addressed before such a transition can take place. These are often linked to the broader socioeconomic context and therefore call for economy-wide solutions, such as energy subsidies for instance. At the same time, there are plenty of lessons the Gulf monarchies can learn from experience in green economy reforms accumulated in other countries.

This book is the collective attempt of a group of scholars and practitioners, coming together from around the world, to address these questions, and to examine how a green economy in the Gulf could look. The concept has sparked numerous debates and is currently inspiring an increasing number of countries in their quest for alternative development pathways. The green economy is something the GCC states simply cannot afford to ignore. It is hoped that this volume will similarly spark new discussions, and inspire policymakers and students of the six Gulf monarchies to look at the future of the GCC through the lens of the green economy.

The emergence of the green economy

Green economy, originally a concept of environmental economics focused on economic policy tools for fixing environmental problems, has over the past years become a key concept on the global sustainable development agenda. The concept was first mentioned in a British government-commissioned sustainable development report from 1989 written by three environmental economists (Pearce *et al.* 1989). However, it was only during the late 2000s' global economic crisis that green economy was brought to international attention as an economic recovery strategy focused on creating 'green jobs' and tackling climate change, promoted by a number of global leaders, including UN Secretary-General Ban Ki-moon and US President Barack Obama (Collina and Pott 2009; UN News Centre 2009). South Korea was the first country to declare 'Low Carbon Green Growth' as its long-term national development vision, in 2008 (Zelenovskaya 2012). A green economy, in its multiple meanings and uses, has since been advocated by numerous international institutions, including the UNEP, World Bank, International Energy Agency (IEA) and G8 and G20 meetings (ibid.). In 2012, signalling the broad attention the concept was receiving globally, the UN Conference on Sustainable Development (UNCSD), or 'Rio+20', debated 'a green economy in the context of sustainable development and poverty eradication' as one of its two main topics (Rio+20 2012).

The concept has not been embraced by all countries without criticism: the developing countries' G77 group has voiced several reservations on its implications for development (TWN 2012), and the Socialist countries of Latin America have referred to it as 'privatization, monetization and mercantilization of nature' (ALBA-TCP 2010). Even the GCC states have remained divided in international fora: whilst the UAE and Qatar have openly embraced the paradigm by joining the Korea-based Global Green Growth Institute (GGGI), Saudi Arabia has repeatedly voiced its scepticism about the approach (Saudi Arabia 2011).

Despite the hype around green economy in the run-up to the Rio+20 conference, owing to the political tensions around its use, the final outcome document 'The Future We Want' only mentions it as one important tool for achieving sustainable development, and focuses more on what green economy policies should and should not do, including: be consistent with international law, respect countries' sovereignty, avoid conditionalities on related finance, and not constitute restrictions on trade. Similarly to the concept of sustainable development, the lack of a common definition allows for both flexibility in its use, including tailoring the concept for the specific context of each country or sector, and confusion, as different actors tend to emphasise different aspects of it, such as environmental or social sustainability.

Importantly, many of the key themes of the green economy agenda, such as renewable energy and energy efficiency, have been openly embraced by the GCC and other states and that otherwise have condemned other aspects of the agenda. Sometimes attitudes have depended on the forum: for example, in the preparations for Rio+20, Saudi Arabia criticised the potential use of green economy policies as a guise for trade protectionism and potential negative effects on energy and food security, but participated shortly after in a G20 statement recognising the importance of the parallel concept of 'green growth' (*The Telegraph* 2012). Resulting from the contestation over the ultimate aims of the green economy agenda, a proposal containing 17 Sustainable Development Goals (SDGs), agreed upon by the UN General Assembly Open Working Group in July 2014 as a key contribution to the UN post-2015 development agenda, did not include any explicit reference to the green economy.

The various green agendas – defining the green economy

Given the concept's recent appearance on the international development agenda and the above-described international controversy, green economy (or growth) has no universally accepted definition. Perhaps the most commonly used definition is that of UNEP (2011, 16), which describes it as an economy that results in 'improved human well-being and social equity, while significantly reducing environmental risks and ecological scarcities'. This definition is the most common one used in this volume, and also one endorsed by the co-editors. Reflecting the fact that green economy does not seek to replace sustainable development, but is intended to serve as the tool for achieving it, the UNEP definition preserves the three dimensions of sustainable development (economic, environmental and social sustainability). The focus on the economy derives from the post-2008 realisation that 'achieving sustainability rests almost entirely on getting the economy right' (ibid., 17). As UNEP eloquently puts it, 'decades of creating new wealth through a "brown economy" model based on fossil fuels have not substantially addressed social marginalisation, environmental degradation and resource depletion' (ibid.). Neither have they provided real investment or green jobs. The UNEP definition encompasses all the above aspects.

Since the launch of the UNEP-led Green Economy Initiative in 2008, many related approaches, concepts and definitions have emerged, or been developed, in parallel. These include the low-carbon (or low-emission) development agenda, sustainable consumption and production (SCP), the circular economy, the ecological economy, green jobs and green growth. A low-carbon economy can be considered a key part of the green economy and is measured by the level of carbon dioxide (CO_2) or GHG emissions in relation to energy production or economic activities. SCP and its implementing 10-year framework of programmes, launched at Rio+20, represent another 'sub-agenda' of the green economy, the central aim of which is to 'do more and better with less', or reducing the use of resources and pollution along the entire life cycle of goods and services while generating new jobs and markets (UNEP-RONA 2014). A concept related to SCP is the circular economy, in which waste from production and consumption processes is circulated as a new input into the same or a different process. Stemming from the Earth's limits thinking, common to many conceptualisations of the green economy, is the ecological economy, in which the economy is subject to ecological principles, such as biodiversity conservation and respecting the Earth's carrying capacity.

Green jobs are commonly understood as jobs that reduce the environmental impact of enterprises and economic sectors, ultimately to levels that are sustainable. As per the definition of the UN Economic and Social Commission for Western Asia, in principle, any job can be 'greened'. Generally, these types of jobs also meet the criteria of 'decent work, adequate wages, safe conditions, workers' rights, social dialogue and social protection' (UNESCWA 2012). Green jobs are also seen as 'a real solution to not only environmental but also economic and social challenges, providing real income generation opportunities' (ibid.).

In addition, many other terms focus on specific aspects of the green economy such as human rights-based economy, holistic growth, inclusive, green and responsible economy, blue economy, de-globalisation, steady state economics (Daly 2005) and de-growth. The latter is very similar to the idea of *Alzohd*, or 'living lightly on Earth', which is rooted in the Islamic culture of the Arabian Gulf region. It simply means avoiding overconsumption in resource usage – extravagant food consumption, for example – and caring about nature and its resources. In other words, the idea recognises that adopting an eco-friendly lifestyle is not only a social responsibility, but also a religious duty as human existence and well-being are dependent on a healthy environment (Abdel Raouf 2010 and 2013).[1]

Green growth is perhaps the concept most closely related to that of the green economy, and is often used interchangeably with green economy. The GGGI's former Director-General has defined 'green growth' as low-carbon, sustainable development that builds on the synergies between economic growth and a 'better environment'. Its characteristics include efficiency and productivity of resource use, fostering of creativity and recognition of the 'planetary boundaries' (Bamsey

2013). Despite the similarities, there is arguably a clear difference between the two, as green economy can be understood as a governance process in all aspects of life of a society, aimed at shifting the whole society from a 'traditional' economy towards a greener one. Green growth, in turn, can be characterised as the increase in the quantity of the goods and services within the economy or specific sectors of that economy. This increase does not necessarily mean the whole economy is green. Another key difference is that, while the green economy comprises a top-down approach, encompassing the transformation of the entire economy, across sectors, green growth can be seen as a bottom-up activity, or measure of progress towards the green economy and may focus on specific sectors or industries of the economy.

Arguably, the main aims of the different green economy agendas, generally speaking, are the full incorporation of environmental and other external costs into the economy, and recognition of the value of natural capital in a way that benefits the economy, society and the environment (UNEP 2011, 18; World Bank 2012, 7). Despite an in-built consciousness of the system's physical limits, within the green economy paradigm, 'sustainable growth' is often considered as positive and possible, and hence not an oxymoron. In sustainable growth, the growth processes are responsibly oriented, and effectively prevent profit-making by companies that continue business-as-usual while merely greenwashing their products and services. Resource efficiency, low-carbon, environmental sustainability and quality of life figure as the core themes of the green economy/growth discourse, and commonly cited policy tools include (economic) incentives and changes in investment patterns and policy (Bowen 2012, 7–8, passim). In Middle East and North Africa (MENA) region-specific literature, the path to green economy has been described as consisting primarily of efforts to decouple economic growth and domestic energy demand and reduce per capita ecological footprints without impairing quality of life (Abdel Gelil et al. 2012, 77, 104).[2]

Greening the brown, growing the green

Despite the recent emergence of the concept on the international development agenda, policy guides for green economy and growth already abound, with a number of international agencies having launched their reports on the topic, including the UNEP, UN Conference on Trade and Development, UN Department of Economic and Social Affairs (UNDESA) and the UNCSD Secretariat (UN SD Knowledge Platform 2014). These policy-oriented manuals generally provide sector- and theme-based analyses and recommendations, including on energy, industry, cities and buildings, transport, waste, water, agriculture and tourism (UNEP 2011; Abaza et al. 2012; WAM 2012). UNEP (2011, 22) has proposed the following policy tools: 'changes to fiscal policy[;] reform and reduction of environmentally harmful subsidies; employing new market-based instruments; targeting public investments to green key sectors; greening public procurement; and improving environmental rules and regulations, as well as their enforcement'. Although framed as a strategy for SCP, a strategy document by the League of Arab States from 2009 prescribes similar policy interventions, namely: reforms in existing energy policies (subsidies, taxes and pricing); improving efficiency, particularly in energy-intensive industries, transport and power generation; promoting large-scale development of renewable energy technologies; and better urban planning for improved air quality (Abdel Gelil *et al.* 2012, 86–88).

Irrespective of the definition and specific approaches to greening the economy adopted, a number of common characteristics and principles are fundamental to achieving the required shift from the brown economy towards the green economy. First, a shift to the green economy requires a multidisciplinary, multi-stakeholder and multi-sectoral approach. For example, while a green economy agenda can be aimed at increasing investment in economic sectors like renewable energy, and sustainable agriculture, tourism, water management, at the same time, green transformations in these sectors should be intimately linked to poverty alleviation goals, and seek positive impacts on human and environmental health, employment and foreign trade.

The green transition has two equally important aspects: 'greening the brown' and 'growing the green'. In principle, all economic sectors can be 'greened', including through the introduction of clean, efficient and innovative technologies. For example, a country can address 'brown industry' and energy-intensive sectors such as cement or construction through new production technologies and more efficient materials. At the same time a country can seek to expand the green economy by developing new green economic sectors, such as renewable energy, energy services or sustainable construction. UNESCWA characterises the two kinds of drivers involved in these transitions as ones that exert a 'push' away from the brown economy through the adaptation of existing economic models, and those that have a 'pull' effect and incentivise participation in the new green sectors (UNESCWA 2013, 19).

Common characteristics of a green economy in any country include, among other things: a low-carbon energy mix; reduced pollution and GHG emissions; resource efficiency; and limited loss of biodiversity and ecosystem services. In terms of policy tools, a green economy is supported by the use of market-based instruments and reduced levels of harmful subsidies, and public investments that are targeted towards greening the economy. In addition, a green economy should be socially inclusive, and be underpinned by a value-based economy. In other words, the green economy aims to encourage new value-based growth by including more social and environmental considerations in the growth process. Of relevance for the GCC countries, it should be pointed out that many of these values are already part of local cultures in the Arab world (Abdel Raouf 2011a).

For measuring progress towards the green economy, new metrics are also required, which should be inclusive of environmental, social and economic aspects of progress. The realisation of the need to use indicators of development that go beyond GDP alone is a further central aspect of the green economy literature. As noted by the European Commission's 'Beyond GDP' project, 'economic indicators such as the gross domestic product (GDP) were never designed to be comprehensive measures of prosperity and well-being' (European Commission

2014). As our understanding of economics has evolved, it has become clear that the GDP, which was introduced over 50 years ago, is simply insufficient to provide a complete measure of a country's or an economy's level of development, prosperity and well-being. Innovative, new indicators are needed for addressing contemporary global challenges, ranging from climate change and resource depletion, to poverty, health and quality of life. Such indicators are essential for governments, policymakers and the private sector to improve their planning and make better development decisions. They can also provide support in the valuation of natural capital assets, calculation of environmental impact, and monitoring of human and environmental health (Abdel Raouf 2014).

Alternative indicators currently being developed include the Genuine Progress Indicator, a project of the US-based Center for Sustainable Economy and the Institute for Policy Studies, that builds on 26 indicators that seek to take into account the positive and negative externalities of economic growth and value quality of life (GPI 2014), and the Organisation for Economic Co-operation and Development's (OECD 2014) 'Better Life Index' that is based on 11 topics deemed essential for well-being in terms of material living conditions and quality of life. Importantly, in order for a green economy indicator to be useful it should be able to monitor and assess both capital assets (including natural and human) and human well-being.[3] Sometimes simple, existing metrics can be used: arguably, the economy of a country is moving in the right direction if there is an increase in green investment, quantity and quality of jobs in green sectors, and in the share of green sectors in GDP. At the same time, there should be a decrease in energy/resource use per unit of production as well as in CO_2 and pollution level/ GDP and wasteful consumption (Abdel Raouf 2010).

Furthermore, the green economy is based on various sustainability principles. Some of the principles present in relevant literature and discourse are the Earth integrity principle (every human has the duty to protect the Earth and its ecosystems), the polluter pays principle (polluters are responsible for the environmental damage they have caused), the dignity principle (every human has the right to livelihood), the justice principle (benefits and burdens should be shared fairly among all stakeholders), the resilience principle (diversity and diversification are preconditions for sustainability as well as quality of life) and the governance principle (establishment of policies, rules and regulations requires a transparent and participatory process that includes all affected people). Respecting the planetary boundaries (see above), or the limited nature of the Earth system, is a further key dimension.

The role of energy in the green economy transition in the Gulf

Perhaps more than in any other region, energy has a pivotal role in any kind of green transition in the GCC. Beyond its unsustainable dependence on fossil fuels, the states of the Arabian Gulf region are currently facing a number of sustainable development challenges, some of which are traditional and others new or emerging. Traditional challenges, which have persisted already for decades or more, include oil export dependency, water scarcity, natural disasters (such as sand storms and cyclones), biodiversity loss, food sovereignty and security issues, desertification, poverty (among migrant populations, in particular), high levels of migration and dependence on foreign labour, unemployment (among GCC nationals), regional instability, and challenges in the provision of health and education services. Among more recent, emerging challenges are the ongoing Arab Spring, the global financial crisis, climate change, waste (construction, household and hazardous) and, perhaps most surprisingly, domestic energy security.

Reflecting a broader global trend in resource management the water, energy and food nexus has been increasingly highlighted as a top policy priority by Arab countries in many regional meetings, including in the context of the Rio+20 follow-up and implementation (CSD 2013). An integrated approach to these three issues is expected to more effectively address the sustainable development goals of improved sustainability, efficiency and equity. Moreover, the nexus approach touches upon practically all the above-described development challenges. In a green economy, the interlinkages between natural resources are better recognised, which, among other things, will enable better harmonisation of energy and water governance, policies and management. Such coordinated local, national and regional policies can lead to more efficient and cost-effective provision of water and energy services as well as rationalisation of their use. This will be key as demand for fresh water and energy is projected to continue increasing significantly in the region over the coming decades.

Most importantly, given the vast potential for solar energy, renewable energy can play a key role in this nexus and the shift towards a greener economy in the GCC. Indeed, given the key role of energy in socioeconomic development, especially in the Gulf, it can be argued that a simultaneous shift in the energy sector is a precondition for any green transition. Since the energy sector affects all other sectors, a green energy sector is very likely to have a positive 'spill-over effect' on the other sectors too. The key dilemma for the GCC states is that a greening of their energy sector is often perceived as inherently in conflict with the basis of their economies, namely the hydrocarbon industry. As some of the main fossil fuel producers and exporters in the world, the relationship of the GCC states with renewables has not been easy (Luomi 2012a). At the same time, as noted above, the region is generally seen as having potential to become a major future exporter of renewable energy especially solar power, and the potential of renewables in boosting domestic supply and liberating further oil and natural gas for exports is increasingly recognised by the GCC governments.

In the late 2000s and early 2010s, pushed by the internal pressures of rising domestic energy and water demand, and external pressures caused by efforts by oil-importing countries to decarbonise their energy supply, the GCC decision-makers were forced to start a re-think of their energy and economic development strategies in order to maintain the high standards of their growing citizen and expatriate populations. Future energy options for the GCC states include an array of technologies that go beyond renewable energy, which – while not the topic of this volume – deserve to be discussed briefly. These include nuclear energy and carbon capture and storage (CCS), which are usually not considered technologies of the green economy and are hence generally excluded in related literature. Nuclear energy and CCS are 'clean' technologies and, together with natural gas (if it is used as a substitute for higher-carbon content fuels), are often regarded as 'bridge' or transition technologies on the road to a zero-carbon economy. However, both bear important environmental risks and uncertainties, including ones relating to nuclear waste disposal and catastrophes, and carbon leakage and related liability issues. Moreover, CCS in particular also carries the risk of perpetuating or delaying the transition into a renewable energy-based, green economy.

Since the mid-2000s, with domestic demand eating into fossil fuel production that could otherwise be exported, some GCC states, most prominently the UAE emirate of Abu Dhabi and Saudi Arabia, took the decision to include nuclear energy in their energy mix. At the time of writing, Abu Dhabi was already constructing two 1.4 GW nuclear reactors, which, along with two further 1.4 GW reactors, are expected to be finalised by 2020 and contribute to the UAE's policy goal of generating 24 per cent of its electricity from clean sources by 2021 (UAE MOE 2014).[4] The GCC states are also testing CCS, with pilot projects located in Abu Dhabi in the UAE and Uthmaniyah in Saudi Arabia (GCCSI 2014). However, the still high cost of these technologies and the lack of economic incentives for their deployment, namely a price on carbon and/or carbon markets, are likely to continue delaying large-scale implementation, in the GCC, similarly to other regions in the world.

Governance of the green economy in the Gulf and green policy

From a Gulf perspective, what are the essential conditions and enablers for a green economy? Arguably, these can be synthesised into governance and financing. Financing will be discussed in the next section. Good governance, accompanied by what this chapter calls 'green policy', consisting of enabling public policies and conditions, is a fundamental requirement for any green economy transition.

It can be argued that governance is key to the success of any country's development. An old term with many meanings in different governing regimes and academic uses, the central idea of governance evolves around a framework for the joint management of the general affairs of a community and its people, or a society and its citizens. In short, governance can be defined as the 'design and execution of common activities in order to achieve a common goal' (Abdel Raouf 2013). In order for governance to be successful, a number of preconditions need to be fulfilled. These include: common agreement on general goals; engagement of all stakeholders in shaping and executing these goals; adoption of various policies to achieve these goals; establishing a clear and correct allocation of authorities and responsibilities; agreeing on common rules, institutions, customs and values; and resorting to negotiation in case of disagreement between stakeholders (ibid.).

Good governance forms the basis for successful policies. Still, it is the governments that can and should take the lead role in encouraging and supporting the shift to the green economy through 'green policies'. A green policy, at the macro level, can be defined as a policy that balances between natural resource consumption and environmental protection, while seeking to achieve social equity and raise the well-being of the society. In simple terms, it is policy that has as its central objective a green economy, with the ultimate goal of achieving sustainable development (ibid.).

It is worth mentioning that ideal green policies are context-specific, with their design and combinations varying from one country to another, and should always take into consideration cultural, economic and social conditions of a country. Also, a country's green policies may and should evolve over time as the above-mentioned circumstances change and develop. Furthermore, a truly effective green policy will not only generate economy-wide impacts, but will also have positive or desired impacts across sectors. Therefore, in designing green policies, a cross-sectoral approach is essential, as a policy with positive impacts in one sector may have negative effects on others. As in any policy, the development of green policies is always bound to involve at least some trade-offs.

A basket of green policy instruments employed in any country, including those of the GCC, may include some or all of the following: market instruments, such as subsidy reform, green taxes and permit markets; legal instruments, including environmental legislation and incorporating sustainable development into trade agreements; government policies and measures, for example sustainable public procurement, sustainable land use and urban policy, integrated management of freshwater, monitoring and accountability measures; and awareness and education campaigns. Most importantly, as the principle of good governance dictates, the design and execution of policies should involve the participation of all relevant stakeholders, starting with all key government agencies, and integrating inputs from non-governmental organisations, academia, businesses and professional organisations, among others (Abdel Raouf 2011a).

Financing the green economy

To date, various multilateral funds have been established to achieve global environmental protection and related benefits. Most of these environmental financial funds, or green funds, provide support to areas relevant for the green economy, including: green technology, green projects and programmes, and measures to shift towards a low-carbon, resource-efficient and climate-resilient economy. At present, the global environmental finance architecture is quite complex. While the existence of several funds and programmes can be considered a merit, it also generates challenges for the coordination of activities, access to funds by recipients, and avoidance of duplication in goals and financing.

Green economy-relevant funding is usually channelled through multilateral funds, such as the Climate Investment Funds, and, starting from 2015, the Green Climate Fund (GCF), established under the UN Framework Convention on Climate Change (UNFCCC). In addition, funds are increasingly channelled through bilateral channels. Some of the recipient countries have also set up national environment/climate change funds that receive funding from multiple developed countries in an effort to coordinate and align donor interests with national plans and priorities. Furthermore, a number of multilateral development banks work on a regional basis that play a key role in supporting green economy transitions, in developing countries in particular. These include the Asian Development Bank, the African Development Bank, the Inter-American Development Bank and the Islamic Development Bank. The focus of this section is on existing global multilateral funds.

The leading, largest and oldest global financial instrument is the World Bank, through its daughter funding programme, the Global Environment Facility (GEF). The GEF finances environmental projects and programmes with the aim of achieving global environmental benefits. Since the 1990s, the Facility has disbursed over USD70 billion in grants and leveraged co-financing for approximately 3,700 projects across the developing world (The GEF 2014). The GEF serves as a financial mechanism for the five main international environmental conventions: the Convention on Biological Diversity (CBD), the UNFCCC, the UN Convention to Combat Desertification, the Stockholm Convention on Persistent Organic Pollutants and the Minamata Convention on Mercury. Consequently, the GEF helps fund initiatives that assist developing countries in meeting the objectives of these conventions, as well as those related to international waters and ozone layer depletion (ibid.). Most recently under its current replenishment period, 'GEF-6', which runs through mid-2018, the Facility is moving from single-technology projects toward programmatic and system-wide, transformative approaches that also increase country ownership. This approach, it is argued, also supports a transition to green economy, which requires not only green technological innovation but also societal and economical innovation, which have an even greater transformative impact than technology itself.

Table 1.1 summarises a number of main multilateral environmental funds globally.

The GCC countries can benefit from these various funds through grants, loans and co-financing. The GCC countries are not yet members of the GEF, with the exception of Kuwait, which joined two years ago, and still have not joined any of the current constituencies in the GEF. Nevertheless, as developing countries (or non-Annex-I in the UNFCCC), in theory they can fully benefit from GEF, as well as GCF financing in various projects related to the five mentioned conventions because the GEF is an instrument for the conventions, and not vice versa.

However, given that all six GCC states are high-income economies, there is plenty of scope for leveraging domestic funding, as well as engaging in partnerships with the private sector – both domestic and foreign. Interestingly, the UAE has already for some years engaged actively in green financing through

Table 1.1 The main global multilateral environmental funds

Fund	Administered by	Focal area	Operation start date	Proposed life of fund
The GEF	The GEF	Climate change; biodiversity; chemicals and waste; international waters; land degradation; sustainable forest management; the ozone layer; persistent organic pollutants	1991	Based on funds replenishment every four years
Adaptation Fund (AF)	The World Bank (interim Trustee of the UNFCCC AF); AF Board	Climate change adaptation	2009	Continuous
The Green Climate Fund (GCF)	The Green Climate Fund Board (part of the UNFCCC financial mechanism)	Climate change adaptation and mitigation; REDD (Reducing Emissions from Deforestation and forest Degradation)	2015	Based upon future UNFCCC negotiations
Least Developed Countries Fund (LDCF)	The GEF (under the UNFCCC)	Climate change adaptation	2002	Indefinite
Special Climate Change Fund (SCCF)	The GEF (under the UNFCCC)	Climate change adaptation	2002	Indefinite
Clean Technology Fund (CTF) – one of the CIF	The World Bank	Climate change mitigation through low-carbon technologies	2008	Based on UNFCCC negotiations
Strategic Climate Fund (SCF) – one of the CIF	The World Bank	Climate change adaptation and mitigation; REDD	2008	Unspecified
Pilot Program for Climate Resilience (PPCR)	The World Bank (under the CIF SCF)	Climate change adaptation	2008	Based on UNFCCC negotiations

Table 1.1 (cont.)

Fund	Administered by	Focal area	Operation start date	Proposed life of fund
Scaling up Renewable Energy Program in Low Income Countries (SREP)	The World Bank (under the CIF SCF)	Climate change mitigation	2009	Based on UNFCCC negotiations
Adaptation for Smallholder Agriculture Programme (ASAP)	The International Fund for Agricultural Development (IFAD)	Climate change adaptation	2012	Undetermined
The Nagoya Protocol Implementation Fund (NPIF)	The World Bank	Genetic resources and the fair and equitable sharing of benefits arising from their utilisation		Continuous
Global Climate Change Alliance (GCCA)	The European Commission	Climate change adaptation and mitigation; REDD	2008	Unspecified
Global Energy Efficiency and Renewable Energy Fund (GEEREF)	The European Commission	Climate change mitigation	2008	15 years
UN-REDD Program	UNDP	Climate change mitigation; REDD	2008	2015

Source: Climate Funds Update (2014); data collected by authors.

its foreign investments and development aid in the renewable energy sector. This funding includes USD350 million in concessional financing to renewable energy projects in developing countries through the national Abu Dhabi Fund for Development, supported by the International Renewable Energy Agency (IRENA-ADFD 2014).

Structure of the book

The international development agenda is amidst major changes, marked by the Rio+20 Summit of 2012, and the launch of the post-2015 development agenda and the UN Paris Climate Change Conference in late 2015. With sustainable development at the centre of global policy debates more firmly than ever, the coming years and decades will be decisive for any country hoping to reap the advantages of being an early mover, and benefiting from the new institutions, policy concepts and tools, and means of implementation support of the emerging post-2015 sustainable development architecture. This book is an examination of how the six GCC states are positioned in this transition. It simultaneously seeks to serve as a source for in-depth and regional context-specific analyses and recommendations on how these states could benefit from building sustainable, green economies that have environmental and social sustainability at their core, and ensure a healthy planet and healthy people for their present and the future generations.

The key questions at the core of this book are: why should the GCC states shift towards a green economy? What are the strengths of the GCC with regard to the green economy? How about the barriers and obstacles, including those emerging from the broader socioeconomic context? What lessons can the GCC learn from experiences in other countries? Most importantly, the chapters of this volume collectively address the core question of how a green economy in the GCC could look.

The volume is divided into four sections. Following the introductory section, a section on energy and water will explore some of the GCC states' most pressing green economy challenges. In an overview chapter of the GCC energy sector (Chapter 2), Dr Ibrahim Abdel Gelil provides a summary of current trends and the socioeconomic context for the region's present energy challenges, and highlights green economy policies and measures in the six GCC member states. He also presents a detailed discussion on the barriers hindering a green energy transition in the region's states, including energy subsidies and insufficient support to renewable energy development, and proposes a detailed list of related policy and regulatory interventions needed to overcome the existing barriers.

In Chapter 3, Tom Moerenhout engages in a detailed exploration of energy pricing in the GCC states, assessing their role in transforming to a green economic model in the GCC, and the difficulties associated with pricing reform. He first explains why the under-pricing of energy is negative for the green economy in the fields of green economy financing, energy efficiency, renewable electricity development, greening transport and energy-intensive water desalination. By calculating opportunity cost subsidies associated with fossil fuels in the GCC, Moerenhout presents a convincing case for energy subsidy reform. In addition, he stresses the importance of the political economy context that needs to be considered while embarking on reforming energy prices.

In Chapter 4, Ghada Abdulla presents a case study on the use of economic instruments for greening the energy sector through the deployment of renewable energy. By examining the Spanish experience with solar feed-in tariffs, as well as energy efficiency programmes, she extracts lessons for Bahrain, and the GCC more broadly. Providing insightful observations on both the successes and failures of the Spanish case, the chapter makes a strong case for the need to learn from lessons elsewhere and tailor policies to the Gulf context.

Completing the energy theme, in Chapter 5, Dr Bandar Alhoweish and Chingiz Orujov present a compelling case for investing in energy efficiency in Saudi Arabia, and the Gulf region more broadly. Departing from the observation that meeting the Kingdom's domestic energy requirements has become not only a national challenge but also a serious factor that may contribute to international oil market instability, Alhoweish and Orujov describe existing energy efficiency initiatives in the country and challenges impeding their effective promotion nation-wide. By calculating the economic value of saved energy, specifically within the power industry, they find that, by investing approximately USD1 billion in energy efficiency through 2021, the country could save more than USD3 billion through energy savings, compared to the business-as-usual scenario.

Making the case that sustainable development through green economy requires that the water sector comprehensively addresses the green challenges faced by it, Drs Mushtaque Ahmed, Salem Al-Jabri and B. S. Choudri examine, in Chapter 6, that economic efficiency, equity and environmental sustainability are lacking in the water management of the GCC countries, and point out that current and future water shortages in the GCC countries necessitate both reducing demand and increasing supply. By focusing on experiences from Oman, they provide detailed examples on how different technical solutions, principally on the supply side, would make the GCC states' water sector 'greener', if implemented widely. Use of renewable energy in the desalination industry, use of treated wastewater and greywater, and managed aquifer recharge with treated wastewater, are some of the solutions proposed by the three authors.

The next part of the volume is dedicated to the urban dimension of the GCC green economy, namely buildings and transport. Given the six states' high rate of urbanisation, estimated by the UNDESA (2014, 22) at 83–99 per cent, cities will play an important role in the green economy transition in this region. Christopher Silva provides, in Chapter 7, a comprehensive overview of the emergence of green buildings in the GCC states. He starts by presenting the history of green buildings in the region, including the appearance of codes and professional organisations, certifications and mega-cities. By using a green building complex in Qatar's Education City as a case study and exploring its challenges in its various stages, Silva identifies roadblocks impeding the emergence of a broader trend of sustainable building in the region, derives lessons learned, and makes suggestions on how to encourage the growth of this sector.

In Chapter 8, Arnd Bätzner argues that, after a phase of rapid expansion and facing high projected growth rates, 'greening' the transport sector has become critical not only for the overall greening of the GCC economies, but also for their long-term prosperity and wealth. Focusing on the constraints that the region's climatic and cultural distinctions set upon transit design, Bätzner proposes a fully integrated urban design approach that is tailored for GCC-specific needs and centres on last-mile connectivity, linking homes to high-capacity rail transit, and combined with a network of shaded walk- and bikeways and design interventions such as increased urban densification.

The chapters of the final part of the book explore various cross-cutting issues relevant for the green economy in the Gulf. Labour and jobs, intellectual property considerations and the international relations of the GCC states are key dimensions of the green economy that cut across economic sectors and nation state boundaries. As in the case of the resource- and sector-specific dimensions addressed in this book, these cross-cutting issues present both opportunities and challenges that the region's policymakers need to take into account while devising future development strategies and policies.

In Chapter 9, Amit A. Pandya and Kristin Sparding examine labour-related questions that should be considered in the context of the green economy in the GCC countries. In particular, the two authors address economic activity directed at mitigation of damaging environmental change and adaptation to the effects of environmental change, and the development of cleaner processes of production and distribution for either of the above purposes. Through a detailed examination of workforce qualifications and skills, labour migration, worker safety and health, and international labour standards, the authors seek to elucidate the particular ways in which the requirements of a green economy should shape our understanding of these, and the ways in which requirements from the world of work should shape our understanding of the green economy.

In a critical examination of the green economy agenda, Nihaya Khalaf, in Chapter 10, argues, through a case study on the development of international law on plant genetic resources for food and agriculture, that the transition to a green economy, as part of the global institutional reform agenda that governs the allocation of rights over these resources, is improper to chart the way towards agricultural sustainability. By examining how international law obligations related to agricultural diversity and intellectual property are enacted in the UAE, she concludes that greening the economy through market-based mechanisms would increase the complexities countries face in implementing national laws that balance the special nature of plant genetic resources and plant-related innovations with national needs.

In the final chapter, Kishan Khoday, Leisa Perch and Tim Scott make two important observations on the transboundary relations of the emerging economies of the Arab Gulf states: firstly, their South-South cooperation, and flows of official development assistance and outward direct investment to developing countries around the world are increasing, which is making the Gulf states' increasingly influential in this sphere. Secondly, given this growing prominence, achieving sustainable development and green economy goals globally in the future will increasingly depend on how and whether these emerging economies pursue green economy goals in their global cooperation strategies and local and foreign investments. The three authors of Chapter 11 examine and evaluate the resource-rich GCC countries' experiences with green economy policies so far, and propose how related lessons could help shape a new era of South-South cooperation and public policy coherent with a comprehensive green economic approach for equitable and sustainable development.

Notes

1 It is also worth mentioning that the concept of caring for the environment here is more comprehensive and deeper than protection as it involves different aspects, such as protection from damage and pollution, as well as allowing for the environment to flourish.
2 On the ecological footprint, see: Global Footprint Network (2012).
3 Green accounting, or inclusive wealth accounting, also plays an important role in this regard.
4 The factors and motives behind Abu Dhabi's decision have been analysed by the authors and include: growing domestic electricity demand; availability of funds; a strong government and government legitimacy; the policy goal of reducing the UAE's carbon footprint; trade promotion and foreign policies of major nuclear technology exporters, including South Korea, the US and France; and the potential for creating jobs in a new, non-oil sector of the economy (Abdel Raouf 2011b; Luomi 2012b).

References

Abdel Gelil, Ibrahim, Farid Chaaban and Leila Dagher. 2012. 'Energy.' In *Arab Environment: Green Economy: Sustainable Transition in a Changing Arab World*, edited by Hussein Abaza, Najib Saab and Bashar Zeitoon, 75–112. Beirut: Arab Forum for Environment and Development (AFED).

Abdel Raouf, Mohamed. 2010. 'From Greed to Green.' *Khaleej Times*, 13 April. http://www.khaleejtimes.com/

Abdel Raouf, Mohamed. 2011a. 'Rio Plus 20 a Window for the Arab World.' *Gulf News*, 28 October. http://gulfnews.com/

Abdel Raouf, Mohamed. 2011b. 'United Arab Emirates (UAE): The Nuclear Program and Renewable Energy Alternatives.' *Ambition and Peril: Nuclear Energy and the Arab World*. Perspectives, No. 1. Heinrich Böll Stiftung, April.

Abdel Raouf, Mohamed. 2013. *Green Policy to Balance Energy and Environment Needs: The Case of the United Arab Emirates*. Abu Dhabi: The Emirates Center for Strategic Studies and Research (ECSSR), June. In Arabic.

Abdel Raouf, Mohamed. 2014. 'UAE Takes the Lead in Going Green.' *Gulf News*, 26 February. http://gulfnews.com/

Abaza, Hussein, Najib Saab and Bashar Zeitoon, ed. 2012. *Green Economy: Sustainable Transition in a Changing Arab World*. Beirut: AFED.

ALBA-TCP. Alianza Bolivariana para los Pueblos de Nuestra América – Tratado de Comercio de los Pueblos. 2010. *Nature Has No Price*. Declaration of the Ministerial Committee for the Defense of Nature of ALBA-TCP at the World People's Conference on Climate Change and the Rights of Mother Earth, 5 November.

Bamsey, Howard. 2013. Interview of the Director-General of the Global Green Growth Institute. *Arirang Today*, 1 July. http://youtu.be/OoibD66jzL0

Bowen, Alex. 2012. '"Green" Growth: What Does It Mean?' *Environmental Scientist* December: 6–11.

Climate Funds Update. 2014. 'The Funds.' Accessed 10 November. http://www.climatefundsupdate.org/the-funds

Collina, Tom Z., and Enca Pott. 2009. *The Green New Deal: Energizing the U.S. Economy*. Fokus Amerika. Washington D.C.: Friedrich Ebert Stiftung.

CSD. Commission for Sustainable Development. 2013. Arab Regional Implementation Meeting for the Twentieth Session of the Commission for Sustainable Development (CSD-20), (Rio+20) follow-up meeting, 29–30 May, Dubai, United Arab Emirates.

Daly, Herman A. 2005. 'Economics in a Full World.' *Scientific American* 293 (September): 100–107.

European Commission. 2014. 'About Beyond GDP.' 10 October. http://ec.europa.eu/

The GEF. 2014. 'What is the GEF.' Accessed 13 October. http://www.thegef.org/gef/whatisgef

GCCSI. Global CCS Institute. 2014. 'Large Scale CCS Projects.' Accessed 7 December. http://www.globalccsinstitute.com/

Global Footprint Network. 2012. 'Footprint Basics – Overview.' 18 July. http://www.footprintnetwork.org/

GPI. Genuine Progress Indicator. 2014. 'Genuine Progress Indicator.' Accessed 12 October. http://genuineprogress.net/genuine-progress-indicator/

IRENA-ADFD. 2014. International Renewable Energy Agency, and Abu Dhabi Fund for Development Project Facility. 'About the IRENA/ADFD Project Facility.' Accessed 13 October. http://adfd.irena.org/facility.aspx

Levin, Kelly. 2013. 'World's Carbon Budget to Be Spent in Three Decades.' *WRI Insights*, 27 September. http://insights.wri.org/

Luomi, Mari. 2012a. *The Gulf Monarchies and Climate Change: Abu Dhabi and Qatar in an Era of Natural Unsustainability.* London: Hurst.

Luomi, Mari. 2012b. 'The Economic and Prestige Aspects of Abu Dhabi's Nuclear Programme.' In *The Nuclear Question in the Middle East*, edited by Mehran Kamrava, 125–158. London: Hurst; New York: Columbia University Press.

OECD. 2014. Organisation for Economic Co-operation and Development. 'What's the Better Life Index?' Accessed 13 October. http://www.oecdbetterlifeindex.org/

Pearce, David William, Anil Markandya and Edward Barbier. 1989. *Blueprint for a Green Economy.* London: Earthscan.

Rio+20. United Nations Conference on Sustainable Development. 2012. 'Objective & Themes.' June. http://www.uncsd2012.org/

Rockström, Johan, Will Steffe, Kevin Noone, Åsa Persson, F. Stuart Chapin III, Eric Lambin, Timothy M. Lenton *et al.* 2009. 'Planetary Boundaries: Exploring the Safe Operating Space for Humanity.' *Ecology and Society* 14 (2): 32.

Saudi Arabia. 2011. Intervention of Saudi Arabia by Aysar Tayeb at the 2nd Preparatory Committee Meeting for the UNCSD 2012, UN Headquarters, New York, US, 7–8 March.

The Telegraph. 2012. 'Mexico City G20 Communiqué: Full Text.' 26 February. http://www.telegraph.co.uk/

TWN. Third World Network. 2012. 'North-South Divide over Rio+20 Outcome Document.' *TWN Update on Sustainable Development Conference 2012*, 3 April.

UAE MOE. Ministry of Energy of the United Arab Emirates. 2014. 'UAE Sets Target of Producing 24% of its Electricity Needs from Clean Sources.' Press release, 27 July.

UN News Centre. 2009. 'Ban Urges Leaders at Davos to Forge "Green New Deal" to Fight World Recession.' 29 January.

UN SD Knowledge Platform. United Nations Sustainable Development Knowledge Platform. 2014. 'Green Economy.' Accessed 18 August. http://sustainabledevelopment.un.org/

UNDESA. United Nations Department of Economic and Social Affairs. 2014. *World Urbanization Prospects: The 2014 Revision, Highlights.* (ST/ESA/SER.A/352) UN.

UNEP. United Nations Environment Programme. 2011. *Towards a Green Economy: Pathways to Sustainable Development and Poverty Eradication.* Nairobi: UNEP.

UNEP-RONA. United Nations Environment Programme Regional Office for North America. 2014. 'What is Sustainable Consumption and Production (SCP)?' Accessed 12 October. http://www.rona.unep.org/

UNESCWA. United Nations Economic and Social Commission for Western Asia. 2012. 'Green Economy for the Arab Region.' Presentation by Riccardo Mesiano at a meeting on Rio+20, National Policy Making and Sustainable Development Policies in Conflict-Afflicted Countries: The case of Lebanon. 2 May.

UNESCWA. 2013. *Mapping Green Economy in the ECSCWA Region. Version 1.* Beirut: ESCWA, June.

WAM. Emirates News Agency. 2012. 'Mohamed Unveils UAE's Green Economy.' 15 January. http://www.wam.ae/en/

The World Bank. 2012. *Inclusive Green Growth: The Pathway to Sustainable Development.* Washington D.C.: World Bank.

Zelenovskaya, Ekaterina. 2012. *Green Growth Policy in Korea: A Case Study.* Venice: International Center for Climate Governance.

Part II

Energy and water

2 Barriers to greening the energy sector in the Gulf Cooperation Council

Ibrahim Abdel Gelil

Energy and economy in the Gulf Cooperation Council

The states of the Gulf Cooperation Council (GCC) sit on nearly 33 per cent of the world's proven oil reserves in 2012 with Saudi Arabia, Kuwait and the United Arab Emirates (UAE) holding the world's first, fifth and sixth largest oil reserves, respectively. In addition, the region holds about 22 per cent of the world's proven natural gas reserves, with Qatar, Saudi Arabia and the UAE holding the third, fifth and seventh largest gas reserves, respectively in the same year (EIA 2014). According to the International Energy Agency (IEA 2013), Saudi Arabia topped the world's lists of oil producers and exporters, while Qatar is the third largest producer of natural gas in the world. Further, Qatar ranked fourth of the natural gas exporters in 2012 and is the world's largest exporter of liquefied natural gas (LNG).

Hydrocarbons have played a vital role in the GCC economies. Due to the relatively low cost of oil production in the region, the size of oil rent is relatively massive and constitutes a big fraction of the region's gross domestic product (GDP). For decades, oil revenues have been used to finance governments' spending, accumulate savings, or invest in non-oil sectors, infrastructure, human capital and social programmes, and to improve human development indicators (Abdel Gelil 2012). The share of hydrocarbon revenues in the GDP of the GCC ranges from 32 per cent in the relatively diversified economy of the UAE to nearly 56 per cent in Qatar. Table 2.1 reveals that the hydrocarbon revenues contributed almost 81 per cent of the GCC's governments' revenues in 2010.

This unprecedented social and economic development and dramatic changes in lifestyle have gradually turned the region into an evolving energy consuming market. Table 2.2 shows the average annual growth in total primary energy consumption and population in the region. The primary energy consumption rose more than five-fold between 1980 and 2009, at a rate of 6.2 per cent annually, outpacing population growth, at 3.7 per cent. During the same period, energy demand of the UAE grew at the highest annual rate, of 9 per cent, in parallel to the highest population growth in the region of nearly 7 per cent. These exceptionally high rates of energy consumption and population growth have been attributed to the booming development of modern infrastructure,

Table 2.1 Contribution of the hydrocarbon sector in the GCC economies (2010)

Country	GDP (million USD)	Hydrocarbon sector (million USD)	Share of hydrocarbon sector in GDP (%)	Share of hydrocarbon revenues in total government revenues (%)
Bahrain	22,945	5,591	24.4	81.8
Kuwait	124,244	64,009	51.5	93.8
Oman	63,199	30,118	47.7	81.7
Qatar	128,593	71,642	55.7	60.8
Saudi Arabia	447,762	214,145	47.8	90.4
UAE	297,648	94,042	31.6	75.9
Total GCC	1,084,391	479,547	44.2	80.7

Source: Fattouh and El-Katiri (2013)

Table 2.2 Primary energy consumption (Mtoe) and population growth in the GCC

Country	1980	1990	2000	2009	Compound annual growth rate (1980–2009)	Population growth rate (1980–2009)
Bahrain	3.4	6.4	9.1	13.9	4.9	4.1
Kuwait	12	11.2	22.7	31.1	3.3	2.9
Oman	1.6	4.6	8.5	18.8	8.8	3.5
Qatar	5.4	8.6	16.1	25.6	5.5	3.6
Saudi Arabia	41.6	83.7	121.3	195.9	5.5	1.4
UAE	6.7	30.7	46.7	81.5	9	6.9
Total GCC	70.7	169.4	261.8	366.8	6.2	3.7

Source: Fattouh and El-Katiri (2012b)

industrialisation, urbanisation, and the huge inflow of foreign workers who currently represent more than 99 per cent of private sector staff in the UAE (Mytelka et al. 2012).

Driven by the same factors, energy consumption of the GCC countries has increased at a remarkable rate. In 2011, the total energy consumption of the GCC was nearly 354 Mtoe, with Saudi Arabia consuming approximately 53 per cent of the total (see Figure 2.1). Electricity consumption has also increased from 391 TWh in 2009 to about 423 TWh in 2011, with Saudi Arabia's share at 54 per cent (see Figure 2.2). Energy demand is expected to continue increasing in line with growing industrialisation in this rapidly developing region. Recent estimates have indicated that if Saudi Arabia continues its current pattern of domestic oil consumption, it would lose the ability to export oil by 2020 and become a net importer by 2038 (REN21 2013).

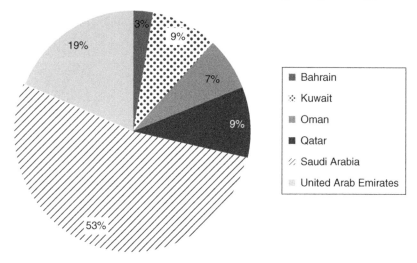

Figure 2.1 Share of total energy consumption by country

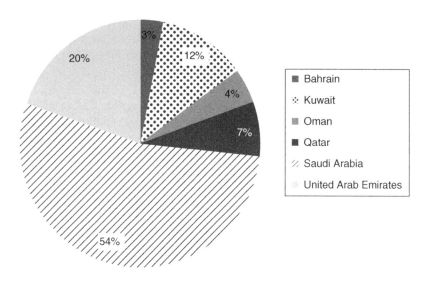

Figure 2.2 Share of total electricity consumption by country

The present electricity generation capacity in the GCC countries is about 80 gigawatts (GW) (EU-GCC Clean Energy Network 2012). Considering current trends, the region must increase its electricity capacity by an additional 60 GW to meet the demand by 2020. In the context of such significant need for new capacity, the region has a unique opportunity to channel future huge invest-ments into a transition to green energy technologies, thus enhancing future

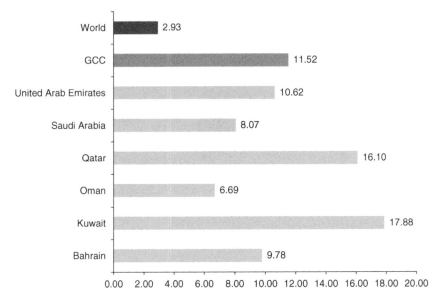

Figure 2.3 Per capita electricity consumption (TWh)
Source: IEA (2013)

energy security and reducing carbon footprints. This would enhance not only the sustainable development of the GCC, but would also integrate these countries' efforts into the broader global effort to address the challenges of climate change.

The GCC economies rely fully on oil and gas to meet domestic energy demand. In 2009–2010, oil accounted for 24.4 per cent of energy used in electricity generation, while gas accounted for 75.6 per cent (EU-GCC Clean Energy Network 2012). However, recently, nearly 136 MW of solar capacity has been added in the UAE and Oman, Qatar, Kuwait and Saudi Arabia (Bachellerie 2013).

It is also worth noting that the energy sector plays a major role in meeting the water and food needs in the region. Fossil fuel-based combined heat and power thermal plants are commonly used for seawater desalination in the region, which hosts nearly 50 per cent of the world's desalination capacity (El-Ashry and Saab 2010). Further, electricity generated from fossil fuel power plants is used to pump and distribute groundwater. Thus, food production in the region, though insignificant, continues to rely on the availability of energy resources.

The average per capita electricity consumption in the GCC was 11,552 kWh in 2011, which was nearly four times more than the world average of 2,933 kWh (see Figure 2.3). The per capita primary energy consumption presented in Figure 2.4 shows that the average is more than five times the world average, while the per capita consumption rates of Qatar and Kuwait are higher than the GCC average. It is worth noting that higher rates of per capita consumption in the GCC are partially attributed to the harsh climate conditions and scarcity of water

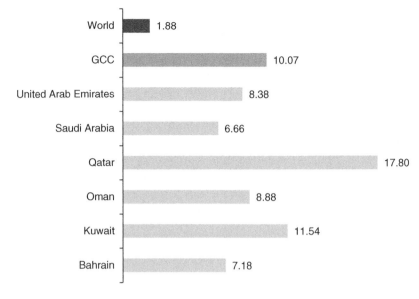

Figure 2.4 Per capita primary energy consumption (toe)
Source: IEA (2013)

resources, which require heavy use of air conditioning and energy-intensive desalination. For example, about two-thirds of residential electricity is used for cooling (Booz&Company 2009). They are also attributable to structural factors of hosting energy-intensive industries, such as petrochemical industries, oil refineries and aluminium smelters. Additionally, energy-pricing schemes in the region are not conducive to rational energy consumption. The region is also well-known for heavily subsidising all forms of energy. This has been sending wrong signals to the market, and impairing, as will be discussed later, the efforts to transition to green energy sectors. The same factors have contributed to high energy and carbon intensities of the GCC economies. Energy intensity, defined as the energy consumption per unit of GDP, is shown in Figure 2.5, which indicates that all six GCC countries are more energy intensive than the world average of 0.19 Kgoe/ (2005) USD.

It is thus obvious there is a need for energy transition in the GCC in order to address a multitude of crucial issues. Although the region has substantial hydrocarbon resources, the escalating demand for domestic energy consumption makes it concerned about future energy supply and the sustainability of its hydrocarbon export revenues needed for development. An energy transition would largely contribute to diversifying the Gulf economies by shifting away from the oil rent-based economies to more sustainable and productive ones. Greening the GCC energy sector would also drastically reduce carbon emissions in a region with the world's highest carbon footprint. The International Renewable Energy Agency (IRENA) has estimated the region's annual carbon emission savings

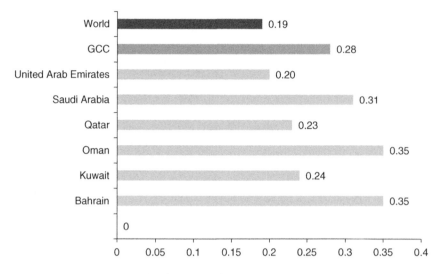

Figure 2.5 Energy intensity (toe/1,000 USD)
Source: IEA (2013)

potential through renewable energy technology deployment at 1,044 million tonnes of carbon dioxide equivalent ($MtCO_2e$) through 2030 (IRENA 2012). As the region depends heavily on seawater desalination to meet the ever-growing water demand, and in the context of expected severe water scarcity due to potential climate change impacts, it is argued that the region needs to shift from fossil-based desalination systems to more sustainable green technologies. Unemployment is another development challenge that green economy would successfully address. According to the International Labour Organization (ILO), 1.4 million new jobs will need to be created in 2015–2020. Green energy technologies are usually labour-intensive and can help create more green jobs across the value chain of engineering, manufacturing, installation, operation and maintenance, and decommissioning. IRENA has estimated that the implementation of the GCC countries' existing renewable energy targets would create between 0.6 and 1.97 million jobs (IRENA 2012).

The International Monetary Fund's report 'Economic Prospects and Policy Challenges for the GCC Countries' (IMF 2013) explains that, due to absent policy reform, a continuous upward trend in energy consumption, in a region that already has some of the world's highest levels of per capita energy consumption, is fuelled by some of the lowest prices. Low gasoline and electricity prices are fuelling domestic oil consumption, while governments are losing out on billions of USD in export revenues. Their recommendation is: 'a gradual upward adjustment in domestic energy prices' to check 'the rapid growth of domestic consumption [and] redirect existing incentives in the growth model away from energy intensive industries' (Kneissl 2014).

Policy options to transition to a green energy sector

The transition towards a green energy sector requires policies and measures, which are well stipulated in the 'The Arab Regional Strategy for Sustainable Consumption and Production' (LAS *et al.* 2010). The strategy identifies a set of strategic objectives to green the energy sector, among which are improving energy efficiency, increasing the share of renewable energy in the fuel mix and disseminating renewable energy technologies. The same strategy pinpoints a whole list of needed policy interventions. These include, but are not limited to: reforming existing energy tariffs so as to integrate environmental and social costs while maintaining energy subsidies for the poor; improving energy efficiency, particularly in energy-intensive industries, transport and electricity generation; developing and wide use of renewable energy technologies; and supporting air quality management through better urban planning and land use.

The current trends in the GCC energy sector are unsustainable in terms of economic, social and environmental dimensions. Adopting green energy policies would, among other things, foster economic diversification, minimise economic vulnerabilities, meet the escalating energy demand cost-effectively, improve environmental quality and address the high carbon footprint. Recently, remarkable but slow policy shifts are noticeable, as are set of strategic objectives that are being adopted in some GCC countries, among which are improving energy efficiency, increasing the share of renewable power in the energy mix, and disseminating energy efficiency and renewable energy technologies. Improving energy efficiency is a major priority in any green economy programme, as it supports the three dimensions of sustainable development through: energy savings and associated reduction of emissions; increasing profitability through a reduction of energy costs; and increasing revenues for oil and gas exporters such as those of the GCC.

Generally, to achieve those policy objectives, government interventions are inevitable. A study by Jalilvand (2012, 13) stated that 'the existing global markets for renewable energy today were all created through political measures'. He also notes that global subsidies for renewable energy are expected to increase from USD66 billion in 2010 to USD250 billion in 2035.

A list of policy interventions are identified in the GCC region, which seek to promote investments in cleaner technologies for oil and gas exploration and production, promote intra-regional electric grid interconnections and natural gas network projects, encourage private sector investment and management of energy facilities, improve energy efficiency, promote production and use of cleaner fuels, and develop and upscale the use of renewable energy technologies. Table 2.3 exhibits a landscape of green energy policy instruments implemented in the region. This 'policy scan' mainly includes two kinds of policy instruments: regulatory policies, such as building codes or minimum energy efficiency standards, and market-based instruments, namely fiscal incentives such as feed-in tariffs (FITs) or tax credits. All GCC countries have national renewable energy targets. These targets include per cent contribution of renewable energy in generated electricity (Bahrain, Kuwait, Oman, Qatar and Dubai), a

Table 2.3 Policy scan of green energy

Country	Regulatory policies									Fiscal incentives		
	RE targets	EE targets	RE strategy/ plan	Competitive bidding	EE appliance standards	EE building codes	FIT	Electric utility quota	Heat obligation	Subsidies/ grants	Tax credits	Public investments
Bahrain	X				X							X
Kuwait	X	X		X	X	X						X
Oman	X	X		X						X		X
Qatar	X	X			X	X					X	X
Saudi Arabia	X	X	X	X	X	X	D					X
UAE	X	X	X	X	X	XX	D	X	X	X		X

XX: Abu Dhabi, D: under discussion

Source: REN21 (2013)

Table 2.4 Energy efficiency and renewable energy targets in the GCC

Country	Renewable energy targets
	Energy efficiency targets
Bahrain	5% by 2020
Kuwait	5% of electricity generation by 2020; 10% by 2030
Oman	10% by 2020
	Reduce transmission and distribution losses in power sector from 14% in 2010 to 10% by 2014
Qatar	At least 2% of electricity generation from solar by 2020
	20% in per capita electricity consumption
Saudi Arabia	25 GW of CSP, 16 GW of solar PV, 9 GW of wind, 3 GW of waste-to-energy and 1 GW of geothermal by 2032
United Arab Emirates	Dubai: 5% of electricity by 2030; Abu Dhabi: 7% of electricity generation capacity by 2020
	Abu Dhabi: reduce electricity peak by 250 MW by 2012
	Dubai: reduce BAU projected power consumption by 30% by 2030

Sources: Lahn *et al.* (2013); Mytelka *et al.* (2012)

per cent contribution of renewable energy in installed capacity (Abu Dhabi[1]) and a percent penetration of renewable energy technologies in the electricity generation mix in Saudi Arabia (see Table 2.4). Three countries (Oman, Qatar and UAE) have energy efficiency targets. These aim to reduce transmission and distribution losses (Oman), reduce per capita electricity consumption (Qatar), reduce electricity peak demand (Abu Dhabi) and reduce total electricity consumption (Dubai). Furthermore, all GCC countries except Oman are adopting energy efficiency standards for home appliances, while all countries except Oman and Bahrain are implementing energy efficiency building codes. The UAE and Qatar currently have the largest share of green buildings in the region. According to the UN Economic and Social Commission for Western Asia, there are 802 LEED-certified green buildings in the UAE. Qatar ranks second, with 173 green buildings, followed by Saudi Arabia, with 145 (UNESCWA 2013).

It is obvious from Table 2.3 that all GCC countries are investing in some way in the development of renewable energy technologies. Two massive public investment programmes are identified in Saudi Arabia and the UAE. It is remarkable that GCC states have been – and continue to be – largely dependent on public funding to invest in renewable energy and energy efficiency. This is attributed to the long history of government dominance in the energy sector and low levels of involvement of the private sector. Only the UAE has one renewable energy project that has been jointly financed by the private sector and the government in the form of a public-private partnership (PPP).

While national targets and strategies constitute an important first step in planning for greening the energy sector, they need to be supported by an appropriate governance system in order to be effective. Otherwise, governments will find it difficult to translate their long-term visions into concrete, actionable plans. Thus, it is generally too early to assess the success of existing policies to achieve the different national targets listed in Table 2.4, as most of these targets are aiming at the year 2020 or beyond. However, the level of success is expected to differ between different countries based on their level of market maturity and success in removing a set of barriers that will be discussed later in this chapter. The importance of reforming the governance system in the region to facilitate the green transition should also be emphasised. For instance, only the UAE and Saudi Arabia have dedicated institutions responsible for promoting renewable energy and energy efficiency at the national level, namely, Masdar in the UAE, and King Abdullah City for Atomic and Renewable Energy (K.A.CARE) in Saudi Arabia. Further, both countries are also discussing the development of FITs to upscale private sector investments.

Green energy initiatives

As noted earlier, although the region has large potential for energy efficiency and ample renewable energy resources, particularly solar energy owing to the high levels of solar radiation, a slow transition to green economy is observable in the past few years. However, at the same time, in spite of their abundant hydrocarbon resources, the GCC states have recently initiated a number of low carbon green initiatives. This section will highlight some of these initiatives.

Bahrain

One of the most alarming energy issues in Bahrain has been the poor level of energy efficiency that leads to a demand growth that surpasses the economic and population growth rates. A set of recent market drivers for energy efficiency and renewable energy can be identified, notably: restructuring the energy sector to attract private investment; corporatisation of some state-owned enterprises; environmental concerns and the need for de-carbonisation of economic development; and the outlook for gas supply in Bahrain. These all have called for more rational energy use and demand-side management. It is worth noting that Bahrain's Vision 2030, launched in 2008, includes a target of a reduction of per capita CO_2 emissions from the current level of 31 tonnes to 10 tonnes by 2014. However, while the National Economic Strategy (2009–2014) established energy efficiency and renewable energy as two strategic options for achieving this objective, there is no clear action plan detailing how, when and who would realise it (Abdel-Gelil 2011). Some major energy players in the country are implementing a few energy efficiency initiatives. Of the total consumption of about 12,000 GWh/year through the Electricity and Water Authority's (EWA) grid, nearly 50 per cent of consumption is by the residential sector, followed by the commercial sector, at approximately 38 per cent. Air conditioning and lighting contribute the most to peak loads in Bahrain. The World Bank is providing technical assistance to the country to support the design and implementation of a large-scale efficient lighting programme for the residential sector. The 'Bahrain Lighting Initiative' supports replacing energy-inefficient incandescent lamps with efficient compact fluorescent lamps (CFL) in the short term and more efficient technologies, such as light-emitting diode (LED)-based lamps, in the medium term (Lia and Ashok 2013).

Waste heat by industrial processes is a major energy saving opportunity in industrial facilities, especially in the aluminium industry because of the high temperature of the exhaust gas in furnaces. The waste heat recovery technique was adopted at Aluminium Bahrain where the flue gas is used to produce steam for seawater desalination. The project thereby increases energy efficiency and decreases energy costs for the Aluminium Bahrain complex while also contributing to the reduction of greenhouse gas emissions (Abdel Gelil 2011).

Other green initiatives have been implemented by the Gulf Petrochemical Industries Co. (GPIC), which owns and operates an integrated petrochemical complex in the country. The company has implemented a carbon dioxide recovery (CDR) project to recover 450 tonnes of CO_2/year from the flue gas that is otherwise being vented into the atmosphere. This is used directly in the manufacturing plants of urea and methanol to increase their production by 30,000 tonnes/year and 44,000 tonnes/year, respectively. In addition, the project will also remove 355 kg/day of sulphur oxide (SOx) from the flue gas leading to better air quality (Nuruddin 2009). GPIC is planning to register the project with the Clean Development Mechanism (CDM), which would earn the company carbon emissions reduction certificates.

Another green initiative by the Government of Bahrain launched in 2011 was the 'Green Building and Sustainability Program', aimed at minimising the sector's negative environmental impacts, optimising energy use and improving overall urban life quality. In the initial pilot phase, focus was placed on public buildings, including new public schools. By applying green buildings specifications in public schools, the programme aims to enhance both work environment and comfort, in addition to resulting in tangible reductions in electricity and water use and CO_2 emissions (Jalilvand 2012).

The 'Bahrain 2030' document acknowledges the need to assess alternative energy resources. Sector strategies of the National Oil and Gas Authority (NOGA), EWA and the Ministry of Municipality have included some measures to promote renewable energy technologies. Currently, some pilot projects are being implemented by different entities. However, these fragmented activities are not being implemented within an integrated policy and institutional framework. These projects include:

- three wind turbines on the World Trade Center, which meets 13 per cent of the building's energy needs;
- assessment of wind power by NOGA in collaboration with a Japanese company;

- a pilot plant by EWA that will generate 3–5 MW of solar and wind energy;
- a pilot street lighting project with solar energy implemented by EWA;
- the 'Petra Solar Project' of NOGA, comprising the installing of 20 MW of grid-connected photovoltaic (PV) panels; and
- the renewable energy educational project 'Princess Sabeeka Park' of the Bahrain Petroleum Company (Abdel Gelil 2011).

Kuwait

As in the case of Saudi Arabia, interest in developing renewable energy resources, and especially solar, was expressed in Kuwait as early as the mid-1970s. Application of solar energy for power generation, desalination and air conditioning were the major areas of research during that period at the Kuwait Institute for Scientific Research (KISR). Those research and demonstration activities were implemented in cooperation between KISR and international research institutions and technology providers. More specifically, those activities included the design, manufacture, supply and installation of solar power systems for communication purposes in cooperation with Ericsson, and a 100 kW solar thermal powered multi-stage-flash desalination unit (Psarras et al. 2009).

The Ministry of Electricity and Water in Kuwait issued an energy conservation code of practices in 1983. This code represents a set of regulations that guides the construction of new buildings and sets minimum requirements for efficient energy use in new and retrofitted residential buildings. Efforts have been under way since 2009 to update the code to energy conservation codes developed by the United States' AHSRAE (Kuwait 2012).

Recently, the Alargan Business Park in Kuwait was awarded Leadership in Energy and Environmental Design (LEED) Platinum certification. The project implemented some energy and water efficiency measures, such as high-performance glazing, energy-efficient lighting and air conditioning, lighting control using motion detectors and daylight sensing, and water low-flow fixtures. Additionally, in 2004, the Kuwait Petroleum Company earmarked USD100 million for development of clean fossil fuels technologies such as fuel cell, carbon sequestration and oil-gasification.

It is worth noting that the total number of LEED registered projects in the GCC in 2020 was 624, of which 27 projects were certified (Seneviratne 2010). Furthermore, a harmonised building code has been under discussion for adoption by 2015 across all GCC countries. The unified code would be in tune with international guidelines and would be drafted taking into account the environmental needs and the region's climate (Ventures Onsite 2014).

Oman

Oman enjoys high renewable energy resource potential, in particular solar and wind. The government, which aims to generate 10 per cent of electricity from solar power by 2020, has recognised this potential. In 2008, the Authority for Electricity Regulation of Oman published a renewable energy study, with the purpose of providing an overview of renewable energy sources in the country and their potential for electricity production. The study assessed the technical suitability of renewable energy technologies for use in the Sultanate. Another feasibility study, by the Public Authority for Electricity and Water (PAEW 2014), from December 2009, found that large-scale commercial solar power projects would be feasible in the country. The study also found that Oman's solar energy potential is sufficient to meet all domestic electricity needs and provide surplus electricity for export by utilising merely 0.1 per cent of the country's land area.

Wind energy in Oman has an estimated total potential of 3 GW of generation capacity (Booz&Company 2009), with over 6.7 full-load wind hours per day, on average. Average wind speeds of 5–6 metres/second at 10 metres' height have been observed along the coastal areas of the country. The government is currently considering six pilot projects in the wind sector. There is also a lot of wind energy available offshore as Oman has a coastline of almost 1,700 km. However, few studies have been made to specify offshore wind energy potential over the last 20 years. Also, private-sector investment in biofuel production from date palms is ongoing, with 80,000 palms allocated for the first phase of the project. In addition, it is estimated that Oman could produce a net 100,000 MWh/year from waste biogas, corresponding to a power capacity of roughly 4 MW (Reegle 2014).

Furthermore, PAEW is working with IRENA towards a renewable energy policy, consisting of a framework for the development of a public policy for upscaling renewable energy through: involving local manufacturers to create jobs and added value to the local economy; using renewable desalination technologies in remote areas; capacity-building programmes; and public awareness campaigns.

Another renewable energy initiative, by Petroleum Development Oman, is using a 7 MW parabolic mirror solar energy plant to produce an average of 50 tonnes/day of steam that feeds directly into the company's thermal enhanced oil recovery (EOR) operations at the Amal West field (Energy Matters 2013). The company is currently conducting a study into using solar energy for power generation on a larger scale.

The first demand-side management (DSM) study in Oman, entitled 'The Study on Demand Supply Management for Power Sector in Sultanate of Oman' and conducted in 1998 by the Japan International Cooperation Agency, identified several strategies for potential load management, including: gas cooling systems for government buildings, hospital, hotels, commercial complexes and large houses; and shifting load from peak time to off-peak time in the industrial and commercial sectors by applying ice thermal storage systems and time-of-use tariffs. However, the study recommendations have never been implemented (Reegle 2014).

Rapid economic and population growth is substantially increasing power and water demand in Oman. A recent utilities demand forecast has estimated that electricity demand could increase by over 73 per cent between 2011 and 2018, with water demand growing at a similar pace. Green construction practices can help the Sultanate grow sustainably by reducing power and water needs while mitigating the environmental impacts. The Oman Green Building Council, part of the World Green Building Council, was set up in 2012 to promote and support green construction in the country.

In 2011, the Research Council of Oman launched a national 'Oman Eco-House Design Competition' in the framework of its 'Adaptation towards Sustainable Development' programme, which targeted higher education students in the Sultanate and aimed to promote awareness on the use of sustainable energy and the adoption of green standards in the design and construction of buildings. The winning project is being built at the winning university campus, and it is conceived to operate at zero net energy, owing to design and material use, and an ability to generate its own electricity supply. The building design further reduces embedded energy in materials, water and planting. The strategies adopted to build the 'Eco House' can be wholly or partly translated into future designs for residential and other projects that aim to save energy and use recycled materials (Oxford Business Group 2013).

Qatar

Qatar's current five-year national development strategy sets 13 efficiency targets for water and energy, which are tied to existing plans in the sector. On the supply side, these include water network leak reductions and expansion of treated sewage effluent networks, whereas on the demand side measures include advancing the adoption of energy-saving technologies, and phased removal of electricity, water and fuel subsidies (GSDP 2011). According to Luomi,

> in 2012, Qatar's Ministry of Energy and Industry announced the launch of a 200 MW solar energy programme, equal to approximately 2% of total demand. In addition, the 2013 Qatar National Food Security Plan recommends the installation of 700–800 MW in solar PV capacity by 2018 to meet the energy requirements of the projects proposed in the plan. This capacity could also be used to fulfil Qatar's pledge to organize a carbon neutral FIFA football world cup in 2022. In parallel, Qatar Foundation has announced a national commitment of 1 GW over the next decade, presumed to be an aggregate of the projects mentioned above.
>
> (Luomi 2014)

Further, she notes that 'Qatar Solar Technologies is setting up a polysilicon plant in the industrial city of Ras Laffan, with an annual production capacity of 8,000t/year, to provide for global PV markets and, later, for domestic use' (ibid.). Exports are expected to commence in 2015 (Qatar Solar Technologies 2014).

As a major natural gas producer, Qatar has joined the World Bank's voluntary Global Gas Flaring Reduction Partnership (GGFR) in 2009 that provides a collaborative framework to increase the use of associated gas by reducing flaring and venting. During the 2012 UN Climate Change Conference in Doha, Qatar signed an administration agreement with the World Bank to participate in the fourth phase of GGFR covering the period 2013–2015. The 'Qatar National Development Strategy 2011–2016' sets out as a key objective the halving of flaring between 2008 and 2016. It also mentions the development of a detailed flaring monitoring tool among the priorities of its environmental strategy for 2016 (World Bank 2012). In the Al-Shaheen project, launched in 2004, Qatar Petroleum worked to capture and use 180 million cubic feet of natural gas/day for electricity generation. The gas, produced as a by-product of pumping 300,000 barrels of oil from 300 offshore wells, had been flared, contributing to greenhouse gas emissions since oil production started at the Al-Shaheen field in 1994. The project was registered in 2007 under the Clean Development Mechanism (CDM) of the Kyoto Protocol, and had issued 3,178 thousand Certified Emission Reduction units as of October 2013 (Luomi 2014). Since then, about 6.2 million cubic metres of associated gas is produced at the field daily. To date, the Al-Shaheen field is Qatar's largest project for reducing emissions, avoiding an average of 2.5 $MtCO_2$/year. However, GGFR still ranks Qatar amongst the global top-20 'flarers' (World Bank 2012). The project is also contributing to the country's energy efficiency efforts by increasing power supply without increasing fossil fuel consumption, and encouraging the development of clean-technology demonstration projects (Abdel Gelil *et al.* 2012). In addition, Qatar Petroleum is working on a USD1 billion project to significantly reduce gas flaring at LNG berths at the industrial city of Ras Laffan. Some estimates place the resulting reductions at 1.8 $MtCO_2$/year (Luomi 2014). Furthermore, Qatar's National Communication to the UN Framework Convention on Climate Change (UNFCCC) describes a national plan for energy efficiency, optimisation and resource utilisation, with aims relating to expanding Qatar's CDM portfolio and increasing energy efficiency (Luomi 2014; Qatar 2011).

In February 2006, Qatar General Electricity and Water Corporation (KAHRAMAA) developed an energy efficiency programme for the country's electricity sector. The aim of the programme was to improve energy efficiency and increase the contribution of the energy sector to the achievement of sustainable development in the country. KAHRAMAA established a department for energy conservation and efficiency and proposed the adoption of a national action plan for energy conservation, which includes: phasing out inefficient lamps in residential areas; reducing electricity distribution losses; enforcing energy efficiency labelling for air conditioning units; and organising a national public education campaign called 'Tarsheed' (Al Kaabi 2012).

In order to promote green buildings, a Qatari research institute has developed the Qatar Sustainability Assessment System (QSAS). The primary objective of QSAS is to create a sustainable built environment that minimises ecological impact while addressing the specific regional needs and environment of the country (GORD 2013). Qatar is also doing the same as per the LEED rating system. New buildings in Education City are sustainably designed and a number hold LEED ratings, including the Qatar National Convention Centre and two halls of residence for students. District cooling is applied in 47 high-rise buildings in Doha's central West Bay district and the Pearl island development project (Luomi 2014).

Saudi Arabia

Interest in developing renewable energy resources, especially solar energy, was expressed in Saudi Arabia as early as the mid-1970s, as the GCC is one of the world regions that have a vast potential of solar radiation per year. To date, there have been few solar projects in Saudi Arabia other than small off-grid uses of PV technology. Saudi Arabia is now attempting to develop its own renewable energy technology hub. There is a research centre for renewable energy at the King Fahd University of Petroleum and Minerals, which focuses on the feasibility of siting of wind or solar facilities. Meanwhile, the King Abdullah University of Science and Technology (KAUST) has developed a 2 MW PV plant near the city of Jeddah, which is able to feed power back into the grid under a special arrangement with the Saudi Electricity Company. Furthermore, in 2010, KAUST was awarded LEED Platinum rating. KAUST buildings utilise 12,000 m^2 of solar thermal and PV arrays, which produce 3,300 MW/year and reduce CO_2 emissions by 1,650 tons/year. The Saudi government has recently announced the development of a number of solar-powered desalination plants using nanotechnology developed by the King Abdulaziz City for Science and Technology, which aims to cut the cost of desalinated water production by 40 per cent. The first plant, with a capacity of 10 MW and serving 100,000 people, will be built at the city of Al-Khafji (KACST 2012).

The K.A.CARE was established in 2010 with the mandate of working towards a sustainable development of Saudi Arabia by gradually shifting toward a greater use of renewable resources. The objective is to generate 54 GW of energy from renewable resources by 2032, to be reached by utilising solar power (almost 80 per cent), with the remaining share coming from a mix of wind, geothermal and waste-to-energy resources (see Table 2.4). In addition, Saudi Arabia has a target to start generating electricity from two nuclear plants in 2023, and gradually increase production to 20 per cent of total power generation by 2032. The Saudi plan of using nuclear power for electricity generation is considered by many to be a strategy that would help diversify the energy mix, increase exports of oil and secure a better position in the global energy market long after the depletion of fossil fuels (Saab 2013). However, whether nuclear energy supports the transition to green economy is still debated. It is true that nuclear power does not directly emit greenhouse gases and could provide an alternative to fossil fuel. Unfortunately, however, there are a great number of concerns about nuclear power that should be addressed before it can be classed as a green power source.

The Saudi Energy Efficiency Center (SEEC) was created in 2010 to promote energy efficiency. It is responsible for the development of energy-efficient technologies and conservation policies. SEEC is currently developing a national energy efficiency programme in the three largest energy-consuming sectors, namely buildings, industry and land transport (SEEC 2014).

The UAE

The UAE's bold initiative to promote clean energy technologies is best represented by the Masdar Initiative, owned by the Government of the emirate of Abu Dhabi. It is guided by the 'Abu Dhabi Economic Vision 2030', which seeks to catalyse the economic diversification of the emirate, drive new sources of income and strengthen Abu Dhabi's knowledge-based economic sectors. Essential components of the initiative are Masdar City and the research-driven graduate university, Masdar Institute for Science and Technology (Masdar 2014). Masdar City is envisaged to be a carbon-neutral community, and 'the silicon valley for clean, green, and alternative energy'. The City's architecture incorporates traditional passive features, such as wind towers and various shading devices, and it relies on alternative energy resources, including solar, wind and geothermal. Mobility within Masdar City is intended to take place through a fully automated electric personal rapid transport system or through walking. Other most significant projects of Masdar include: the 'Shams 1' 100 MW concentrated solar power (CSP) demonstration project using parabolic trough technology; the 'Nour 1' 100 MW PV plant; 10 MW of PV electricity generated by Masdar's headquarters; and a solar power system at the Yas Island Formula 1 racetrack. Furthermore, Masdar has also announced the construction of a 500 MW integrated hydrogen power generation and water desalination plant that will separate natural gas feedstock into hydrogen and CO_2. The hydrogen will be burned and the CO_2 transported and injected into oil fields to enhance oil recovery. The demonstration project will be the first carbon capture and storage (CCS) project of this type in the region.

'Estidama' is another initiative aiming to preserve and enrich Abu Dhabi's physical and cultural identity, and rapidly change the built environment. It is the first programme of its kind that is tailored to the GCC region. An essential tool to advance Estidama is the Pearl Rating System (PRS), which is a framework for sustainable design, construction and operation of communities and buildings. The PRS is specifically tailored to the emirate's hot climate and arid environment. Since 2010, PRS has become mandatory, and all new development projects must achieve, at minimum, a 1 Pearl rating to receive approval from the planning and permitting authorities, while government-funded buildings must achieve a minimum 2 Pearl rating (Estidama 2014). Given the debates that exist amongst practitioners and researchers on the merits and differences between Estidama's PRS, LEED and BREEAM (with the last standing for British Research Establishment Environmental Assessment Methodology), one comparison between the three rating systems concluded that the PRS has many similarities with the LEED and BREEAM rating systems as it has picked certain elements from these systems, but

Table 2.5 Pearl Rating System (PRS) implementation

Developments	Pearl 1	Pearl 2	Pearl 3	Pearl 4	Pearl 5
Projects	152	271	33	3	1
Buildings	192	376	30	3	1
Villas	1,679	8,445	595	0	0

Source: Abu Dhabi UPC (2013)

Table 2.6 Registered Clean Development Mechanism (CDM) projects in the GCC

Country	Registered projects	Renewable energy	Energy efficiency	Landfill gas	Gas recovery
Bahrain	0				
Kuwait	2				2
Oman	2			1	1
UAE	14	5	6	3	
Qatar	1				1
KSA	3	1		2	
Total	22	6	6	6	4

Source: UNFCCC CDM (2014)

still is distinctly local (Elgendy 2010). PRS recognises that significant industry knowledge and capabilities have already been created around the widely adopted BREEAM and LEED. Thus, it endeavours to harmonise the criteria that currently exist within these systems. Consequently, developers and consultants can use existing capabilities and still achieve a Pearl rating. This adds a layer of flexibility and harmonises it with the developments in the rating systems globally (Sharma 2010). Table 2.5 exhibits the evolution of PRS implementation since 2010 until October 2013 (Abu Dhabi UPC 2013).

Furthermore, it is worth noting that the UAE, with a total of 14 registered projects, hosts the largest number of registered CDM projects in the GCC. The CDM is one of the flexibility mechanisms of the Kyoto Protocol. It aims to help developing (non-Annex I) countries achieve sustainable development, and assist industrialised (Annex I) countries in complying with their emission reduction commitments under the Protocol. The registered CDM projects of the GCC are categorised under renewable energy, energy efficiency and recovery of landfill gas projects (see Table 2.6).

Barriers to transition to green energy

A set of barriers often put transition to green energy sector at economic, regulatory or institutional disadvantage relative to fossil-based forms of energy. In the GCC's context, these barriers can be classified as follows:

Policy barriers

Policy barriers to decoupling energy demand from economic growth, decarbonisation of the energy mix and transition to the green economy include:

i. Lack of or weak political will, both at the government and private sector level:

    As has been discussed above, in some countries, governments' commitments are still insufficient to move vigorously to the green economy. Although some, such as the UAE, have moved steadily on a green economic path, others, such as Saudi Arabia, are still hesitant to do so. Discussions in regional and international forums have revealed scepticism by Saudi Arabia on the definitions, drivers and trade impacts of green economy (personal communication). Although Saudi Arabia has the boldest renewable energy strategy in the GCC, many Saudis still believe that green economy poses threats to their fossil-based economy.

ii. Lack of or weak legal and institutional frameworks:

    Several GCC countries are still lacking the proper legal and institutional frameworks conducive to a transition to the green economy. Related problems include incomplete reform of the energy sector, lack of dedicated institutional units to promote green energy technologies and lack of incentives to attract private sector participation, among many.

iii. Slow and/or incomplete liberalisation process of energy and electricity markets:

    In most GCC countries, energy markets are still dominated by public monopolies. Grid connection and access is not evenly provided to renewable energy technologies or independent power producers (IPPs).

iv. Weak or lacking domestic R&D programmes, and low government expenditures in R&D:

    Generally, the gross expenditure on R&D (defined as the share of GDP directed at R&D) in the Gulf region is relatively low compared to the rest of the world. Qatar tops the region with 2.8 per cent in 2013, while Saudi Arabia reached only 0.3 per cent that same year (Battele 2012).

v. Weak regional cooperation:

    Regional and international cooperation is indispensable for achieving sustainable development. In the GCC context, the GCC Secretariat provides the main institutional framework for coordination and collaboration. More needs to be done to encourage stronger regional collaboration between government agencies, research institutions and universities to promote wide dissemination of green economy policies, practices and knowledge.

Market barriers

Energy efficiency and renewable energy markets in the region are distorted due to many underlying causes, including:

    i. Weak capacity to manage and disseminate information about market opportunities for energy efficiency and renewable energy technologies.

    ii. Lack of private sector associations and other market intermediaries promoting energy efficiency and renewable energy technologies.

    iii. Low level of consumer awareness leading to low market demand:

> There has been widespread scepticism about the performance and reliability of renewable energy technologies due to past technology failures, weak product performances and lack of information.

    iv. Lack of national standards, testing and certifications:

> These are crucially needed to secure penetration of high-performance technologies. They are further required to foster technology development and advancement.

    v. Weak capacity of local assembly and manufacturing, distribution, installation and maintenance of green energy technologies.

    vi. Lack of education and training programmes for green energy professionals at all levels.

    vii. Low level of awareness in the financial sector and lack of proper financing schemes:

> Consumers or project developers may lack access to credit to purchase or invest in green energy projects because of lack of collateral, or distorted capital markets.

Economic barriers

Economically, energy efficiency and renewable energy technologies often face unfair competition in the market due to economic barriers. These include:

i.   Heavy subsidies provided by governments to oil and natural gas:

> As discussed, there has been great recognition that heavy subsidies to fossil energy in the GCC form the major stumbling block to a transition to a green energy sector in the region. (A discussion of the subsidy issue will follow.)

ii.   Higher initial capital costs of green energy technologies.

iii.   Lack of consideration of externalities arising from heavy reliance on and use of fossil fuels compared to clean energy technologies:

> The environmental impacts of fossil fuels often result in real costs to society in terms of human health (including loss of work days or health care costs), infrastructure decay (for example from acid rain), declines in fisheries and, ultimately, the costs associated with climate change. Yet, the capacity to internalise these costs into national accounting is lacking in the GCC region.

Energy subsidies

The GCC region has had a long history of subsidising crude oil, oil products, natural gas and electricity (see Table 2.7). Even though there is no agreed-upon

Table 2.7 Energy subsidies in the GCC

Country	Total subsidy (billion USD)	Subsidy as % of GDP	Subsidy as % of cost of supply
Saudi Arabia	43.52	9.8	78.9
Kuwait	7.62	5.8	53.3
Qatar	4.15	3.2	63.2
UAE	18.15	6	55.7

Sources: Abdel Gelil *et al.* (2012); SEEC (2014)

universal definition of 'subsidy', the simplest one is that of De Moor and Calamai which defines subsidy as 'any measure that keeps prices for consumers below the market level or keeps prices for producers above the market level or that reduces costs for consumers and producers by giving direct or indirect support' (Fattouh and El-Katiri 2012a). The rationale for energy subsidies generally differs based on a country's socioeconomic context and political motivation. In the resource-rich GCC region, motives are both economic and political. From an economic stand-point, subsidised petroleum products provided to energy-intensive industries, such as power stations and water desalination, aluminium smelters, and petro-chemicals and cement industries, are likely to benefit those industries as energy constitutes an important component of their production costs. The rationale behind such subsidies is to help protect local industries against foreign com-petition, enhance their export competitiveness and protect local employment. From a political standpoint, fuel subsidies are often introduced or increased, as appropriate, to alleviate popular discontent. In the GCC, the policy of supplying heavily subsidised energy to the domestic market can also be comprehended as a measure of distributing oil and gas rents and, thereby, as a cornerstone of the citizens' participation in the natural resource wealth of their country, with many citizens in these countries considering low-priced energy as a guaranteed birth-right (ibid.).

Despite the obvious negative impacts of fossil fuel and electricity subsidies on the national economy and welfare system, reform of subsidies remains a highly challenging task in all GCC countries. Policy makers often fear public resistance and the impact of increased energy prices on the social well-being of the people in general, and the poor in particular. In addition, the lack of transparency about the size of subsidies, their social and economic impacts, and the difficulties in identifying the main beneficiaries further complicate the initiation of effective and comprehensive energy pricing reform. However, today, these reforms are necessary in order to address not only pressing energy needs of the GCC coun-tries, but also in moving toward a more sustainable energy development path in general. Currently, the issue of reforming energy subsidies is topping the energy political agenda in many GCC countries. Moving to greening the energy sector implicitly suggests removing the above-discussed barriers, with reforming energy prices as a priority.

Policy recommendations

In order to enable a transition to a green economy in the GCC region, a number of policies and measures need to be adopted. It is worth noting that one size does not fit all. Each country should select the policy package that suits its national context. In addition to the first logical step of removing the barriers discussed above, the following policy interventions are inevitable:

Governance

Governance is critical for the achievement of sustainable development. It includes strengthening the institutional and legal frameworks and fostering equitable participation in decision-making by civil society and the private sector. The GCC region needs to revitalise its governance systems for a smooth transition to the green economy. There is a need to consider reviewing the adequacy of national legislative and institutional frameworks, taking into consideration success stories from the region and internationally. Consideration should also be given to the development of, or updating of, existing national strategies for sustainable development, and mainstream green economy concepts into them. It is remarkable that a long-term national initiative to build a green economy in the UAE under the slogan 'a green economy for sustainable development' was launched in 2012. The aims of this initiative are threefold: to make the UAE one of the global pioneers in green economy; to become a hub for exporting and re-exporting green products and technologies; and be a country preserving a sustainable environment that supports long-term economic growth (WAM 2012).

Enabling environment to attract foreign investment

A secure, stable, transparent and accountable economic environment is a necessity for attracting local and foreign investors, particularly for new sectors, such as green energy and venture capital. The financial system should be stable with clear regulations for currency exchange and fund transfers. In addition, the judicial system should be independent and transparent, and the rule of law well instituted. In order to encourage green investment, finance institutions should give priority to green energy projects as opposed to conventional energy technologies. Governments need to create an enabling environment that is conducive to attracting an inflow of foreign direct investments, including through the development of investment roadmaps for a transition towards a green economy. Moreover, governments should support micro-finance in order to encourage small and medium size enterprises to create green jobs. This could be done through the establishment of dedicated loan facilities with low interest rates to provide micro-finance for green energy technologies on preferential terms.

Market incentives

Market incentives, as shown in Table 2.3, have been rarely adopted in the region. These include taxes, subsidies, charges, tradable permits and eco-labelling. The use of a FIT and net metering systems are other incentive tools that encourage investments in renewable technologies, whereby consumers are credited for surplus electricity generation beyond domestic needs. Such tools need to be designed to complement regulations and address environmental, social and economic considerations. Further, there is a need to establish suitable manufacturing standards and specifications and strictly enforce them. Policy instruments and incentives could be introduced to encourage local manufacturers to upgrade their facilities and enable them to export some of their production to regional markets. By targeting the export market, local manufacturers would have an incentive to improve their production quality and would seek to obtain international certification. The local market would, in turn, benefit from better quality products, consumer trust and expanded demand.

Role of the private sector

The active involvement of the private sector and promotion of public-private partnership through finance and expertise is critical for transitioning to the green economy. In order to encourage private sector involvement, governments need to provide the right regulatory and market incentive measures, such as loan guarantees. National capacity is needed to design policies and introduce measures that encourage the involvement of the private sector in support of the green transition (Abaza *et al.* 2012). This could include various forms of concessions and management contracts, private IPPs, contracting out operation and maintenance, billing, metering and bill collection and other services.

Proper financing schemes

Lack of proper financing schemes is one of the major barriers to scaling up green energy technologies. These schemes should be devised involving governments, private sector (including investors and local banks) and international financial institutions. These could also include the creation of national green energy funds to support early market development. Bilateral and multilateral organisations should explicitly consider green energy for development assistance projects. Guarantee funds and refinancing schemes for local banks should also be considered. Furthermore, the region needs to tap more into the potential for carbon finance. Participation of the GCC countries in the CDM is still relatively low (see Table 2.6): the total number of registered CDM projects in the region is 22, the majority of which are hosted in the UAE. Given the complexity of this instrument, low prices of carbon credits and uncertainty of the global carbon market post-2015, substantial capacity building will be needed, among others. Other international climate financing mechanisms available to help ease fiscal pressures and attract private sector participation in green investment include the Green Climate Fund. Furthermore, the Nationally Appropriate Mitigation Action (NAMA) instrument under the UNFCCC provides a means to communicate national needs on finance, technology transfer and capacity building within the current international climate regime.

Subsidy reform

As discussed earlier, fossil fuels subsidies have been a major barrier to expanding the market for energy efficiency and renewable energy technologies in the region. Energy demand is price-sensitive. Most of the GCC countries suffer from a long history of heavily subsidised energy prices. This has impaired the economics of energy efficiency and renewable energy projects, helped increase per capita energy consumption and greenhouse gas emissions, accelerated depletion of natural resources and worsened macroeconomic performance. Energy pricing reform is therefore crucial for improving energy efficiency and promoting renewable energy technologies. The following steps should be taken into account in reforming subsidies:

  i. Replace fossil fuels subsidies with green subsidies. These include direct grants, loans, tax rebates and cuts to encourage investments in green energy technologies;
 ii. Reform subsidies as part of a policy package aimed at reducing negative impacts on the poor and economic competitiveness; and
iii. Develop and introduce a social protection mechanism in order to alleviate negative impacts on the poor.

Capacity building

Strengthening both human as well as institutional capacities would secure the provision of a cadre of professionals capable of designing policy packages aimed at a transition to the green economy. This should be an integral component of education system reforms in the region. Environmental and social considerations need to be integrated into the different disciplines at different levels from primary schools up to higher education institutions. Institutional capacity should be strengthened to support the development of comprehensive national green energy strategies within national planning processes for sustainable development. This should include strengthening the capacity of the energy efficiency and renewable energy agencies at the national level. It should also consider inclusion of renewable energy technologies in school and university curricula, and include human resource training at all levels, including planners, engineers and technicians for the design, installation and maintenance of green energy systems. Raising awareness and building the capacity of the financial sector is also crucial to overcome the financing barrier. Encouraging the creation of industry associations would play a vital role in market development, networking and matchmaking between manufacturers, installers, importers and consumers. This would also catalyse cooperation and public-private partnerships with regulatory agencies and other major players.

Raising public awareness

Low levels of awareness and lack of knowledge about the costs and other benefits of green energy technologies are major barriers to their dissemination.

Development of effective public awareness and promotion campaigns making use of all media can be expected to yield substantial results. Such campaigns should provide information on green energy concepts, technologies and practices, and their costs and benefits. This is crucial for gaining public acceptance and support for a transition to greener lifestyles. Public awareness and promotional campaigns are also needed in order to stimulate local demand for energy-efficient goods and services, and renewable energy technologies. Awareness campaigns and outreach activities should be designed to support the other policy measures. This would aim at enhancing the awareness of major market players of the economic benefits of energy efficiency and renewable energy. Further, increasing public awareness of the environmental, health-related and economic benefits of energy efficiency and renewable energy would increase demand for them.

Research and technology development and transfer

Current expenditure of GCC governments in R&D is relatively low. The GCC countries need to increase their budgetary allocations for R&D. The region's existing research capabilities in clean energy technologies have emerged mainly as a result of collaboration between governments, international technology providers and multilateral organisations, such as the United Nations Development Programme (UNDP), World Bank and European Union organisations. These programmes have been successful in creating human expertise and limited local research capabilities. Enhanced regional cooperation is urgently needed through cooperation between GCCs and other Arab universities with solid and meaningful partnerships for faculty and student exchange and support for long-term interdisciplinary research programmes in energy with multiple partners from various countries. For encouraging private investment in R&D and deployment of green technologies, the policy toolkit includes incentives, such as R&D tax credits or direct subsidies to firms engaging in green activities, as well as public procurement and funding of basic research. The GCC countries have a golden opportunity to invest part of their oil revenue surplus in R&D. Further, green technology transfer could be realised through different schemes, including joint ventures between international technology providers and local firms, and would lead to upgrading and modernising local manufacturing capabilities. Masdar provides an example to be replicated of using oil proceeds to form joint ventures with a number of international technology providers. The same cooperation should be enhanced with research institutions to demonstrate and test green technologies under different national circumstances. The Masdar Institute is also a good example of international cooperation with the Massachusetts Institute of Technology in research, testing and development of renewable energy technologies under region-specific circumstances.

Conclusions

The GCC countries are confronted with a rapidly increasing energy demand in the coming decades resulting from demographic, socioeconomic and resource-related factors. The region has large potential for improving energy efficiency and increasing the use of renewable energy sources, particularly solar, due to its high level of solar radiation. A number of barriers to the development of the green technologies market exist in the region. These prominently include heavy subsidies for competing fossil fuel technologies, lack of or insufficient incentives to support green energy development, costly financing and lack of market intermediaries, such as technology standards. A package of policy interventions needs to be adopted and implemented in order to overcome these barriers. Each country should select the appropriate package from these policies to suit different national contexts. The transition towards green energy systems requires some form of government intervention so as to overcome market distortions favouring fossil fuels. Subsidies for fossil fuels pose a significant barrier to this transition and thus ought to be phased out.

Note

1 Abu Dhabi is one of the seven emirates of the United Arab Emirates. This is not a national target.

References

Abaza, Hussein, Najib Saab and Bashar Zeitoon, eds. 2012. *Green Economy: Sustainable Transition in a Changing Arab World*. Beirut: Arab Forum for Environment and Development (AFED).

Abdel Gelil, Ibrahim. 2011. *Energy Situation in Bahrain: Gap Analysis*. United Nations Development Programme. Unpublished.

Abdel Gelil, Ibrahim. 2012. 'Sustainable Energy Options.' In *Arab Environment: Survival Options: Ecological Footprint of Arab Countries*, edited by Najib Saab, 69–82. Beirut: AFED.

Abdel Gelil, Ibrahim, Farid Chaaban and Leila Dagher. 2012. 'Energy.' In *Arab Environment: Green Economy: Sustainable Transition in a Changing Arab World*, edited by Hussein Abaza, Najib Saab and Bashar Zeitoon, 75–112. Beirut: AFED.

Abu Dhabi UPC. Abu Dhabi Urban Planning Council. 2013. 'Estidama, Sustainability at Large: A Mandate for Success.' Presentation at a conference by AFED. Beirut, 29 October.

Al Kaabi, Fahad. 2012. 'Conservation Plan for Tarsheed.' Presentation SustainableQatar's meeting, 4 June. http://www.sustainableqatar.com/

Bachellerie, Imen. 2013. *Sustainability and Competitiveness: A Programmatic Approach to Solar Energy Transition in the GCC Countries*. GRC Gulf Paper. Gulf Research Center, September.

Battele. 2012. '2013 R&D Magazine Global Funding Forecast.' *Battele R&D Magazine*, 18 December. http://www.rdmag.com/digital-editions

Booz&Company. 2009. *A New Source of Power: The Potential for Renewable Energy in the MENA Region*.

EIA. United States Energy Information Administration. 2014. 'International Energy Statistics.' Accessed 5 October. http://www.eia.gov/

El-Ashry, Mohamed, and Najib Saab. 2010. *Arab Environment: Water, Sustainable Management of a Scarce Resource*. Beirut: AFED.

Elgendy, Karim. 2010. 'Comparing Estidama's Pearls Rating System to LEED and BREEM.' *Carboun*, 17 April. http://www.carboun.com/

Energy Matters. 2013. 'Solar Energy Helps Boost Oman Oil Field Yield.' 24 May. www.energymatters.com.au/

Estidama. 2014. Accessed 6 October. http://estidama.upc.gov.ae/

EU-GCC Clean Energy Network. 2012. *Renewable Energy Readiness Assessment Report: The GCC Countries*. Abu Dhabi: Masdar.

Fattouh, Bassam, and Laura El-Katiri. 2012a. *Energy Subsidies in the Arab World*. Arab Human Development Report Research Paper. New York: United Nations Development Programme, Regional Bureau for Arab States (UNDP RBAS).

Fattouh, Bassam, and Laura El-Katiri. 2012b. *Energy and Arab Economic Development*. Arab Human Development Report Research Paper. New York: UNDP RBAS.

Fattouh, Bassam, and Laura El-Katiri. 2013. 'Arab Oil in the Global and Domestic Contexts.' In *Arab Environment: Sustainable Energy: Prospects, Challenges, Opportunities*, edited by Ibrahim Abdel Gelil, Mohamed Al-Ashry and Najib Saab, 16–35. Beirut: AFED.

GORD. Gulf Organization for Research and Development. 2013. *GSAS/QSAS Technical Guide*. Doha.

GSDP. Qatar General Secretariat for Development Planning. 2011. *Qatar National Development Strategy 2011–2016*. Doha.

IEA. International Energy Agency. 2013. *Key World Energy Statistics*. Paris.

IMF. International Monetary Fund. 2013. *Economic Prospects and Economic Challenges for the GCC Countries*. Annual Meeting of Ministers of Finance and Central Banks Governors.

IRENA. International Renewable Energy Agency. 2012. 'Renewable Energy in the Gulf Region.' Side event at the UN Climate Change Conference in Doha, 12 December.

Jalilvand, David. 2012. *Renewable Energy for the Middle East and North Africa: Policies for a Successful Transition*. Friedrich Ebert Stiftung, February.

KACST. King Abdulaziz City for Science and Technology. 2012. 'Launching the First Phase of the National Initiative for Water Desalination Using Solar Energy.' http://www.kacst.edu.sa/en/

Kneissl, Karin. 2014. 'When Energy Exporters Become Importers and Vice Versa: Many Risks and Some Opportunities for Regional Cooperation.' Presentation at the World Future Energy Summit, Abu Dhabi, UAE.

Kuwait. 2012. *Kuwait's Initial National Communications under the United Nations Framework Convention on Climate Change*. November.

Lahn, Glada, Paul Stevens and Felix Preston. 2013 *Saving Oil and Gas in the Gulf*. Chatham House Report. London: Chatham House.

LAS, UNEP and UNESCWA. The League of Arab States, United Nations Environment Programme and the United Nations Economic and Social Commission for Western Asia. 2010. *The Arab Regional Strategy for Sustainable Consumption and Production*. Cairo: LAS.

Lia, Carol, and Sarkar Ashok. 2013. *Bahrain's Energy Efficient Lighting Initiative*. Washington D.C.: The World Bank.

Luomi, Mari. *Mainstreaming Climate Policy in the Gulf Cooperation Council States*. 2014. OIES Paper MEP 7. Oxford: The Oxford Institute for Energy Studies.

Masdar. 2014. Accessed 12 May. http://www.masdar.ae/

Mytelka, Lynn, Francisco Aguayo, Grant Boyle *et al*. 2012. 'Chapter 25 – Policies for Capacity Development.' In *Global Energy Assessment: Toward a Sustainable Future*, edited by GEA Writing Team, 1745–1802. Cambridge: Cambridge University Press.

Nuruddin, Nour. 2009. 'Production Increase through Environment Enhancement Project.' Presentation at the 22nd AFA International Technology Conference and Exhibition, Morocco.

Oxford Business Group. 2013. 'Going Green: Sustainable Building Practices Should Help to Address Housing Shortages.' http://www.oxfordbusinessgroup.com/

PAEW. Public Authority for Electricity and Water, Oman. 2014. 'Renewable Energy.' Accessed November. http://www.paew.gov.om/

Psarras, John, Alexandros Flamos and Kostas Patlitzianas. 2009. *Enhancing the EU-GCC Relations within a New Climate Regime: Prospects and Opportunities for Cooperation*. Background Paper. Al-JISR Project.

Qatar. 2011. *Qatar's Initial National Communications to the United Nations Framework Convention on Climate Change*. Doha: Ministry of Environment.

Qatar Solar Technologies. 2014. 'Project Update.' Accessed 17 July. www.qstec.com/about/project-update

Personal communication with a Saudi official, 2014.

Reegle. 2014. 'Oman 2012.' Accessed 7 October. www.reegle.info

REN21. 2013. *MENA Renewables Status Report*. Washington D.C.: REN21.

Saab, Najib. 2013. 'The Nuclear Power Option in the Arab Countries.' In *Arab Environment: Sustainable Energy*, edited by Ibrahim Abdel Gelil, Najib Saab and Mohamed Al-Ashry. Beirut: AFED.

SEEC. Saudi Energy Efficiency Center. 2014. Accessed May. http://www.seec.gov.sa/

Seneviratne, Mario. 2010. 'Green Buildings in the GCC Countries.' Presentation on 19 October in Montreal, Canada.

Sharma, Pulkit. 2010. 'ESTIDAMA (Pearl) vs. LEED: A Discussion on Rating Systems and Sustainability in the Middle East.' *MIT Meydan*, 28 February. http://mitmeydan.wordpress.com/

UNESCWA. 2013. *Green Economy Initiatives, Success Stories and Lessons Learned in the Arab Region*. New York: United Nations, February.

UNFCCC CDM. United Nations Framework Convention on Climate Change; Clean Development Mechanism. 2014. 'Project Search.' Accessed 17 July. http://cdm.unfccc.int/

Ventures Onsite. 2014. 'GCC Proposed to Have Unified Building Codes by 2015.' *Onsite Exclusives*, 12 June. https://www.venturesonsite.com/

WAM. 2012. 'Mohammed Unveils UAE's Green Economy.' *Emirates 24/7*, 15 January. http://www.emirates247.com/

World Bank. 2012. 'Qatar, World Bank Extend Cooperation to Further Reduce Emissions from Gas Flaring.' 6 December. http://go.worldbank.org/EI42J8CXF0

3 Energy pricing reform and the green economy in the Gulf region

Tom S. H. Moerenhout

Introduction to the green economy project in the Gulf Cooperation Council

It is widely acknowledged that there is no consensus on what exactly constitutes 'the green economy', and what principles should guide it. The United Nations Environment Programme (UNEP 2011a, 16) defines the green economy as 'one that results in improved human well-being and social equity, while significantly reducing environmental risks and ecological scarcities'. This means a green economy is low-carbon, resource efficient and socially inclusive. The transition from using emission-intensive energy in an energy-inefficient economy, to more sustainable energy use in an efficient economy, is at the heart of the green economy debate (Netzer and Althaus 2012, 3). While a lack of a consensus on the definition of a green economy is a nuisance for international cooperation, it is not necessarily a major point of discussion to address national green economy initiatives in the Gulf Cooperation Council (GCC) context.

The GCC countries have both hinted at, and explicitly moved forward on, a set of green economy objectives (*vide infra*). A transformation to a green economy in the GCC context can be understood as the process through which oil-based economies attempt to shift toward a more sustainable and productive economic model. It is about decoupling welfare creation and economic growth from resource use. The GCC governments are confronted with a number of challenges (*vide infra*) that are slowly but undeniably eroding the political, social, economic and environmental sustainability of their traditional economic model, which is built on export earnings from the sale of conventional energy sources.

Without going into detail on academic and policy assessments about the sustainability (and exact meaning) of the rentier state model, and the challenges posed by the resource curse, it is crucial to understand that the green economy project in the GCC is not merely about transforming the economy, but more about reassessing the valuation of resources within the social contract that shape political dynamics in GCC countries. Energy pricing is at the epicentre of this transformation.

When assessing energy pricing in the broader context of challenges posed to GCC governments and economies, it becomes clear that the green economy project is not just about responding to unsustainable production and consumption patterns through technological innovation, but also about operationalising different consumption and production patterns as a whole (Netzer and Althaus 2012, 5–6). That is not to say that technological innovation does not play a central role in the green economy transformation. On the contrary, technology innovation is a crucial factor in addressing specific policy objectives. The green economy project in the GCC can be understood as one that addresses a set of challenges by setting broad and specific policy objectives and acting upon them. Addressing the aforementioned social contract and trying to lift the resource curse, however, require political economy considerations. Energy pricing reform, within the context of the green economy, therefore has to be an art in political economy.

Challenges in the GCC and green economy investments

To fully understand, and value, the complexity of a green economy transition, it is imperative to see the broader policy challenges in the GCC region. These include poverty, unemployment, food insecurity, water scarcity, energy security and a growing inequitable income distribution. These are exacerbated by uncontrolled urbanisation, rapid industrialisation, and consumption impacts of welfare accumulation in certain strata of the population. Abaza *et al.* (2011, vi) hold that the major reason for not transitioning to a green economy in the Middle East and North Africa (MENA) region is the existence of structural problems such as fragile political systems and demographic challenges. In the GCC, certain political and demographic challenges are aggravated because of a difficult environment, influenced by, among others, the political, social and economic implications of the Arab Spring and the global financial crisis (Abdel Hamid 2012, 22).

Most GCC countries have to contend with certain aspects of the resource curse. Their dependency on fuel exports means that there are insufficient incentives to invest in diversifying the domestic economy, which, in this case, is key to the development of a green economy (UNEP 2011a, 67). The main reform goal, in a green economy context, is to re-invest export earnings in factors that can diversify and enrich the economy, such as infrastructure, human capital and technology innovation (UNEP 2011b, 67). So far, however, under-priced energy has moved investments into energy-intensive industries aimed at exportation (Abdel Hamid 2012, 78). This type of economic diversification is dangerous, as the international prices of such products have often been volatile. These sectors tend to be capital-intensive without generating much employment and thereby exacerbating some of the structural problems of rentier economies (Abaza *et al.* 2011, x). It needs to be noted, however, that among the GCC countries, the United Arab Emirates (UAE), and particularly Dubai, has achieved a higher degree of non-energy-intensive economic diversification.

Another green economy policy objective related to energy pricing is the transformation of energy consumption patterns. Energy efficiency is one side of the coin (*vide infra*); the other side is energy over-consumption in the GCC, particularly in the residential sector. It is well established that energy under-pricing has encouraged over-consumption in a socially regressive manner, with the richer gaining a larger share of energy under-pricing than the poor (ibid., xx). Indeed, the green economy project on energy pricing in the GCC ought to have a large component focusing on demand management to address wasteful consumption. It is about doing more with less, about targeting subsidies more appropriately to the poor, rather than maintaining their availability across the board. Achieving a more equitable distribution of consumption patterns and wealth is indeed a direct objective both of pricing reform and of the green economy at large.

Reforming energy prices is therefore directly linked to green economy investments in three ways. First, by reducing domestic over-consumption, GCC governments are able to sell more fuel on the international market, thereby strengthening revenues and investing power. Second, as under-pricing increases incentives to invest in energy-inefficient energy-intensive industries, the reform of energy prices can serve as catalyst to direct investment flows into high-value sectors. It will also encourage energy-efficiency measures within energy-intensive sectors, hence strengthening competitiveness of the overall economy in the medium term. And third, it will make renewable energy more competitive, which can reduce financing costs in the medium term.

Energy pricing and green economy objectives

Netzer and Althaus (2012, 23) enumerate green economy objectives specific to the MENA region but which also apply to specific GCC countries, including a shift of investment to green economy in urban development, low-carbon transport, renewable energy, energy efficiency, resource-efficient agriculture, and a change in consumption and production patterns. Energy pricing, as previously mentioned, is thus at the heart of these, more specific, green economy objectives. Fossil fuel subsidies are seen as both policy barriers (together with the existence of monopolised energy markets and a lack of renewable energy targets) and economic barriers (Abdel Gelil *et al.* 2011, 88–93). Conflicting policy instruments are regarded as one of the main barriers to green growth innovation. Indeed, the appropriate valuation of resources is not at, but the heart of the green economy.

Energy is improperly priced in two ways. In many developing countries, the retail prices of fossil fuels and electricity are set below a certain reference price. This reference price is either the value of fuel on the international market, or the domestic production cost. A second way in which energy is improperly valuated lies in the fact that most countries around the world fail to price negative externalities from fuel and electricity consumption. This assessment of energy pricing in the GCC will mainly focus on the first type of energy pricing failure, even though a fuel price that is part of a green economy cannot but include negative externalities. This is a crucial note to make, particularly if the international oil price decreases. Indeed, the international oil price is not a market price that reflects the scarcity of the resource, or, for that matter, a sustainable perspective on energy consumption. So even if the 'opportunity cost' of setting low domestic prices (*vide infra*) decreases as a result of lower prices on the international market, this is not in itself an indicator of more sustainable oil management within GCC states.

Methodological note

The calculation of subsidies or the costs associated with the under-pricing of energy is a challenging exercise. The bulk of fossil fuel subsidies in the GCC region are aimed at supporting consumption through price support (in this case, consumption can include the use of natural resources for power generation purposes). The International Energy Agency (IEA) and the International Monetary Fund (IMF), as well as the author of this chapter, estimate support by applying a price-gap approach. This method measures the difference between domestic fossil fuel prices and benchmark prices on the international market. This difference is then regarded as a proxy for total fossil fuel consumption support (Koplow 2009).

The main methodological debate is on the choice of the benchmark or reference price. While the IEA, IMF and the author use international prices as reference prices (IEA 2012b), fossil fuel producing countries and the Organization of the Petroleum Exporting Countries (OPEC) argue that the reference price should be based on the cost of production, since this cost is lower than the international market price in many fossil fuel exporting countries (IEA *et al.* 2010). However, there is insufficient transparency in most of the GCC countries to be able to appropriately estimate the cost of production. Thus, the approach of the IEA, referred to as the opportunity cost approach, is the one most used. This approach refers to the potential revenues lost by selling at low prices on the domestic market, rather than on the international market (IEA 2012b).

Luciani (2014, 11–13) has pointed to a number of disadvantages associated with the opportunity cost subsidy approach. He argues that the balance between domestic consumption and exports, the 'trade off' as he calls it, is something to assess in the long term but not at a given point of time. For him, the opportunity costs need to be assessed in comparing it to the actual costs, starting from a historical perspective. In general, Luciani (ibid., 15) notes: 'If demand growth continues unabated, it will *eventually* lead to a trade off between domestic consumption and exports, increased dependence on imports of refined products, irrational proliferation of capacity in a very inefficient power system' (emphasis added). While many of his critiques are relevant and correct, the author of this chapter disagrees with the time frame of his assessment of opportunity costs, and argues that the *eventual* trade-off is already occurring in many GCC countries today. What is important, however, is to put any opportunity cost estimate in the correct context, which is one of volatile international prices and a rising demand.

However, methodological difficulties do not need to impede cooperation. First, not all GCC countries are net exporters across the board, but often import one or more energy products such as diesel or natural gas (Fattouh and El-Katiri 2012). Second, fuel producing countries increasingly recognise that price

Table 3.1 Total fossil fuel subsidies in the GCC (2011)

	USD billion	*USD/capita*	*% of GDP*	*% of pub exp*
Bahrain[ac]	2.05	1,819	7.94	25.89
Kuwait[b]	11.10	3,015	6.90	17.90
Oman[a]	8.09	1,407	5.97	18.80
Qatar[b]	5.98	3,382	3.45	13.01
Saudi Arabia[b]	60.94	2,163	10.21	25.94
UAE[b]	21.82	4,060	6.38	26.72
Total GCC	109.98			

Sources: IEA (2012a); IMF (2013); author's calculations

Notes: IEA figures (a) were used when complete. In case of incomplete IEA estimates, IMF estimates (b) were reported. Both estimates are based on a similar opportunity cost approach. Other calculations were done by the author based on IMF country statistics; the Bahrain subsidy estimate (c) is incomplete because of the unavailability of natural gas subsidy estimates.

support is the cause of wasteful over-consumption and, subsequently, fiscal stress (Moerenhout 2013).

Overall subsidies, green economy financing and energy efficiency

The under-pricing of energy reduces financial resources available for investing in other areas, including a green economy diversification project. In 2011, subsidies calculated according to an opportunity cost approach to oil, natural gas and electricity in the GCC region have reached around USD110 billion. A little more than half of these subsidies have been allocated to oil, with the remainder distributed between electricity and natural gas (approximately 27 and 20 per cent respectively) (IEA 2012a). These subsidies have become fiscally unsustainable for most Gulf countries, and amount to between 5 and 10 per cent of the gross domestic product (GDP), and between 15 and 25 per cent of government expenditure in most GCC countries (see Table 3.1).

Most definitions of the green economy, including some of those applied in the Arab region, do not only include a transformation of consumption and production patterns, but also call for the inclusion of negative social and environmental externalities in, among others, the setting of prices. For example the Arab Forum for Environment and Development has included the non-inclusion of externalities as a problem in achieving green economy objectives (Abaza et al. 2011, 88–93). The IMF (2013) has for the first time put forward such a post-tax analysis of fossil fuel subsidies. While their methodology is still under development, initial results show that there are high costs associated with the over-consumption of energy resources in the GCC. Overall subsidies (again estimated based on the opportunity cost approach) increase from USD110 billion to USD179 billion, representing between 8 and 17 per cent of GDP and between 20 and 48 per cent of public expenditure.

These numbers, with or without externalities included, demonstrate that the under-pricing of energy incurs high opportunity costs for GCC governments. In most GCC countries, the opportunity costs of under-pricing have doubled in a period of only three years between 2009 and 2011 (IEA 2012a). This is because of high fuel prices on the international market. This also led to high fuel export revenues for GCC countries. While certain GCC countries may not have exported certain fuels more in the absence of under-pricing, opportunity costs remain a valid indicator because of the high domestic consumption, and therefore more limited resource availability, for future exports. While this may appear as a distant poten-tial threat, Gastli and Armendariz (2013, 10) have estimated that oil reserves in Bahrain and Oman could be depleted within as little as 20 years. Those in Qatar and Saudi Arabia could follow closely on their heels, with reserves disappearing in around 60–70 years. The UAE (especially Abu Dhabi) and Kuwait have large resources compared to domestic consumption patterns and would respectively last 92 and more than 100 years. While different estimates exist, these numbers illustrate the problem of current consumption to reserve and production ratios. It must, how-ever, be noted that the pressing trends do not have similar dynamics when natural gas is considered. In this case, for example, Qatar has amongst the world's highest reserves with a much more healthy consumption to reserve and production ratio.

Available financing, within which fuel exports play an important role, is key to the green economy project, since a serious transformation to the green econ-omy requires large investments sustained through time. Fuel export security also serves to demonstrate long-term fiscal strength to investors. On a global level, investments in solar energy reached USD114 billion in 2013. Only USD9 billion of this was invested in the entire Middle Eastern and African regions, despite both possessing enormous solar resource potential (Bachellerie 2012; Bloomberg New Energy Finance 2014b). Besides pumping money into energy-inefficient, energy-intensive industries, low energy prices can lead to energy-inefficient investments in infrastructure. Such investments are often capital-intensive and result in a lock-in effect in which energy-efficiency investments are more difficult and costly to make (Meltzer *et al.* 2014, 26). Cheap energy and electricity reduce incentives to achieve energy efficiency in different sectors including industry, agriculture, residential appliances and transport.

Without pricing reform, the energy-efficiency measures that are taken might not always pay off. Jevon's paradox holds that more energy efficiency in com-bination with low and fixed tariffs might actually increase energy consumption relative to what would have been consumed without these gains. UNEP has put forward that rebound effects are larger when prices are smaller and constant (UNEP 2011a, 68–69). Therefore energy pricing reform is needed to make sure that energy-efficiency measures indeed lead to actual gains.

Competitiveness of renewable electricity

The demand for electricity is increasing, and providing subsidies while simultan-eously constructing conventional energy infrastructure to meet that demand is economically unsustainable (Abaza *et al.* 2011, x). Between 2002 and 2011, electricity consumption in the GCC grew by an average of nearly 7 per cent per year (author calculations based on IEA data). The Chief Executive Officer of Saudi Aramco noted that if nothing changes, domestic fuel consumption could more than double by 2030 (El-Katiri 2014, 8). The move toward economic diversification with a focus on energy-intensive industrialisation has meant that industry is the largest growing consumer, at a compound annual growth rate (CAGR) of over 9 per cent between 2002 and 2011 (author calculations based on IEA data). However, electricity demand in industry grew by 12 per cent annually between 2007 and 2011. In Oman, industrial consumption growth between 2007 and 2011 reached as much as 28 per cent per year (ibid.). This demonstrates that demand management in GCC countries is not only about managing the residential sector, but also about incentivising energy efficiency in industry (and in desalination, *vide infra*).

Even though there has been a relative decrease in the share of residential power consumption, the sector still represents the highest consumer of electricity. Almost half of all electricity produced in the GCC is consumed by the residential sector (53 per cent in 2002 to 47 per cent in 2011), which is significantly more than in other countries. In Qatar, residential electricity consumption grew by an average 17 per cent per year between 2007 and 2011. This is in contrast with countries such as Spain, Tunisia and Morocco where residential power consumption in 2011 was around 30 per cent of total power consumption (author calculations based on IEA data). Most GCC countries have begun efforts to manage demand in the last few years. Between 2007 and 2011, the CAGR of total electricity consumption was 5.5 per cent, as opposed to 6.8 per cent between 2002 and 2011. Residential sector power consumption only grew by 3.8 per cent annually between 2007 and 2011, as opposed to 5.6 per cent annually in the period 2002–2011. However, it must be noted that this decreasse in growth rates corresponded to a period of economic slowdown, which begs the question whether the decrease is truly a result of demand management.

Many GCC governments are planning steps to diversify their energy mix and reduce consumption in the residential and industrial sectors through energy-efficiency measures as well as behavioural change. Aside from the subsidisation of electricity tariffs, the subsidisation of inputs to electricity production also places renewable energy development and deployment at a disadvantage. Subsidised inputs for electricity generation, and directly subsidised electricity retail prices (see Figure 3.1), create a restrictive environment for the competitiveness of renewable sources of electricity generation to be showcased, and, thereby, limit incentives to invest in them.

Most GCC countries apart from the UAE have retail electricity prices of under USD0.05/kWh (Krane 2013, 14). The opportunity cost is particularly high in cases where oil products (such as diesel) are used for power generation. Mondal and Khalil note that electricity tariffs below 0.05 USD/kWh are considerably unattractive for the development of renewable energy. In all GCC countries, average consumer costs fall well below generation cost (Mondal and

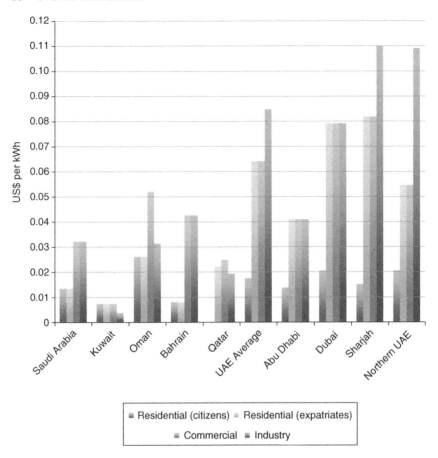

Figure 3.1 Electricity retail prices in the GCC (USD per kWh)
Source: Provided (2014) by Jim Krane (collected 2011–2014)

Khalil 2013, 44–45). An incomplete estimate of average electricity production costs in a number of GCC countries show that they are at the level of between USD0.09 and 0.13 per kWh. These numbers can, however, vary significantly between countries and are mainly dependent on the purchasing cost of fuel inputs. It is conceivable that the production cost of electricity lies much lower in, say, Saudi Arabia that is known to provide subsidised inputs for power generation. While these figures are rough ballpark figures, it is helpful to understand that a price gap between production cost and retail price is at the level of between USD0.07 and 0.11 per kWh (author calculations). Again, in certain specific countries, this price gap may be lower as a result of subsidised inputs. Even when disregarding subsidised inputs, however, retail electricity tariffs are often not cost-reflective, and harm the competitiveness of renewable energy (El-Katiri 2014, 11).

While, to date, it is common to primarily focus on government-set tariffs, the subsidisation of inputs is a crucial factor in lowering the production costs of conventional electricity. On average in the GCC, 40 per cent of total domestic supply of natural gas is used in power plants. This 40 per cent is associated with a natural gas subsidy of at least USD8 billion in 2011. This figure leaves out Bahrain and Saudi Arabia for whom there were no natural gas subsidy estimates available. Saudi Arabian power plants, however, consume around 40 per cent of all natural gas used in power plants in the entire GCC region (IEA 2012a).

In addition to natural gas, many GCC countries have started using diesel for electricity generation in power plants and in industry. Given the fuel price trends in international markets, the opportunity cost associated with diesel consumption for electricity generation is high. In the GCC, 35 per cent of diesel was used in power plants, and 10 per cent for electricity generation in industry. This was associated with a total diesel subsidy of over USD14 billion for electricity generation in the GCC in 2011. Kuwait, Oman and Saudi Arabia each use over 50 per cent of domestic diesel supply for electricity generation in power plants and industry. Also Luciani (2014, 12) agrees that the use of diesel is a high-cost solution.

If we take these subsidised inputs together, we find that in the GCC there has been an opportunity cost subsidy of USD0.28/kWh of conventional electricity on average. This does not include estimates for subsidised crude oil and fuel oil used in power plants in Kuwait and Saudi Arabia, and subsidised natural gas used in power plants in Bahrain and Saudi Arabia. It is important to understand that this figure is not equal to a direct transfer to power producers or utilities. It does, however, reflect the high opportunity cost of subsidising inputs.

Electricity production costs vary widely as a result of the different uses of materials, differing environments and resource availabilities, and so on. IEA estimates solar photovoltaic (PV) production costs to be between USD0.11 and 0.49 per kWh for ground mounted models and USD0.14 and 0.69 per kWh for rooftop installations. The King Abdullah City for Atomic and Renewable Energy (K.A.CARE) estimates that rooftop installations could reach around USD0.224/kWh in Saudi Arabia. For concentrated solar power (CSP), IEA estimated a levelised cost between USD0.18 and 0.30 per kWh, while K.A.CARE estimates reached USD0.175/kWh. Onshore wind was estimated by the IEA at between USD0.040 and 0.16 per kWh (El-Katiri 2014, 44). From 2009 to 2014, solar PV levelised costs per MWh strongly decreased by around 50 per cent for PV using crystalline silicon and by around 34 per cent for PV using thin film (Bloomberg New Energy Finance 2014b). This has been partially responsible for a drop of investments in solar energy technology by 20 per cent since 2013 (Bloomberg New Energy Finance 2014a, 11).

The opportunity cost subsidy of under-priced inputs (diesel and natural gas) can be estimated at around USD0.28/kWh, and the under-pricing of tariffs at roughly between USD0.07 and 0.11 per kWh. This is clear evidence of the significant negative impact of under-pricing on renewable energy development and deployment. In the absence of subsidised inputs and subsidised final electricity prices, or, said differently, if opportunity costs would be fully accounted for (even without the inclusion of negative externalities), renewable energy would be able to reach competitiveness much more easily. As El-Katiri (2014, 1) has emphasised, this would undoubtedly be the case if renewables were to replace fuel-driven power generation (i.e. by diesel, crude oil and fuel oil), as opposed to natural gas-based power production.

On average in the GCC, there is a solar PV potential of close to 2,083 kWh/m^2/year and a CSP potential of 2,208 kWh/m^2/year (Mondal and Khalil 2013, 36). These are more than sufficient resources available both to drive domestic replacement of fuel-based power plants by renewable energy, and to drive forward medium-term technology innovation. The U.S. Energy Information Administration has estimated levelised costs of electricity for new generation resources for the year 2019. While electricity generation via natural gas (conventional combined cycle) only costs around USD0.0663/kWh, solar PV and solar thermal remain more expensive at respectively USD0.130 and 0.243 per kWh (EIA 2014). There is thus still potential to surf down the learning curve. GCC countries could deliver a resource-rich platform to drive innovation in the solar sector (see: Bachellerie 2012).

Most countries need renewable energy targets and subsidies to attract investors. If GCC governments were to indicate that the era of under-pricing energy and electricity is to be reformed, this commitment would suffice to kick-start the reorientation of capital flows toward the renewable energy sector.

Greening transport

Transport policy has consistently favoured infrastructure development that benefits individual, rather than public, transportation. Two of the main steps forward toward a 'greener' transport sector are the development of mass public transit systems, and the introduction of fuel efficiency standards (Abaza *et al.* 2011, x–xi). Moreover, fuel efficiency standards represent only one side of the balance, with the other being fuel pricing. To date, the under-pricing of transport fuels has led to a dramatic increase in consumption. In the period 2002–2011, CAGRs for gasoline and diesel consumption in transport in the GCC have both been around 5.5 per cent (author calculations based on IEA data). In particular Oman and Qatar have experienced high CAGRs of around 9 per cent for both gasoline and diesel.

A high average annual growth rate in consumption, combined with an increase in gasoline and diesel prices on the international market, have led to an increase in the opportunity cost of selling under-priced transport fuels. Together, the gasoline and diesel opportunity subsidies reached around USD32 billion in 2011, which represented over 50 per cent of the total opportunity cost subsidy associated with oil products. In 2004, the opportunity cost subsidy associated with the under-pricing of gasoline and diesel only reached slightly over USD2 billion (see Figure 3.2).

It is important to understand the story that these figures tell. In 2002, transport fuel prices in the GCC were, in most cases, on par with those on the international

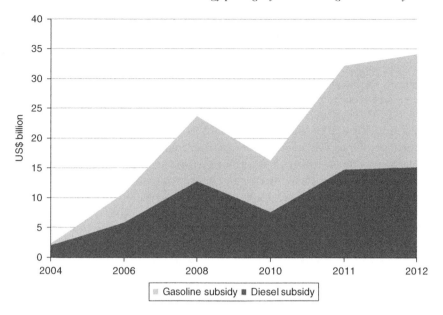

Figure 3.2 Transport fuel opportunity cost subsidies in the GCC (USD billion)
Source: Author's calculations
Note: 2012 subsidy estimates are based on 2011 consumption figures; diesel represents only the share of diesel used as transport fuel, not the share used for electricity generation.

market, thereby nullifying the potential opportunity cost subsidy. Since then, however, transport fuel prices on the international markets have increased. This indicates that over-consumption on the domestic market (as a result of under-pricing) is negative both because it leads directly to resource waste, and, more significantly, because the opportunity cost has increased as a result of the price difference. Thus, when considering the green economy at large, and the financial resources needed for the transformation to such a system in particular, it is imperative to place opportunity costs at the centre of the debate.

In a world of increasing international fuel prices, every next unit of over-consumption on the domestic market as a result of fixed low prices represents a higher opportunity cost for the oil exporting state than the unit before. While the CAGR of consumption of gasoline and diesel was around 5 per cent, the CAGR of associated subsidies in the period 2004–2012 was around 40 per cent. This reality makes the transport sector a key sector in need of reform, not only to transform to a green economy in that sector, but also to open up short- and medium-term financial capacity that can be re-invested in the diversification of the domestic economy and energy system. For example, the estimated capital investment for the GCC railway (a rail connection between all six GCC countries) is reported at USD200 billion (Marcellin 2014). Individual countries are also moving forward with expensive rail projects such as the Etihad Railway

Network in Abu Dhabi, the Jeddah Metro (both USD11 billion), the Riyadh Metro (USD23 billion) and the Qatar Integrated Rail Project (USD40 billion) (ibid.).

Even though there is little transparency with regard to fuel and vehicle usage, it appears well established that fuel consumption in transport in GCC countries is mainly driven by passenger vehicles. In an analysis on Bahrain, AlSabbagh *et al.* (2013) reveal that passenger vehicle growth reached around 7.3 per cent per year between 2000 and 2010 (AlSabbagh *et al.* 2013, 6). In 2010, over 80 per cent of all road vehicles were for passenger transport (ibid., 17). Investing in public transport can be beneficial, given that the average car age in Bahrain is 10.5 years (ibid., 17). In addition, without fuel economy standards, the country is prone to increased energy consumption by transport, in particular given that there is a trend toward larger engine sizes and heavier vehicles (ibid., 25–26). Unfortunately, current data deficiencies do not allow verification of whether the trends in Bahrain are representative for the entire GCC region.

All of these factors mean that it is '5 to 12' for the transformation of GCC transport systems. Hard measures will be necessary to encourage efficiency and wider use of public transport. One large survey in the GCC pointed out that GCC citizens strongly prefer private passenger cars to commute to work, rather than available public transport (Attwood 2010). Besides fuel efficiency standards for passenger vehicles, clear fuel price signals will be needed to move citizens to use public transport.

Energy pricing and energy-intensive water desalination

Electricity and energy pricing reform needs to take into consideration energy-intensive desalination processes (Meltzer *et al.* 2014, 37). Desalinated water will be increasingly needed for residential and industrial use, and thus also potentially for agricultural use in case more investments are made in the primary sector. At the same time, the water intensity of fuel extraction is rising, making the energy sector a growing consumer as well (Economist Intelligence Unit 2010, 13). Again, pricing reform is at the centre of available options to encourage efficient consumption. In the residential sector, where the water usage per capita in the GCC countries is often around six times higher than in certain industrialised countries (Algethami 2013), pricing reform could help reduce domestic water wastage and excessive consumption. Further, it would encourage the agricultural sector to switch to less water-intensive, and perhaps more resilient, crops better suited to the local environment. It is precisely because of the huge potential impact of these demand shifts that most studies mention demand management as the key priority (World Bank 2012, 1).

It has been widely reported that the GCC is investing at least USD100 billion in desalination projects from 2011 to 2016 (Algethami 2013). Like electricity generation facilities, this type of infrastructure investments will soon be unsustainable if they are not linked to more efficient consumption patterns. Almost 60 per cent of the world capacity for desalination is currently located in the

GCC region (Dziuban 2011, 2). To date, many desalination plants are of the co-generation type, producing both water and energy. For this particular type of plant, however, it is technologically more difficult to transform to new, more energy-efficient desalination technologies (Saif 2012).

The need to rationalise conventional energy use in power production, industry and transport is only made clearer by the burden that GCC governments are already bearing with energy-intensive desalination. While it remains technologically challenging, some GCC governments have started to implement alternative energy desalination projects (Dziuban 2011, 6–7). The cost of conventional energy inputs to desalination will be a key factor in encouraging renewable energy-driven desalination. Although costly in the short term, desalination and renewable energy are the *only* choices for medium-term economic and political sustainability.

Simply put, since both water and energy facilities are tapping from the same fossil fuel resources, energy rationalisation in one sector will be needed to assist the sustainability of the other – and vice versa. The most unsustainable scenario is one in which both sectors tap into fossil fuel resources as if they were infinite. Without pricing reform, one would have reason to fear such a 'business as usual' scenario.

Political economy considerations

Abaza *et al.* (2011, xx) hold that in a green economy, natural resource governance is inclusive of all stakeholders, including those with weak institutional power. This is in stark contrast to the manner in which politics are conducted in many GCC countries. However, far too often, the complexities of the allocation state model in GCC countries are falsely reduced to a static model in which a uniform government conducts politics independently from other stakeholders. This fallacy disregards the complex political economy of energy policy and policy reform in the GCC. An understanding of this political economy, however, is necessary to understand the potential for political action of different stakeholders, which in itself determines the space within which pricing reform can move.

The following does not attempt to give a comprehensive overview of the aforementioned political economy. This would require an extensive analysis of stakeholder motives, trade-offs and institutional structures as is touched upon in William Ascher's (1999, 244–279) analysis in *Why Governments Waste Natural Resources*. Rather, the ensuing section attempts to describe a few noteworthy dynamics between different stakeholders that are common to multiple GCC countries and that are relevant to understanding the available reform space.

Dynamics within government

Leadership is important in energy pricing reform. Without a consensus, efforts in general, and longer-term strategies in particular, often fail. Top officials in Gulf countries have acknowledged the pricing problem. Saudi Arabia's Minister of Economy and Planning mentioned in 2014 that fossil fuel subsidies are increasingly distorting the economy (Meltzer *et al.* 2014, 29). A few months earlier, the UAE Minister of Energy, and Oman's Minister of Oil and Gas, stated that low fossil fuel prices are responsible for wasteful consumption (Moerenhout 2013). While there is growing recognition at the top governmental level that reform is needed, this cannot be extrapolated to politics at large.

Curiously, a higher level of democratisation is not necessarily linked to sounder economic policy-making. The Kuwaiti Parliament, for example, undermined economic and institutional reform in favour of extended rent distribution policies. Elected parliaments in GCC countries can indeed be more populist, preferring rent distribution through low prices. Theoretically, this is in sharp contrast to appointed technocratic regulators, which favour diversification. Conversely, in more authoritarian regimes, there are often weaker links between different stakeholders, which often allowed government and technocratic bodies to pursue a more rational policy (Hertog 2013b, 40). Populist rent distribution policies of different institutions indeed depend on where the power of those institutions' members comes from. For example, in Qatar, the parliament is more of a consultative assembly that has limited powers and its members are appointed by the Emir. While it was initially foreseen that in the first ever general elections in 2013 two-thirds of the parliament would be directly elected, these elections were postponed by the Emir when he handed over power to his son (Khalaf 2013).

Further, in Kuwait, the lack of development of natural gas projects is likely to run the country into supply shortages in the not too distant future. Indeed, projects concerning the importation of gas have received greater support in parliament than those allowing foreign involvement to develop the domestic gas sector, despite the former being more expensive. The parliament can sanction ministers (who are appointed by the Emir) and hold them accountable for decisions within the oil sector. With a complex oil sector, and associated political and economic system, and the selection of ministers being constantly prone to change, there is little opportunity for ministers to push through durable decisions (Stevens 2011a, 346). These dynamics are highly relevant for fuel pricing, and equally for the development of renewable energy, which would also benefit from the input of foreign partners and expertise.

It is well understood among energy price reformers that a political consensus is most often a necessity, albeit insufficient in isolation from other factors, for success. In countries with some type of political pluralism, the support of parliament is mandatory for the follow-through of reforms, in particular when such a parliament is playing a large role in energy policy and enterprises. Moreover, the establishment of sound communication channels is often associated with practices of consensus building and policy coordination. However, in the GCC communication between ministries, and within the bureaucracy at large, as well as between different levels (micro, meso, macro) is severely limited (Hertog 2010).

To understand dynamics within, and access to, governments, it is important to value informal networks, or what Hertog calls 'brokers'. These are persons that are able to make the bureaucracy accessible to claimants. Most often, they can do this because of a privileged position. Access to such brokers is uneven. Though this may seem contradictory to how authoritarian regimes are often understood, internal hierarchies in fact contain numerous players with some level of power over policy consensus or implementation. These networks and client–patron relations operate vertically, which makes it difficult to achieve horizontal coalitions for policy reform (Hertog 2013b, 26–31). To achieve consensus, GCC governments will need to invest in developing horizontal brokers that can push for coordination and reform.

Dynamics between government and the private sector

Hertog has convincingly described the asymmetry in the interaction between the government and the private sector. The government is instrumental to business in two ways. First, it provides under-priced inputs that are important to production processes, and particularly important in the Gulf's energy-intensive industries. Second, governments are the drivers of broad public sector employment, which is associated with higher salaries than those earned in the private sector. This means that business relies on high public sector wages to generate demand for their products, particularly since there is not sufficient international demand for the Gulf's products. Hertog has quantitatively demonstrated that private sector contribution to GDP is associated with public spending (ibid., 8). From its side, the private sector is less useful to government. It does not contribute to state budgets via taxation (ibid., 11–13), and it does not generate private sector jobs for GCC nationals, relying on foreign labour instead.

Private businesses have garnered a certain degree of independence from the government since it invested in private overseas resources, which have grown faster compared to revenue from the local sale of products or services (ibid., 4). Generally, however, the private sector remains in an inferior position. Most of the large companies have links to the government, either as a previous owner, as a minority, or often, a majority shareholder. There is no broader shareholder culture. Some national business associations in the Gulf are well organised, but overall lobbying practices are not strongly developed, and the private sector, while retaining a greater influence over governmental policy than other segments of society, nevertheless tends to fall in line with economic policy set out by the governments. For example, chambers of commerce are often dominated by multiple members of a few large families that are appointed by the government, rather than business associations (ibid., 28–32).

Overall, business is isolated and therefore seeks protection from, and alliances with, government. This alliance is fairly deep-seated, with business often siding with the government against domestic opposition movements (ibid., 37–38). That said, the private sector continues to have the possibility of moving its capital elsewhere if local policies turn to its disadvantage (Hertog 2013a, 69). Lobbying activities, as far as they go, are often reactive, but also include a defensive angle with regard to the privileges of industry. For example, the Omani Chamber of

Commerce has explicitly asked for lower utility tariffs. Similarly, lobbying activities of Saudi chambers have focused on reacting to the 2010 electricity tariff rises (Hertog 2013b, 34–35).

Nevertheless, in the time of crises, citizens' interests have taken precedence over those of the private sector, with the private sector often being required, for example, to pay higher tariffs (ibid., 43). Because of the aforementioned reasons, the private sector indeed does not play a prominent role in the social contract of GCC states. If the private sector seeks greater influence, a more independent position and new markets, they will inevitably have to negotiate with governments to construct a more competitive environment. It is this dynamic that will determine whether business can eventually deal with, and potentially even be an ally of, energy pricing reform.

Dynamics between government and society at large

Like business, large parts of society have internalised what Beblawi called the 'rentier mentality', in which the link between productive work and income is broken and the acquiring of wealth has become dependent on oil revenue distribution, without work (Hvidt 2013, 42). It is through the clientilistic use of bureaucratic employment that the bureaucracy has become fragmented and corruption occurs. Low retail energy prices have long been a cornerstone of this system. Any increase in these prices, therefore, threatens an age-old status quo and could undermine the belief in this system and affect its function. Though these increases may not immediately affect everyone, they would represent a paradigm shift in policy that, if successful, could be perceived as a threat to the positions of certain powerful patrons. Hence, the timing of these reforms is crucial. A large proportion of the population in GCC countries is very young, well educated and desirous of jobs. It is psychologically easier to accustom this group to a changing regime now, rather than later, when they have fully internalised the rentier mentality.

Rising living standards that have led to wasteful consumption patterns form another critical part of this rentier mentality. The structure of demand is one of the key issues that reforms should target. Costs of satisfying peak load demand are higher than those for base load and are often not covered by domestic prices. Seasonal variations in commercial and residential demand (due to air conditioning) incur high capital costs for installations with lower utilisation rates (Luciani 2014, 15). In this regard Luciani has, rightly so, argued that increasing prices without addressing seasonal variations and peak load demand patterns might reduce costs but would not target the actual cost problems.

To understand the dynamics between government and society, of course, one cannot disregard the impact of regional political instability. The looming fear of a contagious Arab Spring transforming into a Gulf summer, in many ways, strengthened the social contract in the Gulf states in favour of society. The fact that state capture has been strengthened by the Arab Spring has been demonstrated by what could be referred to as the 'rentier reflex'. This notion refers to how GCC governments react to political unrest by extending patronage packages that not only ignore medium-term economic transition but also aggravate current unsustainable practices. In the aftermath of the Arab Spring such reflexes included cash transfers, additional job creation in the public sector, increasing salaries and benefits of public workers and the military, and so forth. The two hardest hit countries, Oman and Bahrain, also received military and financial aid from other GCC countries. In total, spending by GCC governments increased by 20 per cent during 2011 (Ulrichsen 2013, 36–40). Most governments also repressed pluralistic voices. For example in Saudi Arabia, Shia oppression was intensified (Heydarian 2014, 139–146).

The classic rentier reflex, however, is not only fiscally but also politically unsustainable. Growing discontent over citizenship rights may become a larger problem for governments if they want to pursue controversial reforms. The success or failure of such reforms may depend on whether or not a certain political tipping point is reached. Such tipping points are more sensitive to a series of factors (including the activities of marginalised groups) that historically never were able to challenge the stability of the political regime.

Among others, Hertog has argued that the state has lost autonomy in reforming and guiding policy. Not only were citizens co-opted into a client–patron system, but, within the very same system, the government found itself in a quagmire. In addition, on a micro-level, many of the so-called 'clients' entered state institutions through employment, making change even more difficult. This is why it is easier to affect policy when new bodies are created (Hertog 2013b, 18–19). This is a key conclusion to understand the need for new technocratic institutions and structures to achieve energy reform.

Dynamics between the private sector and society at large

Dynamics between the private sector and society are driven by a zero-sum conflict over resources, and a lack of interdependence. Industrial development has generated little employment, no tax base and hardly any investment opportunities (ibid., 2). In the GCC, one of the major problems is indeed the existence of a very young educated population, and a severe lack of skilled, well-paying jobs with the private sector mainly providing low-paid jobs to expatriates. A lack of an autonomous private sector has been to the disadvantage of the GCC population. Earlier attempts to reform service and utility prices have failed mainly because of strong political opposition from both businesses and the wider population (Hertog 2013a, 72). As previously indicated, however, rather than a structured opposition, both groups mainly compete over tariff policies. The zero-sum game is thus a result of two quasi-independent groups of stakeholders that desire the lowest tariffs possible over increasingly more limited and valuable government resources.

One of the key messages for the green economy will be to create interdependence between an active private sector and society through employment. This could break the zero-sum game and assist in reaching a compromise on resource valuation at large. In this regard, it is important to demonstrate to both national investors and the society that pricing reform can favour a renewable energy sector that is able to offer high-skilled, high-wage jobs for GCC nationals. One key but often unspoken issue is the standard of work many GCC workers are used to in the public sector (Hertog 2013b, 16). If state-owned enterprises are to play a role in the renewables sector, it will be necessary to condition support upon technological innovation and productivity gains. Allowing private participation, alongside this kind of conditioning, would signify a cultural shift in the electricity model, which will make the planning and implementation of it particularly challenging.

The role of energy companies

Most energy companies are vertically integrated, state-owned enterprises, offering few opportunities for private companies to participate, particularly in transmission and distribution (Ferroukhi *et al.* 2013, 28–29). Even though they are linked to the government, some energy companies are semi-independent technocratic bodies that can balance the rentier state project with the objective of running a successful export-oriented business. This makes them allies for the government in terms of pursuing and communicating about pricing reform. National oil companies (NOCs) would generally prefer higher prices in order to sustain a more profitable business. For example, Saudi Aramco has already voiced concerns over the distribution system and its impacts on the sustainability of their business (Hertog 2012, 242). Since they have a direct link to the consumer, utilities in particular could play a role in energy reform and efficiency campaigns (Meltzer *et al.* 2014, 38).

Significantly, the potential role of NOCs can vary considerably across the GCC. Saudi Aramco, for example, is a corporately strong, technocratic body which has largely evaded corruption scandals (Stevens 2011b, 193). As Hertog frames it, it is an island of efficiency still shielded from the brokerage system (Hertog 2013b, 28). Other NOCs, however, are more politicised. Kuwaiti nationals working for the Kuwait Petroleum Company have been reported to have asked political favours of their members of parliament, which is seeking for more influence over the energy sector (Losman 2010, 436). The company is bureaucratic, politicised and unable to make and implement reforms that would improve its performance (Stevens 2011a, 334). National oil companies play an important role as collectors and distributors of rents. Aside from discounted energy prices, they are often under political pressure to support other welfare-distribution agencies (Losman 2010, 437). For example middle-level managers in the Kuwait Petroleum Company have often been politically appointed (Stevens 2011a, 335).

Energy sector coordination and reform

There is no streamlined and coordinated energy policy that can address pricing as a whole. This makes communication about the energy sector complex. Many states have recently started attempts to better coordinate policies, including most governmental, and some private sector, stakeholders. Institutional coordination however, remains minimal, which, according to Lahn *et al.*, is the greatest barrier to policy reform (Lahn *et al.* 2013, 10–18). There have, however, been many more advancements in the electricity sector, with some autonomous regulators appearing on the scene. For example Saudi Arabia, Oman, Dubai and Abu Dhabi have all delegated the power of regulation of the electricity sector to independent bodies (ibid., vii). As mentioned, these types of technocratic islands of efficiency can play a crucial role in the communication, planning and implementation of energy pricing reform.

In general, energy sector coordination and reform requires more transparency. Often, oil revenues and distribution are not transparent, with a powerful elite holding a large share of the pie. What is often called corruption is also a power distribution mechanism of the rentier state model, which is not only about establishing a relationship between citizens as clients, and the leading elite as patrons, but also includes the element of power distribution within that select elite. There is also corruption in the allocation of extraction and distribution contracts. Oil is often used to favour certain types of recipients, who then re-sell the fuel elsewhere at higher prices. But contracts are also 'smuggled', in that they are allocated to a specific contractor, who then subcontracts a cheaper (and often low-quality) foreign firm to execute the contract (Losman 2010, 440).

It must be noted that a lack of transparency is a larger characteristic of the rentier state culture, without necessarily immediately a negative connotation. For example, even the more corporatised and less corrupt Saudi Aramco is famous for lacking transparency. Another example is that the energy price advantage that consumers receive is still not consistently communicated in various GCC countries (Lahn *et al.* 2013, 15). Increasing transparency will indeed be a key aspect of pricing reform.

Regional coordination and reform

What neighbours are doing is often important in how domestic measures are perceived. In the context of a green economy for the wider MENA region, it has been well recognised that a shared vision would help the green economy project forward (Netzer and Althaus 2012, 24). Since state capture may be the strongest political economy factor determining energy sector reform, it could be argued that regional initiatives can help overcome that barrier. In this frame of mind, the GCC could virtually serve as a legitimate vehicle outside of the individual rentier member states that is able to assist in pricing reform. A unified GCC price for petroleum products was discussed in a September 2013 meeting of oil ministers. It was reported that while feasibility studies were still being prepared, there was no strong objection to the idea of unified fuel prices (Jeddah: Arab News 2013). They are seen as a response to fuel smuggling, which is particularly common from Saudi Arabia to the UAE.

Since prices of petroleum products are different in some countries, a unified GCC price would mean a price increase for consumers in some states. It is believed that this would help to rationalise consumption in those states that would observe these price hikes. One oil analyst has estimated that a unified price could save up to 30 per cent of fuel consumption in Saudi Arabia (Arab News 2013). The plan to implement a unified fuel price is one designated for the medium term. To achieve successful implementation, it is imperative for GCC governments to provide the necessary services to cope with price increases. This particularly requires investments into public transport and social safety nets in order to assure equitable access.

One of the main obstacles to discussing a unified fuel price could be the decision regarding a roadmap to price adjustment in the future. While a combined GCC strategy may hold a lot of potential, it is also possible that such cooperation would be inflexible if regional decision-making policies are unclear or ineffective. A clear vision of the path the GCC ought to, or will, pursue is more obscure than is often assumed, especially given inconsistencies in, among others, the role of oil in political identity. For example in Abu Dhabi, the government is strongly accepted as a medium-term strategy developer, which shapes its interaction with the Abu Dhabi National Oil Company (ADNOC). Further, low production-to-reserve ratios are used to preserve Abu Dhabi oil for the future (Rai and Victor 2011, 490–491). This is one of the reasons why prices have been higher in the UAE than in other GCC countries, in which production has often been intensified to gain higher revenues. In addition, the fact that Dubai holds a weak resource base and has strongly diversified, while Abu Dhabi needs to manage supply to six other emirates, has also led to more rational pricing. It must be noted, however, that ADNOC also recently increased its production targets. Nevertheless, these types of different 'oil identities' in the various GCC countries may make it difficult to accept regional participation and actually decide on its longer-term content.

One notable initiative that in time may demonstrate potential as well as difficulties associated with the integration of fuel pricing policies at the GCC is the Gulf Cooperation Council Interconnection Authority (GCCIA). Some of the ambitious objectives of the GCCIA include the interconnecting of national grids, the improving of the economic efficiency of power systems and the coordination of the operations of existing electricity companies and authorities. So far, the GCCIA project appears to have been successful in dealing with political issues such as financing and cost-sharing, the creation of the Interconnection Authority and the awarding of contracts. A more in-depth study of the political aspects associated with the integration of these markets into one trading market is however yet to be elaborated.

Conclusions

The Gulf states examined in this chapter have never borrowed significant amounts from international financial institutions and they will not need to do so to achieve pricing reform. This chapter has demonstrated that such reform will be necessary for GCC states that desire to move successfully toward a new, productive and green economic growth model. Inappropriate energy pricing negatively affects green economy objectives such as the development of renewable energy, a transformation of the transport sector, the management of demand patterns, the expansion of energy efficiency investments and the so-far elusive aspiration to achieve a sustainable water and energy future. The under-pricing of energy has high opportunity costs and pricing reform could open up financial capacity that is needed for longer-term sustainable investments into the green economy.

Reform, however, will not be easy and touches upon the core foundation of the social contract in GCC states. Therefore, careful preparation is needed. Central to reform is not just the technical capacity to achieve it, but more so the interplay of different political economy considerations. The foregoing analysis has touched upon a number of them, starting with the need to achieve political consensus and find allies for pricing reform. Building a horizontal consensus will require managing the various vertical patron–client relations. In particular, populist bodies that promote excessive rent distribution may pose a problem. In the first place, communication within government would need to be modernised.

While the private sector may generally be opposed to pricing reforms, it is not inconceivable that parts could become allies of reform if government offers business incentives to achieve actual autonomous privatisation. Also society is expected to be opposed to pricing reform. However, in a time with soaring unemployment and an educated young population, good policies could slowly alter a rentier mentality if it is able to create skilled and well-paying jobs. This will require the participation of the private sector and a government whose incentives are dependent on productivity gains. Since rentier dynamics within the bureaucracy are culturally locked, the creation of independent, technocratic bodies that can regulate reform outside of the client–patron dynamic may be desirable.

National oil companies can be important allies given that their profitability is suffering under low domestic prices. However, corruption will need to be targeted to achieve some type of trust. GCC states are also in need of streamlined energy sector and policy coordination. Increasing transparency can be a factor that serves both of these goals. Also regional cooperation through the GCC can help achieve reform. However, coordination through unified fuel prices would need careful planning in order to have a longer-term strategy that allows for policy flexibility and adjustment to new circumstances.

To conclude, it is the impact on and perception of a variety of stakeholders that will determine the reform space. Successful reform will therefore not only require investments to safeguard and improve equitable distribution and access to water and energy, but will also ask for a thorough understanding of the political economy dynamics within and between GCC states. Let there be no doubt, it is '5 to 12' for GCC states to transfer to a new economic development model. More than a regional threat, the Arab Spring ought to be considered as the alarm clock to avoid a Gulf Summer. A now woken-up Gulf elite has the financial capacity and policy means at hand to courageously start turning the wheel, starting with the direly needed economic transformation.

References

Abaza, Hussein, Najib Saab and Bashar Zeitoon, ed. 2011. *Arab Environment: Green Economy*. Beirut: Arab Forum for Environment and Development (AFED).

Abdel Gelil, Ibrahim, Farid Chaaban and Leila Dagher. 2011. 'Energy.' In *Arab Environment: Green Economy*, edited by Hussein Abaza, Najib Saab and Bashar Zeitoon, 72–112. Beirut: AFED.

Abdel Hamid and Mohamed Abdel Raouf. 2012. 'Green Economy Challenges in the MENA Region.' In *Green Economy: Turning over a New Leaf Towards Sustainable Development?*, edited by Nina Netzer and Judith Althaus, 21–26. Friedrich Ebert Stiftung, June.

Algethami, Sarah. 2013. 'GCC Must Improve Agriculture Technologies, Agra Middle East 2013 Hears.' *Gulf News*, 26 March. http://gulfnews.com/

Alsabbagh, Maha, Yim Ling Siu, John Barrett and Ibrahim Abdel Gelil. 2013. CO_2 *Emissions and Fuel Consumption of Passenger Vehicles in Bahrain: Current Status and Future Scenarios*. SRI Paper. Leeds: University of Leeds.

Arab News. 2013. 'GCC to Discuss Single Fuel Price.' *Zawya*, 20 September. https://www.zawya.com/

Ascher, William. 1999. *Why Governments Waste Natural Resources: Policy Failures in Developing Countries*. Baltimore, MD [etc.]: The Johns Hopkins University Press.

Attwood, Ed. 2010. 'Survey Shows Lack of Interest in GCC Public Transport.' *Arabian Business*, 19 August. http://www.arabianbusiness.com/

Bachellerie, Imen Jeridi. 2012. *Renewable Energy in the GCC Countries: Resources, Potential and Prospects*. Jeddah: Gulf Research Center.

Bloomberg New Energy Finance. 2014a. *Global Trends in Renewable Energy Investment: Executive Summary*.

Bloomberg New Energy Finance. 2014b. *Global Trends in Renewable Energy Investment 2014: Figures*.

Dziuban, Michael. 2011. *Scarcity and Strategy in the GCC*. Gulf Analysis Paper. Center for Strategic & International Studies, February.

Economist Intelligence Unit. 2010. *The GCC in 2020: Resources for the Future*.

EIA. United States Energy Information Administration. 2014. *Levelized Cost and Levelized Avoided Cost of New Generation Resources in the Annual Energy Outlook 2014*.

El-Katiri, Laura. 2014. *A Roadmap for Renewable Energy in the Middle East and North Africa*. OIES Working Paper MEP 6. Oxford: Oxford Institute for Energy Studies.

Fattouh, Bassam, and Laura El-Katiri. 2012. *Energy and Arab Economic Development*. Arab Human Development Report Research Paper Series. New York: United Nations Development Programme Regional Bureau for Arab States.

Ferroukhi, Rabia, Haris Doukas, Stella Androulaki, Emanuela Menichetti, Andrea Masini and Arslan Khalid. 2013. *EU-GCC Renewable Energy Policy Cooperation: Exploring Opportunities*. Jeddah: Gulf Research Center.

Gastli, Adel, and Javier San Miguel Armendariz. 2013. *Challenges Facing Grid Integration of Renewable Energy in the GCC Region*. Jeddah: Gulf Research Center.

Hertog, Steffen. 2010. *Princes, Brokers, and Bureaucrats: Oil and the State in Saudi Arabia*. Ithaca, NY: Cornell University Press.

Hertog, Steffen. 2012. 'Good, Bad or Both? The Impact of Oil on the Saudi Political Economy.' In *The Political Economy of the Persian Gulf*, edited by Mehran Kamrava, 221–250. London: Hurst.

Hertog, Steffen. 2013a. 'The Evolution of Rent Recycling During Two Booms in the Gulf Arab States: Business Dynamism and Societal Stagnation.' In *Shifting Geo-Economic Power of the Gulf: Oil, Finance and Institutions*, edited by Dr Bessma Momani and Professor Matteo Legrenzi, 55–74. Burlington, VT: Ashgate Publishing.

Hertog, Steffen. 2013b. *The Private Sector and Reform in the Gulf Cooperation Council*. London: London School of Economics and Political Science.

Heydarian, Richard Javad. 2014. *How Capitalism Failed the Arab World: The Economic Roots and Precarious Future of the Middle East Uprisings*. London: Zed Books.

Hvidt, Martin. 2013. 'Economic Diversification in the Gulf Arab States: Lip Service or Actual Implementation of a New Development Model?' In *Shifting Geo-Economic Power of the Gulf: Oil, Finance and Institutions*, edited by Dr Bessma Momani and Professor Matteo Legrenzi, 39–54. Burlington, VT: Ashgate Publishing.

IEA. International Energy Agency. 2012a. 'Fossil-fuel Consumption Subsidy Rates as a Proportion of the Full Cost of Supply, 2011.' http://www.iea.org/subsidy/index.html

IEA. 2012b. 'Fossil-fuel Subsidies – Methodology and Assumptions.' http://www.iea.org/publications/worldenergyoutlook/resources/energysubsidies/methodologyforcalculatingsubsidies/

IEA, OPEC, OECD and the World Bank. 2010. *World Bank Joint Report. Analysis of the Scope of Energy Subsidies and Suggestions for the G-20 Initiative*. Report Prepared for Submission to the G-20 Summit Meeting Toronto, Canada, 26–27 June.

IMF. International Monetary Fund. 2013. *Energy Subsidy Reform: Lessons and Implications. Executive Summary*. 28 January.

Jeddah: Arab News. 2013. 'No Objections Voiced to GCC Unified Fuel Prices.' *Arab News*, 26 September. http://www.arabnews.com/

Khalaf, Roula. 2013. 'Abdication of Qatar's Ruler Avoids Risky Elections.' *Financial Times*, 25 June. http://www.ft.com/

Koplow, Doug. 2009. *Measuring Energy Subsidies Using the Price-Gap Approach: What Does It Leave Out?* International Institute for Sustainable Development, August.

Krane, Jim. 2013. *Stability Versus Sustainability: Energy Policy in the Gulf Monarchies*. EPRG Working Paper. Cambridge: University of Cambridge.

Lahn, Glada, Paul Stevens and Felix Preston. 2013. *Saving Oil and Gas in the Gulf*. London: Chatham House.

Losman, Donald L. 2010. 'The Rentier State and National Oil Companies: An Economic and Political Perspective.' *The Middle East Journal* 64(3): 427–445.

Luciani, Giacomo. 2014. 'The Political Economy of Gulf Energy Reform.' In *Political Economy of Energy Reform: The Clean Energy-Fossil Fuel Balance in the Gulf*, edited by Giacomo Luciani and Rabia Ferroukhi, 7–24. Berlin: Gerlach Press.

Marcellin, Frances. 2014. 'A Window of Opportunity – Inside the GCC Rail Revolution.' *railway-technology.com*, 11 March. http://www.railway-technology.com/

Meltzer, Joshua, Nathan Hultman and Claire Langley. 2014. *Low-Carbon Energy Transitions in Qatar and the Gulf Cooperation Council Region*. Washington D.C.: Brookings Institution.

Moerenhout, Tom. 2013. 'Ministers UAE and Oman Place Spotlight on Low Fossil-fuel Pricing in the GCC.' *Global Subsidies Initiative*, 14 November. http://www.iisd.org/gsi/news/

Mondal, Alam, and Huden Serenat Khalil. 2013. *Renewable Energy Readiness Assessment Report: The GCC Countries 2011–2012*. Abu Dhabi: Masdar Institute of Science and Technology.

Netzer, Nina, and Judith Althaus. 2012. 'Introduction.' In *Green Economy: Turning over a New Leaf Towards Sustainable Development?*, edited by Nina Netzer and Judith Althaus, 3–8. Friedrich Ebert Stiftung, June.

Rai, Varun, and David Victor. 2011. 'Awakening Giant: Strategy and Performance of the Abu Dhabi National Oil Company (ADNOC).' In *Oil and Governance*, edited by David Victor, David Hults and Mark Thurber, 478–514. Cambridge: Cambridge University Press.

Saif, Omar. 2012. *The Future Outlook of Desalination in the Gulf: Challenges & Opportunities Faced by Qatar & the UAE*. Ontario: McMaster University/United Nations University Press.

Stevens, Paul. 2011a. 'Kuwait Petroleum Corporation (KPC): An Enterprise in Gridlock.' In *Oil and Governance*, edited by David Victor, David Hults and Mark Thurber, 334–378. Cambridge: Cambridge University Press.

Stevens, Paul. 2011b. 'Saudi Aramco: The Jewel in the Crown.' In *Oil and Governance*, edited by David Victor, David Hults and Mark Thurber, 173–233. Cambridge: Cambridge University Press.

Ulrichsen, Kristian Coates. 2013. 'Domestic Implications of the Arab Uprisings in the Gulf.' In *The Gulf States and the Arab Uprisings*, edited by Ana Echague, 35–46. Madrid: FRIDE and the Gulf Research Center.

UNEP. United Nations Environment Programme. 2011a. *Decoupling Natural Resource Use and Environmental Impacts from Economic Growth*. Nairobi: UNEP.

UNEP. 2011b. *Towards a Green Economy: Pathways to Sustainable Development and Poverty Eradication*. Nairobi: UNEP.

World Bank. 2012. *Renewable Energy Desalination: An Emerging Solution to Close the Water Gap in the Middle East and North Africa*. Washington D.C.: World Bank.

4 Spanish renewable energy and energy efficiency: lessons for Bahrain reforms?

Ghada Abdulla

Introduction

The hot climate of Bahrain, together with the rising rate of population growth, rapidly rising incomes and the dependence on the hydrocarbon sector, have caused energy consumption to rise sharply over the past couple of decades. According to the Bahrain Central Informatics Organization, the total energy consumption in Bahrain rose from 6,454 GWh in 2002 to 13,350 GWh in 2013 (see Figure 4.1).

Currently, Bahrain produces the majority of its electricity output from natural gas (around 85 per cent) with the rest supplied by oil (15 per cent) (Bachellerie 2012, 30). However, Bahrain is a small producer of natural gas and the rising rates of extraction have resulted in a large fall in gas reserves. According to the United States Energy Information Administration, natural gas reserves in Bahrain were around 6.5 trillion cubic feet in 1990, fell to 3.25 trillion cubic feet in 2002, and has remained constant since (see Figure 4.2). Power production and consumption also have large effects on the environment, with power generation alone accounting for 35 per cent of carbon dioxide (CO_2) emissions (Bachellerie 2012, 33). Due to Bahrain's small size, polluters are located in areas close to residential areas, resulting in significant environmental and health hazards. Falling natural gas reserves, together with the environmental threats resulting from high fossil fuel consumption, have led Bahrain to start implementing policies to increase energy efficiency and to consider alternative sources of energy.

Solar and wind power are the renewable energy sources that have the highest potential in Bahrain. However, as can be seen from Table 4.1 these are still not utilised. Many countries have focused on renewable energy support together with energy efficiency enhancement, and remarkable results have been achieved. Such countries can offer a wide range of lessons for Bahrain. Among the most successful countries in terms of solar and wind installations are Germany, Spain and Denmark. Of these countries, Spain is the country with a gross domestic product (GDP) per capita closest to that of Bahrain (see Figure 4.3). Spain is also the country with a climate most similar to Bahrain's.

The Spanish experience can offer a variety of lessons for Bahrain both in terms of its successes and failures. Spain has a long experience in promoting the green economy. It has two decades of experience in renewable energy support. Hence,

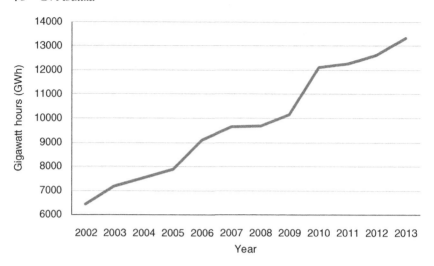

Figure 4.1 Total electricity consumption in Bahrain
Source: Bahrain Central Informatics Organization (2014)

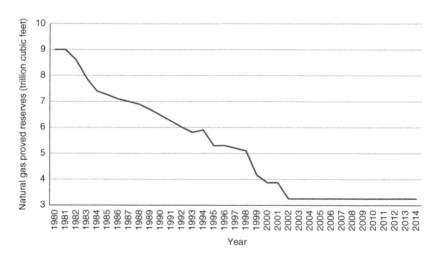

Figure 4.2 Natural gas reserves in Bahrain
Source: EIA (2013)

both the short- and medium-/long-term effects of its policies can be analysed. Spain has supported renewable energy through a system of feed-in tariffs (FITs) where renewable energy producers received guaranteed payments in order to induce investors to enter the renewable energy sector. Spain's system of FITs was very effective, making the country a leader in solar and wind energy. However,

Table 4.1 Installed capacity in Bahrain by type of generation (2013)

Year	Steam	Gas	Combined cycle	Diesel	Coal	Hydro	Wind	Solar	Others	Total
2013	100	700	3,134	0	0	0	0	0	0	3,934

Source: Arab Union of Electricity (2013)

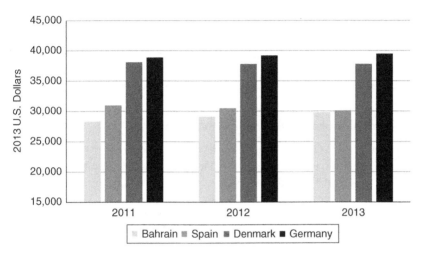

Figure 4.3 Gross domestic product (GDP) per capita (PPP)
Source: CIA (2014)

over the medium term, problems started appearing, as a large tariff deficit started accumulating due to the system's excessive costs. While FITs are used by many countries worldwide, Spain has had an extreme experience with them, and therefore its experience provides accentuated lessons for a country like Bahrain where renewable energy is only entering the energy agenda. Spain has also implemented a wide range of policies and undertaken a variety of measures to improve energy efficiency, which have resulted in large energy savings. Many of these measures could be easily implemented in Bahrain.

As a result of the policies adopted in Spain to promote the green economy, the green economy sector in Spain has grown to account for around 2.5 per cent of the Spanish GDP while 2.2 per cent of the country's total workforce is employed in the green economy sector (Sustainlabour *et al.* 2012, 7). In this chapter, the author will study the policies and legislations undertaken by Spain to support renewable energy and increase energy efficiency. The effects of these policies will be analysed, and lessons for Bahrain will be drawn from the Spanish experience. The majority of literature published on renewable energy in Bahrain studies its potential and analyses the source from an environmental point of view. This chapter differs from previous literature in that it provides an economic analysis and policy recommendations. Also, this is the first study that aims to draw renewable energy and energy efficiency policy recommendations for Bahrain from the experience of another country. The chapter concludes with a number of findings: first, FITs could be successfully implemented in Bahrain to encourage the installation of renewable energy. It is recommended that fossil fuel energy support be redirected towards renewable energy in the form of FITs. Second, in terms of energy efficiency, policies could easily be executed in Bahrain to simultaneously achieve both monetary and environmental benefits. These policies include increasing the energy efficiency of buildings through further regulations, and the use of energy-efficient lighting for indoor lighting, outdoor lighting and for traffic lights. Also, measures could be implemented to increase the energy efficiency of the transport sector through improvements in public transport and through increasing public awareness regarding pollutant emissions of different transport vehicles.

The potential for renewable energy in Bahrain

Due to the high solar radiation and long days, Bahrain's potential for solar energy is very high. Bahrain has an average of 3,350 hours of sunshine per year (Alnaser 1995, 26). The global horizontal irradiance (GHI) (which measures the total amount of shortwave radiation received by a surface parallel to the ground and is the most important parameter used to find the average electricity yield from solar photovoltaic (PV) power systems) is nearly 2,160 kWh per meter squared per year in Bahrain (Bachellerie 2012, 35). This can be compared to the GHI in Spain, where the regions with the highest potential for solar PV have an average GHI of 1,900 kWh (Solargis 2014). In Bahrain, the GHI is highest between April and September (Bachellerie 2012, 35). This is also when the electricity demand is highest (Bahrain Electricity and Water Authority 2014a). Climate conditions, such as high humidity and dust, must be taken into consideration as these reduce the efficiency of solar installations and increase their maintenance costs (Alnaser 1995, 26). Regular cleaning of the mirrors will be required which requires large amounts of water, which is an important challenge due to water scarcity in Bahrain. Also, extremely high temperatures, such as those reached in Bahrain in the summer, could reduce the efficiency of solar installations (ibid., 26). Solar energy is also relatively expensive when compared to other renewable energy sources, such as wind (IRENA 2012).

The potential for wind energy is moderate in Bahrain. Al Jowder (2009) studies wind speed data for the years 2003–2005, and uses different methods to estimate the country's wind energy potential. He calculates the average wind speeds at different heights and found that the average wind speeds are 4.56 m/s for 10 m, 6.96 m/s for 30 m and 8.65 m/s for 60 m. He finds that the average annual wind power density (a parameter that measures the mean annual level of power available per square meter area) is 114.54 W/m^2 for a height of 10 m, 433.29 W/m^2 for 30 m and 816.70 W/m^2 for 60 m. Hence, with these levels of power density, and especially for a height of 30 m and more, Bahrain could successfully install wind capacity. Alnaser and Al-Karaghouli (2000) also find that the potential for wind energy in Bahrain is moderate. However, they state that the use of small-sized (2-metre diameter or less) wind turbines located near the sea-shores could help Bahrain meet the high electricity demand during the summer peak hours. Because of the relatively low wind speeds and variant wind direction, they conclude that small wind turbines are most suitable for Bahrain. Variant wind direction allows spacing between wind turbines to be reduced. However, the high intermittency of wind in Bahrain could be problematic if large amounts of wind installation are to be incorporated in the electricity system. Other types of renewable energy, such as biomass, hydropower, water current power and tidal power, are impractical in Bahrain.

Theoretical analysis of renewable energy support

Green economy is a concept that has gained popularity in recent years. It aims to achieve economic prosperity together with environmental conservation so that sustainable economic growth can be achieved. Green growth policies include promoting renewable energy, increasing energy efficiency, green buildings, sustainable transport, waste management and water management.

Green growth policies aim to correct for the market failures that arise as a result of continuing business as usual. The consumption or production of fossil fuels results in a negative externality, as third parties are harmed by such activities. This is due to the emission of pollutants, which result in health and environmental costs to society. The polluter does not face the full cost of its actions, and the cost to society is higher than the cost to the polluter. Because polluters are not internalising the cost of their emissions, pollutants are emitted at unsustainable levels. To correct this market failure, policy-makers can either use market-based instruments or command-and-control regulations. Command-and-control regulations are specific measures set by policy-makers to be achieved by polluters. Hence, a polluter does not have the flexibility to choose the most efficient method to accomplish the objective of pollution reduction. Alternatively, 'market-based instruments are regulations that encourage behaviour through market signals rather than through explicit directives regarding pollution control levels or methods' (Stavins 2003, 358).

Market-based instruments are the most efficient tools to achieve green growth, as they allow polluters to choose the most cost-effective method to achieve the goal of the policy-makers (Menanteau *et al.* 2003, 810). Hence, polluters can choose between using renewable energy and implementing energy saving measures. Market-based instruments include environmental taxes, subsidies and tradable permits. Market-based instruments, such as carbon pricing, raise the cost faced by polluters. If the carbon price were to be set at a level where marginal private costs are equalised with the social benefits of abatement the market failure would disappear. Hence, a carbon price would be sufficient on its own to remove the market failure and no other measure would be required.

If the sole objective is the preservation of the environment then policies that support renewable energy would be inefficient. Such policies, by artificially lowering the price of renewable energy, encourage the support of specific technologies that may not be sufficiently developed at the expense of other more efficient methods. This raises the social cost of carbon abatement. However, market-based instruments are not sufficient to stimulate the learning process that will bring the prices of renewable energy down. Support for renewable energy can be justified if a positive externality of technological spill-overs exists. Due to technological spill-overs there will be underinvestment in developing renewable energy sources. Policies that support renewable energy lead to an increase in production and the proliferation of renewable energy, which in turn brings about the required learning effects. Political constraints are another reason why different countries have supported renewable energy as opposed to environmental taxes.

The most widely used system for renewable energy support is the FIT scheme. A FIT scheme is a price-based approach where payments are guaranteed to renewable energy producers at a level determined by public authorities for a predetermined period of time. Alternatively, quantity-based approaches can be established where the public authorities set an objective amount of renewable energy output to be reached, and then launch a competitive bidding process or a tradable green certificates scheme.

It has been shown by many studies that FITs are more effective in renewable energy deployment, especially when the share of renewable energy in electricity is low. Butler and Neuhoff (2004) compare FITs, quotas and auction mechanisms, and find that FITs result in larger deployment and may lead to cost reductions to consumers. Held et al. (2006) find that FITs ensure the fastest deployment of renewable energy at the lowest cost. Bürer and Wüstenhagen (2009) survey 60 professionals from European and North American venture capital and private equity funds and find that investors perceive FITs to be the most effective renewable energy policy. Sijm (2002) shows that FITs offer investment certainty and hence are very effective. However, FITs are not cost efficient because premiums are fixed by public authorities who do not have complete information of the development of the renewable energy costs. He also states that FITs distort market competition, but notes that the administrative demands of the system are low. He hence concludes that a system of FITs can be effective in the short run to promote renewable energy but, in the long run, the system can become unsustainable as the share of renewable energy in electricity rises. Menanteau et al. (2003) also explain that price-based approaches are very effective in terms of the quantity of renewable energy deployed, but quantity-based approaches are more effective in controlling the costs of the system since the amount of renewable energy is known a priori.

Therefore, although many of the prevailing renewable energy support systems could be used in Bahrain, the author believes that a FIT system is the most suitable renewable energy support system for the country, given that it has only recently started encouraging renewable energy projects. At this early stage, FITs could be more effective in encouraging renewable energy production. FITs reduce uncertainty to investors, which is important in encouraging renewable energy deployment in Bahrain.

Evolution of Spain's renewable energy policies

Spain first introduced a system of FITs in 1994. In 1997, the government established the 'Special Regime', whereby renewable energy and non-renewable cogeneration (mainly by natural gas) were given high levels of support compared to other sources. A year later, Royal Decree 2,818/1998 established the basic administrative framework for renewable energy producers. Levels of support were differentiated based on the type of technology. Producers could choose to sell their output directly in the market, have bilateral contracts or add their output to the grid. Renewable energy producers could also choose between either fixed premiums above electricity prices or a fixed total price. The premiums were to be reviewed every four years. The reason for setting both fixed premiums and fixed tariffs was to encourage participation in the market while at the same time guaranteeing certain remuneration to investors.

In 2004, support for renewable energy was increased especially for solar photovoltaic and wind energy. Support was also differentiated by the size of installation; smaller installations received higher support. Installations that supplied energy at peak hours also received higher support. Participation of generators in the market was also encouraged. If they chose to sell their output, generators received the market price of electricity, an incentive for participating and a premium. To reduce the risks faced by renewable energy generators and to reduce the system's costs, Royal Decree 661/2007 was introduced, replacing the previous FIT with a tariff linked to the consumer price index. It also introduced caps and floors on the levels of support in an attempt to prevent windfall profits as a result of falling renewable energy costs. However, high levels of support to different types of renewable energy were maintained. Payments to solar PV installations with capacity between 0.1 MW and 10 MW were increased. This resulted in a much larger than expected expansion of the solar power capacity. To limit this growth of solar PV, FITs received by new solar plants were reduced in 2008, and a quota was set on the number of new solar PV installations. Tariffs for new installations were cut by 30 per cent, while tariffs for installations registered before 2008 were maintained.

With the rise of renewable energy installations, the cost burden of renewable energy support started rising sharply, and a large tariff deficit started accumulating. Hence, in 2009, a cap was set on the level of deficit to be achieved in the next few years. In 2010, the Spanish government legislated measures to manage costs by reducing remuneration for renewable energy installations and setting more stringent rules on installations that qualify for support. Remuneration for wind and solar PV plants was sharply reduced. A ceiling was set on the number of hours in which solar PV or wind plants were eligible for support: if the plant exceeded this number it received the market price for these hours.

The measures taken to reduce the increasing costs of renewable energy support in 2010 were not sufficient to bring down the large amount of the accumulated deficit. Hence, in 2012, the Spanish government imposed a 7 per cent tax on electricity regardless of the source, plus an additional tax on electricity differentiated by the type of technology. This was the first time that wind and solar PV installations were taxed in Spain. Also in 2012, all support for new renewable energy installations was stopped, while FITs for existing installations were maintained. In 2013, support was removed from existing and new installations. Instead, renewable energy plants would receive the maximum of either the market price or a subsidy above market price, such that the return of renewable energy investors is equal to the rate of return of a 10-year Spanish treasury bond plus 300 basis points.

In conclusion, the Spanish renewable energy legislation was initially mainly driven by the motivation to encourage renewable energy production. Legislation was frequently modified to deal with challenges as they appeared and improve the efficiency of the system. However, the main challenge that remained is the excessive costs of the renewable energy support system, as will be discussed in the section below.

Analysis of Spain's renewable energy policies

FITs, together with other supporting policies, and combined with low interest rates until 2007, have caused a rapid rise in the amount of renewable energy produced in Spain (see Figures 4.4 and 4.5). Spain has become a leading country in renewable energy production worldwide. In 2013, 42 per cent of the country's electricity demand was covered by renewable energy (Red Eléctrica de España 2013). Wind power was the largest contributor to demand coverage, reaching 21 per cent of energy production (ibid.) (see Figure 4.6). In 2009, the renewable energy sector contributed around EUR10.283 billion to the Spanish GDP, which is around 0.98 per cent of the total GDP that year (Sustainlabour et al. 2012, 10).

Job creation has been one of the main reasons to support renewable energy. The FIT system resulted in a large increase in the number of jobs available in the renewable energy sector. From 1998 to 2009, the number of people employed in the renewable energy sector rose from 3,500 to 109,000 people (ibid., 8). The International Renewable Energy Agency (IRENA), in its Renewable Energy and Jobs Annual Review 2014, estimated that, by 2013, a total of 114,000 direct and indirect jobs have been created in the renewable energy sector in Spain. Forty-four thousand of these jobs are in biomass, 28,000 in concentrated solar power (CSP), 24,000 in wind power and 11,000 in solar PV. Moreover, the jobs created in the renewable energy sector are generally high-wage jobs. Sustainlabour et al. (2012) estimate that the salaries in the renewable energy jobs sector in Spain are 52 per cent higher than the national average. Hence, the FITs in Spain have resulted in socio-economic benefits.

Moreover, the large levels of support for renewable energy and the consequent increase in renewable energy capacity in Spain have had large benefits in terms of learning effects and technological progress. Spain grew to become one of the leading renewable technology manufacturers. According to the Organisation for Economic Co-operation and Development (OECD), renewable energy patents granted in Spain as a percentage of total patent applications filed under the

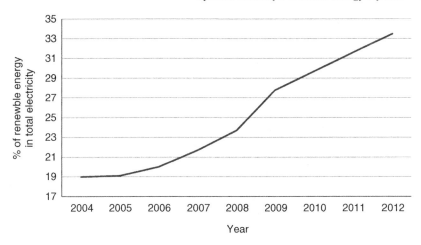

Figure 4.4 Share of renewable energy in electricity in Spain
Source: Eurostat (2014a)

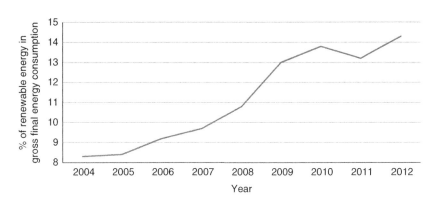

Figure 4.5 Share of renewable energy in gross final energy consumption in Spain
Source: Eurostat (2014a)

Patent Corporation Treaty rose from 1.4 per cent in 1995 to 6.7 per cent in 2009. According to the Spanish Patent and Trademark Office (Oficina Española de Patentes y Marcas 2013), Spanish applications in the renewable energy sector grew constantly during the 2000–2012 period. The most significant growth took place in solar PV applications: from 14 applications in 2000 to 122 in 2012. Solar energy patents formed 48 per cent of all renewable energy patents in 2012. Wind patents grew from 13 applications in 2000 to 83 in 2012, and accounted for 33 per cent of all renewable energy applications. Spain is considered one of the top three countries in Europe for renewable energy patent applications and one of the top five worldwide.

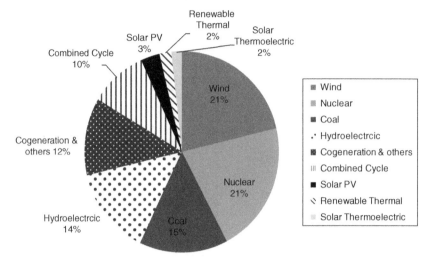

*Figure 4.*6 Electricity demand coverage in Spain (2013, %)
Source: Red Eléctrica Corporación (2013)

However, since 2000, mainly due to the support for special regime generation, the regulated revenues in the electricity sector have not been equalised with the cost of production, resulting in the accumulation of a tariff deficit (see Figure 4.7). The growth of the deficit was reinforced by the reform of the renewable energy support in 2007. The level of yearly tariff deficit more than tripled from 2007 to 2008 (Comisión Nacional de Energía 2013a). According to the Spanish National Energy Commission (Comisión Nacional de Energía 2013b) the accumulated debt of the electricity sector reached EUR26 billion by 2013. Factors that contributed to the increase of the tariff deficit include an increase in FIT premiums relative to market prices, and a larger than expected growth of renewable energy supply together with lower than expected demand for energy as a result of the economic crisis. These led to an overcapacity in energy production. In 2012, total electricity generation capacity in mainland Spain was 100,000 MW while peak demand only reached 45,000 MW (Red Eléctrica de España 2013).

One of the main factors that contributed to accelerating the growth of the tariff deficit is the improper design of support for solar photovoltaic installations. The reform of renewable energy legislation in favour of solar PV installations in 2007 led to a large entry of generators into the electricity market. Solar PV capacity grew by 806 per cent in 2007 and 903 per cent in 2008 (Álvarez *et al.* 2010, 15). In 2009, the share of solar PV support was 40 per cent of the support received by all special regime energy sources, while solar output was only 8 per cent of the special regime output (Federico 2011, 96). Even after a significant reduction of support by mid-2008, investors continued installing new solar PV even though the remuneration to solar PV producers was reduced by more than the fall in prices of solar technology (ibid., 98). The installed solar PV capacity reached 3.8

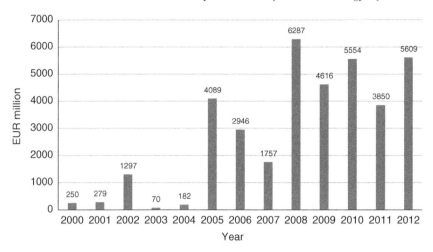

Figure 4.7 Yearly deficit generated by the electricity system in Spain
Source: Comisión Nacional de Energía (2013a)

GW in 2010 making Spain the second largest country in terms of installed solar capacity after Germany (US Department of Energy 2011, 2). The growth of solar power was well above the target set in the Spanish renewable energy Action Plan 2005–2010, which was only 400 MW. This shows that FITs for solar PV were set at levels far higher than the level required to encourage investment in solar PV energy, which resulted in high profit margins for solar PV producers. Furthermore, the majority of Spain's solar capacity was introduced at an early stage – 2.7 GW installed in 2008 (ibid.) at a EUR450/MW tariff (Ministerio de Industria, Energía y Turismo 2013) – when this technology was not fully developed. Other countries that encouraged the installation of solar PV capacity at a later stage were able to do so at a much lower cost due to the fall in technology prices. For example Germany increased its solar PV capacity by 64 per cent between 2010 and 2011 and did so at a EUR250/MW tariff (ibid.). Additionally, the solar PV support system in Spain before the 2007 reform was progressive: plants with installed capacity above 100 kW received much lower remuneration than those with capacity of 100 kW or less. This was justified based on economies of scale. However, some large-scale PV power stations started to break up into units of less than 100 kW connected together and managed by a single firm. Such procedures further contributed to increasing transaction costs of solar PV producers and inefficiency (Álvarez *et al.* 2010, 13).

According to the Council of European Energy Regulators (CEER 2013), the total expenditure on support to renewable energy in euros per unit of energy consumed in Spain in 2010 was EUR20.61/MWh – the highest when compared to other European Union (EU) member states (see Figure 4.8). The European average level of support was EUR6.85/MWh. Solar PV installations in Spain received EUR399/MWh, amounting to the highest level of support per unit of energy

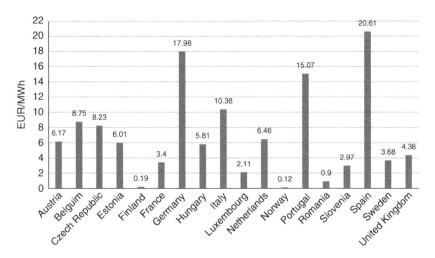

Figure 4.8 Renewable energy electricity support per unit of final energy consumed
Source: Council of European Energy Regulators (2013)

consumed among all technologies. The second highest support per megawatt hour of energy was for biomass EUR77.51/MWh, followed by wind and hydro, at EUR45.55/MWh and EUR44.01/MWh, respectively (ibid.). These numbers fell moderately after 2010 when support for renewable energy was reduced.

In order to assess the renewable energy support scheme in Spain, the cost of renewable energy support must be compared to the environmental benefits achieved. Federico (2011) compares the amount of avoided CO_2 emissions from renewable energy with the cost of the renewable energy support scheme in Spain. He finds that, in 2010, the cost of renewable energy support per unit of avoided CO_2 in Spain was around EUR200–250/t, and which was between 14 and 17 times higher than the market price for CO_2. He hence concludes that the expansion in renewable energy output in Spain has been achieved at an excessive social cost. The opportunity costs of remuneration of renewable energy have been high, and these excessive costs could have been used to stimulate other sectors of the economy.

The high share of renewable energy led to a rise in electricity prices in Spain (see Figure 4.9). According to the Ministry of Industry, Energy and Tourism (Ministerio de Industria, Energía y Turismo 2013), Spanish households in 2012 paid electricity prices 30 per cent higher than the EU average, while industrial consumers paid electricity prices 18 per cent higher than the EU average. Energy costs form a significant part of the costs of firms, and hence energy prices affect their international competitiveness. This has led many firms, most notably energy-intensive industries such as the metallurgy and chemical industries, to relocate to nearby countries. For example, companies such as Hoechst Ibérica, Marcial Ucín, Sidenor and Ferroatlántica redirected part of their investments to countries abroad (Álvarez *et al.* 2010, 33).

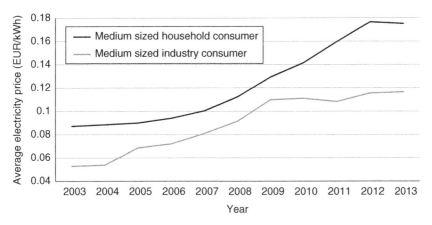

Figure 4.9 Electricity prices in Spain

Source: Eurostat (2014b)

Note: Medium sized household consumer: annual consumption between 2500 and 5000 kWh. Medium sized industry consumer: annual consumption between 500 and 2000 MWh.

In conclusion, the Spanish FIT system proved to be very effective in encouraging investors to install new renewable energy capacity. This led to job creation in manufacturing, installation, operation and maintenance of renewable energy installations. Significant progress has been achieved in terms of technological advances, reflected by the number of renewable energy patents Spain achieved. However, renewable energy support generated excessive costs that are proven to be higher than in other European countries due to the higher profit margins received by Spanish renewable energy producers.

Renewable energy lessons for Bahrain from the Spanish experience

Due to the wide use of FITs in many countries all over the world and their proven success in many of these countries, and because numerous studies (Sijm 2002; Butler and Neuhoff 2004; Held *et al.* 2006; Bürer and Wüstenhagen 2009) show that FITs are more effective in terms of renewable energy deployment than other support systems (especially when renewable energy production levels are low), the author believes that a FIT system is the most suitable instrument to be used in Bahrain to support renewable energy. The Spanish example is unique and can serve as a benchmark, whereby Bahrain can learn from both the successes and the drawbacks of the Spanish renewable energy support system. The excessive costs faced by Spain due to renewable energy support must not be viewed as a deterrent to renewable energy support. As explained in the previous section, costs have been large due to improper policy design. Therefore, Bahrain must be very careful when designing the FIT system. Identifying the appropriate level of support is difficult and, consequently, thorough studies must be undertaken. Before initiating a FIT system, a careful study must be carried out both on the potential of renewable energy at different sites in Bahrain, and on the renewable energy market to identify potential suppliers in order to introduce renewable energy in the most cost-effective way. Also, a study must be undertaken on both the institutional and human capacities required for the renewable energy sector, and measures must be set to tackle the challenges. Targets on the amount of renewable energy to be installed must also be set, and these must be set at reasonable levels in order to be credible.

After the initiation of the FIT system a careful monitoring of the progress of the renewable energy sector and especially of the profits of renewable energy producers is required. Large profits signal that support levels must be reduced. In Spain renewable energy investors were making large windfall profits while the tariff deficit continued to grow, but major actions to reduce the tariff deficit were taken only after a large tariff deficit had been accumulated. The amount of support must decline gradually over time due to learning effects and technological advances, which reduce the cost faced by renewable energy producers. Although it is difficult to directly link support for renewable energy to the change in the cost of renewable energy technologies, Spain failed to adjust its renewable energy support scheme with the falling costs of renewable energy technologies. Consequently, large cuts in the levels of support and the legislations undertaken recently were inevitable. However, this led renewable energy investors to question the credibility of the Spanish renewable system, and uncertainty has increased regarding future policies, which has resulted in a fall in investments in the renewable energy sector and a consequent fall in employment in the renewable energy sector. Therefore, the reduction of renewable energy support must be designed in a way that does not affect the credibility of the system. A certain period of time must be given before changes in support take place so that renewable energy producers can make adjustments and plans based on the new levels of support.

The main barrier against renewable energy deployment in Bahrain is constituted by the high prices of solar and wind technology when compared to those of fossil fuel sources. Unlike Spain, which imports oil and gas at relatively high prices, the prices of oil and gas in Bahrain are low, and do not reflect the real cost of energy. This is because conventional energy sources such as oil and gas receive high amounts of subsidies in Bahrain and in the other Gulf Cooperation Council (GCC) countries. If FITs are introduced, support levels need to be high to make renewable energy competitive with the under-priced fossil fuel energy (see Table 4.2).

As shown in Figure 4.10, Bahrain and the GCC countries in general are among the countries with the lowest electricity prices in the world. Fossil fuel energy priced significantly lower than their economic value in international markets, together with further subsidies on electricity generated from these sources, makes it extremely difficult for renewable energy to compete in the energy market. To solve this problem, fossil fuel subsidies should be redirected to renewable energy.

Table 4.2 Electricity tariffs in Bahrain

Domestic residential electricity tariff	Non-domestic electricity tariff
1–3,000 unit at 3 fils 3,001–5,000 unit at 9 fils 5,001 & over at 16 fils	Each unit at 16 fils

Source: Bahrain Electricity and Water Authority (2014c). Note: Electricity unit = 1 kilowatt hour (kWh). 1000 fils = 1 Bahraini dinar

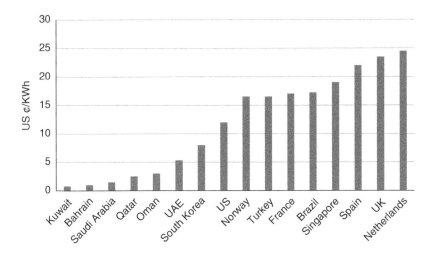

Figure 4.10 Average residential electricity prices (2008)
Source: El-Katiri (2014)

Redirecting fossil fuel subsidies towards FITs to support renewable energy producers could help mitigate many of the problems that Spain faced as a result of renewable energy support. Renewable energy could be encouraged without imposing additional financial expenses on the budget. Hence, the emergence of a large renewable energy deficit, such as that of Spain, can be avoided. Also, resources to finance renewable energy support would not be deducted from the budget allocated to other sectors of the economy. Hence, growth in the renewable energy sector would not be at the expense of other sectors.

The renewable energy sector in Bahrain could lead to an increase in job opportunities as happened in Spain. Renewable energy jobs worldwide reached 6.5 million in 2013, with solar PV energy being the largest source of employment with 2.3 million people employed in the sector (IRENA 2014, 2). Hence, installing renewable energy plants in Bahrain could create new job opportunities with high wages. However, education and training are important factors in job creation and therefore Bahrain must also develop a workforce with the required skills for the renewable energy sector by providing incentives for people to choose this area of specialisation. As IRENA (2014, 3) highlights: 'skill shortages can also act as a major barrier to renewable energy deployment and thus to associated employment'.

Redirecting subsidies from fossil fuel energy to renewable energy might lead to a rise in electricity prices. Nonetheless, this does not necessarily mean that society would be harmed. Under-pricing of fossil fuels and electricity has high opportunity cost and distorts markets. A rise in electricity prices to a level that reflects the true market price of electricity will encourage more efficient use of energy, especially since energy consumption patterns of both households and industries in Bahrain are considered wasteful precisely due to low electricity prices (Bachellerie 2012, 22).

Energy subsidies are regressive since industries and the rich are the largest energy consumers and therefore benefit proportionately more than the poor. Nevertheless, low energy prices create a safety net for the poor, and any attempt to raise energy prices will reduce their real income. Raising energy prices will also reduce the competitiveness of certain industries. Most notably the petrochemical and aluminium industries will be harmed because they are energy intensive. These are the main industries in Bahrain, which raises the question of whether such measures will be socially acceptable. To tackle this problem, the government must increase awareness of the benefits of renewable energy as opposed to conventional sources of energy. The government should also compensate those industries and households harmed through carefully designed compensation measures that specifically target the poor and assist the economy in its long-term adaptation.

Bahrain's international competitiveness may be harmed by a rise in domestic energy prices, if energy prices remain low in the other GCC countries. This may lead firms to relocate to neighbouring countries as firms did in Spain. Hence there must be coordination between the GCC countries in terms of support for renewable energy and electricity prices. The recommendations mentioned above for Bahrain can be applied to other GCC countries due to the similarity in their economies. If the GCC countries increase their support for renewable energy they can increase their exports of fossil fuels, while these increased revenues also offset the costs of renewable energy support. Also, if technological progress in renewable energy continues at the current rate, it can soon be competitive with conventional sources. This way, in the long run, support for all energy sources can be removed and renewable energy can still remain competitive.

Bahrain is now on the right track. The National Oil and Gas Authority (NOGA 2010) has agreed with the Japanese Inter-Domain Company to cooperate in evaluating the potential of wind energy in the country. As a result, in January 2009, a 50-metre-high mast was installed for measuring wind power. NOGA has also cooperated with the United States-based Petrosolar to explore Bahrain's solar power potential. In July 2011, the Minister of Energy signed a renewable energy consultancy contract with Fichtner Consulting Engineers of Germany to provide field measurements, data-collection and verification, and a full investigation to determine the adequacy of solar and wind energy in the country. Under agreement, Fichtner was to provide a techno-commercial feasibility study that explains both the advantages and disadvantages of solar and wind technologies and identify optimal areas in Bahrain. Soon after, the Bahrain Electricity and Water Authority (2014b) announced plans to install a 3–5 MW solar PV and 2 MW wind energy pilot plant to help study more carefully the potential of renewable energy in Bahrain and consider further expansion. In June 2014, a 5 MW solar plant was inaugurated, at a cost of USD27 million: 3 MW of the power produced will be consumed by the Bahrain Petroleum Company, 1.5 MW by the city of Awali and 0.5 MW by the University of Bahrain (*Gulf Daily News* 2014a). The project is expected to reduce CO_2 emissions by 6,900 Mt/year. In 2014, the Electricity and Water Authority also announced it was studying the potential for constructing a solar plant at Hawar to meet the electricity needs of the island. Bahrain aims to produce 5 per cent of its energy from renewable sources by 2020.

Spain's energy efficiency policies and lessons for Bahrain

The first steps for moving towards a green economy in Bahrain should be through increasing energy efficiency. An increase in energy efficiency can achieve the same objectives of using renewable energy but at a significantly lower cost. The potential of increasing energy efficiency in Bahrain is high. Increasing energy efficiency not only leads to a reduction in pollutant emissions, but also boosts the profitability of firms and incomes in general. Spain has focused on increasing energy efficiency as a policy that goes hand in hand with renewable energy support policies. The different energy efficiency policies undertaken in Spain can offer important lessons for Bahrain.

Buildings

Due to the warm climate in Bahrain, Bahraini citizens spend most of their time inside buildings. In 2013, electricity consumption of the domestic sector was almost 50 per cent of the country's total electricity consumption (Bahrain Central Informatics Organization 2014). The commercial sector accounted for 36 per cent of the total electricity consumption (ibid.). Increasing electricity efficiency of buildings can therefore lead to large energy savings. Spain has implemented a number of measures to increase energy efficiency in buildings, which have led to a significant reduction in energy consumption. Royal Decree 314/2006 established the Technical Building Code, which sets the regulatory framework of the minimum requirements to be met by new buildings and those undergoing renovation of more than 25 per cent of their area (Martín 2013, 341). It contains a Basic Energy Saving Document, which sets requirements of energy efficiency and renewable energy in buildings (IEA 2013). Periodic inspections of energy efficiency have been implemented since 2007 (Martín 2013, 342). A software program has also been used to classify buildings based on their energy efficiency and CO_2 emissions, and provides a detailed assessment of possible energy efficiency improvement measures (ibid., 344). The Spanish Institute for Energy Diversification and Saving (IDAE) together with the Spanish Technical Association of Air-Conditioning and Refrigeration has published a number of guides to increase awareness about measures to enhance energy efficiency in buildings.

To provide appropriate thermal insulation, buildings in Spain must have a thermal envelope with specific features depending on the climate of the area of the building and solar radiation exposure (IDAE 2014a). This reduces the amount of energy required to reach and maintain the appropriate indoor temperatures. Measures to increase the insulation of equipment and piping of heating, cooling and hot water production system installations are also promoted (ibid.). To further reduce energy consumption, Royal Decree 1,826/2009 introduced limits on indoor temperatures in summer and winter for administrative, commercial and public buildings that use fossil fuel sources of electricity. In these, the indoor temperature values should be placed in a visible place (Martín 2013, 342). The Decree also introduced an obligation to use a mechanism that keeps doors directly connected with the outdoor closed in buildings using fossil fuel sources of electricity (ibid.). Such measures, if implemented in Bahrain, would lead to large energy savings, especially since the majority of electricity consumed in buildings in the country is used for cooling.

In 2014, the Bahrain Electricity and Water Authority announced a new regulation ruling that all new residential and commercial buildings must be equipped with thermal insulation. This important step is expected to save 15–30 per cent of electricity consumed in buildings (Gulf Daily News 2014b). Many buildings in Bahrain are designed with glass glazing, which forms a poor heat insulator. This together with high solar radiation leads to a rise in indoor temperatures and significantly increases the need for energy to cool the building. Also, due to glass glazing and reflective windows, outside temperatures in the city centres are found to be higher than in rural areas in Bahrain (Alnaser and Flanagan 2007, 499). Radhi (2008) studied a typical public building in Bahrain with glass glazing, and found that the cooling load can be reduced by 35 per cent and total electricity consumption by 22 per cent by using more efficient glazing. Spain started increasing energy efficiency in public buildings so as to save public funds and set an example for the private sector (IDAE 2014b). Bahrain can do the same. The built environment should also be designed with an aim to reduce the amount of surfaces exposed to solar radiation.

Lighting

The Technical Building Code also sets lighting requirements in new buildings and those to be refurbished, with certain compulsory efficiency standards. Also, lighting installations should have a control system that allows switching on and off depending on the occupation of the area (IDAE 2014c). Buildings in Spain should also optimise the exploitation of daylight (ibid.). IDAE has published a number of guides on the use of natural light for indoor lighting in buildings, and on efficient lighting in offices, hospitals and health centres and educational establishments. These are aimed at increasing public awareness and providing a set of recommendations on energy efficiency procedures that may be carried out. Inefficient light bulbs have been phased out (ibid.). High-efficiency light bulbs such as compact fluorescent lights (CFLs) use only a quarter to a fifth of the energy used by incandescent bulbs. Light-emitting diodes (LEDs) are 15 times more efficient than incandescent bulbs. They also last longer: LEDs have a lifetime of 100,000 hours while CFLs have a lifetime of 10,000 hours and incandescent have a lifetime of 1,000 hours (Humphreys 2008, 470). Hence, the higher prices of efficient light bulbs can be quickly regained, and large amounts of money can be saved. LED lights also do not cause heat build-up, which is important in Bahrain as it allows for air-conditioning costs to be reduced.

In April 2014, the Cabinet of Bahrain announced a ban on importing and manufacturing of incandescent bulbs with tungsten filaments, and that these will be replaced by CFLs (*Gulf Daily News* 2014c). Also, energy efficiency standards for air conditioning equipment will be raised. Such measures are expected to bring broad environmental and economic benefits. While this is a step in the right direction, further measures, such as those undertaken by Spain to control the switching of lights and optimise the use of natural light, should be undertaken. Nevertheless, it should be taken into account that increased natural light raises the temperature of the building, and therefore an efficient balance between lighting and cooling must be chosen.

Measures to increase the efficiency of street lighting constitute a further area to be considered. A pilot project was undertaken in the cities Alcorcón, Soto del Real and Teruel in Spain, where high lighting levels were cut back and lamp posts replaced with more efficient ones, which reduced light emissions towards spaces other than the lighting focus (IDAE 2014d). This proved to be very economical as electricity consumption was significantly reduced as a result. It was estimated that, if implemented across Spain, the payback period would be around six years (ibid.). Consequently, Royal Decree 1,890/2008 was established regulating energy efficiency of street lighting in Spain. It sets obligations on the type of light bulbs and on reducing glare and limiting the wasted energy from unnecessary lighting. The Decree requires all towns with over 25,000 inhabitants to install efficient street lighting within five years (ibid.). This has had significant effects, and it is argued that similar legislation is required in Bahrain, as the potential for increasing energy efficiency of street lighting in Bahrain is large.

One of the main focuses of IDAE has been on the substitution of sodium vapour traffic lights with efficient LED technology. The Institute provided EUR 30 million to 600 municipalities for replacing traffic lights with LED technology. A total of 462,300 traffic lights were replaced leading to an 87,760 MWh annual saving (IDAE 2014e). Such action is estimated to reduce CO_2 emissions by 622t/year (ibid.). Similar large-scale replacement of traffic lights in Bahrain could lead to significant environmental and economic benefits as the replacement of a typical traffic light in Bahrain with LED technology can lead to an energy saving of more than 75 per cent. Also, given their greater brightness, LED lights are more suitable for Bahrain's dusty and foggy weather.

Transport

The transport sector is the largest sector in terms of energy consumption in Spain, accounting for 39 per cent of national consumption (IDAE 2014f). While the share is lower in Bahrain, transport is still a significant energy consumer, and energy efficiency improvements in this sector would therefore lead to a large reduction in pollutant emissions. In 2003, the Spanish Saving and Energy Efficiency Strategy was approved, which sets the basic framework and goals regarding energy efficiency. Later, the 2008–2012 Action Plan was published, which sets the measures to be taken to achieve these goals (IDAE 2007). For the transport sector, these revolve around moving from private car transport towards more sustainable methods of transport such as walking, cycling or public transport. The Action Plan sets several legislations in favour of public transport, and includes planned projects to enhance bicycle lanes and pedestrian areas, as well as ones to improve inter-modality. Spain has also sought to increase awareness through several campaigns. The government has published a transport to work plan and has promoted the use of bicycles by subsidising cycling and installing a public bicycle system for daily mobility (IDAE 2014g). Investments have been made in the improvement of the rail network and promoting the shift of freight from road to rail (ibid.). Bahrain faces a larger challenge than Spain due to its hot weather, and modes of transport such as walking and cycling can therefore not gain popularity as means of daily mobility. However, improving public transport, such as buses and trains, is feasible. Bahrain plans to expand and improve its bus services together with the planned GCC railway project, which is expected to result in a significant reduction of pollutant emissions in the air, since these will replace private car use.

In its Action Plan, Spain has also focused on renewing the transport fleet. An increasing number of cars and light trucks are fuelled by diesel instead of gasoline. Implementation of the Plan has resulted in improvements in energy intensity (Mediluce and Schipper 2011, 6468). Tax incentives are being used to promote low CO_2-emitting cars through the car registration tax where tax levels are based on CO_2 emissions per km (ibid., 6473). Spain also promotes the use of alternative energy cars, such as hybrid and electric vehicles. The IDAE has developed a database where car buyers can assess different models based on their emissions and fuel consumption. Since 2002, according to Royal Decree 837/2002, cars should be labelled depending on their fuel consumption (IDAE 2014h). In Bahrain similar measures should be taken to increase the public awareness of the efficiency of different cars and to help consumers make an informed choice.

Conclusion

The widespread success of the FIT scheme makes it an important potential tool for renewable energy support in Bahrain. In Bahrain a system of FITs will be costly due to existing support for fossil fuel energy. These subsidies, however, could be redirected towards renewable energy support. This way, many of the problems faced by Spain could be avoided. Bahrain is now on the right track, with thorough studies being undertaken and pilot projects planned. Implementing a FIT scheme can be only considered after sufficient information is available regarding these projects.

In terms of energy efficiency a lot can be achieved, and the public authorities in Bahrain are aware of this potential. Measures to improve energy efficiency of buildings must be undertaken, especially regarding the use of glass glazing. Starting with government buildings, as did Spain, can serve as a benchmark for the private sector to follow. In terms of lighting, Bahrain has issued legislation to increase energy efficiency of lighting in buildings. These measures should be extended to street lighting and traffic lights. In the transport sector public transport should be developed, and public awareness raised regarding the benefits of using public transportation and the emissions and fuel consumption of different cars.

Many of the policy recommendations given throughout this chapter can be applied to other GCC countries due to the similarity of their economies. Similarly to Bahrain, all other GCC countries too support fossil fuel energy and have, as a result, low electricity prices. Industry activities in all six states are also concentrated in energy-intensive industries. Electricity consumption patterns too are very similar, with the GCC region sharing very high energy consumption per capita rates. Energy intensity growth rates are also rising very fast in the GCC. Hence, there is a strong urge to find alternative sources of energy to meet this rising energy demand and to maintain the current levels of energy exports. Increasing renewable energy capacity and implementing measures to increase energy efficiency is therefore not only important from an environmental perspective, but also for securing the Gulf states' future energy supply.

References

Al Jowder, Fawzi. 2009. 'Wind Power Analysis and Site Matching of Wind Turbine Generators in the Kingdom of Bahrain.' *Applied Energy* 86: 538–545.

Alnaser, N. W., and R. Flanagan. 2007. 'The Need of Sustainable Buildings Construction in the Kingdom of Bahrain.' *Building and Environment* 42, No. 1: 495–506.

Alnaser, W. E. 1995. 'Renewable Energy Resources in the State of Bahrain.' *Applied Energy* 50: 23–30.

Alnaser, W. E., and A. Al-Karaghouli. 2000. 'Wind Availability and Its Power Utility for Electricity Production in Bahrain.' *Renewable Energy* 21: 247–254.

Álvarez, Gabriel Calzada, Raquel Merino Jara, Juan Ramón Rallo Julián and José Ignacio García Bielsa. 2010. 'Study of the Effects on Employment of Public Aid to Renewable Energy Sources.' *Procesos De Mercado* VII, No 1.

Arab Union of Electricity. 2013. *Statistical Bulletin 2013, Issue 22.*

Bachellerie, Imen Jeridi. 2012. *Renewable Energy in the GCC Countries: Resources, Potential and Prospects.* Jeddah: Gulf Research Center.

Bahrain Central Informatics Organization. 2014. 'Development of Electricity Consumption for the Various Sectors, in GWh (2003–2013).' Accessed April. http://www.cio.gov.bh/

Bahrain Electricity and Water Authority. 2014a. 'Electricity Statistics.' Accessed April. http://www.mew.gov.bh/

Bahrain Electricity and Water Authority. 2014b. 'H.E. the Ministry [sic] of Energy Signs a Contract for Conducting Feasibility Study for Renewable Energies and Supervision of Establishment of a Pilot Power Plant." Accessed April. http://www.mew.gov.bh/

Bahrain Electricity and Water Authority. 2014c. 'Tariffs & Services Rates.' http://www.mew.gov.bh/

Bürer, Mary Jean, and Rolf Wüstenhagen. 2009. 'Which Renewable Energy Policy is a Venture Capitalist's Best Friend? Empirical Evidence from a Survey of International Cleantech Investors.' *Energy Policy* 37, No. 12: 4997–4950.

Butler, Lucy, and Karsten Neuhoff. 2004. 'Comparison of Feed-in Tariff, Quota and Auction Mechanisms to Support Wind Power Development.' *Cambridge Working Papers in Economics CWPE 0503*, CMI Working Paper 70.

CIA. Central Intelligence Agency. 2014. *The World Factbook*. Accessed April. https://www.cia.gov/library/publications/the-world-factbook/

Comisión Nacional de Energía. 2013a. *Nota resumen del saldo de la deuda del sistema eléctrico*. Madrid, 29 May.

Comisión Nacional de Energía. 2013b. *Spanish Energy Regulator's National Report to the European Commission 2013*.

CEER. Council of European Energy Regulators. 2013. *Status Review of Renewable and Energy Efficiency Support Schemes in Europe*.

EIA. United States Energy Information Administration. 2013. 'Bahrain.' Updated 30 May. http://www.eia.gov/countries/

El-Katiri, Laura. 2014. *A Roadmap for Renewable Energy in the Middle East and North Africa*. MEP 6. Oxford: Oxford Institute for Energy Studies.

Eurostat. 2014a. 'Share of Energy from Renewable Sources.' Updated 14 April. http://appsso.eurostat.ec.europa.eu/

Eurostat. 2014b. 'Electricity Prices by Type of User.' Updated 28 May. http://epp.eurostat.ec.europa.eu/

Federico, Giulio. 2011. *The Spanish Gas and Electricity Sector: Regulation, Markets and Environmental Policies*. Barcelona: IESE Business School.

Gulf Daily News. 2014a. 'Bahrain Boost as Bapco Launches Key Solar Plant.' 26 June. http://www.gulf-daily-news.com/

Gulf Daily News. 2014b. 'Heat Insulation Guidelines for New Buildings.' 24 March. http://www.gulf-daily-news.com/

Gulf Daily News. 2014c. 'Saving Energy.' 28 April. http://www.gulf-daily-news.com/

Held, Anne, Mario Ragwitz and Reinhard Haas. 2006. 'On the Success of Policy Strategies for the Promotion of Electricity from Renewable Energy Sources in the EU.' *Energy & Environment* 17, No. 6: 849–868.

Humphreys, Colin J. 2008. 'Solid-state Lighting.' *MRS Bulletin* 33, No. 04: 459–470.

IDAE. Instituto para la Diversificación y Ahorro de la Energía. 2007. *Saving and Energy Efficiency Strategy in Spain 2004–2012: Action Plan 2008–2012*. July.

IDAE. 2014a. 'Insulation in Building.' Accessed March. http://www.idae.es/

IDAE. 2014b. 'Public Buildings.' Accessed March. http://www.idae.es/

IDAE. 2014c. 'Lighting in Buildings.' Accessed March. http://www.idae.es/

IDAE. 2014d. 'Street Lighting.' Accessed March http://www.idae.es/

IDAE. 2014e. 'Announcement of the Aid Scheme to Replace Traffic Lights Optics with New LED Technology.' Accessed March. http://www.idae.es/

IDAE. 2014f. 'Transport.' Accessed March. http://www.idae.es/

IDAE. 2014g. 'Modal Change Enhancement Measures.' Accessed March. http://www.idae.es/

IDAE. 2014h. 'Consumo de carburante y emisiones de CO_2 en coches nuevos.' Accessed March. http://coches.idae.es/

IEA. International Energy Agency. 2013. 'Technical Building Code.' Updated 15 March. http://www.iea.org/

IRENA. International Renewable Energy Agency. 2012. *Summary for Policy Makers: Renewable Power Generation Costs.* Abu Dhabi: IRENA.

IRENA. 2014. *Renewable Energy and Jobs Annual Review 2014.* Abu Dhabi: IRENA.

Martín, Aitor Domínguez. 2013. 'EPBD Implementation in Spain: Status at the End of 2012.' In *Implementing the Energy Performance of Building Directive (EPBD): Featuring Country Reports 2012.* Porto: Portuguese Energy Agency (ADENE).

Mendiluce, María, and Lee Schipper. 2011. 'Trends in Passenger Transport and Freight Energy Use in Spain.' *Energy Policy* 39, No. 10: 6466–6475.

Menanteau, Philippe, Dominique Finon and Marie-Laure Lamy. 2003. 'Prices Versus Quantities: Choosing Policies for Promoting the Development of Renewable Energy.' *Energy Policy* 31, No. 8: 799–812.

Ministerio de Industria, Energía y Turismo. 2013. *The Reform of the Spanish Power System: Towards Financial Stability and Regulatory Certainty.* Presentation slides. http://www.thespanisheconomy.com/stfls/tse/ficheros/2013/agosto/Power_System_Reform.pdf

NOGA. National Oil and Gas Authority (of Bahrain). 2010. *Annual Report 2009.*

Oficina Española de Patentes y Marcas. 2013. 'Spain and Renewable Energy Patents 2000–2012.' http://www.oepm.es/

Radhi, Hassan. 2008. 'A Systematic Methodology for Optimizing the Energy Performance of Buildings in Bahrain.' *Energy and Buildings* 40: 1297–1303.

Red Eléctrica Corporación. 2013. *Corporate Responsibility Report 2013: Towards a Sustainable Energy Future.* Alcobendas, Madrid.

Red Eléctrica de España. 2013. *The Spanish Electricity System Preliminary Report 2013.*

Sijm, Johannes Paulus Maria. 2002. *The Performance of Feed-in Tariffs to Promote Renewable Electricity in European Countries.* Petten: Energy Research Centre of the Netherlands.

Solargis. 2014. 'Global Horizontal Irradiation – Spain.' Accessed 21 May. http://solargis.info/

Stavins, Robert N. 2003. 'Experience with Market-based Environmental Policy Instruments.' *Handbook of Environmental Economics* 1: 355–435.

Sustainlabour, Biodiversity Foundation, and International Labour Organization. 2012. *Green Jobs for Sustainable Development: A Case Study of Spain.*

United States (US) Department of Energy. 2011. *2010 Solar Technologies Market Report.* November.

5 Promoting an effective energy efficiency programme in Saudi Arabia: challenges and opportunities

Bandar Alhoweish and Chingiz Orujov[1,2]

Introduction: economic challenges in Saudi Arabia

Global energy security has intertwined with the Kingdom of Saudi Arabia for decades. Its historic role as the largest oil exporter the energy market has ever known and the high oil prices in recent years have contributed to the recognition of Saudi Arabia as one of the best-performing G20 economies. During 2008–2012, its real gross domestic product (GDP) growth averaged at 6.25 per cent per annum, just behind China and India. Saudi Arabia has also continued to play the role of a stabilising force in the global oil market by increasing its oil production to avoid any supply shocks resulting from, for example, geopolitical tensions in Libya, Nigeria, Angola and elsewhere (IMF 2013). This has greatly assisted in preventing a detrimental impact on global economic growth. The country owns the world's largest conventional oil reserves, of around 266 billion barrels (16 per cent of the world's proven and recoverable reserves). It also produced 13.3 per cent of total world oil production in 2012, with a refining capacity of more than 3.5 million barrels per day (mbpd) (BP 2013). The country's official policy target is to maintain a spare capacity that ranges at least 1.5–2 mbpd: in 2012, it averaged at 2.2 mbpd. This makes Saudi Arabia the only country with such a significant spare production capacity. Its current total crude oil production capacity is 12 mbpd (IEA 2013a). Yet, given the oil market's supply-demand volatility, several major projects are currently under way in the Kingdom to secure further immediate supplies once needed to ensure the market's stability. This indicates the country's continuing emphasis on its role in preventing oil supply shocks.

The Saudi government has indeed seen historic budgetary surpluses since 2003 as a direct result of high oil revenues (except in 2009). This significantly contributed to reduce the government's public debt-to-GDP ratio to as low as 3.5 per cent in 2012 – a significant reduction from 82.9 per cent in 2003. Oil revenues have also supported the government's foreign reserves, which reached USD711 billion in September 2013 (97 per cent of estimated 2013 GDP). These are further projected to increase to USD767.5 and USD841 billion in 2014 and 2015, respectively. These figures are equivalent to 37.7 and 38.2 months of imports of goods and services, respectively (IMF 2013).

Despite the recognised national economic performance when compared to the international average, the Kingdom is facing important socio-economic challenges. These challenges, among others, have forced a sharp increase in the break-even oil prices needed to generate revenue to cover government expenditure from USD37/barrel in 2008 to USD84.4/barrel in 2013 (Bailey and Willoughby 2013). This is extremely significant given that oil revenues account for more than 80 per cent of Saudi Arabia's export revenues and over 90 per cent of budget revenues. In other words, the Saudi economy depends heavily, and almost solely, on oil market developments, demonstrating the country's extreme vulnerability to any price shocks (IMF 2013).

One example of these highly complex challenges is the high national unemployment rate, which has reached 12 per cent, and remains much higher for youth (30 per cent) and women (35 per cent). This is despite the fact that the labour force survey recorded a two-million increase in employment between 2009 and 2012 (ibid.). Knowing that three-quarters of these jobs have gone to non-Saudis while the Saudi labour force is projected to increase 3.5 per cent a year over the course of next decade demonstrates the magnitude of the challenge (EIU 2014). It also indicates, as a consequence, that the economic growth rate needs to increase even further than the current high rate (approximately 6 per cent in recent years) to solve the issue of unemployment since the rate of labour entering the market is growing (IMF 2013).

Another serious challenge for the country's decision makers is the food and water security issue. The fact that over 85 per cent of the country's food requirements are imported exposed Saudi Arabia to supply disruptions during the global food crisis in 2007 and 2008. This is coupled with the fact that the rate of domestic food consumption increases at a very fast pace of 8 per cent annually. This challenge is driven by the high annual total population growth of 2.7 per cent, as well as the increasing purchasing power of the population. As for the water scarcity issue, the country's renewable freshwater resources are among the lowest in the world and, yet, water desalination costs the government USD1 per cubic metre while the population pays as little as 3 USD cents. This is in spite of the amount of energy required to avail this scarce resource, which receives even more generous subsidies (Bailey and Willoughby 2013). The amount of energy subsidies alone is reported to cost the government over 10 per cent of the country's GDP (Lahn and Stevens 2011, 49).

The most serious challenge facing the Kingdom is its apparent unsustainable energy consumption behaviour. The country currently consumes just over a quarter of its total oil production, which is equivalent to 2.9 mbpd. According to its national oil company, Saudi Aramco, if the business-as-usual scenario persists, the crude oil export capacity will fall by about 3 mbpd, to under 7 mbpd by 2028 (Alhoweish 2011, 365). This particular fact is threatening the Kingdom's ability to maintain its defining international role as the most reliable oil exporter. The decision makers have realised the need to address this particular challenge to maintain the country's oil export capacity, and are currently striving to formulate sustainable and 'painless' plans of action to reverse the effects of the collective challenges described above. One of these action plans is promoting and enforcing a nation-wide energy efficiency programme as an effective tool to decelerate the widening domestic energy supply-demand gap. Although this high-profile programme is principally driven by the need to better control the extremely high domestic consumption of fossil fuels, it presents a unique opportunity to establish a substantial 'green energy market' (Wittmann 2013, 959–965) through promoting energy saving investments. The Kingdom has exceptional factors for adopting successful 'green investments', including availability of financing (Eyraud et al. 2013, 852–865), but these require an institutional enabling environment that is still being developed. If the green energy market potentials were even partially realised in the Kingdom, this also would demonstrate the country's political support for climate change actions and agreements proposed under the United Nations Framework Convention on Climate Change (UNFCCC) (Barnett et al. 2004, 2077–2088).

This chapter provides a comprehensive explanation on how meeting domestic energy requirements in Saudi Arabia became a national challenge as well as a threat to international oil market stability. The chapter examines the government's recently adopted approach to address this highly visible challenge. The country has for many decades made – and still makes – substantial investments to add new power plants and expand capital-intensive infrastructure. However, since it has become evident that this approach has not been sufficient to address the growing demand for energy, the government has finally decided to support a highly ambitious programme to increase energy efficiency. The chapter describes the present energy efficiency initiatives in the Kingdom and associated challenges impeding their effective promotion nation-wide. Moreover, since energy efficiency programmes need adequate financial incentives and subsidies to sustain and maximise their potentials, the chapter discusses the economic value of saved energy units specifically within the power industry. The results serve as recommendations and a basis for the decision makers regarding the size of required incentives needed to sustain the programme's promotion.

Balancing energy demand and supply challenges: foundation of energy efficiency drivers in Saudi Arabia

Energy efficiency has tremendous potential to reduce Saudi Arabia's increasingly widening energy supply-demand gap through curbing any excessive demand for the service. It is also argued that the current challenges facing the Saudi energy industry have been evolving since the industry's early development. Therefore, it is necessary to take a holistic view of the various challenges affecting the whole industry on both the demand and supply sides. This will provide an understanding as to how and why energy efficiency, as a discipline adopted to balance the electricity supply-demand, is currently being resisted and challenged.

Demand-side challenges: forces influencing electricity tariffs

When electricity was first introduced in Saudi Arabia in the 1930s, consumption was modest and it was mainly used for lighting. Residential consumers were slowly introduced to new electrical appliances and population growth took off, which was when loads started increasing. The country saw rapid economic and demographic developments during the oil price boom in the early 1970s. Apart from the load increase pattern, it is important to understand the industry's anatomy. Before the government took over the ownership of the private supply industry, electricity businesses produced very generous profits for private producers (MIE 2000).

Tariffs varied from one producer to another depending on the cost of production and operation. The government's first intervention was in 1954 when it set the electricity tariff in Jeddah (the second largest city in Saudi Arabia) from 0.55 Saudi riyals (SR) per kilowatt hour (kWh) (14.67 USD cents) to SR0.325/kWh (8.7 USD cents, with USD1 = SR3.75) (ECRA 2008). The level of tariff adjustment was believed to offer a very reasonable return to the service producers. In the 1970s, however, Saudi consumers became familiar with more electrical appliances, including air conditioners, as a result of increased per capita income. This was immediately reflected in a further electricity demand increase, in addition to the development plans that encouraged ambitious construction, industrial and agricultural growth (MIE 2004).

The increased oil revenues in the 1970s shifted the Saudi lifestyle dramatically, both socially and economically. This was when electricity, as a service, was transformed from a privilege into a social right. The government was financially very stable and thus able to promote further reductions in the tariff and guarantee the private producers subsidies that covered their operating costs in addition to providing a guaranteed profit margin of 15 per cent. The tariff was subject to even more modifications, in which additional subsidies were offered, adding financial burdens to the government's budget required to operate and expand the service accordingly (ibid.).

In the late 1980s and early 1990s, oil revenues significantly dropped, which affected the government's fiscal budgets. Moreover, the First Gulf War, during 1990–1991, brought unexpected additional, and very intensive, costs. To act upon necessary budget spending cuts, the Saudi Ministry of Industry and Electricity suggested in 1995 there was a necessity to restructure the entire industry and merge all regional electricity companies into a single entity. This was the first step to introducing a liberal and free electricity market. The Council of Ministers approved the recommendation in 1998, and the newly established Saudi Electricity Company (SEC) became operational in April 2000 (Alhoweish 2011).

Table 5.1 shows the tariff structure that offered a reasonable financial income where the company – as was perceived by the government – could manage its operational and maintenance costs, repay the substantial credit facilities and loans inherited from the previous companies, and finance required expansive capital investments along with the support of government subsidies.

Table 5.1 The SEC tariff (April 2000)

Monthly consumption (kWh)	Residential, commercial, government (SR/kWh)	Agricultural, charitable (SR/kWh)	Industrial (SR/kWh)
1–2,000	0.05	0.10	0.12
2,001–4,000	0.10		
4,001–5,000	0.13	0.12	
5,001–6,000	0.18		
6,001–7,000	0.23		
7,001–8,000	0.28		
8,001–9,000	0.32		
9,001–10,000	0.36		
+10,001	0.38		

Source: ECRA (2008)

Table 5.2 The SEC tariff (October 2000)

Monthly consumption (kWh)	Residential, commercial, government (SR/kWh)	Agricultural, charitable (SR/kWh)	Industrial (SR/kWh)
1–2,000	0.05	0.05	0.12
2,001–4,000	0.10	0.10	
4,001–5,000	0.12	0.12	
5,001–6,000			
6,001–7,000	0.15		
7,001–8,000	0.20		
8,001–9,000	0.22		
9,001–10,000	0.24		
+10,001	0.26		

Source: ECRA (2008)

The tariff was then changed in less than seven months, as shown in Table 5.2. A review of the official documents that described the history of tariff changes in Saudi Arabia revealed an apparent lack of explanation for understanding the forces surrounding these changes. When the Deputy Minister of Electrical Affairs and Chairman of the Board of SEC was asked to explain, he stated 'those who were able to pay [without having their life-style affected] were the ones who complained and influenced the decision makers to reduce the tariff'. The Deputy Minister explicitly pointed out that these influencers complained to top decision makers, calling for reinstating the older tariff (ECRA 2008).

A closer look at the last two tariff schemes shows that the amended tariff affected only residential users who consumed over 4,000 kWh per month, in addition to agricultural users. This demonstrated evidence supporting the Deputy

Minister's statement that financially 'capable' consumers were the ones who influenced the reduction of the (seemingly) commercial tariff introduced just seven months before (ECRA 2008).

Government officials strongly believed that subsidies and control of service prices were necessary for productive manufacturing processes and improved standards of living for the people. Moreover, the introduction of low tariffs attracted foreign investments to base their industries in Saudi Arabia, thus boosting non-oil businesses. Several automobile manufacturers, for example, placed investments in Saudi Arabia in 2012 and 2013. The central problem remains that the extent of these tariff subsidies did not reflect the operational cost of the SEC and, most importantly, did not encourage efficient electricity usage, creating another deep challenge (ibid.).

Inefficient appliances

Coupled with the above challenge, and demonstrating the extent of this particular challenge, the Minister of Water and Electricity announced in a press conference, in 2008, that Saudi Arabia was flooded with non-compliant and highly inefficient electrical appliances with a striking share of 80 per cent of the local market. Although the Saudi Standards, Metrology and Quality Organization has suggested specific electrical appliance standards, it has not had the authority to enforce these standards. In fact, even these standards were considered to be very low when compared to the current international average (Alhoweish 2011). In an attempt to tackle this issue, the Ministry of Water and Electricity undertook several campaigns for electricity rationalisation, but they were largely ineffective as no attractive incentives were offered, especially given such a low tariff.

Supply-side challenges

Energy efficiency is an effective tool to manage the demand side of the energy industry. However, both the demand and supply sides of the industry are naturally interlinked and, therefore, the causes and effects of both sides normally overlap. Figure 5.1 shows the breakdown for the total energy supply and final use in Saudi Arabia. It demonstrates that the largest share of energy usage is accounted for by electricity – the main focus of this chapter.

Fossil fuel supply subsidies

Governments provide many forms of energy subsidies to stimulate productive economic growth and to enhance the security of energy supply along with keeping the prices affordable to consumers. This is especially true for countries blessed with an abundance of energy resources like Saudi Arabia. Subsidies comprise all measures that keep prices for consumers below market level, keep prices for producers above market level, or reduce costs for consumers and producers by giving direct or indirect support.

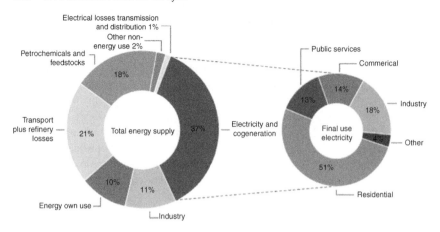

Figure 5.1 The Saudi Arabian energy supply system

Table 5.3 Saudi oil production and consumption during 2002–2012 (mbpd)

	2002	2003	2004	2005	2006	2007	2008	2009	2010	2011	2012
Production	8.93	10.16	10.64	11.11	10.85	10.45	10.85	9.71	10.08	11.14	11.53
Consumption	1.63	1.76	1.88	1.99	2.07	2.21	2.39	2.61	2.79	2.84	2.94

Source: BP (2013)

Table 5.4 Saudi natural gas production and consumption during 2002–2012 (Mtoe)

	2002	2003	2004	2005	2006	2007	2008	2009	2010	2011	2012
Production	51.0	54.1	59.1	64.1	66.2	67.0	72.4	69.7	78.9	83.0	92.5
Consumption	51.0	54.1	59.1	64.1	66.2	67.0	72.4	69.7	78.9	83.0	92.5

Source: BP (2013)

Table 5.3 and Table 5.4 show the country's total production and consumption of oil and natural gas.

The above tables provide evidence that the Saudi oil and natural gas production levels fluctuated in the quoted period, driven by the global oil demand, while domestic oil consumption was growing steadily and, most importantly, intensively. If this scenario persists, this may reduce oil availability for exports in the future. The government has expressed on several occasions its determination to reduce wastage in demand and increase oil production capacity, if needed. From a national economics context, however, Saudi Arabia has been identified to offer the third highest level of energy subsidies in the world, which is equivalent to over 10 per cent of its GDP (Lahn and Stevens 2011).

For example, the retail price for a litre of gasoline and diesel stands between 16 USD cents and 6.7 USD cents, respectively (ibid.). In 2011, the land transport sector consumed at least 765 thousand barrels of oil equivalent per day, and this is projected to increase to 1.7 million barrels of oil equivalent per day by 2030 (SEEC 2014). Moreover, although Saudi Arabia sits on the fourth largest natural gas reserves in the world, the entire production is consumed locally in order to meet the growing domestic needs, mainly for power generation and manufacturing feedstock (BP 2013). However, the fact that the natural gas retail price is set at USD0.75/million British thermal units (MMBtu) while the global market prices are much higher (USD4/MMBtu in 2011), makes any further gas exploitation (in other words, additional upstream investments) highly unprofitable. In fact, knowing that the cost of extracting gas from new fields would range between USD3.5 and 6/MMBtu indicates inevitable operational losses if retail prices were not to be reviewed.

Fuels used for power generation

The government has also offered the SEC, which accounted for over 76 per cent of total power generation in 2012, heavily subsidised fuel prices that are far below international market prices. The fact that the growth rate of local demand for electricity is among the highest in the world (8 per cent annually up to 2032) indicates the amount of subsidies will keep mounting up significantly (ECRA 2008; 2012). In 2006 the Council of Ministers issued a Royal Decree to have Saudi Aramco, the national oil company, set the fuel price for the oil supplied to the SEC. The government capped the price for heavy fuel oil supplied to the SEC by Saudi Aramco at USD2–2.64/barrel subject to its grade (SEC 2009). This also entailed that private investors and developers involved in the independent power producer or independent power and water producer business structures would receive the fuel from SEC (which is already struggling to pay back the government for the fuel) at no cost. Knowing that Brent oil averaged at a price of USD111.67/barrel in 2012 gives a good indication of how much revenue the government would have generated from the oil had it been sold on the international market (BP 2013). Another serious concern facing the power supply industry is that the average cost of a unit of electricity in the Kingdom is SR0.15/kWh (4 USD cents/kWh) while the average price collected from consumers by the SEC in 2012 was SR0.141/kWh (3.76 USD cents/kWh) (ECRA 2012). This was the case even after applying the 'Time of Use' tariff scheme in 2010, which is applied to industrial and commercial users encouraging them to shift their loads outside the peak hours (1–5 pm) for the period June–September. The enforcement of this scheme, although it provided even more generous tariffs during off-peak hours, received significant resistance from the concerned commercial and industrial users since, according to them, tariffs were increased significantly during peak hours, affecting their operational costs.

Table 5.5 SEC projected achievements and required resources during 2014–2023

Projected period	Power generation (MW)	Power transmission and distribution		Total investment (USD)	Number of customer additions
		Transmission lines (km)	S/S (number)		
2014–2017	18,000	20,000	234	66 billion	2 million
2018–2023	22,000	30,000	260	100 billion	3 million
Total	40,000	50,000	494	166 billion	5 million

Investment pressure

The SEC is currently under tremendous pressure to meet the growing demand for electricity through substantial and urgent expansive investments. Table 5.5 demonstrates that the required investment for the coming decade totals around USD166 billion, which is expected to serve over five million additional customers. In 2012, the SEC served over 6.7 million customers and its generation capacity stood at 53.6 GW (SEC 2012). To support this highly ambitious programme, the government has provided substantial soft loans to avoid costly delays. In 2010, it injected USD4 billion to the SEC's treasury, followed by USD13.6 billion in 2011 (Alhoweish 2011) and USD13.3 billion in early 2014, in order to finance urgent expansion projects.

Seasonal supply-demand profile

In addition to the SEC's financial struggle to provide the required investment capital from its own resources, Saudi Arabia's extremely fluctuating power demand profile, stemming from high seasonal demand in the summer, questions the economic and financial returns of such substantial investments. For example, in 2012, the summer load peaked at 44 GW, while it dramatically dropped to as low as 25 GW during the other seasons (ECRA 2012). The extreme weather in the summer of 2010, with temperatures in some parts of the Kingdom exceeding 50°C, spiked the electricity demand and exceeded the SEC's forecasts as demand grew just over 10 per cent compared to the peak load in 2009. Currently, 5 per cent of the generating capacity operates for only 48 hours per year, demonstrating the extremely low capital return on such mega projects (Lahn et al. 2013). This obviously significantly decreases the cost-benefit ratio of these almost non-operating projects.

The above-described collective demand- and supply-side challenges provide profound evidence that Saudi Arabia is bearing extremely intensive and non-productive costs just to meet its growing demand for electricity in order to keep its lights and, most importantly, air conditioners on. The adopted energy policy has clearly contributed to extremely wasteful consumption behaviour, and, therefore, any attempt to reverse this will benefit the national economy.

Table 5.6 Per capita electricity consumption in Saudi Arabia (2002–2012)

Year	2002	2003	2004	2005	2006	2007	2008	2009	2010	2011	2012
kWh/ capita	5,980	6,460	6,400	6,570	6,760	6,810	7,020	7,260	7,700	7,740	8,230

Source: ECRA (2012)

Energy efficiency: Saudi Arabia's untapped fuel

Table 5.6 demonstrates the pattern of increasing per capita electricity consumption in Saudi Arabia. If it persists, one major consequence would be limiting the country's oil exports, threatening international oil market stability. Dramatic political will, however, was observed when King Abdullah announced in 2010 the establishment of the King Abdullah City for Atomic and Renewable Energy as an explicit indication that the government has considered adopting a mix-generation policy.

It will take years to realise the first nuclear power plant or a plant running on renewable energy. This ambitious supply-side alternative energy approach is already facing some serious challenges for effective implementation, which are beyond this chapter's scope. As with managing the demand side of the energy industry, the Council of Ministers also established the same year the Saudi Energy Efficiency Center (SEEC). The Center is composed of representatives from related stakeholder organisations (totalling over 20 governmental and non-governmental organisations), and aims at unifying and consolidating the efforts required to rationalise the Kingdom's energy usage, enhancing energy efficiency and achieving the lowest possible energy intensity. This entails preparing a nation-wide energy efficiency programme, and developing relevant policies, regulations and rules that govern energy consumption and support the programme's effective implementation (SEEC 2014).

Saudi energy efficiency programme

Before SEEC's establishment, King Abdulaziz City for Science and Technology (KACST) partnered with the United Nations Development Programme in 2003 to develop a National Energy Efficiency Program. The programme assisted in improving institutional and human capacities to set relevant policies, regulations and targets for various sectors and consumers (UNDP 2009). The programme was further developed through the establishment of SEEC, which launched a nation-wide programme in 2012 targeting demand-side management in three main energy-consuming sectors. The buildings, land transport and industry sectors together represent more than 90 per cent of the total national energy consumption in Saudi Arabia, and hence these were identified as the focus of the programme. The programme measures the current energy consumption behaviour, examines international benchmarks and best practices, and customises these to the local context. It will then develop the relevant initiatives accordingly with proper implementation mechanisms. The programme was launched in 2012 with active participation of the government and non-governmental stakeholders. The programme has formed nine specialised integrative teams, each of which reviews the roles required by each stakeholder involved (government and non-government) and coordinates the activities required for an effective implementation of its corresponding initiative. Three teams are responsible for managing the three main energy-consuming sectors: buildings, land transport and industry. The remaining six teams are cross-functional, supporting the three main teams. The themes of the cross-functional teams are: urban planning; financing; awareness; energy efficiency regulations; testing, inspection and certification; and energy service companies (ESCOs). The financing team is headed by a representative from the Ministry of Finance, and the testing, inspection and certification team is headed by a representative from the Saudi Standards, Metrology and Quality Organization, and so on (SEEC 2014).

The buildings sector

This sector alone accounts for 80 per cent of total electricity consumption and includes residential, governmental and commercial buildings. The Energy Efficiency Program focused on modifying and enhancing the technical specifications of household electrical appliances, such as air conditioners, freezers, refrigerators, washing machines and lighting fixtures, as well as enforcing thermal insulation for new buildings. Air conditioning alone represents 50 per cent of the building sector's total electricity consumption and therefore received significant attention. Consequently, the programme raised the minimum efficiency performance standards (MEPS) for the energy efficiency ratio of air-conditioning units allowed onto the market from 7.5 in 2006 to 8.5 (or three stars for window units) and to 9.5 (or four stars for split units) in September 2013. All air conditioners now carry accurate labels using stars as efficiency level indicators. Each additional star demonstrates that the air conditioner is 10 per cent more efficient than one at the previous level. The MEPS will be raised once again (effective from January 2015) to 9.8 (window) and 11.5 (split). The latter target is equivalent to the American Society of Heating, Refrigerating and Air-Conditioning Engineers standard. Washing machines and electric water heaters will also have MEPS, effective from January 2015 (ibid.).

The industrial sector

The industrial sector consumes 15 per cent of total energy consumption and 18 per cent of total electricity consumption in Saudi Arabia. Petrochemicals, steel and cement factories account for 85 per cent of the entire industrial energy consumption and therefore remain the focus of the energy efficiency programme. The remaining industries will be targeted in the next phase, which will include setting new specifications for common equipment, such as engines and boilers, among others. These efforts are coordinated with experts from international agencies and organisations such as the International Energy Agency (ibid.).

Land transport

As mentioned above, the land transport sector consumed at least 765 thousand barrels of oil equivalent per day in 2011, and this is projected to increase its demand to 1.7 million barrels of oil equivalent per day by 2030. This excessive consumption is driven by the extremely low retail prices for gasoline and diesel, as Saudi Arabia provides the third lowest prices in the world just after Venezuela and Iran. This has naturally encouraged wasteful consumption behaviour. Another aspect that may have contributed to this excessive consumption is the lack of public transportation systems. In 2012 alone, the number of land transport vehicles reached 10.3 million, for a population of nearly 30 million, and this is projected to increase to 25–27 million vehicles by 2030, if the business-as-usual scenario persists. The government has already awarded several mega rail-networking projects spread over the Kingdom but these normally take several years to be realised. Therefore, the programme will focus on enhancing vehicle fuel economy. The fuel economy average of land vehicles in the Kingdom is very low (12.2 km/l) when compared to countries like Japan, China and Mexico (19.7, 15.0 and 13.4 km/l respectively). The programme aims at this stage to achieve the United States (US) average of 13.1 km/l (SEEC 2014).

Barriers and challenges undermining energy efficiency efforts and key success factors

Above, the study demonstrated various interlinked barriers impeding an effective promotion of energy efficiency in Saudi Arabia. The most apparent barrier is created by the extremely low energy prices imposed by the government. Government officials believed that lowering energy prices would enhance the competitive advantage of local manufacturing, attract foreign investments for job creation and technology transfer, and improve people's standards of living. However, this persisting policy has not only contributed to extremely wasteful consumption behaviour but has also created a culture of resistance against any attempt to reverse this phenomenon. Especially commercial and industrial consumers demonstrate such resistance. Although increasing energy prices would encourage more responsible consumption behaviour, and hence significantly curb unnecessary demand, the social risks of this course of actions create apparent disincentives to the government. Therefore, the SEEC is not mandated to recommend raising energy prices, and only focuses on raising the MEPS of electrical appliances, increasing land transport fuel economy standards and improving energy intensity rates, especially for large consumers (public utilities and commercial and industrial consumers). In fact, even the recent progressive attempts to raise the MEPS have faced severe resistance from the private sector trading electrical appliances.

Despite all these barriers, the SEEC has achieved its planned milestones so far with great success. The key factor contributing to this success was its exceptional ability to create an environment of harmony and high level of coordination between many representatives of stakeholders to develop a national energy efficiency plan for the country. Managing the multiple authorities and agencies involved in this ambitious programme is a huge challenge in its own right. However, the administrative committee of SEEC embraced the programme's objectives and succeeded in spreading a spirit of ownership among the entire set of governmental stakeholders involved. This is a significant success given the government's history of poor enforcement of regulations at such scale. In fact, enforcing regulations still remains a challenge that needs to be properly addressed by the SEEC for its ongoing and future initiatives. For example, 70 per cent of residential buildings are not thermally insulated, largely because of an apparent lack of supervision mechanisms (SEEC 2014). The SEEC's building sector team is currently developing a stringent supervision mechanism that would deprive any non-thermally insulated building from an electricity connection. While the programme enjoys apparent political support, control on the energy demand side is highly fragmented. In order to overcome this particular challenge and to maintain its current momentum, the programme will need to upscale its potential. Given the potential of these measures to significantly reduce energy wastage, an innovative set of solutions is required. This study therefore attempts to estimate the economic size of financial incentives the government may consider to maximise the programme's potential. Naturally, gaining political support in this context will require a strong economic case, as will be described below.

International best practices

Energy efficiency measures applied worldwide are based on firm and clear policy objectives. Successful schemes associated with energy efficiency obligations – a regulatory mechanism that requires obligated parties to meet quantitative energy saving targets by delivering or procuring eligible energy savings produced by implementing approved end-use energy efficiency measures – have produced significant results in the US, Canada, Australia, the UK, Italy, Denmark and China. Best practices suggest keeping the policy objectives of the scheme simple and clear, and focused on achieving energy savings (RAP 2012).

Energy efficiency in the United States

In the US energy efficiency spending is strongly driven by government policies. Policies drive energy efficiency spending in two ways: by compelling spending to comply with regulatory requirements (such as building energy codes and appliance standards); and by stimulating spending through economic instruments or market mechanisms (including direct procurement and tax incentives). Energy efficiency standards for new buildings have been progressively tightened in the US over the past decade, culminating in the recent introduction of two new model building energy codes: the 2012 International Energy Conservation Code covering residential buildings; and the 2010 American Society of Heating, Refrigerating and Air-Conditioning Engineers standard 90.1–2010 covering commercial buildings. These codes are projected to produce a 30 per cent improvement in the energy efficiency of new buildings compared to buildings constructed to comply with the 2006 model code. The Pacific Northwest National Laboratory estimates today's savings from building code changes over the past two decades to total 42 TWh (Satchwell *et al.* 2010).

Energy service companies in the United States

The US is home to the world's most developed ESCO market, extensive energy efficiency programmes funded by utility customers, and a steadily expanding portfolio of energy performance standards for appliances, vehicles and buildings. The American Recovery and Reinvestment Act, adopted in 2009, supported these developments by directing over USD10 billion of additional government spending into energy efficiency. The US ESCO industry is expected to see continued annual growth of 10 per cent in the coming years. A report by the Lawrence Berkeley National Laboratory forecast that the sector will more than double in size over the medium term, reaching annual turnover of USD13 billion by 2020. Because energy saving measures implemented by ESCOs are typically long-lived, the annual energy savings delivered by this industry are expected to grow even faster than annual investment, reaching an estimated 770 TWh by 2020 (IEA 2013b).

Overall, electric efficiency programmes saved over 112 TWh in 2010, which is enough to power over 9.7 million US homes for one year, and avoided the generation of 78 million metric tonnes of carbon dioxide (CO_2). Electric efficiency savings (including both traditional energy efficiency as well as load control programmes) were achieved at an average cost of 4.3 USD cents/kWh saved in 2010. Focusing on energy efficiency only (excluding and assuming no savings from load control programmes), savings were achieved at an average cost of 3.5 USD cents/kWh in 2010. The actual cost is likely to be between 3.5 and 4.3 USD cents/kWh of saved electricity (IEE 2012).

Energy efficiency programmes in Australia

The Australian government introduced the Energy Efficiency Opportunities programme in 2006. This decision was based on the realisation that the greatest potential for energy efficiency savings resided with the largest energy-using corporations, and a general lack of uptake of energy efficiency opportunities by firms in response to market forces. The programme addresses information failures that stand in the way of businesses' benefitting from cost-effective energy efficiency opportunities (IEA 2013b).

Over 300 corporations are covered by the Energy Efficiency Opportunities programme, representing two-thirds of Australia's primary energy consumption. Since 2011, the programme has included companies from the electricity generating sector. Participation in the programme is mandatory for all corporations that use more than 0.5 petajoules (12,000 toe) per year. The programme aims to build industrial capability and capacity to identify, assess and implement cost-effective energy efficiency opportunities with a payback period of four years or less. It mandates reporting of efficiency opportunities to the public and the corporate board (ibid.).

An independent review of the Energy Efficiency Opportunities programme undertaken in 2013 identified that it:

- had been effective in addressing information-type market failures;
- was complementary to current government policies, and addressed information failures not addressed by carbon pricing policies;
- had facilitated the identification of an additional 40 per cent in energy savings, above and beyond what would have been achieved in its absence; and
- had been highly cost-effective, with a benefit-to-cost ratio of almost 4:1 (ibid.).

A key element of the Australian government's AUD42 billion 2009 Nation Building and Jobs Plan for economic stimulus was the provision of AUD3.9 billion for the Energy Efficient Homes Package, including the Home Insulation Program. Under the programme, homeowners and landlords with eligible dwellings were able to claim the cost of installing ceiling insulation. Eligible dwellings included homes built before the mandatory thermal performance requirements introduced in the 2003 building code, as well as dwellings that had little or no ceiling insulation. Under the programme, around 1.1 million roofs were insulated at a cost of AUD 1.45 billion (ibid.).

An evaluation of the Energy Efficiency Opportunities programme in 2013 estimated that 40 per cent of reported energy savings by participants had been realised above what would have been achieved in its absence. This additionality estimate equates to annual net energy savings of 34.6 petajoules (0.8 Mtoe) being directly attributable to the programme between 2006/2007 and 2010/2011 compared to business-as-usual (ibid.).

Analysis of the impacts of the partially completed Home Insulation Program indicates national energy savings of 230,000 toe per year by 2020, despite the programme's short duration. These savings could equal cumulative economic benefits of AUD3.9 billion from avoided space heating and cooling energy requirements by 2020. In addition, peak demand reductions of 400 MW could have a value of avoided infrastructure investment of AUD1.7 billion (ibid.).

From the two countries' experiences reviewed above, the US is found to be relatively more relevant for Saudi Arabia, for two reasons: both countries are large oil producers; and the Saudi currency is pegged to the US dollar at a fixed rate.

Calculating economic value of energy saving in Saudi Arabia: methodology and approach

The key objective of this study is to define the economically justifiable incentive schemes for boosting energy efficiency measures in Saudi Arabia. It addresses the question of what is the optimal size for a financial allocation to energy efficiency measures by taking into account that such an allocation should yield more benefits than costs for society? The key determinant of the incentive's size is the economic cost of saved unit of electricity (ECSUE). ESCUE serves as a yardstick for policy makers to determine the required scale of intervention and the size of energy efficiency programmes and policies. Any expenditure less than ECSUE per unit of electricity allocated by policy makers to energy efficiency interventions ultimately results in the society being better off while achieving the target of electricity saving.

The Saudi Electricity and Co-Generation Regulatory Authority (ECRA) has set a target of reducing consumption of electricity in Saudi Arabia by 8 per cent compared to the forecasted increase in 2021 (Lahn *et al.* 2013). Based on the demand forecasted by ECRA, which indicates demand reaching 325 TWh in 2021 in the most likely scenario, an 8 per cent reduction of consumption in 2012 implies a 26 TWh electricity saving by 2021 (CER 2006). This value is set as the targeted saving for the purpose of this study. For the purpose of defining the volume of incentives that would make society better off, the analysis looks into the opportunity cost of saved energy and cost-benefits of energy efficiency measures to identify socio-economic gains from energy efficiency improvements.

The cost-effectiveness methodology is used by different countries for determining the cost and benefits of energy efficiency measures by assessing the cost of a saved unit of energy by energy efficiency measures. Reviews of energy efficiency programmes in the US and Australia were conducted to determine the cost effectiveness of programmes. The purpose of these reviews is to determine the scope of energy efficiency programmes and average cost of saving an electricity unit by the programme.

First, the economic cost of saved energy is determined to indicate cost to society. It will also enable to determine the margins of incentives, which would maintain the society better off provided that the total value of incentives is less than the opportunity cost of a saved unit of electricity. For this purpose, economic cost of unit of saved energy is multiplied by the targeted domestic consumption. The subjects of this analysis are demand-side energy saving measures for the residential and public sectors in Saudi Arabia, which jointly occupied a share of 62 per cent in domestic electricity consumption in 2012. As noted above, demand-side management of electricity consumption has seen limited intervention from the Saudi government.

Economic cost analysis of saved unit of electricity in Saudi Arabia

The calculation of ECSUE (kWh) lies at the core of the methodological approach of this analysis as it is a key determinant of the scale of government incentives. The value of saved electricity is derived from three factors:[3]

- value of saved fuel per unit in power generation (VSFU);
- saving on capital investment (SOC); and
- avoided CO_2 emissions.

The value of saved fuel emerges from the generation of electricity by the four types of fuels used in Saudi Arabia, namely natural gas, oil, diesel and fuel oil. In 2012, natural gas and oil accounted for 74 per cent of generation, with shares of 35 per cent and 39 per cent in the fuel mix, respectively. Diesel accounted for 20 per cent and heavy fuel oil for 6 per cent of total power generation in 2012.

Average input of fuel for unit of electricity production could be simply calculated as below:

Average value of fuel input for generation of unit of electricity (AVF) = Total fuel consumption at the plants/Total electricity generated by power plants   (1)

However, lack of data for fuel consumption by power plants led the authors to derive the volume of fuel input for power generation by using the average thermal value of plants and energy content of each fuel type (see equation 4 below). By determining both AVF consumed for generation of unit of electricity and applying the difference between world market price (WMP) and domestic market price (DMP or DP), the value of saved fuel is calculated for each category of fuel by applying the weight of each fuel in the generation mix:

$$VSFU = AVO \times (WMPO - DPO) \times 39\% + AVG \times (WMPG - DPG) \times 35\% + AVD \times (WMPD\text{-}DPD) \times 20\% + AVHF \times (WMPHF - DPHF) \times 6\% \quad (2)$$

Where:

VSFU = Value of saved fuel per unit of saved electricity, USD/kWh
WMPO = World market price of oil, USD/MMBtu
WMPG = World market price of natural gas, USD/MMBtu
WMPD = World market price of diesel, USD/MMBtu
WMPHF = World market price of heavy fuel, USD/MMBtu

Domestic prices paid by local power generators are well below the world prices. They receive fuel at subsidised prices by the government.

As suggested by data in Table 5.7, the opportunity cost of diesel in power generation in the Kingdom (equal to the difference between the international market price and the price paid by producers), is the highest (USD21.09/MMBtu), followed by crude oil (USD18.53/MMBtu). This implies that policy should support the reduction of consumption of these two types of fuels in power generation more than that of others. For the calculation of the average value of input of fuel per unit of electricity (AVF) generation at SEC plants the study employed statistical data on power generation by each fuel type (EPF), average thermal value

Table 5.7 Prices paid by power producers in Saudi Arabia compared to international market prices in 2012 (USD/MMBtu)

Type of fuel	Price paid power producers	International market prices
Heavy fuel oil	0.43	15.43
Natural gas	0.75	9.04
Diesel	0.67	21.76
Crude oil	0.73	19.26

Source: ECRA (2012)

(ATV) at the grid, and energy contents of each fuel type (ECF). The following formula was engaged in defining the AVF for each category of the fuel:

$$AVF = \{(ATV \times EPF) \div ECF\} \div EPF \qquad (3)$$

Where F = fuel (oil, heavy fuel oil, natural gas and diesel)
By simplifying (3), it is obtained that:

$$AVF = ATV \div ECF \qquad (4)$$

By dividing the average thermal value of power plants by the respective fuel energy content the average value of fuel input per unit of electricity generation is obtained. AVF, which is measured by kg/kWh, is converted to the thermal value (MMBtu/kWh) by using the respective energy content of each fuel to match the measuring units (USD/MMBtu) of fuel prices in formula (2) above.

Saving on capital cost

Energy efficiency measures can lead to significant savings. They also reduce absolute demand or growth of demand in the power generation sector. Reduced demand for power translates into a lower generation capacity requirement than in the absence of energy efficiency measures. Hence, additional capacity saving occurs, which is measured in this calculation by USD/kWh. The source of data for this purpose was a study undertaken by King Fahd University for ECRA in 2005. The study looked at the levelised cost of electricity at over 30 power plants in the Kingdom. Capital cost makes up a minor part of the levelised cost. The results revealed that for power plants with combined cycle running on crude oil (1,090 MW Rabigh A power plant) the capital cost per kWh was 0.552 USD cents. For combined cycle gas power plants (1,417 MW PP9) the capital cost of electricity was 1.24 USD cents, whereas for diesel-fired power plants (Jeddah PP3) it was 0.33 USD cents, and for heavy fuel oil (HFO)-fired power plants (Rabigh A ST) is was 0.40 USD cents/kWh. For the purpose of this study, the following values are used for counting saving on the capital cost (SOC):

$SOC_{Gas\ plant} = USD0.0124/kWh$
$SOC_{Diesel\ plant} = USD0.0033/kWh$
$SOC_{Crude\ plant} = USD0.00552/kWh$
$SOC_{HFO\ plant} = USD0.004/kWh$

SOCs are allocated by applying the weight determined by the share of each fuel type as per the following formula:

$$SOC = 39\%\ SOCO + 35\%\ SOCNG + 20\%\ SOCD + 6\%\ SOCHF \qquad (5)$$

Emission reductions

Energy efficiency measures lead to lower consumption of electricity and, in Saudi Arabia, given its energy mix, also to lower emissions accounted in the power grid. For accounting of emission reductions the approach taken is to quantify emission reductions per kWh by multiplying the national grid emission factor by the unit of saved energy. World market prices per tonne of CO_2 are applied to derive the monetary value of emission reductions. The grid emission factor value is taken from the Saudi Clean Development Mechanism (CDM) Designated National Authority's official publication where it is identified as 0.654 kg/kWh (DNA 2011). The price of certified emission reduction units[4] has been volatile since the inception of the European Union (EU) emissions trading system in 2005, given interlinkages between the two and volatility in the latter. It saw a peak of EUR24/tCO_2 in 2008 and traded at around EUR2/tCO_2 in 2013. For the purposes of this study, a conservative price of EUR2 per tonne is applied, which equates to USD0.175/kWh (EEX 2014).

Costs and benefits of energy efficiency improvements

The failure to properly evaluate the benefits of energy efficiency results in under-investment in energy efficiency. The foregone benefits represent the 'opportunity cost' of failing to adequately evaluate and prioritise energy efficiency investments. This opportunity cost may be very large and, in particular in the contexts of increasing global energy demand, stress on resources, and climate change-related concerns, may represent a cost that society cannot afford to bear. Evaluation of energy efficiency programmes is challenging due to the complexity of calculations on savings occurring directly from the impact of the programme. There are several published studies on the evaluation of energy efficiency programmes in the US and EU. Generally, the evaluations are based on the cost versus volume of saved energy by the programme thus looking at USD cost per saved kWh.

Results and discussion

Calculations for AVF were based on generation data of SEC-operated plants in 2012, which represent around 77 per cent of the entire power generation in Saudi

Table 5.8 Data and parameters employed in calculations

Fuel type	Share in the fuel mix (%)	Electricity generated by each fuel type (TWh)	Energy content (lower heating values in BTU/kg)	Estimated fuel consumption by SEC plants	Average thermal value of fuel input per unit of electricity (MMBtu/kWh)	Average volume of fuel input per unit of electricity
Natural gas	39	80.8	50,426	23 billion cubic metres	10.3	0.284 m3/kwh
Crude oil	35	72.5	39,700	19.08 million tonnes	10.5	0.263 kg/kwh
Diesel	20	41.4	40,568	10.66 million tonnes	10.4	0.257 kg/kwh
Heavy fuel oil	6	12.4	40,345	5.23 million tonnes	10.4	0.421 kg/kwh

Arabia. That year, the SEC-operated plants generated 207.13 billion kWh of electricity, of which 35 per cent was generated by crude oil combustion, 39 per cent by natural gas combustion, 20 per cent by diesel and 6 per cent by HFO combustion. Generation by each fuel type was: 80.8 billion kWh from natural gas; 72.5 billion kWh from crude oil; 41.4 billion kWh from diesel; and 12.4 billion kWh from HFO. By applying the thermal average value of SEC in 2012, which reportedly was 10,451 Btu/kWh, and energy content for each fuel type, it is concluded that, in 2012, SEC consumed 23.0 billion m³ of natural gas, 136.3 million barrels of oil, 10.66 million tonnes of diesel and 5.23 million tonnes of HFO. Average volume of fuel input per unit of electricity is then found by dividing the total fuel volume of a particular fuel by the generation volume of the same fuel type. Table 5.8 summarises the data and key findings.

Hence, by applying data provided in Table 5.8 and 'plugging in' formulas (1), (2) and (3), the obtained value for VSFU is USD0.1589. This implies that every unit of electricity saved by the energy efficiency programme saves fossil fuels to a value of USD0.1589. In the context of the targeted savings of 26 TWh, the value of saved fuel can be USD4.13 billion.

Saving on capital cost is calculated according to formula (5) and it is found that SOC is USD0.0073/kWh. Total cost of saved electricity including the cost of CO_2 emissions is found to be USD0.3412/kWh, and USD0.1662/kWh excluding the cost of CO_2. The results suggest that a nation-wide programme aiming at energy conservation can spend up to USD0.1662/kWh in tackling energy waste in an economically viable manner. Hence, the economic cost of the targeted 26 TWh electricity saving is USD4.3 billion.

By extrapolating the cost of saved units of energy by energy efficiency programmes in the US, which was reported above to be in the range of 3.5–4.3 USD cents/kWh, it is envisaged that the government of Saudi Arabia can achieve its targeted 26 TWh saving by spending as much as USD0.9–1.11 billion, which is almost four times less than it costs the economy (USD4.3 billion) in a business-as-usual case.

Conclusions

Saudi Arabia is facing significant domestic energy challenges. Focusing on the power sector, demand-side challenges include forces influencing electricity tariffs and allowing inefficient electrical appliances in the Kingdom. Supply-side challenges include the extent of fossil fuel supply subsidies for domestic consumption, investment pressure on SEC to allocate adequate financial resources to meet the growing demand for electricity, and the seasonal supply-demand profile in the Kingdom undermining economic and financial returns on these investments. To address these challenges, the government has finally supported a highly ambitious programme to increase energy efficiency. This chapter has argued that there is a need for adequate financial incentives and subsidies to sustain and maximise the Saudi energy efficiency programme's potential. However, it was noted that gaining political support in this context would require a strong economic case. Calculations of the value of a saved unit of electricity revealed it can be a powerful tool for policy makers by serving as a determinant of the required size of public resources allocation to tackle energy waste in an economically viable way. Although ESCUE has volatile variables, such as oil prices, it can still be applied for short- and mid-term policy planning. The empirical analysis showed that financial allocations for energy efficiency programmes can pay back benefits which would exceed the cost of not having these programmes. It was shown that in a business-as-usual scenario Saudi Arabia's energy consumption would grow without any energy conservation measures with the opportunity cost of energy increasing depending on the price of hydrocarbons. The challenge remains of designing and implementing successful energy efficiency programmes by channelling incentives so that a market for energy efficiency services can be stimulated and can emerge. An energy efficiency market will also require a legislative framework to regulate activities of all actors. Experience of the US and perhaps the EU can provide a wide spectrum of knowledge for policy makers for designing national energy efficiency legislation. There is also a significant role for a regulator to define size and mechanisms of incentives, as well as introduce monitoring and verification standards.

This study has explained how Saudi Arabia's current nature of energy generation (100 per cent fossil fuel-based) and inefficient consumption necessitates the government to allocate resources for incentives to tackle existing energy efficiency challenges. It was empirically demonstrated that, based on the results of energy efficiency programmes in the US, as much as USD1.1 billion is required to reach Saudi Arabia's saving target of 26 TWh by 2021. This is four times less than it costs to the economy at a business-as-usual demand scenario. This study has demonstrated that as much as USD3.2 billion can be saved through energy savings by energy efficiency programmes in Saudi Arabia. The chapter therefore calls for exploring innovative forms of financial incentives to maximise the Kingdom's energy efficiency potential and reach ECRA's targeted saving.

Notes

1 The views and opinions in this chapter are solely those of the authors and do not necessarily reflect the view of the Islamic Development Bank.
2 The authors would like to express their sincere appreciation to the Saudi Energy Efficiency Center for providing comments and feedback that significantly enhanced the quality of this chapter.
3 There are intangible benefits from ensuring energy security in global markets by additional available supply that are not quantifiable and, hence, not part of this work.
4 The tradable carbon reduction units allocated for registered CDM projects by the United Nations Framework Convention on Climate Change (UNFCCC) in developing countries.

References

Alhoweish, Bandar. 2011. *Addressing the Project Implementation Challenges in the Saudi Arabian Power Supply Industry: An Investigative Approach towards Improving Project Delivery*. Doctoral thesis in Applied Engineering and Science. Birmingham: Aston University.

Bailey, Rob, and Robin Willoughby. 2013. *Edible Oil: Food Security in the Gulf*. London: Chatham House.

Barnett, Jon, Suraje Dessai and Michael Webber. 2004. 'Will OPEC Lose from the Kyoto Protocol?' *Energy Policy* 32 (18), 2077–2088.

BP. British Petroleum. 2013. *BP Statistical Review of World Energy*. London.

CER. Center for Engineering Research. 2006. *Report on Updated Generation Planning for the Saudi Electricity Sector*. Riyadh.

DNA. Saudi Arabia's Clean Development Mechanism (CDM) Designated National Authority. 2011. *Baseline Determination for the Electricity Grid in the Kingdom of Saudi Arabia*. Accessed 27 December 2014. http://cdmdna.gov.sa/GEF.pdf

ECRA. Electricity and Co-Generation Regulatory Authority of Saudi Arabia. 2008. *Annual Report 2008*. Riyadh.

ECRA. 2012. *Annual Report 2012*. Riyadh.

EEX. European Energy Exchange. 2014. 'Grey Certified Emissions Reductions.' Accessed 27 December. https://www.eex.com/

EIU. The Economist Intelligence Unit. 2014. *Healthcare in Saudi Arabia: Increasing Capacity, Improving Quality?*

Eyraud, Luc, Benedict Clements and Abdoul Wane. 2013. 'Green Investment: Trends and Determinants.' *Energy Policy* 60, 852–865.

IEA. International Energy Agency. 2013a. *World Energy Outlook*. Paris.

IEA. 2013b. *Energy Efficiency Market Report*. Paris.

IEE. Institute for Electric Efficiency. 2012. *Summary of Ratepayer-Funded, Electric Efficiency Impacts, Budgets, and Expenditures*. IEE Brief. Washington D.C., January.

IMF. International Monetary Fund. 2013. *IMF Country Report, Saudi Arabia.* Washington D.C.

MIE. Ministry of Water and Electricity of Saudi Arabia. 2000. *Electricity Development in the Kingdom of Saudi Arabia through 100 Years.* Riyadh.

MIE. 2004. *Electricity Growth and Development in the Kingdom of Saudi Arabia.* Riyadh.

Lahn, Glada, and Paul Stevens. 2011. *Burning Oil to Keep Cool: The Hidden Energy Crisis in Saudi Arabia.* London: Chatham House

Lahn, Glada, Paul Stevens and Felix Preston. 2013. *Saving Oil and Gas in the Gulf.* London: Chatham House.

RAP. Regulatory Assistance Project. 2012. *Best Practices in Designing and Implementing Energy Efficiency Obligation Schemes, International Energy Agency Demand Side Management Program.* Task XXII Research Report. Montpelier, Vermont.

Satchwell, Andrew, Charles Goldman, Peter Larsen, Donald Gilligan and Terry Singer. 2010. *A Survey of the U.S. ESCO Industry: Market Growth and Development from 2008 to 2011.* Berkeley: Ernest Orlando Lawrence Berkeley National Laboratory.

SEC. Saudi Electricity Company. 2009. *Annual Report.* Riyadh.

SEC. 2012. *Annual Report.* Riyadh.

SEEC. Saudi Energy Efficiency Center. 2014. *Opinion Leaders' Meeting.* Presentation by the SEEC Technical Team, Riyadh, 10 May.

UNDP. United Nations Development Programme. 2009. *Saudi Arabia: National Energy Efficiency Program in Saudi Arabia.* Riyadh.

Wittmann, Nadine. 2013. 'OPEC: How to Transition from Black to Green Gold.' *Energy Policy* 62, 959–965.

6 Green challenges and some technological solutions in the water sector of the Gulf Cooperation Council countries

Mushtaque Ahmed, Salem Ali Al-Jabri and B. S. Choudri

Introduction

Water is essential for life. It is vital to every civilisation and any process of development. Water problems have always remained an issue of concern to the governments in arid countries, especially in the Gulf Cooperation Council (GCC) countries where the key causes of water problems are population growth and increasing demand for water. Climate change is expected to make the current situation even worse: the key predictions of the Intergovernmental Panel on Climate Change (IPCC 2001a; 2001b; 2007a; 2007b; 2014) for the region include high incidence of reduced flows, declines in rainfall and higher temperatures. Such predictions are based on the agreement of the vast majority of climate models. These changes will make water management even more difficult than today. When renewable surface and groundwater resources are not sufficient to meet the ever-increasing demands from agricultural, industrial and domestic sectors, finding alternative water resources becomes a priority.

The green economy agenda strives for poverty alleviation, social justice, human wellbeing, reduced environmental risks and conservation of ecological resources (UNEP 2011), whereas proper management of water resources will require environmental sustainability, social equity and economic efficiency. Green economy has also been described as the practical and operational framework for implementing the three pillars of sustainable development: environmental, economic and social. Water has been described as the 'bloodstream of the green economy' by the Stockholm Statement of 2011 (GWP 2013). In the current global context, water connects three critical issues of food, energy and climate change (UN-Water 2011). Green economy measures in the water sector include economic instruments (taxes, fees and water markets), financing of infrastructures through rates charged for water services, dissemination of innovative technologies, improved water resources planning and strengthening of institutional capacities (ibid.).

Current status of water management and environmental sustainability in the GCC countries

Basic features of the current status of water management in the GCC countries include:

- On a per capita basis, the GCC countries consume considerably more water than the world average (816 m^3 per capita/year compared to 500 m^3 per capita/year, PwC 2014).
- They are the world's biggest consumers of desalinated water.
- High energy consumption in the desalination sector has put the GCC countries among the highest greenhouse gas (GHG) emitters in the world, on a per capita basis.
- The price of water is heavily subsidised, with the gap between costs and revenues at 92 per cent (ibid.).
- Eighty per cent of the region's water is used for agriculture, with 22 per cent of domestic water not being unaccounted for (ibid.).
- Apart from the huge amounts of GHGs the GCC countries emit into the atmosphere, other environmental problems associated with the water sector in the region include seawater intrusion into the coastal aquifers due to excessive groundwater use, increased soil and groundwater salinity, and contamination of groundwater due to excessive fertiliser and pesticides use.
- The major management issues in the sector are excessive water demand, inadequate water supplies and ineffective institutional frameworks.

According to a report by the World Bank (2005), per capita freshwater availability in the GCC fell from about 680 m^3 in 1970 to about 180 m^3 in 2000, ranging from 60 to 370 m^3. These figures are much lower than the 1,000 m^3 figure that is considered the borderline for water stressed regions. Tables 6.1–6.4 provide some basic information on the water sector of the GCC countries. Table 6.1 provides data on sectoral water use changes during 1990–2000. Table 6.2 provides sectoral shares of total water resources in the region. Tables 6.3 and 6.4 provide a summary of water availability in the GCC countries.

Green challenges in the GCC water sector

One of the major pillars of green economy is to reduce environmental risks and conserve natural resources. Challenges in terms of environmental sustainability in the water sector of the GCC countries are numerous. Some of the major ones are: water shortage; energy-intensive desalination; high water consumption in the domestic sector; unsustainable groundwater use in the agricultural sector; misdirected subsidy; and the lack of appreciation of integrated water resources management (IWRM) principles by the decision-makers.

Table 6.1 Sectoral water use changes between 1990 and 2000 (in Mm³/year)

Country	1990			2000			Growth rate (%)		
	Municipal water	Agriculture water	Total water	Municipal water	Agriculture water	Total water	Municipal water	Agriculture water	Total water
Bahrain	103	120	223	132	137	269	128%	114%	121%
Kuwait	303	80	383	772	221	993	255%	276%	259%
Oman	86	1,150	1,236	179	1,124	1,303	208%	98%	105%
Qatar	85	109	194	163	270	433	192%	248%	223%
Saudi Arabia	1,700	14,600	16,300	2,500	18,300	20,800	147%	125%	128%
UAE	540	950	1,490	1,344	2,162	3,506	249%	228%	235%
Total	2,817	17,009	19,826	5,090	22,214	27,304	181%	131%	138%

Source: World Bank (2005)

Table 6.2 Sectoral shares of total water resources

Country	1990		1994*		2000		2003*	
	Municipal water	Agriculture water	Municipal water	Agriculture water	Municipal water	Agriculture water	Municipal water	Agriculture water
Bahrain	46%	54%	39.33%	56.49%	49%	51%	49.78%	44.54%
Kuwait	79%	21%	37.61%	60.22%	78%	22%	43.86%	53.87%
Oman	7%	93%	4.57%	93.87%	14%	86%	10.14%	88.42%
Qatar	44%	56%	23.13%	73.92%	38%	62%	39.19%	59.01%
Saudi Arabia	10%	90%	8.91%	89.95%	12%	88%	8.99%	-
UAE	36%	64%	23.72%	66.79%	38%	62%	15.43%	82.84%

Source: World Bank (2005); *FAO (2014 (Aquastat))

Table 6.3 Water resources endowment in the GCC countries

Country	Area (km²)	Average annual rainfall (mm)	Groundwater recharge (Mm³/year)	Non-renewable reserve (Mm³)
Bahrain	652	30–140	110	negligible
Kuwait	17,818	30–140	160	n/a
Oman	212,460	80–400	900	102,000
Qatar	11,610	20–150	50	negligible
Saudi Arabia	2,149,690	30–550	3,850	428,400
UAE	83,600	80–160	190	n/a

Source: World Bank (2005)

Table 6.4 Changes of annual renewable water per capita between 1970 and 2000

Country	Renewable groundwater	Population (millions)				Annual renewable water per capita					
	(Mm³/year)					(m³/year/capita)					
		1970	1980	1990	2000	1970	1980	1990	2000	2007*	2012*
Bahrain	110	0.2	0.3	0.5	0.7	524	329	219	164	112.4	88.01
Kuwait	160	0.7	1.4	2.1	2.2	215	116	75	73	7.82	6.15
Oman	900	0.7	1.1	1.6	2.4	1,245	817	553	373	544.7	422.5
Qatar	50	0.1	0.2	0.5	0.6	450	218	103	85	50.35	28.28
Saudi Arabia	3,850	5.7	9.4	15.8	20.7	670	411	244	186	92.61	84.84
UAE	190	0.2	1.0	1.8	3.2	864	182	107	59	25.88	16.29
Total	5,260	7.8	13.5	22.3	29.8	678	391	236	176	833.76	646.0

Source: World Bank (2005); *FAO (2014 (Aquastat))

Water shortage in the GCC countries

The Arabian Peninsula, which includes the GCC countries, comprises several arid and semi-arid countries, and is marked with extremely high summer temperatures, low intensity of rainfall, and declining groundwater table levels due to over-pumping and obviously high evapotranspiration rates. The area has more than half of the world's proven oil and natural gas reserves, which enable most of its countries to adopt state-of-the-art technology in the desalination of seawater. However, oil and natural gas reserves are not likely to be sustained forever, and the region is under the threat of having climate change further exacerbate the already high temperatures and low rainfall (Tolba and Saab 2009). Groundwater in most of the countries in the region is not renewable according to many sources and, therefore, continuous abstraction is lowering the water table depth, and in some cases deteriorating water quality due to seawater intrusion. For example, in Oman agricultural demand for water increased from 1,152 million cubic metres (Mm³) in 1990 to 1,546 Mm³ in 2011 and, consequently, supply from groundwater aquifers increased from 899 Mm³ in 1990 to 1,269 Mm³ in 2011 (Zekri *et al.* 2014).

High water consumption in the domestic sector

The GCC countries have the highest per capita water consumption in the world. The values are: Bahrain 511 litres/day, Kuwait 503 l/d, Oman 203 l/d, Qatar 744 l/d, Saudi Arabia 300 l/d and the United Arab Emirates 631 l/d (World Bank 2005). The increase in domestic water demand can be attributed to a lack of conservation measures, low pricing of water, misdirected subsidy and lack of awareness. Domestic water use in all GCC countries increased from around 2.8 billion m³ to 5.1 billion m³ during 1990–2000. Drinking water use alone is expected to reach around 8.5 billion m³ in 2025 (ibid.). Such increase in water consumption will require the establishment of costly new desalination and wastewater treatment plants, which ultimately will result in greater GHG emissions.

Unsustainable groundwater use in the agricultural sector

Agriculture is the biggest consumer of water resources in the GCC countries, although it plays a relatively insignificant role in the region's gross domestic product (GDP). The over-extraction of groundwater beyond safe yield levels has resulted in the pollution of the existing groundwater aquifers due to intrusion of seawater and the upcoming of brackish and saline water supplies from lower aquifers. This is particularly problematic in Oman, Bahrain and Qatar. The use of groundwater for irrigation of low-value agricultural crops in GCC countries had resulted in the wastage of both non-renewable and renewable resources that would be better reserved for present or future high-value uses. Only limited attempts have been made to control groundwater demand through the use of water charges, restrictions on groundwater pumping, limitations on groundwater development and the introduction of advanced irrigation systems. Use of treated wastewater in agriculture (Alkhamisi and Ahmed 2014), a rapid increase in the number of greenhouses, use of salt-tolerant crops, rising yields, adoption of dry farming and increased private investments are some of the positive developments in the GCC agricultural sector (NCB Capital 2010).

The average irrigation water use in the region has increased from around 17 billion m³/year to 22 billion m³/year in just over ten years (1990–2000) (see Table 6.1). Irrigation water is mainly supplied by groundwater, and a rapid expansion of irrigated areas has resulted in substantial increases in groundwater abstraction volumes. In all GCC countries, this volume far exceeds the renewable amounts of groundwater, and has depleted aquifers in many areas. In Saudi Arabia, a rapid expansion of irrigated areas has led to extensive mining of deep non-renewable aquifers – although the total irrigated area has started to decline since 2000 due to government policy changes.

Energy-intensive desalination

Worldwide desalination capacity is increasing at a rapid pace. According to the International Desalination Association, in June 2011, 15,988 desalination plants operated globally, producing 66.5 Mm³/day and providing water for 300 million people (Henthorne 2009). In the GCC states, the desalination industry is expanding at a rapid pace due to the scanty rainfall, rapid population growth, and industrial and tourism developments in the region. Seventy-six per cent of the global desalination capacity is already located in the three enclosed sea areas of the Middle East and North Africa region: the Arabian Gulf, the Mediterranean Sea and the Red Sea. In Oman the demand for desalinated water was predicted to rise from 88 Mm³ in 2007 to 236 Mm³ in 2014, at average annual rate increases of 15 per cent per year (Al-Barwani 2008). In 2010, the total desalination capacity in Oman was already nearly

600,000 m³/day. The importance of desalination in Oman is enormous as most of the country's habitants' drinking water requirements are met by desalinated water. As such, population increase will continue to further increase demand for desalinated water in the coming years.

Thermal processes have been a major part of the desalination market in the GCC countries (80 per cent of desalination capacity is thermal-based) and continue to be an important source of water supply in some specific areas where energy is relatively cheap, cogeneration steam from power production is available, and feed water conditions are not suitable for reverse osmosis. A number of desalination projects proposed or in the pipeline are also based on this type of distillation concept. Hybrid systems coupling different technologies are also being adopted in the design of integrated systems that are more economically efficient and environmentally friendly, opening up the possibility of tailored solutions for each type of industrial problem. Selecting appropriate technologies to meet specific needs at specific locations is essential. This is due to the peculiarities of the sea and brackish waters, especially in the GCC region. The biggest challenge, however, remains in the capability to successfully operate desalination plants once installed. In spite of the technological advances and successes in reducing energy requirement, mainly in membrane-based processes, desalination remains an energy-intensive process, hence contributing to climate change. In the GCC region, the situation is the worst as thermal-based processes, mainly multi-stage flash and multi-effect distillation, are dominating the market.

There are serious green or environmental sustainability issues that concern the desalination industry. Concerns mainly revolve around the concentrate and chemical discharges into the sea and the air pollutant emissions attributed to the energy demand of the desalination process. Most of the desalination plants discharge their brine directly into the sea. In some cases, the brine is partially treated or mixed with seawater before disposal into the sea in order to meet local environmental regulations mainly on salinity, temperature and chemicals. In inland brackish water applications, the brine is typically discharged into evaporation ponds or injected into the ground, while coastal brackish water plants discharge their brine into the sea as well. If evaporation ponds are constructed properly, they are much more environmentally friendly than the option of dumping into the sea.

Other important environmental factors are the emissions of GHGs and air pollutants, as desalination is an energy-intensive process using fossil fuels. The desalination approach is in danger of shifting the problem from water scarcity to energy dependency, and from the stressed freshwater ecosystems to the marine environment. In order to safeguard a sustainable use of desalination technology, the potential environmental impacts of desalination projects need to be evaluated, adverse effects mitigated as far as possible, and the remaining concerns balanced against the impacts of alternative water supply and water management options. Environmental restrictions are expected to increase with time in order to mitigate the impact of desalination plants on the environment. Other challenges faced by the desalination industry in the GCC countries include managing cost, sustainability and capacity development.

Misdirected subsidy

The GCC countries are among the richest countries of the world. According to the World Bank (2014) their per capita GDP on purchasing power parity basis ranges from USD44,000 to USD132,000, and their citizens are blessed with much government assistance in their lives. Many subsidies are provided in the water sectors of the GCC countries that benefit nationals, industries and businesses. These sometimes result in unwanted, environmentally negative consequences. Subsidies and free water to the nationals of some of the GCC countries have resulted in high per capita consumption levels of domestic water. It is generally accepted that sustainable pricing of water and water-related services can signal the scarcity of the resource, promote efficiency and manage demand. Targeted social support is more effective than low tariffs (or their absence) to combine with investment in water supply and sanitation systems, and affordability for poor households (OECD 2008). Unfortunately, the GCC countries are extremely inefficient in recovering the cost of production in the water sector. In Kuwait, for example, water charges cover less than 10 per cent of the costs of production (*Arab Water World* 2014).

Lack of appreciation of integrated water resources management principles by the decision-makers

Another negative aspect of water management in the region is the absence of the principles of IWRM. Economic efficiency, equity and environmental sustainability, which are the bedrock of IWRM, are lacking. UNEP (2011) defines green economy as an economy that leads to improved human well-being and social justice, while environmental risks are to be reduced and natural resources to be conserved. As such, IWRM and the green economy can complement each other. There are various reasons for the lack of an IWRM approach in the GCC countries, which include lack of trained manpower, reliance on expatriate consultants and professionals, reliance on engineering solutions (as funding is relatively abundant) and lack of participation of stakeholders in decision-making.

Some innovative technical ideas from Oman for making the water sector 'green'

In the following section, the authors will discuss possible ways to increase the supply of water in the most efficient way for the various sectors. The examples given are mostly from Oman and are mostly technical in nature. The examples are overwhelmingly 'supply-side' solutions. This in no way signifies that 'demand-side' solutions are not important. In fact, demand-side solutions are preferable in most cases over supply-side solutions as they have longer-term effects and are more cost-effective. Below, consideration will be given to the environmental sustainability, or 'greenness', of alternative sources of water. In general, a green water sector has the following attributes: a decreased water footprint; increased water conservation; greater efficiency in water use; and augmented reuse and recycling of water.

Wastewater treatment and reuse

Wastewater treatment is a process wherein the contaminants are removed from wastewater as well as household sewage to produce a waste stream or solid waste suitable for discharge or reuse. Presently, reuse is given a lot more emphasis than just disposal after treatment. In Oman the expected production of treated wastewater (TWW) could be 100 Mm³/year in 2012 and this amount would increase to 220 Mm³/year from 2020 onwards. In order to maximise the utilisation of this resource, several studies were conducted from 2004 to 2010 targeting the use of tertiary treated wastewater in the cultivation of forage and other field crops. These studies were divided into the following: (i) utilisation of TWW in irrigation of annual forage (maize, sorghum and barley); (ii) yield and water use efficiency for maize under TWW; (iii) effect of no-tillage agriculture on different field crops under TWW conditions; and (iv) use of TWW in irrigation of wheat.

In the first study, three experiments were conducted to test the performance of crop varieties under TWW. In the second, two experiments were used to test the yield and water use efficiency of forage maize under TWW. In the third, two experiments were used to test forage crops under two tillage systems (no-tillage and conventional tillage) under TWW. Finally, two experiments were conducted to test the performance of three varieties of wheat under TWW. The results showed that the plant height (cm), forage and dry matter yield (t/ha) increased under the influence of TWW. No significant difference was found between the two tillage systems for forage production under TWW. Wheat grain yield (t/ha) under TWW was twice the average wheat production under freshwater irrigation. Regarding the heavy metals and microbial quality of TWW, it was found that heavy metals and the microbial population were very low or within the Omani standard.

Research in many countries has shown that it is safe to use TWW under most conditions, and most governments encourage such use by enacting necessary guidelines and standards to ensure public safety. Therefore, treated wastewater can be used as an alternative source to improve the situation of water scarcity as well as to increase the area of wheat and forage crop production for sustainable agriculture in Oman and the other GCC countries (Alkhamisi and Ahmed 2014). The Omani government is currently building pipe networks to bring treated wastewater to the farmers on a pilot scale and, if successful, treated wastewater reuse is likely to become a common feature of Omani agriculture.

Greywater treatment and reuse

A way of saving water around the home that has grown in popularity over the last few years is the installation of greywater systems. Greywater systems reuse and recycle wastewater from the home for use in the garden or even in the home for toilet flushing or washing clothes. Usually, only wastewater from the bathroom and laundry is suitable for greywater as kitchen wastewater contains too many fat and oil residues and food scraps that can potentially pose health and environmental risks. Greywater systems need to be well set up and maintained to ensure that they do not have any negative effects on the environment or human health. All greywater systems require some behavioural changes and a maintenance regime; therefore, careful consideration is needed before installing a system. Greywater quality, quantity, treatment and other related issues have been widely discussed. Surendran and Wheatley (1998) reported approximately equal volumes of greywater and lavatory flush water, on average, in the United Kingdom. Hodges (1998) reported that about two-thirds of domestic water is greywater. In Oman, 80 per cent of wastewater produced from households is considered greywater (Prathapar *et al.* 2005). Griggs *et al.* (1998) identified greywater reuse for irrigation and toilet flushing as a major water conservation measure. Increasing water availability by treating and reusing wastewater, particularly for irrigation, is a long-term government policy in Oman (Al-Obaidani and Atta 2003).

Greywater reuse reduces the amount of freshwater needed to supply a household and wastewater entering the sewer or a septic system. Related benefits include water savings, and reduction in wastewater treatment costs and the threat to groundwater pollution from septic tanks. With proper management, greywater reuse will bring significant environmental and economic benefits. A simple calculation shows that, for example, 20,000 houses with greywater systems with each treating a modest 1 m³/day will save 20,000 m³/day in the consumption of desalinated water. This is equivalent to the capacity of a mid-sized desalination plant. A greywater system was designed, which consisted of settlement pond, underground greywater storage tanks, a small trap filter and the main multi-layer filter (Ahmed *et al.* 2008). The treatment unit's performance efficiency was enough to satisfy Omani regulations on reuse of wastewater in irrigation. The financial analysis showed the internal rate of return for such a system after ten years to be attractive (14.9 per cent) considering the prevailing bank interest rates in Oman. Costs of the systems and the amount of greywater treated were the main factors affecting the internal rate of return. Based on this study, the authors concluded that, under certain conditions, greywater treatment and reuse is technically and financially feasible in Oman and the GCC countries (Ahmed *et al.* 2008).

Use of low-quality surface water

The treatment system designed for greywater was also used for improving low-quality surface water in a mountain village in Oman. Al Jabal al Akhdar (Green Mountain) in arid Northern Oman has freshwater resources that had supported small communities for hundreds of years. Al Jabal al Akhdar receives more rainfall annually (300–400 mm) compared to the desert plains. Over the last decade, this region underwent enormous changes due to rapid development. There are 24 retention reservoirs in the area, but most are eutrophic, with the nutrient loading caused by input of animal fecal matter via surface run-off. As expected, these waters are contaminated with coliform bacteria and some also have pathogenic *Escherichia coli*. Drinking water needs of all the villages and the requirements of at least one large farm and a hotel are met by groundwater extraction. Because of poor quality, the surface water in the reservoirs is under-utilised.

A treatment system similar to the greywater systems discussed previously, that is low-cost and low-maintenance, was designed, constructed and operated in one village to clean the reservoir water for non-drinking human use (Ahmed *et al.* 2010). The treatment unit improved the major water quality parameters. A survey among the adult male population of the village showed their eagerness to adopt this system and use the treated reservoir water for uses other than agriculture. Establishment of these treatment units in other villages should reduce the pressures on groundwater extraction. Such systems are relatively easy to build and can be adapted to local conditions (Jashoul and Ahmed 2008).

Managed aquifer recharge

Managed aquifer recharge (MAR) is practised widely to store water during periods of surpluses and withdraw during deficits from an aquifer. MAR implies the acceleration of aquifer recharge by altering natural soil surface conditions to increase infiltration, or the injection of water directly via recharge wells. Aquifers are very good means of storing water. With reasonable care the water is protected from pollution. They use minimum land area and cause no environmental damage. Recharged water is distributed across the aquifer due to natural gradients. When practised along coastal aquifers, MAR mitigates seawater intrusion. It is less expensive and easier to operate and maintain compared to surface dams, and always available on demand. On the other hand, MAR has some disadvantages. In most cases, only a part of the recharged water is recovered. Some impurities, such as microbes, heavy metals or trace elements, if present in recharging water, will contaminate the aquifer, and are very expensive to contain and clean. In order to avoid these problems, the injected water usually undergoes a treatment process to satisfy drinking water standards.

In Muscat, the Oman Wastewater Services Company currently has approximately 14 per cent of the households on its sewer network, which will increase to 80 per cent by 2015, with a surplus of 100,000 m³/day of treated wastewater (treated effluent) during winter months. The aquifer along the northern coast of Oman is conducive for MAR. Data show that treated effluent volumes will increase from 7.6 Mm³ in 2003 to 70.9 Mm³ in 2035. 'HYDRUS 2D' simulations show that areas with sandy loam soils are suited for infiltration ponds. If soils are loamy sands or heavier, injection may be necessary. Numerical simulations with 'Visual MODFLOW' show that the limited aquifer thickness in the upstream part makes that area unfavourable for artificial recharge. The proximity to the coast in the downstream part may pose a threat to the quality of the recharged water, and the shorter travel distance may cause a loss of these waters. Therefore, the middle zone, where the aquifer is relatively thicker and is distant from the coast, is the most suitable. The cost of MAR in Oman after membrane bioreactor treatment of wastewater has been estimated as USD0.353/m^3 and USD0.371/m^3 under two different electricity costs, a 30-year life span, and 85 per cent recovery and 5 per cent interest rates (Zekri *et al.* 2014).

Biosaline agriculture

The use of saline water, which is in abundant supply in the GCC countries, will make agriculture more resilient to climate change and help tackle the existing shortage of water in general. Findings from a research project (Al-Rawahy *et al.* 2010) on the management of salt-affected soils may be a guide to the GCC countries facing the prospect of living with soil salinity resulting from the use of saline groundwater. This project identified salt-tolerant crops, proper management techniques to combat soil salinity as well as policy directions whose implementation will not only benefit the farmers presently but will help them with future climate change-related challenges in Omani agriculture. This project was undertaken as soil and groundwater salinity has emerged as the most significant problem of present agriculture of Oman. Scanty rainfall coupled with high temperature is always conducive to accumulation of salts. These conditions are predominantly found in Oman and other GCC countries. However, human activities of the past proved a driving factor and secondary soil salinity has increased at a very rapid rate due to persistent use of saline groundwater, the concentration of which is increasing with time because of increased pumping in the Al Batinah region. The region has been the most important area of agriculture in Oman encompassing an area of 80,000 ha. The balance existing before the 1990s between total pumping and annual recharge has been greatly disturbed resulting in reduction of crop yields in the beginning and abandoning of lands gradually. Saline water intrusions are also present in some areas of the region that are nearer the sea, as the result of over-pumping. The estimated values for salt-affected lands are 44 per cent of the total geographical area and 70 per cent of the agriculturally suitable area of the country.

Annual financial losses due to salinity have been reported as 7.31–13.97 million Omani riyals (2005 data). When the lands go out of cultivation, the owners of salt-affected lands become unemployed. This socio-economic problem has many negative impacts on the society. Thus, the salinity problem is a huge threat to the sustainability of agriculture in Oman, especially in Al Batinah, and is likely to become progressively worse as the impacts of climate change begin being felt in the coming years. Findings from the project confirmed the following: (i) salt-tolerant varieties of tomatoes, barley, sorghum and pearl millet can be grown successfully in saline soils of the Al Batinah coast; (ii) mulching surface soil with a thin layer of shredded date palm residues resulted in less salt accumulation in the soil resulting in more crop yield than other methods; (iii) fodder grown in saline soils with saline water has no negative effect on growth or meat quality of goats; and (iv) the incorporation of aquaculture in saline areas was proven feasible (Ahmed *et al.* 2013). It will be relatively easy to implement findings of this project with active involvement of the concerned government departments in Oman. Once successful in Oman, this project could be replicated in other GCC countries.

Recharge dams

In arid countries the potential evaporation exceeds the annual rainfall. Surface storage dams are mostly unsuitable. Groundwater recharge dams are used in arid countries to enhance the natural groundwater recharge by a controlled infiltration of stored flood events. The efficiency of this recharge process has been evaluated, and the management of the dams has been optimised with regard to a maximum recharge volume. The concept of establishing underground recharge dams in Oman first arose about 1978. The main purpose of these dams is to enhance groundwater storage through utilising *wadi* flood water, which often wasted into the sea or desert. This can be done by storing such water in the underground layers for use later for all purposes. Recharge dams are constructed on alluvial *wadi* channels to store flood water for temporary periods not exceeding three days to prevent evaporation losses and health risks. The stored and purified water is released slowly, so that it can penetrate through the thick alluvium downstream of the dam and, accordingly, be withdrawn for use in due time. Thirty-two underground recharge dams have been constructed in Oman, and work is currently under way to establish another 11 (MRMWR 2007).

The amount of groundwater recharge by dams can be increased by many times compared to natural recharge. This positive effect occurs mainly due to the prevention of flow losses beyond the recharge area, and due to the extended duration of the infiltration. Depending on site-specific boundary conditions and the magnitude of flood events, dams allow the possibility of recharging more than 80 per cent of the stored water to the aquifer. Case studies show that recharge percentages of even 95 per cent are achievable.

Storage dams

Large water storages (also called reservoirs or impoundments) can be formed in-stream by constructing dams or off-stream by lining natural or artificial depressions with impermeable liners. The stored water may be used during periods when surface water flows are insufficient to meet water demand. One important aspect to be considered when using this technology is the need to prevent in-stream storages from rapidly silting up, thus reducing the effective storage capacity. Siltation problems can be reduced by constructing siltation ponds upstream of the main storage to trap silt that would otherwise enter the storage reservoir, and by ensuring that land use practices within the drainage basins feeding these storages are such that they minimise sediment loss from the land surface. In Oman the first surface storage dam with a significant amount of storage is now under construction. The Wadi Dayqah Dam is one of the major water projects in the region and in the Sultanate, and will provide water supply for the Governorate of Muscat after the completion of its second phase (ibid.).

Energy-efficient desalination

Desalination produces water at a known and regular rate in respect to both quantity and quality. Rejected brine can possibly serve as raw material in the manufacture of fertilisers and other products (d'Orival 1990). The main constraint of desalination is the cost of desalinated water. This cost is mostly determined by the costs of energy used in the desalination process. However, desalination techniques are progressing rapidly, and there is a good chance of reducing the cost further during the next few years (Mohsen and Al-Jayyousi 1999).

Desalination for water supply globally has grown steadily since the 1960s. In fact, seawater desalination currently meets most, if not all, requirements for domestic freshwater supply for some countries (including the GCC countries), and is a supplemental source for others. Based on the process, desalination plants can be categorised into two types. The first involves plants that employ a phase-change process. In such plants, desalination takes place while there is a change of phase (that is, evaporation or freezing). Plants that follow such a process include multi-stage flash, multi-effect distillation, vapour compression distillation, solar humidification/dehumidification desalination and freezing-melting. The second type of desalination plant comprises those that involve no phase change. In such plants, the extraction of water or salt takes place while the salts or pure water remain in the solution phase. These include reverse osmosis and electrodialysis.

There have been recent developments and advances in energy-efficient and low-cost desalination systems. One such example is the new solar-driven desalination systems that will support socio-economic development in rural areas by elevating social conditions in remote locations that lack water supply, and thereby stem the movement of people to cities. These systems are very suitable for such locations as they are very easy to operate, low-cost, and do not need extensive maintenance.

In recent years, several institutions such as the Water Desalination and Reuse Center at King Abdullah University of Science and Technology (KAUST) are looking at developing new emerging low- and renewable-energy-driven desalination technologies that can use low-grade waste heat, and solar and geothermal energies, which are available in the region. These mainly involve forward osmosis, membrane distillation and adsorption desalination processes, with and without conventional desalination processes, such as multi-effect distillation and reverse osmosis, targeting to meet operational, economic and environmental challenges. In Abu Dhabi, a pilot project is under way, with four international companies contracted to build small-scale desalination plants using renewable energy. The Emirati company Masdar is taking the lead role, and, at the time of writing, production from the renewable energy desalination plants was expected to commence in early 2015 and continue through June 2016. At the end of this trial period, Masdar will choose to go forward with the technology of one of its four partners, or even four, if all prove successful (*Khaleej Times* 2014).

Desalination for high-value agriculture

In the GCC countries the use of desalination units for providing freshwater in agriculture is an increasing trend. Small-scale desalination units for agriculture are simple to operate and require a minimum set of maintenance levels. Depending on the desired quality of desalinated water, the running cost of chemicals and membranes is relatively low. Costs of desalination can be regulated with the optimisation of the seasonal crop water requirements. Moreover, desalination inland usually uses brackish water, in which the salinity level (about 10,000 mg/l) is relatively lower than that of seawater. Therefore, the cost of desalinating brackish water is lower than that of seawater. Furthermore, Ayers and Westcot (1994) have noted that irrigation water standards by the Food and Agriculture Organization of the United Nations allow salinities of up to 2,000 mg/l, which has a positive impact on the cost of desalination for irrigation water. One of the main challenges for adopting this technology for agriculture is the cost of energy required. With the advancement in desalination technologies, the energy requirements, and hence cost, are reduced dramatically (FAO 2014; Kabell and El Said 2012). Energy requirements were reduced to about one-sixth from the 1970s to 2002, with a cost of about EURO.428/m^3 (about 0.25 Omani riyals) in 2002. The technology provides a positive social impact by enabling farmers to reclaim and recover their salt-affected farms.

The major environmental impact of the use of desalination technologies relates to the amount and quality of the brine discharge. Desalination units produce brine of about 60 per cent of the intake water, with almost twice the salinity level of the intake water (FAO 2014). Disposal of such brine in agricultural lands is associated with huge environmental concerns, and adds to the overall cost of the technology. In 1997, the Spanish government established a network of pipelines to collect brines from various desalination units and dispose them into a protected estuary. Brine disposal from inland desalination plants in Oman has been extensively discussed, but no such studies have been conducted for the desalination plants used for agriculture (Ahmed *et al.* 2000; Ahmed *et al.* 2001a; 2001b; Ahmed *et al.* 2002). Brine disposal into the sea may require diluting it first.

Produced water from desalination units has an electrical conductivity of about 0.2–0.3 decisiemens(dS)/m. This is within the recommended level for the use for irrigation water. However, desalination for agriculture requires extra efforts to remove boron and total dissolved salts. Seawater has a boron concentration of about 4.5–6.0 mg/l. Recommendations for irrigation water includes a boron concentration of less than 0.50 mg/l, total dissolved salts at less than 450 mg/l and chloride concentration of less than 105 mg/l (Shaffer *et al.* 2012). Boron in neutral and acidic environments passes through the reverse osmosis filters. Without any additional filtration, boron in produced water is about 2.0 mg/l, which is toxic to many fruit crops. Some crops that are grown in Oman are 'semi-tolerant' to boron at about 1.0 mg/l (Zarzo *et al.* 2012). Such extra restriction on water quality for agriculture requires additional costs for the seawater reverse osmosis technology. Another issue is that desalination removes important ions that maintain the structure of the soil and serve as plant nutrients, such as calcium (Ca^{2+}), magnesium (Mg^{2+}) and sulphates (SO_4^{2-}). Further re-mineralisation is thus required to supplement such ions for the plants and soils, which adds additional costs for the process.

Water saving and conservation in domestic use and agriculture

Demand management through water savings, conservation, education and awareness will have a better long-term effect than increasing supply. Securing an adequate supply is only half of the water equation, and managing the demand side is just as crucial. Saudi Arabia has a substantial water shortage problem where water demand far exceeds water resources' sustainable yields. This fact has motivated the Saudi Ministry of Water and Electricity to launch a massive water conservation awareness programme to enhance water use efficiency in the country (Ouda *et al.* 2013). Another leading concern facing the future of agricultural production is the availability of water, and it is expected that climate change will cause more extreme climate events including droughts, floods and shifts in plant growing zones (TWDB 2014). As populations grow, more efficient use of water in growing food will be of key importance. For example, in Oman agricultural water usage has exceeded freshwater recharge for many years now, and the effects of over-pumping water for agriculture are apparent both in Al Batinah and on the Salalah Plain. Groundwater levels have fallen steeply, and seawater intrusion of the coastal aquifers is well-established; coastal date gardens have perished, and much of small-scale agriculture has been abandoned. Even if all pumping ceased tomorrow, it would take decades for a freshwater balance to be achieved (Hutton 2003). Experts suggest that if agriculture is to continue efficiently, it should focus on high-quality, high-value crops that require relatively small water inputs, and are closely controlled and monitored by high-technology drip irrigation systems. Thus, the present imbalance between the available water resources and water demand is chronic in the GCC countries, and is expected to escalate in the future unless major positive steps are taken soon to rationalise and manage water demand, increase and augment water supply, and impose realistic controls on water use (Al-Zubari 2003).

Fog collection

This innovative technology is based on the premise that water can be collected from fogs under favourable climatic conditions. Fogs are defined as a mass of water vapour condensed into small water droplets at, or just above, the Earth's surface.

The small water droplets present in the fog precipitate when they come into contact with objects. Present research suggests that fog collectors work best in coastal areas where water can be harvested as the fog moves inland driven by the wind. However, the technology could also potentially supply water for multiple uses in mountainous areas, should water present in stratocumulus clouds at altitudes of approximately 400–1,200 m be harvested (Abdul-Wahab and Lea 2008).

Full-scale fog collectors are simple, flat, rectangular nets of nylon supported by a post at either end or arranged perpendicular to the direction of the prevailing wind. The one used in a pilot-scale project in the El Tofo region of Chile consisted of a single 2 m by 24 m panel with a surface area of 48 m^2. Alternatively, the collectors may be more complex structures, made up of a series of such collection panels joined together. The number and size of the modules chosen will depend on local topography and the quality of the materials used in the panels. Multiple-unit systems have the advantage of a lower cost per unit of water produced, and the number of panels in use can be changed as climatic conditions and demand for water vary.

This technology should be adopted after a pilot project is first carried out to quantify the potential rate and yield that can be anticipated from the fog harvesting rate of the area under consideration. Community participation in the process of developing and operating the technology in order to reduce installation, operating and maintenance costs is necessary. In Oman the possibility of fog water collection has been investigated by Abdul-Wahab and Lea (ibid.). They observed that fog collection has the potential to reduce dependence on groundwater and improve the quality of life in some mountain areas (such as the Dhofar Governorate) of Oman.

Rooftop water harvesting

Rooftops of urban structures in arid and semi-arid countries can be turned into rainwater harvesting systems. Rainwater harvesting is the process of collecting and storing rain for future productive use. Harvesting is done on the rooftop. In the case of sloping roofs, a well-designed gutter system will pick up the rain and bring it to the filters. In the case of flat roofs, the down pipes will convey the water to the filter. The gutters and down pipes are usually made of polyvinyl chloride (PVC) for want of an environmentally safer material. Storage could occur in manmade tanks or the aquifer could be the sink. In cases where houses and apartments have a sump built to store water from the main, the same sump can be used to harvest rainwater too. Alternatively, inverted wells may be constructed to receive rain water from gutters and serve as a transient storage for recharging water. Water collected from such systems could be utilised for home gardening.

Cloud seeding

This expensive technology encourages efficient raindrop formation through a collision – a coalescence process, which is enhanced or accelerated by the introduction of hygroscopic nuclei into a storm updraft at cloud base. Silver iodide crystals are most commonly used as nuclei for raindrop formation, and are released by rocket or aeroplane into an appropriate cloud formation. The requirements are that the air must be cooled, or vapour must be added, until the air becomes saturated, and the air must contain particulate nuclei to enable the phase transition from vapour to water or ice to occur without great supersaturation. Some of the water particles formed must grow large enough to fall out of the cloud. In Oman cloud seeding experiments were conducted by the Ministry of Water Resources, which reported that the formation of summer cumulus clouds in the Eastern and Western Al Hajr Mountains encourages the implementation of such project. The preliminary tests indicate a potential increase in rain rates of 10–20 per cent more than the current normal rate (MRMWR 2007). *Arabian Business* (2011) reported in January 2011 that scientists working for the Abu Dhabi government created 52 rainstorms in Al Ain in July and August of 2010 during the peak of the emirate's summer months. They further reported that such rainstorms were only possible when the atmospheric humidity reached a minimum level of 30 per cent.

Policy recommendations

Based on the data and information presented in the previous sections of this chapter, the authors are making a number of policy recommendations. Implementing these policies would result in a 'greener' water sector, which is compatible with the green economy principle of reducing environmental risks. The recommendations are rather general in nature, as cost-benefit analyses were not carried out. It is expected that before any recommendations are adopted by the relevant governments, in-depth policy analysis and economic analysis, including social and environmental impact analyses, will be undertaken. The recommendations are divided into three categories: demand side, supply side and others.

Demand side

- Water pricing should reflect the true cost of production.
- Subsidies provided to consumers must be targeted to the needy and incentives given for water savings by consumers.
- Installation of water saving devices must be made compulsory for all new residential, commercial and industrial buildings.
- Urban water demand management should be given highest priority as this sector uses water that is produced and delivered at high cost. The tariff structure should encourage conservation. Subsidies for retro-fitting, compulsory installation of water saving devices in new buildings, leakage detection and education campaigns should be part of a comprehensive water demand management action plan.
- Groundwater abstraction should be regulated, including for farmers, and all should pay for such water depending on its use.

Supply side

- MAR should be encouraged with strict control over the quality of injected water.
- Collection and utilisation of treated wastewater should be given high priority. Such uses can include not only irrigation but also managed aquifer recharge, industrial uses, saline water intrusion control and toilet flushing.

Others

- Governments should encourage the use of alternative sources of energy in the desalination industry. If direct use is not possible, energy use for water production must be compensated by producing the same amount of energy through alternative sources, and supplied to the grid.
- Maximum overall savings in the water sector will result from improved water use in the agricultural sector. Use of good quality groundwater for non-economic high water consuming agricultural production is to be avoided. Biosaline agriculture should be encouraged. Use of smart technology (such as hydroponics, drip irrigation, metering and controlled environment agriculture) should be encouraged, and desalinated water for agriculture should be permitted only for high-value crops making economic sense.
- Adopting IWRM should be made compulsory through the adoption of water management plans that reflect the IWRM principles. All alternative water resources that are cost-effective and environmentally sound should be brought under the integrated management plans.

Conclusion

Current and future water shortages in the GCC countries necessitate both reducing demand and increasing supply. There are numerous green, or environmental sustainability, challenges that affect the management of this vital sector. In order to overcome these challenges, besides conservation, use of unconventional supplies should be seriously looked into. This chapter has introduced some of the options with green credentials, with particular reference to Oman. Such options include rooftop rainwater harvesting, greywater and wastewater treatment and reuse, managed aquifer recharge, fog collection, cloud seeding and water desalination. Using these sources appropriately and continuing to maximise water conservation opportunities will help us tackle the water shortages in the GCC countries in a 'green' way.

References

Abdul-Wahab, S., and V. Lea. 2008. 'Reviewing Fog Water Collection Worldwide and in Oman.' *International Journal of Environmental Studies*, 65 (3), 487–500.

Ahmed, M., W. Shayya, D. Hoey, A. Mahendran, R. Morris and J. Al-Handaly. 2000. 'Use of Evaporation Ponds for Brine Disposal in Desalination Plants.' *Desalination*, 130 (2), 155–168.

Ahmed, M., W. Shayya, D. Hoey and J. Al-Handaly. 2001a. 'Brine Disposal from Reverse Osmosis Plants in Oman and the United Arab Emirates.' *Desalination* 133 (2), 135–147.

Ahmed, M., A. Arakel, D. Hoey and M. Coleman. 2001b. 'Integrated Power, Water and Salt Generation: A Discussion Paper.' *Desalination* 134 (1–3), 37–45.

Ahmed, M., W.H. Shayya, D. Hoey and J. Al-Handaly. 2002. 'Brine Disposal from Inland Desalination Plants: Research Needs Assessment.' *Water International* 27 (2), 194–201.

Ahmed, M., S. Al Sidairi, S. A. Prathapar and S. Al-Adawi. 2008. 'Evaluation of Locally Manufactured and Commercial Greywater Treatment Systems: A Case Study from Oman.' *International Journal of Environmental Studies*, 65 (1), 33–41.

Ahmed, M., R. Victor and M. Jashoul. 2010. 'Groundwater Demand Management in Al Jabal Al Akhdar Region of Oman by Utilization of Low Quality Surface Water.' *Proceedings of Global Change and the World's Mountains, 2010*, Perth, October.

Ahmed, M., N. Hussain and S. Al-Rawahy. 2013. 'Management of Saline Lands in Oman: Learning to Live with Salinity.' In *Developments in Soil Salinity Assessment and Reclamation, Innovative Thinking and Use of Marginal Soil and Water Resources in Irrigated Agriculture*, edited by Shabbir A. Shahid, M. A. Abdelfattah and F. K. Taha, 265–282. Netherlands: Springer.

Al-Barwani, H. 2008. 'Seawater Desalination in Oman.' *Arab Water World*, 32 (12), 41–42.

Alkhamisi, S. A., and M. Ahmed. 2014. 'Opportunities and Challenges of Using Treated Wastewater in Agriculture.' In *Environmental Cost and Face of Agriculture in the Gulf Cooperation Council Countries*, edited by S. A. Shahid and M. Ahmed. Netherlands: Springer.

Al-Obaidani, S. B. S., and T. H. A. Atta. 2003. *Water Resources Management in Oman*. Country paper presented at the Ministerial Conference on the Occasion of the 3rd World Water Forum, Kyoto, Japan, 22–23 March.

Al-Rawahy, S. A., M. Ahmed and N. Hussain. 2010. 'Management of Salt-Affected Soils and Water for Sustainable Agriculture: The Project.' In *Management of Salt-affected Soils and Water for Sustainable Agriculture*, edited by A. Mushtaque, S. A. Al-Rawahy and N. Hussain. Oman: Sultan Qaboos University.

Al-Zubari, W. K. 2003. 'Alternative Water Policies for the Gulf Cooperation Council Countries.' In *Water Resources Perspectives: Evaluation, Management, and Policy*, edited by A. S. Al-Sharhan, and W. W. Wood, 155–167. Amsterdam: Elsevier Science.

Arab Water World. 2014. 'Kuwait's High Water Consumption Levels Require Instant Measures.' *Arab Water World*, XXXVII(7), 44.

Arabian Business. 2011. 'Abu Dhabi-backed Scientists Create Fake Rainstorms in $11m Project.' 3 January. http://www.arabianbusiness.com/

Ayers, R. S., and D. W. Westcot. 1994. *Water Quality for Agriculture, Irrigation and Drainage*. Paper 29, Rev. 1. Rome: Food and Agriculture Organization of the United Nations.

d'Orival, M. 1990. *Water Desalting and Nuclear Power*. München and Paris: Verlag Karl Thiemig.

FAO. Food and Agriculture Organization of the United Nations. 2014. *Aquastat* database. Accessed 31 October. http://www.fao.org/nr/water/aquastat/main/index.stm

Griggs, J. C., M. C. Shouler and J. Hall. 1998. *Water Conservation and the Built Environment*. Research Publication (21AD/WATER). Oxford Brookes University, UK.

GWP. Global Water Partnership. 2013. *Water in the Green Economy*. Perspectives Paper. Stockholm.

Henthorne, L. 2009. *The Current State of Desalination*. Presented at the International Desalination Association World Congress, Dubai, November.

Hodges, D. 1998. 'Safe Use of Household Greywater.' *Water and Environment Manager*, 13(6), 15–17.

Hutton, S. 2003. 'Saving the Future: Water in Oman.' *Oman Economic Review*, March.

IPCC. Intergovernmental Panel on Climate Change. 2001a. *Climate Change 2001: The Scientific Basis*. Contribution of Working Group I to Third Assessment Report of the IPCC. Cambridge, UK: Cambridge University Press.

IPCC. 2001b. *Climate Change 2001: Synthesis Report*, edited by R. Watson and the core writing team. Cambridge, UK: Cambridge University Press.

IPCC. 2007a. *Climate Change 2007: Impacts, Adaptation and Vulnerability*. Contribution of Working Group II to the Fourth Assessment Report of the IPCC. Cambridge, UK: Cambridge University Press.

IPCC. 2007b. *Climate Change 2007: The Scientific Basis, Summary for Policymakers*. Contribution of Working Group I to the Fourth Assessment Report of the IPCC. Cambridge, UK: Cambridge University Press.

IPCC. 2014. *Climate Change 2014: Impacts, Adaptation and Vulnerability*. Cambridge, UK and New York: Cambridge University Press.

Jashoul, M. and M. Ahmed. 2008. *Improving Quality of Hajamta Reservoir Water Using a Custom-made Treatment System*. Proceedings of the First International Conference on Water Resources and Climate Change in the MENA Region, Muscat, Oman, 2–4 November.

Kabeel, A. E., and M. S. E. El Said. 2012. *A Hybrid Solar Desalination System of Air Humidification Dehumidification and Water Flashing Evaporation. Part I. A Numerical Investigation*. 16th International Water Technology Conference, Istanbul, Turkey, 7–10 May.

Khaleej Times. 2014. 'Use of Renewable Energy for Desalination Plants in UAE.' Accessed 18 June. http://www.khaleejtimes.com/

Mohsen, M. S., and O. R. Al-Jayyousi. 1999. 'Brackish Water Desalination: An Alternative for Water Supply Enhancement in Jordan.' *Desalination*, 124, 163–174.

MRMWR. Ministry of Regional Municipalities and Water Resources of Oman. 2007. 'Recharge Dams in Oman.' Accessed 15 July 2014. http://www.mrmwr.gov.om/en/

NCB Capital. 2010. GCC *Agriculture*. Saudi Arabia.

OECD. Organisation for Economic Co-operation and Development. 2008. 'Green Growth and Water.' Accessed 23 June 2014. http://www.oecd.org/greengrowth/

Ouda, O. K. M., T. Shawesh, T. Al-Olabi, F. Younes and R. Al-Waked. 2013. 'Review of Domestic Water Conservation Practices in Saudi Arabia.' *Applied Water Science*, 3, 689–699.

Prathapar, S. A., M. Ahmed, A. Jamrah, S. Al Adawi, A. Al Harassi and S. Sidiari. 2005. 'Overcoming Constraints for Greywater Reuse in Oman.' *Desalination*, 186, 177–186.

PwC. PricewaterhouseCoopers. 2014. *Achieving a Sustainable Water Sector in the GCC: Managing Supply and Demand, Building Institutions*, by Tarek El Sayed and Johnny Ayoub.

Shaffer, D. L., N. Y. Yip, J. Gilron and M. Elimelech. 2012. 'Seawater Desalination for Agriculture by Integrated Forward and Reverse Osmosis: Improved Product Water Quality for Potentially Less Energy.' *Journal of Membrane Science*, 415–416, 1–8.

Surendran, S., and A. D. Wheatley. 1998. 'Greywater Reclamation for Non-potable Reuse.' *Journal of Chartered Institution of Water and Environmental Management*, 12, 406–413.

Tolba, M. K., and N. W. Saab, eds. 2009. *Arab Environment: Climate Change: Impact of Climate Change on Arab Countries*. Beirut: Arab Forum for Environment and Development.

TWDB. Texas Water Development Board. 2014. *Agriculture Water Conservation: Overview of Best Management Practices*. Austin: TWDB Conservation Division.

UNEP. United Nations Environment Programme. 2011. *Towards a Green Economy: Pathways to Sustainable Development and Poverty Eradication: A Synthesis for Policy Makers*.

UN-Water. 2011. *A Water Toolbox – or Best Practice Guide of Actions*. Stockholm.

World Bank. 2005. *A Water Sector Assessment Report on the Countries of the Cooperation Council of the Arab States of the Gulf*. Report No. 32539-MNA.

World Bank. 2014. *World Development Indicators*. Accessed 15 August. http://data.worldbank.org/

Zarzo, D., E. Campos and P. Terrero. 2012. 'Spanish Experience in Desalination for Agriculture.' *Desalination and Water Treatment*, 59 (1–3), 53–66.

Zekri, S., M. Ahmed, R. Chaieb and N. Gaffour. 2014. 'Managed Aquifer Recharge Using Quaternary Treated Wastewater in Muscat: An Economic Perspective.' *International Journal of Water Resources Development*, 30 (2), 246–261.

Part III

The urban environment

7 Green buildings in the Arabian Gulf

Christopher Silva

Introduction

Green buildings, or sustainability-focused constructions, can be defined as any structure that during its construction or operation focuses on reducing its impact on the natural environment and on human health (EPA 2014). Green buildings usually try to achieve this goal by encouraging integrated design processes, aimed at reducing construction waste, overall carbon footprint, operational redundancies and surpassing established limits or benchmarks related to the usage of energy, water and other resources. These types of constructions also take into account the location of a building relative to general services such as stores, community organisations and leisure centres, with the hope to reduce carbon emissions due to transportation, and also support local economies.

While the idea of being more efficient during construction or the goal to improve the performance of a building has been present throughout the ages, the appearance of green buildings can be associated with the rise of the environmental movement in the late 1960s, the increased costs of water and electricity in various Western nations after the oil crisis of the 1970s, and more significantly with the development of the first green building codes (Korkmaz 2009). The two most commonly known and used codes are the Leadership in Energy and Environmental Design (LEED), developed by the United States Green Building Council in 1998, and the Building Research Establishment Environmental Assessment Methodology (BREEAM) code developed by the Building Research Establishment in the United Kingdom in the late 1980s. In this chapter, green building codes and certification standards available in the Arabian Gulf will be used to showcase the progress of the green building movement in the region.

The presence of green buildings in the Arabian Gulf can be linked to its fast population growth occurring in the past 20 years, and the construction boom of the early 2000s. The Gulf Cooperation Council (GCC) countries want to continue their development and ensure that they have a working economy when their resources of fossil fuels run out. In countries such as the United States, green buildings are playing a major role in the shift to a green economy. For example, it was expected that 2013 would bring a total of eight million jobs to the American market (USGBC 2013). Green buildings are an essential element of the transition to a green economy for the GCC countries for the following reasons:

1) While rich in hydrocarbons, all GCC countries lack natural sources of fresh water. These water needs are currently met by the extremely expensive, energy-intensive and time-consuming process of desalination. Second, a great percentage of the water produced by desalination is lost in leakages during transmission and due to overuse. Alarmingly, overuse of water in households in Qatar accounts for nearly 30 per cent of the total water needs of the country (GSDP 2009). Design elements and efficient fixtures, provided inherently by a green building, are simple, direct fixes and one of many examples on how these types of constructions can help curb some of these losses of resources.

2) All of the six GCC countries currently rank in the top eleven countries with highest carbon emissions per capita in the world (World Bank 2014). One of the main culprits for their high ranking is their intense electricity usage, in part by inefficient buildings that require extreme amounts of power for cooling, accounting for nearly 50 per cent of their energy usage. Improved building insulation and energy efficient equipment, along with greater reliance on renewable energy sources, all of which are commonly provided in a green building, can significantly help reduce carbon emissions from power generation.

3) Green buildings take into account their placement within a community by giving preference to settling a new construction near existing businesses and community resources. This encourages local economies, along with reducing the carbon emissions from the commute with vehicles. Furthermore, the site selection can help encourage the use of public transportation and other alternative methods, encouraging greater physical mobility with positive health impacts as well as reducing carbon emissions.

Due to these previous issues and others, the GCC countries have noted the development of sustainable construction codes and guidelines as a national development priority. Some headway has been made in some nations, with the United Arab Emirates (UAE) ranking in 2014 as the ninth country in the world, not counting the United States, in total amount of building area based on cumulative gross square meters that is LEED certified (USGBC 2014). Qatar and Saudi Arabia also have their share of unique green buildings, with large university campuses holding world rankings for the largest number of Platinum certified buildings in one location or largest university campus in the world to be LEED certified, respectively. Besides a few examples, however, not much headway has been made into making these construction types the norm in all GCC countries. The State of Qatar, for example, highlights in its national development strategy that a shift to sustainable construction is essential for achieving its 2030 Vision (GSDP 2011). However, as of 2014, only new government building designs have had to follow these codes.

The emergence of green buildings in the GCC

The modern idea of green buildings can be linked to the growth in the GCC countries that took place in the early 2000s due to high oil and natural gas prices, as well as the increased publicity for green buildings occurring in the United States and the United Kingdom during that same time. The large availability of construction projects, especially in the UAE, caused numerous foreign design firms to set base in the region, which henceforth influenced building construction. Architects flocked from various parts of the world, most significantly from the United States and United Kingdom, bringing with them their knowledge of existing green building standards. It is important to note that energy and water usage or carbon emission reductions were not requirements at first given by the building owners of the GCC. Several of the architects and engineers bidding for projects in the region found in the Arabian Gulf a unique opportunity to enhance not only the name of their clients, but also their own firms, by pushing boundaries suggesting bold designs aimed at achieving higher standards and green building certification. This idea of achieving renown in building design and performance, perhaps called 'bragging rights' over other companies and countries, has been an essential decision-making element continually 'sold' to many building owners in the GCC. For example, in Qatar, the possibility of having 'the largest collection in the world of LEED Platinum buildings in one university campus' was, based on personal communications between the author and his colleagues, an essential element that drove the selection process of the design firm and helped maintain targets of one of their most iconic construction projects.

One of the first green buildings of the GCC was the Pacific Controls headquarters in Jebel Ali, in the Emirate of Dubai in the UAE. The building was awarded the LEED Platinum certification by the United States Green Building Council in 2006. Bahrain followed with the Bahrain World Trade Center in 2007, a significant landmark of the green building movement in the GCC and the world. It did not seek any green building certification but, with its three large wind turbines, it was the first building in the world to have a building-integrated wind turbine system. Amongst the list of first certified green building projects in the region are projects such as the Kuwait English School, in Kuwait City, and Wafi City, in Dubai. Once again, these early buildings, and so many still today, were erected not simply to reduce energy or water usage but out of desire to surpass standards and bring fame to the organisation or building owner. Some buildings or large projects never left the blueprint, such as the Bahrain University City.

While the number of registered projects in the various green building standard websites can evidence the presence of green buildings, it is important to note that the idea of sustainable and efficient design has been present in the Arabian Gulf region for quite some time. In the times before the discovery of oil and natural gas, it was common for houses to be built according to the orientation of the movement of the sun, to maximise daylight, as well as to include passive design concepts that served as insulation such as recessed windows and thick mud walls. Buildings were placed in close proximity to each other so that shade could be used as a cooling technique. Families shared smaller homes and water conservation was a basic ethic. Among the various passive green building technologies, one truly stood out: the wind tower. The wind tower was an airflow unit, which helped ventilate and cool a house during the hot months. Using very simple construction characteristics, the tower was simply a common tower with an inner shaft and four inlets at the top, one for each wind direction (north, south, east and west). Wind hit the top of the tower and immediately made a sharp curve, flowing down a cement shaft, cooling the air along the way. The cool air reached the bottom of the tower and helped maintain the temperature of the room.

The discovery of oil and natural gas in the various GCC countries, along with the establishment and maintenance of the social contracts to support its political regimes, encouraged governments to provide free or nearly free water and electricity as well as other resources to its citizens and all individuals living in their countries. For example, the residential cost of electricity per kilowatt-hour is approximately US dollar 3 cents in Qatar and 6 cents in the UAE, in comparison with over 13 cents in the United States (EIA 2014). The cost of water in Qatar is USD1.20 per cubic meter (Qatar General Electricity & Water Corporation 2014). While the provision of essential resources by a country to its citizens can be laudable, these allowances for utilities in turn have led to a most inefficient building era, which was based on the overt, unintentional, basic idea that usage of water and electricity should not be taken into account in the design, construction or operation of a building. This disregard for resource management led, for example, to the extreme usage of air conditioning units as cooling element of a house. This is seen even in somewhat comic and superfluous uses, such as cooling outdoor water tanks. In the GCC of today, the intelligence of the passive sustainable concepts like the use of shade or the wind tower serves only as decorations and memories of a time long past. A shift to more intelligent building design is essential if these countries are to make the leap to a new, lasting, economy that is not solely reliant on fossil fuels.

Green building standards of the GCC

Nearly a decade after the first LEED certified building in the region, the GCC boasts not only many more registered and certified buildings in both LEED and BREEAM, but several countries also have their own certification standard. The development of such codes can be seen as a move to show to the world that the GCC can also create knowledge, as opposed to just being simple users or copiers of Western countries. Furthermore, design firms understood, from experience, that standards like LEED and BREEAM were not originally designed with considerations for extremely hot climate areas or regions with lower-than-usual construction resources such as stone, wood or metal.

The Emirate of Abu Dhabi, in the UAE, developed its own set of guidelines called Estidama. The word Estidama means 'sustainability' in the Arabic language and this set of requirements is not simply a building code. Estidama sets itself as a list of principles that drives the construction of the built environment of this emirate of the UAE and is part of the government's master plan, Plan Abu Dhabi 2030 (Estidama 2014). Inside the Estidama concept there is a green building code, called the Pearl Rating System (PRS), and all Abu Dhabi buildings must achieve its minimum rating of one pearl. Keeping the idea of integrated design in mind, and transferring voluntary building codes to the norm, both Estidama and the PRS can be seen as the most successful of the GCC efforts to transform simple construction standards into integrated legislation that takes into account green building codes. The PRS is unique as it bridges both LEED and BREEAM when it comes to documentation and inspection, requiring vast amounts of information to be collected regarding the building, both before and after construction, with the addition of site visits of an inspector to ensure the facility is truly operating as planned. This is a major difference from LEED, which only requires the online submission of documentation for certification to be reviewed and awarded.

In 2009, the construction company Barwa hired a research centre of the University of Pennsylvania to develop a Qatar-specific green building design standard, which became known as the Qatar Sustainability Assessment System (QSAS). This standard was later renamed the Global Sustainability Assessment System (GSAS), and is now managed by the Gulf Organization for Research and Development (GORD). By having gathered information from nearly 30 of the most well-known green building standards around the world, GSAS has a solid scientific foundation and aims at being used not only in the GCC but by also other countries, hence the switch in the name from QSAS to GSAS (from Qatar to Global).

It can be argued that the development of country-specific certification codes is related to abundance of funding, the perceived need for each GCC country to showcase to the world its own developments, and their unfortunate lack of collaboration due to historical tribal competition, considering that developing country-specific codes is 'reinventing the wheel' since these six nations have very close environmental issues, and especially similar climatic patterns. While Bahrain, Kuwait, Oman and Saudi Arabia do not have any codes of their own, discussions are taking place in all these countries for the development of country-specific codes.

News articles reference the visit from representatives of GORD, the developers of GSAS, to encourage the use of its standard in Kuwait (Balbo 2012), as well as assessments under way for the potential development of a country-specific set of guidelines. A report to the National Committee of Building Codes of Kuwait in 2012 discussed the benefits of such a programme, and identified that most of its members had experience with either GSAS, LEED or BREEAM (Al-Sayegh 2012). In Bahrain, news articles from late 2012 mention the interest of the Central Municipal Council in embedding international green building practices in the country's construction codes, and that a new set of guidelines would be released sometime in early 2013 (*Trade Arabia* 2012). Oman does not currently have a country-specific code nor does it enforce any international code, however technical material from a major construction company informs that there is interest in the development of such programmes or codes (Courtney-Hatcher *et al.* 2013). Saudi Arabia is unique in choosing to simply suggest that all buildings comply with LEED requirements. This is not a mandate at the moment, however in a meeting of the Saudi Green Building Council in 2013, it was announced that over 200 Saudi engineers were becoming LEED Accredited Professionals and that the Kingdom would begin to enforce green standards in all its new construction (McCullough 2014).

It is argued that challenges in the dissemination and use of local standards, such as the GSAS or the PRS, are linked to their lack of foreign recognition and the potential bias in the award of certification. Both LEED and BREEAM are known and have been widely used worldwide, while GSAS or PRS have not. This is the case for Qatar Foundation and its LEED projects. Even though the head office of GORD, the developer of GSAS, is based on the Qatar Foundation campus, the construction division of the latter has consistently informed designers that all buildings must minimally follow LEED Gold rating requirements. The bias or fairness in certification issue is related to the small number of registered projects. There is a possibility that companies or individuals applying for building certification with GSAS and those overseeing the certification know each other, making the process unfair and influenced by relationships as opposed to true building performance. Questions of transparency and accurate rating could be asked of the large development of Lusail, owned by Barwa, the parent construction company which paid for the development of QSAS before the creation of GORD. This is the same for Estidama and its PRS. The LEED standard, on the other hand, has a multitude of experts from various parts of the world and works with blind document submissions, making it impossible for someone submitting a project for certification to know or even directly contact the expert conducting the assessment.

Green building councils

In the United States, green building councils serve as meeting points for those interested in further developing their skills in sustainable design, showcasing best practices in construction, as well as for lobbying groups to discuss how to push forward the green building agenda within their local or national legislative bodies. For example, the Cascadia Green Building Council, in the State of Oregon, used to produce a study guide for individuals interested in earning the credential of LEED Accredited Professionals as a means to fundraise for their operations, as well as other educational online tools. Furthermore, this council was instrumental in moving legislation forward to embed green building guidelines into the construction codes of their state. Green building councils in the GCC countries originated differently, and also serve a different purpose.

Since 2007, there has been an observed increase in the presence of interest groups and educational events on the topic of green buildings in the GCC countries. This increased activity can be compared to the arrival of more design firms, bringing individuals who were seeking to further their knowledge about the field as well as to share information on common issues being faced in GCC projects.

Currently, in Qatar, there is an organisation called Qatar Green Building Council, which was founded in 2009 (QGBC 2014a). Based on the website of the organisation, the Council's goals are to disseminate the usage of any green building code in Qatar, as well as provide educational opportunities and help further the sustainable construction agenda in the country. The organisation began as an informal networking group chaired by the previous chief executive officer of the Msheireb Properties (previously DohaLand) group, which the author of this chapter used to attend. Today, it has become a semi-governmental organisation, with its own building (also at the Education City campus), several high profile board and founding members, and a cadre of permanently funded staff members. While not formally associated with any green building certification standard, its board members are directly linked and funded by Qatar Foundation, which has a commitment to build according to LEED Gold as opposed to the local standard GSAS. It encompasses several meeting and discussion groups, called 'interest groups', each with a different mission and whose members meet frequently (QGBC 2014b).

All other GCC countries also have their distinct green building groups, with the UAE being the most unique with the Emirates Green Building Council, which was founded in 2006 and serves all the various states of that country, providing training events and conferences. It does not sponsor one building code but suggests the use of BREEAM, LEED or PRS. Both Kuwait and Saudi Arabia have been noticed organising local conferences to discuss the topic of sustainable construction, such as the Kuwait Green Building Forum of 2013 and a GSAS training in Saudi Arabia in early 2014.

Being funded or sponsored by governments means that green building councils in the GCC serve a more educational and social function as opposed to a place for civil society to organise and engage with governments to further green building legislation. Conferences and classes are frequently organised to showcase local and visiting professionals, or on a rare occasion, inform about a new local concept. One of these elements has been the work done by the Qatar Green Building Council on a passive house for Qatar, which uses the internationally known German *Passivhaus* concept, along with being designed according to GSAS.

Sustainable neighbourhood developments

Along with the increased appearance of green buildings in the Arabian Gulf, there has also been a growing notion of sustainable cities or developments. These mega projects originated around 2006, during the peak of oil prices, at the same time as the various Palm islands developed in the Emirate of Dubai in the UAE. The GCC countries are, each in their own way, trying to be at the forefront of sustainable construction by promoting green cities with new commercial land development companies, creating country-specific green building standards and aiming to break world rankings with advanced building performance.

Masdar City, on the outskirts of Abu Dhabi, in the UAE, was the first to appear, in 2006. It is argued that it originated as a reaction to negative press this country received due to the assumed massive environmental impact caused by other large construction projects in the UAE. However, other sources suggest that it surfaced as another way to help Abu Dhabi gain further international recognition and acceptance via the environmental movement (Reiche 2010). Masdar City is not the first mega city of its type in the world, but it has been lauded by some as a true example of sustainable community design due to its size. This development is connected to the Masdar Institute of Science and Technology, a higher education institution awarding degrees in various engineering fields. Masdar City aimed to be a carbon-neutral development with nearly 100,000 daily commuters, 40,000 of those being residents of the city itself. Early projections suggested that the city would be completed by 2016. However, due to the financial crisis of 2008 and subsequent budget cuts, new targets point to the city being ready sometime between 2020 and 2025 (Attwood 2010).

The next development, first called DohaLand, appeared in 2008 as a means to reshape the old downtown area of Doha. With over 100 buildings and now called Msheireb, this project has its buildings achieving at least LEED Certified and many LEED Gold and aims to be the largest collection of LEED buildings anywhere in the world. As of 2014, only three buildings were nearing completion and a school, Qatar Academy Msheireb, was also not completed but already had plans to hire teaching staff that same year. The Msheireb community is more like a real estate development than a carbon-neutral city like Masdar, while using the LEED brand to verify its performance. One main criticism of the Msheireb Downtown Doha project has been its impact on the population who previously lived in the current construction area. Thousands of shop owners and workers have struggled to find new homes as this new sustainable construction project progresses (Badawi 2014).

Education City, an educational campus located on the outskirts of Doha, is another complex focused on sustainable design. Its early master plan did not require world-famous architects such as Arata Isozaki and Ricardo Legorreta, to follow green building codes. However, since 2007, all its buildings need to be designed to achieve LEED Gold. In its final phase, the City will be a car-free campus with an advanced bicycle-share system, a tram system and home to a large solar energy testing facility in its science and technology park. Buildings designed prior to 2007 are now being retrofit with solar panels with the aim of producing around 15 per cent of the energy needs of each building.

One example from Saudi Arabia is the massive King Abdullah University of Science and Technology (KAUST), which received Platinum rating in 2010 and, at that time, was the largest LEED project in the world in terms of its total built area. Bahrain also intended to build a sustainability-focused university city, called Euro University, as plans were announced in 2005 (ITP 2005). While the expected completion was 2007, as of 2014, no more information on the project could be found, indicating that it most likely did not go forward. While these examples are interestingly unique to the GCC and seek to provide an example to the world, many question their portability not only to other regions, but also to other parts of the GCC, especially due to their high cost. Furthermore, as of

2014, none of these large mega green cities were completely finished so that common users could test their various expected impacts.

Case study: Qatar Foundation Student Housing

In 2007, Qatar Foundation began the design of a new university student housing facility to support its main umbrella university, Hamad bin Khalifa University, on its campus, Education City. This new facility, completed in late 2013, was intended to house 1,200 students attending one of its various international branch universities that provide undergraduate and graduate degrees in Doha. Students who attend this campus come from over 65 countries, mainly from Qatar, the Arab countries, and also India and Pakistan. Based on communications with various early project members, this iconic collection of buildings was the first in Qatar that sought to achieve Platinum rating according to LEED and was designed by engineering firm Burns & McDonnell and Treanor Architects, both from the United States.

The project architects and engineers informed that the student housing project sought to maximise water efficiency by using various types of low-flow elements, as well as installing the first grey water filtration system in Qatar. Water used in showers and room sinks is filtrated in a container-size grey water system then used for irrigation, toilet flushing and for display water fountains. The electricity usage of the complex is offset by nearly 15 per cent renewable energy, with approximately 12 per cent originating from photovoltaic (PV) panels and 3 per cent from wind turbines. Furthermore, this collection of 12 buildings boasts a unique, thick insulation system, aimed at maintaining a tight building envelope helping reduce its electricity consumption from air conditioning needs. The project also achieved points for sourcing local materials, with all its stone originating from within 800 kilometres from the site, coming from Oman, Saudi Arabia and Iran.

The facility is commonly known for being a highly complex project due to being the first endeavour seeking LEED certification in Qatar. For nearly two years, the construction division of Qatar Foundation, called Capital Projects, in its role as the project owner, spent time holding workshops for contractors as means to build capacity and help identify a company to construct the buildings. In the end, the construction phase was deemed so complex that it had to be split into two parts: an enabling works phase, focused on grounds preparation, foundation and structure; and a main works phase, aimed at the mechanical, electrical, plumbing and fit-out elements.

On-going discussions with engineers from the construction companies from both phases highlighted the challenge of building the first LEED Platinum buildings in Qatar. Some of these difficulties were the lack of experience of the construction workers on how to handle requirements, such as waste segregation, installation of delicate bamboo wooden flooring and the ban on smoking inside or in the vicinity of the building. Furthermore, the extra requirements of document tracking to comply with LEED submittals had not been done by these contractors in Qatar. Due to the lack of interest from contractors because of the abundant availability of easier construction projects in the region, as well as the lack of experienced contractors, the project was delayed by nearly two years and was only fully occupied in July 2014, nearly five years after breaking ground.

Post-construction issues have been observed with the maintenance and upkeep of complex equipment. For example, early in the occupancy of the building, the grey water filtration system was damaged due to a mistake by an untrained technician. This first caused a water outage and later the need to use common city tap water for over a week to address the needs of the building. Second, the campus electricians are not used to maintaining either solar panels or wind turbines, nor do they have the experience or information to ensure that the renewable energy is being produced at the expected rate. Contracts with foreign firms are necessary to check and maintain these new pieces of equipment. Another issue is the maintenance of the green cleaning programme, as such products are not easily accessible in Qatar and custodial staff requires extra training on the handling of the equipment. Users also complain, expecting the traditional, flowery scent commonly found in places after they are cleaned, which is not the case when using green cleaning products. Furthermore, elements like a parking lot spot to be used for low-emissions vehicles or carpool vans are often misused as individuals cannot buy such a car type and are not used to carpooling practices. Finally, the building users are still adapting to the various conservation aspects that require their action. One of these is the room electricity activation, which is turned on when students place their room key cards in a slot near the room door. Residents frequently leave other cards when they leave the room, trying to maintain certain lights on, therefore bypassing the system and causing unnecessary electricity waste. Another element is the participation in the recycling programme. Due to a requirement with all LEED buildings, this facility collects paper, plastic, cardboard, glass and aluminium. However, at the time of writing, participation in the programme was still low. Students living in the complex frequently ask the staff if the recyclables collected are truly being sent to recycling plants, as they do not fully believe this occurs in the Arabian Gulf.

Challenges and barriers for green building development

While there may be challenges with equipment availability and operational knowledge, perhaps the most concerning element hindering the construction of green buildings in the region is related to the support and directives from the government. In general, the cost of building a green building is still not facilitated by policies, exemptions or rebates, making it so that sustainable projects become a boutique item as opposed to a standard. An exception to this case is Abu Dhabi, where the Estidama guidelines are helping re-shape the construction market. One of the main issues with the lack of government efforts is connected to the energy and water policies and price subsidies given to the residents of GCC countries. In some countries, residential or commercial buildings owned by citizens as well as government facilities will never see a bill for their usage of water or electricity. This practice not only encourages their increased usage, which leads to more environmental degradation and financial costs, but it also fails to set an encouraging tone for the reduction of the usage of resources. In many countries outside of the GCC, the idea of saving money due to using less water and electricity is sufficient to incline some to build green.

Furthermore, the lack of cooperation from local production and transmission organisations plays a significant role in this problem. For example, the electricity company of Qatar, KAHRAMAA, does not allow for electricity to be put back into the grid, which is an essential element for the installation of a renewable energy source like PV cells or wind turbines. This practice forces anyone considering renewables to also have to pay a premium on a large battery system, so that all energy produced on site stays on site. In Qatar especially, this issue will have to be tackled by the designers and builders of the stadiums for the 2022 football World Cup, as all facilities have a requirement to produce on-site renewable energy. Finally, even if electricity could be sent back into the grid, the challenge of low-cost electricity due to subsidies will also make the renewables market not interesting for investment. Simple return-on-investment calculations are usually based on a 7–20-year pay-back time, however, which given the above-mentioned challenges means that those wanting to build green in the GCC may find themselves with much longer pay-back time, making it unfeasible for the large expansion of this market. Site-specific solutions can make this work in a neighbourhood or area, such as Masdar or Education City, since they may rely on their independent status to develop a common, shared energy grid. However, they are not applicable to the common homeowners in those countries.

Surrounding infrastructure and associated businesses to support the green building movement are also lacking in the GCC. For example, in LEED, it is a requirement for any building applying for certification to collect general waste along with recyclables like paper, plastic, cardboard, glass and aluminium. In Qatar, for example, there are only two small paper-recycling plants, as well as one for plastic and one for aluminium. No company currently processes glass, forcing anyone wanting to collect this item to ship it to another country for processing once they have collected enough to fill a shipping container. Stores that sell equipment for solar panels or grey water filtration systems are also not widely available and operate on a monopoly and 'boutique' style, once again driving prices up. Intelligent technology, like smart metering, began being installed in Abu Dhabi in 2010 and Qatar in 2013. However, this trend is being driven by the power companies who are paying for the installation of the equipment (Nassouri 2010; Siemens 2012). The issue of availability of construction materials for green buildings has also been highlighted by a GCC forum of construction companies (Omar 2014). During the forum, various GCC officials encouraged the issue of collaboration, and there was even a promising announcement of a survey to develop a sustainable materials outlook in the region that would cover over 400 companies.

Lastly, the lack of conservation policies in most countries and the lack of enforcement of consumption reduction policies in others, on top of poor-quality awareness campaigns, are also hindering the development of these types of constructions. One example is Qatar, where local officials have publicly discussed how difficult it is to enforce local conservation codes, which are very strict and have existed since 2008 (Scott 2014). An increase in fines is being considered (Khatri 2014). Nevertheless, the resource usage issue in the GCC begs the question of whether people would indeed reduce resource consumption in such wealthy countries, given the high average income levels. Furthermore, the local electricity and water companies do not publish a set list of energy-saving light bulbs that one should use for a reduced electricity bill, nor an educated data-driven programme to incentivise a family to reduce consumption. Reduction programmes have been mostly linked to publicity campaigns with very little or no impact. One of those is the Tarsheed campaign, which has been launched twice, and even so both water and electricity consumption in households in Qatar has continued to rise. This has even been announced by the Ministry of Energy and Industry (*Doha News* 2013). Moreover, utilities consumption in Qatar is expected to increase by over 50 per cent by 2022 (Kemp 2014). Awareness programmes that analyse usage, comparing pre- and post-campaign electricity or water data, would especially benefit the government, given that it would enable saving of large amounts of financial and environmental resources.

Conclusion

All the GCC countries have tremendous potential to be role models as it relates to the green economy concept. They have relatively young nations, and their governments are interested in leaving a mark and becoming role models to the world. If well planned, green buildings could serve well in this journey to ensure that the GCC states' financial and development wellbeing are maintained well past the age of oil and natural gas. To be able to achieve these goals, there are a number of limitations that need to be addressed first. Required actions include the following:

1) A major overhaul in the subsidies for water and electricity must occur. Currently, the GCC countries provide these basic resources at very low cost, so that there is little encouragement for individuals and businesses to choose water and electricity conservation and green building technology, over traditional, business-as-usual methods. Return on investment must make sense.
2) Government buildings and planning codes must shift to more detailed and sustainability-focused guidelines that incorporate norms from these local or international voluntary green building standards. So far, the State of Qatar has informed that all new government buildings must comply with a local green building code, and that residential and commercial buildings must comply after 2016. The Emirate of Abu Dhabi, in the UAE, also included a green building code in its Estidama guidelines, and is making strides to ensure that local construction codes embed these practices. Similar practices should be undertaken by other GCC nations as well.

3) Power companies should leap forward and update their practices, equipment and codes, encouraging distributed power generation and allowing users to send electricity 'back into the grid'. This practice will encourage renewable energy investment by both businesses and individuals. The current inability to feed electricity to the grid is a major roadblock for the installation of renewable energy sources, which in turn are key to ensure a post-oil, green economy.

4) Governments must provide information as well as incentives on the use of green building technology, such as low interest loans for the purchase of renewable energy equipment or the installation of a grey water filtration system. The GCC countries should also encourage greater collaboration between each other on the trade of goods and construction materials, with a higher focus on green building-related goods.

5) Collaboration between already established codes of the region is a must. The GCC is a small region, with its countries and states sharing many similarities. The development of niche codes, like Estidama and its PRS, and the GSAS, while laudable, only increases competition between 'brands' and reduces the overall efficacy of regional standards.

References

Al-Sayegh, Alia. 2012. 'Overview on the Development of Green Building Codes for Kuwait.' Presented at the Forum on Green Buildings, College of Technologies Studies, Kuwait City, Kuwait, 27 March. http://www.paaet.edu.kw/mysite/Portals/88/Files/Alia_AlSayegh1.pdf

Attwood, Ed. 2010. 'Masdar to Delay Final Completion Until at Least 2020.' *Arabian Business*, 10 October. http://www.arabianbusiness.com/

Badawi, Nada. 2014. 'Expat Workers in Musheireb Struggle with New Electricity Cuts.' *Doha News*, 8 April. http://dohanews.co/

Balbo, Laurie. 2012. 'Qatar's GSAS Turns Other Rating Systems Green.' *Green Prophet*, 22 June. http://www.greenprophet.com/

Courtney-Hatcher, David, Steven Tee, Dianne Hamilton and James Barton. 2013. *Construction and Projects in Oman: An Overview*. Construction and projects. Multi-jurisdictional Guide 2013/14. Practical Law Company.

Doha News. 2013. 'Water, Electricity Consumption in Qatar Jump Amid Efforts to Reduce Usage.' 6 February. http://dohanews.co/

EIA. United States Energy Information Administration. 2014. *Electric Power Monthly*. Updated on 27 October. http://www.eia.gov/electricity/monthly/

EPA. United States Environmental Protection Agency. 2014. 'Green Building.' Updated 9 October. http://www.epa.gov/

Estidama. 2014. 'Frequently Asked Questions.' Accessed 24 October. http://estidama.upc.gov.ae/

GSDP. General Secretariat for Development Planning of Qatar. 2009. *Qatar's Second Human Development Report: Advancing Sustainable Development*. Doha: GSDP, July.

GSDP. 2011. *Qatar National Development Strategy 2011–2016: Towards Qatar National Vision 2030*. Doha: GSDP.

ITP. 2005. 'Bahrain Set to Build Multi Million-Dollar Green City.' *ITP.net*, 11 June. http://www.itp.net/

Kemp, Kim. 2014. 'Qatar Water Demand to Increase by 56.5%.' *Construction Week Online*, 30 September. http://www.constructionweekonline.com/

Khatri, Shabina. 2014. 'Qatar Mulls Doubling Penalty for Water Wastage to QR 20,000.' *Doha News*, 3 October. http://dohanews.co/

Korkmaz, Sinem. 2009. 'A Review of Green Building Movement Timelines in Developed and Developing Countries to Build an International Adoption Framework.' Paper presented at the Fifth International Conference on Construction in the 21st Century (CITC-V), Istanbul, Turkey, 20–22 May. http://www.cedbik.org/images/kaynak/citc-v-finalpaper1.pdf

McCullough, Deborah. 2014. 'Saudi Arabia's Green Degree Brings Hopes of Sustainability.' *The Guardian*, 12 May. http://www.theguardian.com/

Nassouri, Saeed. 2010. 'Smart Metering Initiative ADWEA Program.' Presentation. December. http://www.metering.com/wp-content/uploads/Saeed_Nassouri.pdf

Omar, Ebrahim. 2014. 'Gulf Construction Experts Urge Green Practices, Better Regulation.' *Al-Shorfa*, 21 April. http://al-shorfa.com/en_GB/

Qatar General Electricity & Water Corporation. 2014. 'Tariff.' Accessed 24 October. http://www.km.com.qa/

QGBC. Qatar Green Building Council. 2014a. 'Vision & Mission.' Accessed 6 November. http://www.qatargbc.org/

QGBC. 2014b. 'Interest Groups.' Accessed 6 November. http://www.qatargbc.org/

Reiche, Danyel. 2010. 'Renewable Energy Policies in the Gulf Countries: A Case Study of the Carbon-neutral "Masdar City" in Abu Dhabi.' *Energy Policy* 38: 378–382.

Scott, Victoria. 2014. 'Kahramaa Official: Conservation Laws Difficult to Enforce in Qatar.' *Doha News*, 8 January. http://dohanews.co/

Siemens. 2012. 'Siemens Provides Energy Supplier in Qatar with Turnkey Smart Metering Solution.' Press release, 2 April. www.siemens.com/press/en/

Trade Arabia. 2012. 'Bahrain Launches Green Buildings Drive.' 1 July. http://www.tradearabia.com/

USGBC. United States Green Building Council. 2013. 'A Green Economy is a Growth Economy.' *Market Brief*. Accessed 7 November 2014. http://www.usgbc.org/Docs/Archive/General/Docs10759.pdf

USGBC. 2014. 'U.S. Green Building Council Releases Ranking of Top 10 Countries for LEED Outside the U.S.' Accessed 1 May. http://www.usgbc.org/

World Bank. 2014. *World Development Indicators*. Online database. Accessed 24 October. http://data.worldbank.org/data-catalog/world-development-indicators

8 Greening urban transport in the Gulf Cooperation Council countries: localised approaches to modal integration as key success factors

Arnd Bätzner

Introduction

This chapter focuses on different aspects of an integrated Gulf Cooperation Council (GCC) urban transport system based on urban design parameters, taking into account mid- and long-term social, demographic and economic perspectives. Focusing on the constraints that the GCC countries' climatic and cultural distinctions set upon transit design – such as extreme levels in sun radiation, religious constraints, and particularly high expectations regarding comfort and service levels in travel – the limits of best-practice approaches from other contexts are discussed and suggestions are made for their adaptation for GCC countries.

In a systemic approach, special attention is given to 'last mile' coverage between transit hubs and residents' homes without which no sustainable shift to green transportation will be efficient in a long-range perspective. Learnings from other parts of the world also suggest 'door-to-door' offers to be critical for fundamental acceptance by citizens. Intermodality thus needs to be re-thought from a GCC perspective, enabling it to reach up to the precise location of a user at any given time. Some preliminary elements of this are empirically confirmed by recent experiences, for example with the metro and bus network in Dubai.

On an urban scale, proposed solutions must efficiently address current conditions of sprawl and similarly support upcoming efforts to halt and reverse it, densifying settlement areas. It is crucial to understand that green transport is both a key driver of, and a prerequisite for, green cities. A brief discussion of perceptions and particularities of Gulf urbanism in this chapter will point towards a set of distinctive features that will impact design aspects and functionalities of urban transit systems in the region.

Considering the prevailing social and economic parameters in the GCC states, elements for a fully integrated approach based on last-mile connectivity, linking homes to high-capacity rail transit, are proposed, combined with a network of shaded walk- and bikeways and urban design interventions such as increased densification. Recommended components include shared vehicles and last-mile door-to-door shuttles. It is also crucial that this network be fully interconnected between modes in order to maximise its potential benefits, reducing or eliminating congestion thus ultimately contributing to securing the GCC's economic competitiveness on a global scale.

Transportation design and Gulf urbanism

Urban transport in large parts of the GCC member states today is almost entirely dependent on the use of private motor vehicles. This increasingly leads to undesirable secondary effects, such as heavy congestion, loss of time and over-consumption of resources, but also the perpetuation of a car-dependent design of the built environment. As such, transportation, by its connection to virtually every aspect of daily life, stands in the focus and at the crossroads of many of the challenges that Gulf societies face in terms of a transition to greener, more live-able environments centred around long-term perspectives for a family-oriented, twenty-first century Gulf modernism and globally competitive conditions for business developments.

Given that the *status quo* is unsustainable both in terms of energy use and spatial planning, it calls for solutions that raise the efficiency and attractive-ness of GCC city spaces. Future urban design concepts need to function under the special social and cultural conditions of the GCC. Key success factors include feasibility under the given climatic conditions and result-oriented aspects, such as coverage of the entire door-to-door travel chain, travel time savings over car-based solutions, a high standard of social acceptance, and a level of comfort on par with expectations and standards derived from other areas of daily life.

For any novel ground transport concept to offer ease of use and good accessibility, it can be inspired by experiences in other parts of the world but needs to take them further, developing localised solutions adapted to GCC-specific needs. One of the key suggestions made in this chapter is a novel on-demand, short response-time paratransit service, that is, a demand-responsive, highly flexible local transport offer allowing for an easy access to high-capacity transportation modes such as urban rail. The idea behind this is to turn transport into a commodity available literally at resi-dents' doorstep and at any demanded frequency. A blend of a 'black car'-style luxury minibus and an upscale hotel shuttle, the availability of such a service as a com-plement to upmarket mass transit is a prerequisite for the reduction of private car use, and eventually car ownership. It is the missing link between homes and transit stations that act as local transportation hubs, ultimately reacting to existing deficits in the built environment, primarily urban sprawl. In denser populated areas and for short-distance links, a series of complementary designs, such as covered, ventilated walk- and bikeways, are proposed. While these primarily act as intra-neighbourhood links, they can also provide access to transit stations wherever a reasonable exten-sion of station catchment areas can be achieved.

Also, declared government ambitions in the Gulf tourism sector call for power-ful urban transport solutions that support growth of the sector beyond its current limitations, giving it a broader regional scope: the GCC states' high-capacity air travel infrastructure needs a complement on the ground.

Based on the opportunities of the GCC states' geographical position, economic development agendas and tourist attractions, any transportation planning will have to comply with, anticipate and support various existing and upcoming spatial developments. Derived from these is the need to define mid-term territorial strategies in a trans-national GCC master plan. Both urbanised areas as well as major tourist sites need to be either destinations or hubs in a future ground transportation network. Transportation planning thus receives a role as a major spatial development tool. Focusing the development of housing, industrial, business and tourism facilities along the axes defined by transport infrastructure and transport availability is a prerequisite for a shift towards greener economies in the Gulf region.

Previous analysis of current and forecasted urban mobility in GCC states shows that the overall reduction of vehicle miles travelled is a target that will translate into significant improvements in trip times, and liveability of both urban and suburban territories, as well as energy savings, in line with mid-term development schemes declared by political leaders.

The following chapter starts by giving a short overview of results from previous literature on urban transport in the GCC states relevant for the questions raised. In the subsequent section, some particularities of Gulf urbanism, as highlighted in previous architectural discussions, are highlighted. Based on these insights, the suitability of different transport solutions and modes is discussed, and the necessity for full integration is underlined.

Urban transport in the GCC: *status quo*

Forecasts for the Middle East and North Africa region see an urban population growth of 25 per cent by 2020, with over 80 per cent of the GCC population residing in cities by that year (Muttoo 2010). The past years have seen several initiatives aimed at increasing the liveability of the region's urban centres through deployment of transit systems. The launch of the Emirate of Dubai's Metro in 2009 and the subsequent introduction of a complementing public bus network sparked off rapid growth in ridership, resulting in over 10 million passenger trips per month taken in 2014 on the two rail lines (RTA 2014). Saudi Arabia's Makkah Metro is also of a high-capacity design with an hourly capacity of up to 80,000 patrons needed for the *Hajj* pilgrimage (Muttoo 2010). This sets the pace for other projects: while the trans-GCC railway is currently under construction, with its first segment open (see the section on the GCC railway), the regional linkage it creates cuts per-passenger carbon dioxide (CO_2) emissions by up to 90 per cent in comparison to air travel (ibid.). Beyond this, to augment its impact, the railway will need to be complemented by a performing and coordinated urban transport offer. Muttoo (ibid.) refers to calculations by the Gulf Research Center indicating that expected yearly CO_2 reductions by Dubai Metro alone amount to 1.6 million metric tonnes.

It is important to note that a broad acceptance of transit requires educational efforts. Riding transit and planning daily activities accordingly is part of a lifestyle that users have to adopt and the inherent advantages of which they have to discover, as illustrated by the Dubai Roads and Transport Authority (RTA) Director of Rail Operations Mohammed Al Mudharreb who has referred to 'people [that] have started to perceive and grasp the benefits and advantages of using mass transit systems, including the psychological and physical relief in having smooth mobility' (*Gulf News* 2014). The ultimate goal would be to have the use of transit accepted as a social norm, with private vehicle use limited to functions that cannot be covered by public transportation or to situations where it brings a net advantage for the user's comfort. To achieve this, transit offers need to be perceived as attractive and their usage as socially desirable, which directly translates into quality standards and service levels that are to be met.

One of the key success factors behind the Dubai Metro is the development of novel approaches in careful consideration of social, economic and cultural parameters, the most prominent of which is the declared luxury layout of the entire system that includes air-conditioned walkways from parking structures to stations and a first class titled Gold Class. While Elsheshtawy and Al Bastaki (2011), in their research on Dubai Metro, find the upscale layout of the system reflecting 'no attempt at subtlety', they draft a remarkable long-term social expectation, namely: 'yet even with this focus on grandeur and spectacle there is still the possibility … that the Metro will indeed cater to the city's various social classes and that it will somehow unify the disparate districts constituting its urban fabric' (ibid., 3). Indeed, RTA's consequent linkage of transport modes, the expansion of its bus network and unified ticketing are all factors working in this direction. Similar design innovations have facilitated in partially overcoming the social stigma of the transit bus, namely that bus patrons are mainly low-income groups with no other choice of transportation – a bias that had previously contributed to an almost total lack of interest in public transportation by the middle classes.

A decade ago, when the Sharjah–Dubai intercity bus service was first introduced, riders mainly came from shared taxis, not from private cars (*Gulf News* 2004), which implicitly indicates that bus ridership mainly consisted of workers who did not drive due to lack of access to a car or for financial reasons. RTA Dubai, on the other hand, sees the fact that about 80 per cent of metro patrons do not own a car as a proof of the metro's positive effect on the decrease of private car ownership (*Gulf News* 2013). While the interurban bus service's impact on motorised traffic at the time of its introduction was considered 'slight', ten years later ridership has reached an average of 17,000 passengers per day (ibid.). The deployment of Dubai's touch-and-go public transport access card, 'Noi', to interurban routes signals a paradigm shift: integrated ticketing means easier accessibility for riders, better visibility of the offer and, for operators and planners, better tracking of passenger streams. The Sharjah–Dubai buses illustrate that if transit is to have significant effects on modal choice and incentivise behavioural change, it needs to offer smooth and integrated connections between urban, interurban and international routes. Understanding the success factors for urban mobility thus requires a broad view including peri- and interurban travel. It cannot be uncoupled from the understanding of intercity buses, intercity rail and, particularly in the GCC, the development of regional aviation. The latter currently is, despite its lack of environmental sustainability especially on short routes, one of the primary means of intra-GCC travel and is itself facing a whole set of capacity-related challenges (see the section on Gulf airspace development).

Also in this context, it is important to note that transit cannot be successful without proper integration of its conception with urban redevelopment. Elsheshtawy and Al Bastaki (2011, 5) point out that Dubai's RTA has 'embarked on an extensive study involving … transit-oriented development, inspired by world-wide practices'. Dubai continues to set the pace in terms of innovative public transport in the GCC: its first tram line was opened in November 2014. The highly positive results from Dubai have inspired Abu Dhabi and Qatar, among others, to develop comparable strategies for integrated public transport network with heavy urban rail as their backbone, and have led to similar projects being aggressively driven forward in Kuwait and Bahrain (updated from: Global Mass Transit 2009).

Gulf urbanism: specificities and infrastructural challenges

In its contemporary form, urbanism in the GCC region comes in two major flavours: suburban sprawl and representative business district landmarks. As in many rapidly expanding cities in the world, the drain on existing infrastructure increasingly becomes challenging in terms of providing capacities, and dealing with spatial and environmental constraints of underperforming or underdeveloped utilities and transport systems, their development not having in many cases kept pace with observed growth in population and wealth. The gross domestic product (GDP) per capita in the GCC states is among the highest in the world (CIA 2014). It contributes to a largely car-dependent lifestyle that in a historical perspective used to mimic what is widely perceived as material expression of an 'American dream', but is better described as a globally observable, middle-class' *clichéd* and often naïvely backwards-oriented notion of a desirable daily life. Lacking economic as well as ecological sustainability, the part of GCC urbanism that is dominating by surface is largely based on the elements of a suburban lifestyle, such as free-standing scattered homes, made possible by the availability of comparably cheap land and fossil fuels, which in turn catalyses associated phenomena such as big box retailing and the absence of adequate transit offers. It leads to increased demand for travel, translating into traffic jams, or even permanent gridlocks, paralysing conurbations and seriously affecting economic performance. Learning from structurally comparable dynamics previously observed in other parts of the world – for example Asian metropolises such as Bangkok, Jakarta and virtually all larger cities in China – it is obvious that, without adequate governance interventions, addressing the negative externalities of urban sprawl by encouraging densification and retrofitting transit, the GCC states can expect to face serious efficiency and reliability challenges affecting both passenger and freight transportation.

As mentioned, another widely visible aspect of current Gulf urbanism is constituted by landmark buildings in existing or newly created city centres or urban densification areas. Heavily marketed and benefitting from tremendous public attention, it is interesting to ask what the drivers of contemporary GCC 'city-making' are: what creates these new cities' attractiveness for residents and visitors, and how do they cope with infrastructural challenges?

Dutch architect Rem Koolhaas, one of the earliest and most prominent reviewers of contemporary Gulf urbanism, pointed out already in 2006 that some Gulf cities essentially build on elements of a repertoire of established urban prototypes. He cites examples borrowed from originally different environments and their 'urban radicalization' (Koolhaas 2006a) when applied to a GCC context: 'community (themed and gated), hotels (themed), skyscrapers (tallest), shopping centres (largest), airports (doubled)' – linked by public spaces, later extended 'with boutique, museum franchise and masterpiece'. Despite generating 'sometimes disappointing results', he first and foremost identifies 'a farewell performance of an "urban" that has become dysfunctional through sheer age and lack of invention' (Koolhaas 2006b). Lacking the possibility to use established urban forms as a toolbox in the Gulf, Koolhaas thus advocates for an analysis and perception of early twenty-first century Gulf urbanism that be detached from intuitively learned patterns and vocabulary of Western origin. Classifying the 'refusal to take seriously something actually originating in the West and, subsequently, an inability to detect a rising global phenomenon' as a mixture of intellectual laziness and arrogance, Koolhaas (2006a) cites a number of highly unflattering pictures that GCC urbanism has been labelled with even in publications of high renown: 'Lawrence of Suburbia' (Pinkerton 2005); 'Las Vegas in Arabia' (Molavi 2005); 'Skyline on crack' (Toshens 2006); or 'Walt Disney meets Albert Speer' (Davis 2005).

Arguing that contemporary developments in Dubai are highly different from Davis' sinister vision for a Los Angeles destroyed by corporate greed and a lack of civic action (Davis 2002), Koolhaas identifies a pioneering role for Gulf cities, each of which 'has been synthesising versions of the 21st century metropolis and now exports its own versions on an equally colossal scale to parts of the world modernity has not reached so far' (Koolhaas 2006b): if they are to pioneer 'a new kind of urbanism' that is to be exported 'to places immune to or ignored by previous missions of modernism' (ibid.), a specific Gulf urbanism, in consequence, is to become an export product of the GCC economies, generating new types of answers under a specific set of border conditions for which the architectural repertoire as we know it offers no historical models.

This observation is key for assessing the importance that a proper configuration of transportation systems gains for Gulf cities. Efficient urban and regional mobility has been identified as being critical for metropolitan areas to be successful in the decades to come. Thus, GCC urbanism, as understood by Koolhaas, needs to come up with credible, efficient, highly generic and adaptable – in short: customised – solutions in this field, especially if it is to be an archetype for newly and rapidly urbanising areas across the globe.

At this point, a key problem with Koolhaas' 'tabula rasa' theory emerges. Interpreting the United Arab Emirates' (UAE) pavilion at the 2006 Venice Biennale as 'a sign of integration, perhaps, or at least coordination between the different emirates' (ibid.), the timid wording seems to hide the urgency of facts: if the GCC countries want to further progress towards a twenty-first century model region with a strong perception and own identity, true intra-GCC collaboration is to be intensified, making it function on more levels than it does today. From this point of view, the approach of seemingly unlimited extravagance in urban planning is an outdated 1990s-era concept. For almost three decades, it had been a radical marketing tool – brand building by using heavy construction equipment and pouring concrete (ibid.). The result ultimately became self-referential and a tourist attraction by itself. Over time, the principle of 'more' as novelty driver has lost part of its lustre since some of its side effects and the failure to address basic functionality issues have led to serious concerns about the overall concept's sustainability. Today, the insufficient capacity, or total absence, of a transport infrastructure on par with the declared ambitions is one of the major concerns.

In the period 2015–2025, the diversity of political and economic conditions of the surrounding world call for a new perception of the GCC states as a territorial, economic and conceptual entity that, as of today, is a prerequisite for global visibility (ibid.). After two decades of what could be perceived as an urban playground in the most positive sense of the term – with liberties translating, among others, into efficiency and speed of project realisation – a phase of consolidation, integration and coordination is now required, consisting of keeping the strengths while addressing additional dimensions reflecting new priorities.

Under this agenda, a strongly performing intra-GCC transportation system, led by the trans-GCC railway, is one of the most iconic projects. Symbolising integration towards the interior as towards the exterior, it breaks the ground for a set of related measures, going far beyond primary economic efficiencies and deeply into the political and social fields. Koolhaas' assertion that Western media's widespread criticism of the GCC development model in the first financial crisis followed an intention to make it 'a definition of what cannot be done anymore' (ibid.) and be intolerant against 'experimentation that is Dubai or that is the Middle East' (ibid.) tends to hide a much simpler observation. The public criticism – shared by some prominent intellectuals – was less brute 'Dubai bashing' than the expression of a general resentment that, after 20 years of 'radical difference' and 'anything goes' urbanism, a lack of penetrative, up-to-date innovation management that reflects the requirements of the twenty-first century had become obvious.

Infrastructural and economic developments cannot be separated from social and political evolutions. Political stability is the foundation for sustainable economic success. Yet, the draft of a regional network among the GCC states and also within their metropolitan areas remains largely theoretical to date. As Reisz (2010) remarks, a 'collaborative effort among the cities' is not visible as such, but 'an extreme amount of duplication'. Given the declared ambitions of the region in terms of building sustainable futures for the coming age of oil depletion, the present outcome, despite laudable isolated initiatives, to date is still unsatisfactory. The population in the Arab world is expected to grow some 40 per cent over the next two decades, which means roughly 150 million additional people (*The Economist* 2008). In terms of transport, this indicates that existing road infrastructure and any linear extension of it will not be able to cope with the demand to come. Also, social changes will result in demand for individual mobility within the Arab world rising further, resulting in more travellers in absolute numbers, multiplied by the higher number of trips each person will take.

Yet in design and layout of transportation systems, a paradigm shift has happened in recent years. The planned GCC railway running along the Gulf coast and into Oman (see the section on the GCC railway), and metro systems in Medina and Dubai, under construction in Abu Dhabi and sketched in Doha, stand for highly contemporary and successful approaches to urban transport that have been brought to, and implemented in, the Gulf region. For the GCC states to stay at the crossroads of global business, to further modernise their societies, and extend their capacity to welcome travellers, trade partners and tourists from all over the world, individual initiatives in transport planning need to be extended, coordinated, linked and integrated beyond simple 'copy-paste applications'. Similar to Koolhaas' observation that Gulf urbanism needs to detach itself, and be considered detached from, historic models, innovations in GCC transport need to emancipate themselves from previous applications by enhancing them, taking their designs further. Bespoke transportation solutions, such as e-bike-sharing systems combined with shaded bikeways, will no longer be a utopia, but make essential contributions to more liveable Gulf cities, enhancing non-car transport usability and leveraging local connectivity. Bespoke innovations, like Dubai Metro's 'Gold Class' or air-conditioned bus shelters, are not mere 'nice to have' options, but highly serious approaches and critical success factors in tailoring urban transport to local needs. From this point of view, and regarding their potential future application to contexts where similar approaches will be needed, they must now be considered historic models of their own.

GCC tourism and transportation infrastructure

The GCC countries' geo-strategic position as a natural transport hub in an economic 'force field' between Europe and Asia results in a growing number of travellers arriving in, or flying through, the Gulf region. This also allows for active government strategies supporting strong growth rates in exposition, fair and congress tourism, or 'MICE'. Travel times, time shifts and lodging costs can in some cases be significantly reduced by choosing the Gulf region as an event location, especially for events attracting a global audience. The international airports of the GCC region appear as key elements of this strategy, and air infrastructure likewise is the backbone of religious tourism to the Kingdom of Saudi Arabia. Saudi Arabia today is the only GCC state with functioning intercity passenger rail services, whereas other GCC states currently have no high-capacity ground transportation options connecting to airports, with the exception of the Dubai Metro.

Historically, the UAE Emirate of Sharjah was the GCC area where leisure travel took its origins after the first Imperial Airways flight landed in 1932 (Pirie 2009). As noted in the section above, it was, however, neighbouring Dubai that – through lustre and extravagance turned into sights in themselves – pioneered much of today's tourism development in the GCC region, turning itself into a genuine regional model. While the other GCC states have set different accents and identified distinct target groups in the regional and global tourism markets, such as Saudi Arabia's strong focus on religious tourism or Qatar's focus on medical tourism through its master plan for the Hamid bin Khalifa Medical City, great and iconic infrastructure works remain a common identifier that the majority of these projects share.

Given its prototyping role, a brief historical round-up given below for illustrative reasons will focus on key developments in Dubai, admitting that – with local variations, as described previously, and with different degrees of intensity due to differences in policy or in specific target groups among sub-segments of the touristic market – developments in some GCC states, for example in the majority of the UAE's emirates have, from a systemic point of view, taken basically comparable evolutions. As Davidson (2008, 119) explains in a historical analysis of Dubai, 'attracting non-oil related foreign investment and boosting the domestic economy has been Dubai's commitment to building up a luxury international tourist industry since the 1990s'. Destination marketing started out with a high-quality, resort-based 'sun and beach' product for leisure and recreation-oriented vacationers. To follow were healthcare and educational tourism, fuelled by investments in world-class museums, opera houses and discovery offers such as desert trips. Further initiatives included themed parks (such as Ferrari World in Abu Dhabi) and the organisation of seasonal festivals, large-scale events, exhibitions and concerts. Finally, shopping – facilitated by low taxation – and large sports events (such as the 2022 Qatar soccer World Cup) also function as attractors for leisure tourism. In parallel, business tourism is attracted by industry fairs, exhibitions and congresses of global outreach, such as the Arabian Travel Market or Dubai Air Show (based on Davidson 2008).

The above segmentation illustrates that GCC tourism cannot be considered uncoupled from the development of transportation offers and transport infrastructure. Of the touristic sub-segments above, every single one is reliant, in a very specific way, on the availability and reliability of efficient and comfortable transportation.

Also, the typology of visitors is broadening: throughout the late 1990s, incoming leisure tourism in the GCC states focused on the luxury segment. Four- and five-star hotels showed comparably high occupancy rates and housed about two-thirds of all tourists visiting Dubai (ibid.). Local trips were essentially made by private-hire vehicles or taxis, since public transport at that time was rudimentary, essentially consisting of a set of infrequently served bus routes with often no marked pedestrian access to roadside stops. A significant opening of the tourist market to middle-class target groups occurred in the early 2000s, when domestic airline capacities expanded and prices became competitive enough to broaden the customer base. This was also reflected by the opening of the first economy hotel of an international chain in the GCC region: in 2003, the French Accor group opened their first Ibis hotel in Dubai. Others followed quickly in an expansion to other GCC states (Accor 2014). The customer groups targeted by this segment of hotels include a rising number of travellers used to riding transit instead of relying on taxicabs. According to Dubai RTA Director of Rail Operations Mohammed Al Mudharreb, rapidly growing ridership on the Dubai Metro – 12.4 million passengers in August 2014 – is seen as a major contributor to 'boosting tourist activities and … the competitiveness of Dubai in staging international conventions [and] sport events … besides conserving the environment through minimising pollution generated by private vehicles' (*Gulf News* 2014). Greening transport thus appears as a major factor in locally greening tourism.

At this point, it is crucial to understand the role of transportation on a social, non-infrastructural level. In a tourism context, the medium-to-top tier customer segment does not accept transportation to be considered as 'lost time'. Transport, if it is to be attractive, thus needs to be made an integral and credible part of the daily life of a tourist experience. Likewise, a seamlessly integrated transport network will coincidentally have repercussions that strongly affect urban, regional and social development.

The GCC railway: actual status

The Shah–Habshan–Ruwais section of the UAE's Etihad Rail, totalling 270 km which are to be part of the future trans-GCC railway, has been undergoing testing since 2014, with commercial freight operations expected to start in 2015 (Etihad Rail 2014a). Operational management and maintenance have been contracted to Deutsche Bahn, which temporarily transferred 60 German expert staff such as engineers to Abu Dhabi to start up train test runs and operations (Deutsche Bahn 2014). Passenger services, integrated into a trans-GCC network, have been publicly announced but, at the time of writing, no time frame had yet been communicated regarding their introduction (Etihad Rail 2014b). In a historical comparison, it is interesting to note that, over the past 150 years, motivations for building railway lines in Arabia have shifted from colonial-led geostrategic (Baghdad Railway) and religious-geostrategic (Hejaz Railway) reasons to more efficient freight transportation and facilitated exports (Saudi Arabian railways) and, in recent times, back to a focus on passenger transportation (Frost and Sullivan 2011, 1; JHR 2014). Besides the *Hajj*, facilitated circulation of travellers on trains has in the past decade been identified as a means to create political ties (Frost and Sullivan 2011, 2–3).

While rail transport is expected to play a major role in intra-GCC travel (MOT 2014), it is interesting to ask whether long-distance connections to Turkey and beyond are imaginable. From a commercial perspective, and contrary to the ongoing withdrawal of intra-European overnight trains, it is noteworthy that, in 2012, the Russian Railways started introducing a series of 200 new, state-of-the-art sleeping cars with all contemporary amenities, such as air conditioning, showers and entertainment systems (*Railway Gazette* 2012). Other railway systems in the former Soviet Union states ordered similar rolling stock (*Railway Technology* 2014). Largely built in Western Europe and designed to operate both on Russian and European tracks (ibid.), these carriages highlight that a market for modern long-distance rail travel does exist. A potential sleeping car train linking Europe with the Gulf would represent a revival of the glorious but defunct Orient/Taurus Express trains in a contemporary form.[1]

It is essential to understand that while long-distance rail transport can help reduce intra-GCC air travel, the GCC railway will be unable to unlock its full potential without its passenger stations fully integrated in efficient urban transportation networks that will carry passengers to and from their long-distance trains. Decades of experience from Europe and the United States show that offering decent travel solutions for the last mile – from a passenger's home or office to the rail transport hub – is one of the modal shift triggers making residents opt for rail rather than car (UITP 2014) or, by analogy, air. From this point of view, it is noteworthy that Dubai's RTA has been declared a 'key partner' of Etihad Rail (Etihad Rail 2014b), demonstrating that reflections of integration with urban transportation have been a firm part of the GCC passenger rail project from the very beginning.

An integrally connected mobility system acts as an incubator and facilitator for business travel, leisure travel and tourism. Integrating regional and urban transportation will strongly affect urban development, 'turning the growing metropolises … into a network of innovative nodes' (Brillembourg *et al.* 2011, 17).[2] In terms of investments, establishing integrated urban mobility, and setting up heavy urban rail systems, new interchange facilities and other required infrastructure, generates significantly lower external costs in a long-term perspective than current, road-only-focused infrastructural expenses. Kinninmont (2010, 9) mentions that much of the GCC's growth in recent years 'was driven largely by double-digit increases in government spending'. She reminds that 'these levels of spending growth cannot be sustained indefinitely', and that the International Monetary Fund has 'advised the GCC states to plan their exit strategies from the recent "fiscal stimulus" policies' (ibid.).

Gulf airspace development and ground transportation

The fabulous growth story of the major GCC airlines is propelled by, and based on, their self-assigned functions as global connectors, an ambition well illustrated by Dubai's duplicated, new mega-hub airport that opened in 2013 and is identified by the International Air Transport Association code DWC for 'Dubai World Central'. Connecting passengers changing planes in Dubai, Doha or Abu Dhabi represent by far the largest share among GCC long-distance carriers' patronage – up to 75 per cent in a long-term expectation of Doha's new airport, opened in 2014 (*The Economist* 2010). However, most flyers will not see more of the Gulf than attractively priced duty free shops in the respective airport's sealed-off transit area.

With a prediction of GCC tourist arrivals rising to 1.8 billion a year over the next two decades (Booz & Company 2013), there is a limit to expanding even well-located airports. Even if there is no shortage at present, both the recent history and projections for world air travel via the Gulf show that what right now looks like spare capacity can, and will, fill up quickly (*The National* 2014). Also, there is a limit to expanding air transport hubs: facilities lose in attractiveness with increased size, since both air-to-air and ground-to-air connections become time-intensive and cumbersome, with longer walks, and use of shuttles or terminal changes involved. On a map of global competitiveness, this turns into a negative site-related factor, affecting local economic efficiency. Also, and particularly in the GCC context, a hub less appealing to those air-to-air connecting travellers that are at the heart of the GCC airlines' business strategies puts at risk the economic success of the carrier whose home base it is.

Dubai International Airport's passenger rate currently grows at about 20 per cent per year (*The Economist* 2010). 'DXB' handled over 66 million passengers in 2013, making it the second airport in the world ranked on international passenger traffic, and the seventh in the world by total passenger traffic (Airports Council International 2014). With its Terminal 3, opened in 2008 and exclusively used by Emirates Airline, expanding into the largest building in the world by floor space, it will ultimately be able to handle 43 million passengers a year, up from 30 million in 2010 (*The Economist* 2010).

Despite the success and the state-of-the-art quality of the existing Dubai International Airport, a new, even larger one started operations in 2013. 'DWC', Dubai Al Maktoum Airport, is projected to fully open in the early 2020s and is planned to have a passenger capacity of over 160 million per year, making it by far the world's largest airport (ibid.).

Meanwhile, in the nearby emirates of Abu Dhabi (part of the UAE) and Qatar, two other airports within less than 300 kilometres' distance from Dubai have also announced projected yearly passenger numbers of 40 million and 50 million, respectively, by 2015 (ibid.). For comparison, Europe's busiest airport, London Heathrow, counted 72 million passengers arriving and departing in 2013 (Heathrow Airport Holdings 2013), and Europe's third busiest airport Frankfurt/Main counted 58 million passengers (Fraport 2014). On the carrier side, now-established GCC airlines, such as Qatar Airways, Emirates Airline, Gulf Air and Etihad Airways, as well as comparatively young ones such as Oman Air, count among the best airlines in the world regarding the level of service offered to the passenger, all of them being awarded four or even the maximum of five stars in reference rankings (Skytrax 2014). Emirates Airline, the largest and the blueprint model for most other GCC carriers, currently flies to over 120 destinations on all continents and is projected to count around 400 wide-bodied planes by 2020 (Emirates Airline 2014). These figures illustrate that the current projects in GCC countries will, within a few years, deeply affect market conditions and geographies in a significant portion of global long-distance air travel. They combine into a geostrategic set of advantages crucial for understanding the interdependencies between future transport

Table 8.1 Airport expansion projects in the GCC region: forecasted passenger capacities

State	IATA code	Name	Capacity 2014	Capacity planned
Abu Dhabi	AUH	Abu Dhabi International Airport	10 million	20 million (2017) 30 million (2030) 50 million (2050)
Bahrain	BAH	Bahrain International Airport	7 million	28 million (2030)
Dubai	DXB	Dubai International Airport	47 million	80 million (2015) 100 million (2020)
Dubai	DWC	Dubai Al Maktoum International Airport	–	87 million (2025) 160 million (2035)
Kuwait	KWI	Kuwait International Airport	8 million	13 million (2016)
Oman	MCT	Muscat International Airport	4.5 million	12 million (2015) 48 million (2025)
Qatar	DOH	Hamad International Airport	24 million	50 million (2025)

Source: Airport websites (2014)

infrastructure and scenarios for urban developments within the GCC states. Even if a major share of future passengers will be in transit, developments as previously discussed will result in growth rates of GCC-bound arriving or departing local passengers proportionally lower, yet still important in absolute numbers. While greening the air transport business is an issue now tackled on a global scale, expected GCC air traffic expansions, as mirrored by planned airport capacity evolution (see Table 8.1), illustrate the urgency of designing and providing a sustainable and efficient ground transportation infrastructure to cope with demand to come.

As outlined earlier, in a GCC context it is critical to include aviation when discussing the interrelations between the evolution of transportation and tourism.[3] A common GCC airspace will not come to existence without further political integration. The current fragmentation of air traffic control in the GCC region is emerging as a major challenge and, to date, no single body regulating and coordinating air traffic exists. In the UAE, aviation is expected to account for a quarter of the total GDP by 2016 (Deakin 2014). In neighbouring Qatar, across the Gulf but sharing the same airspace, and with regard to the ever-increasing number of movements, Qatar Airways Chief Executive Officer Akbar Al Baker has called for 'a single air traffic management system similar to Eurocontrol to monitor and operate a very congested airspace' (Siddiqui 2014). Successful air space management is closely tied to matters of national sovereignty and security, but also to a powerful complement in ground transportation. The GCC railway's planned passenger services, seen as a regional integration project and integrated with urban transit as explained above, will serve as backbone for greening regional transport. Helping curb intra-GCC air traffic growth, its integrated conception lets it affect the full door-to-door transportation chain, coincidentally fostering a modal shift towards the use of transit in urban areas. Greening intercity transport thus implicitly means greening urban transport; any disincentive to private car use is welcome, since any journey that does not commence in a private car is less likely to end in one.

Taking green urban transport further: suggested innovations

A coordinated, holistic approach to mobility planning, in the widest sense of the terminology, will simultaneously benefit trade through more efficient freight transport and support national integration through facilitated mobility of individuals. The main benefits for patrons are easier accessibility and less hassle in air and coach travel, resulting in higher comfort and quality perception, and translating into better acceptance.

Current intra-GCC ground transport lacks capacity, attractiveness and efficiency. As an example, in May 2014, the ground transport offer between Dubai, UAE, and Muscat, Oman, consisted of between two and four coaches per day in each direction, while up to 28 flights were scheduled.[4] Coach travel takes six to eight hours while flying takes less than one. A well-developed ground transport offer would result in increased sustainability, time and cost efficiency, allowing for a better allocation of resources. Also, long-term GCC-wide spatial planning would greatly benefit since it could rely on a solid accessibility design framework. Residential and commercial real estate, and business and leisure facilities could be concentrated in areas well-served by transport, leading to overall sustainability gains in the built environment that make an important contribution to hard-wiring the benefits of a greener lifestyle into GCC societies.

While state-of-the-art transit solutions around the world have inspired implementation in the GCC, a key success factor is bespoke approaches and localised adaptations of proven concepts that build on recognising local needs, values and special needs.

Based on the different factors and elements discussed above, the following aspects of GCC transit systems have proven to deliver good results:

- Heavy urban rail, such as metro lines, serve as a high-capacity backbone of urban public transport. Light rail/tram systems or bus rapid transit and local bus systems can precede and/or complement such systems on secondary axes (Keilo and Montagne 2012).
- Localised solutions, such as the availability of a luxury class on trains or full air conditioning, including walkways linking stations to adjacent buildings, can help make systems attractive to new social groups of patrons and help fight prejudice against transit as 'transport for the underprivileged' (Jaffe 2013).
- Full integration of modes for easy access, extended to include regional and interregional transport, has proven to boost ridership (UITP 2012).

With demand for individual mobility on the rise and urbanisation proceeding at a fast pace, future developments will require solutions that build on these success factors and take them further. Based on the idea that a trip does not start at the bus stop or metro station, but at the resident's door, the author suggests the future focus to be on last-mile connectivity. This includes:

- *General on-demand transportation*, such as taxis, black car services and private hire cars (globally operating transportation network companies, such as Uber, Lyft and Sidecar, among others). While this is the most traditional and established mode of last-mile coverage, its future application will need to rely on real-time planning through smartphone-enabled applications that bring a one-stop trip planning integrating car services with high-capacitive modes, such as metro or bus, and a one-stop ticketing process.
- *Local on-demand transportation*, such as community shuttles, last-mile shared luxury vans or other door-to-door modes operating with shared vehicles or small buses. Based on community shuttles, such modes, in order to be successful in a GCC context, require a novel type of full-service, full-luxury approach bringing them to a new level of acceptance. Critical elements are pickup time (for example within 10 minutes from issuing a pickup request), level of comfort (for example leather seats, water and tea on board, and broadband WiFi) and a level of integration with the main network that makes their use attractive. Solutions that have to be developed include dedicated air-conditioned pickup/dropoff points at metro stations and dedicated fast-track access to trains.
- *Full integration* – infrastructure and tariff-wise – with other modes such as waterborne transit, which, on top of its technical capacity to provide cost-effective high-capacity transport, brings 'fun' elements into the mobility chain by offering a particularly appealing experience (and which, for the tourist part of ridership, illustrates the rich maritime tradition of GCC countries).

As Jaffe (2013) notes, context and travel experience matter when winning over car drivers. In a GCC context, if social acceptance of potential patrons is to be won, a transit journey in the overall experience needs to be as attractive as a journey in a luxury sedan. Operating areas of local pickup vehicles would typically include clearly delimited zones, making them a tool to serve housing estates of suburban type. The same is valid for large parts of the functionality of ride-sharing modes that, in their United States or European layouts, might have difficulties in gaining acceptance in a GCC environment due to social factors.

While from a cultural point of view this can be seen as a contemporary, 'teched-up' version of the traditional 'Baiza' bus,[5] it reaches unparalleled levels of comfort and customer service, the trip quality reference being 'black car' services. This system would be designed to accommodate self-driving vehicles at a later stage, namely as soon as these become available and acquire full permission to operate.

Consequently, other suggested last-mile connectivity features include:

- *Self-drive shared vehicle systems*, such as bike or car sharing networks. Special attention should be given to e-bike sharing systems: while electrical bikes have shown to have usage profiles closer to those of cars than to those of traditional bikes, they require less physical effort while offering shorter travel times. E-bikes can positively support general public health efforts in the GCC, such as fighting obesity-related type 2 diabetes, while conveying the image of a modern, high-tech transport mode. A prerequisite is a separate network of shaded, dedicated walk- and bikeways. In dense urban areas, this can be implemented as an elevated second or third layer, enhancing independence and travel speeds while reducing potential conflicts with other modes.
- *Smart infrastructure systems*, such as one-stop traveller information smartphone apps, road pricing (tolling), congestion charging and smart parking. While the GCC's first electronic travel planner was introduced in Dubai in 2009, future systems need to integrate road traffic in order to be truly multi-modal and to develop a steering effect on modal choice. Clarke (2014) emphasises both the provision of 'reliable transport infrastructure' as well as 'higher levels of satisfaction' that such systems can offer, if properly designed. Advanced models integrating planning and capacity management of both transit and private cars exist for example in London (managed by Transport for London) and Singapore (managed by the Land Transport Authority of Singapore).

Thus, in a systemic view, the suitability of possible future solutions and modes for urban application in GCC cities include the ability to provide:

- *Cross-modal routing*: at the core of this needs to be an integrated network travel planning tool that indicates the best routing – integrating all modes, both scheduled, route-based transport such as air, rail, interurban coach, urban rail, bus, cable-propelled modes, and on-demand or flexible services, such as shared vehicles, vans, taxis and people movers. For the latter, such as the integration of Omani 'Baiza' buses, a new definition and understanding of paratransit is needed.
- *Dynamically adapted real-time travel planning*, or adapting routing to the real conditions in real time. This calls for mapping to be integrated, with a first approach potentially based on the current Google Transit data format – the only global industry standard existing at the time of writing in matters of live travel data exchange. As explained above, any true intermodality calls for smartphone apps acting as routers, superordinate to the individual modes, intelligently linking and integrating the diversity of transport offers.
- *Ticketing and revenue management*: critical to the solutions suggested here is the availability of integrated ticketing. In less than a decade, touch-and-go

travel passes such as Dubai's Noi will be replaced by powerful smartphone apps guiding riders to boarding points and simultaneously taking over new forms of ticketing, making it easier even for first-time users in non-familiar environments. At a later stage, this functionality can be part of a global transit interface, ultimately addressing the problem of thousands of different transit pricing systems around the world – one of the main barriers to more extensive use of public transport systems by incoming business people or tourists (Koenig 2012). Also, integrated ticketing eases the challenges posed by a supra-national system in making it compatible with multi-operator competition. With no necessity to have just one administrative body or transit agency running all operative entities, the routing function simultaneously acts as an integrator and as a centralised user interface. This corresponds to historical experiences from Europe where urban tariff communities have acted as first steps of an integration that has been further implemented and optimised over the past two decades.

Outlook

In 2006, Koolhaas formulated a radical thesis of the countries of the GCC as 'an untainted canvas [providing] the final tabula rasa on which new identities can be inscribed' (Koolhaas 2006a). Starting out from the unparalleled *status quo* of the region, the ideal of a 'futurized present' is suggested as a primary tool to sketch a new type of urbanism. Like the Dubai Metro itself, an integrated GCC ground transport system integrating urban transit has the potential to be an iconic representation of a new, contemporary GCC urbanism.

Globally, the requirements set by the increasingly palpable threat of transit gridlocks in metropolitan areas ask for a next level of integrating transit, which is made possible at present by the rapid advances in mobile information and communication technologies and their trivialisation on the front end. The ground transport network turns itself into a tool interconnecting citizens' mobility, boosting trans-national trade, reflecting the political economy of the territories and ultimately strengthening the GCC region as a whole, enhancing and shaping its identity.

Still, in order to define and fine-tune adequate solutions, careful monitoring of ongoing developments and further research is needed: what kind of car trips do metro journeys substitute? How exactly does intra-modal connectivity have to be designed in order to be compliant with women's travel requirements? How can luxury-conscious patrons be won over on a long-term basis? How can the value of the family be mirrored in transit offers?

As previously discussed, a long-term perspective would include that, in a time horizon of several decades, the GCC states' current profiles in developing locally rooted plans to conceive and implement a set of strategic measures for combined advances in transportation lead the countries into a future-oriented, twenty-first century infrastructural constitution. The latter would provide a solid base for all further development of the region, and would be a prerequisite for a successful evolution of GCC urbanism and a backbone for the economic and social development of Gulf societies.

Urban transport concerns every urban resident, every day – actively as a consumer of urban mobility and passively through the dependence on the efficiency of transport of fellow citizens and the availability of goods and services. While the latter – a good performance of logistics – is vital for current and future economic performance, the capacity of others to get around town in a fast and convenient way directly affects the quality of every individual's mobility. Congested roads and overcrowded, delayed trains are inhibitors to any other person's possibility to move around in decent conditions. Greening transport thus is synonymous, not contradictory, to enhancing the transport sector's economical performance and attractiveness to users.

The GCC cities compete on a global scale in offering attractive conditions to existing and prospective residents and businesses, and a backbone of economic performance and potential economic development. After a phase of rapid expansion in the past decades and facing projected growth rates, solving the challenges in the field of urban transport has become a critical factor for the GCC countries' long-term capacity to keep and expand prosperity and wealth. This chapter has explained how urban, regional and global transport are interconnected in their implications for GCC residents' quality of life. Ultimately, 'greening' the transport sector is critical for the overall greening of the GCC economies. Its role as key infrastructure for the future development of the region implies that there is no other alternative.

Notes

1 The nametag 'Taurus Express' still exists and is used for an internal Turkish train running on parts of the old route.
2 Brillembourg et al. (2011) discuss structurally comparable examples in the Southern Hemisphere.
3 With the continuing expansion of low-cost air transport and its increasing integration into transportation chains, such considerations will also be necessary in other environments to get a full picture.
4 Sources: visitoman.org, kayak.com, searches by the author during five days in September 2014.
5 Baiza buses are functional mixtures between transit buses and shared taxis that in 2014 are the backbone of public transport in Muscat, Oman. They are generally operated with Toyota Hiace vehicles seating up to 14 passengers in a school bus-style configuration. While Baiza buses' strength is their flexibility and capacity to instantly adapt themselves to riders' demand by adapting their routes to ridership in real time, their weakness is their lack of efficiency on longer urban routes, mainly due to their low capacity and slow boarding procedures.

References

Accor. 2014. 'Accor Development in North Africa and Middle East.' Accessed 12 August. http://accor.com/

Airport websites. 2014. Data for table taken from respective airport websites. Accessed 20 December.

Airports Council International. 2014. 'International Passenger Traffic for Past 12 Months.' Accessed 24 July. http://www.aci.aero/

Booz & Company. 2013. 'Reinventing the GCC's Tourism Ecosystems – The Key to Reaping the Sector's Full Benefits.' Accessed 22 September 2014. http://www.booz.com/

Brillembourg, A., H. Klumpner and D. Schwartz. 2011. 'Build Simply: South of The Border.' *MAS Context Magazine* 10(Summer), 14–27.

CIA. US Central Intelligence Agency. 2014. *The World Factbook*. Accessed 13 December. https://www.cia.gov/

Clarke, R. 2014. 'Investment in GCC Smart Transport Requires Carefully Crafted Master Plan.' *The National*, 24 September.

Davidson, Christopher M. 2008. *Dubai: The Vulnerability of Success*. New York: Columbia University Press.

Davis, Mike. 2002. *Dead Cities: And Other Tales*. New York: The New Press.

Davis, Mike. 2005. 'Tomgram: Mike Davis on a Paradise Built on Oil.' *TomDispatch*, 14 July. Accessed 30 December 2014. http://www.tomdispatch.com/post/5807/

Deakin, R. 2014. 'Time to Secure the Gulf's Aviation Future.' Accessed 31 July. http://nats.aero/

Deutsche Bahn. 2014. 'DB fährt Güterzüge in den Emiraten.' ('Deutsche Bahn Runs Freight Trains in the Emirates.') Accessed 21 December. http://www.deutschebahn.com/

Elsheshtawy, Y., and O. Al Bastaki. 2011. 'The Dubai Experience: Mass Transit in the Arabian Peninsula.' In: *Global Visions, Risks and Opportunities for the Urban Planet*. Singapore: The 5th International Conference of the International Forum on Urbanism.

Emirates Airline. 2014. 'Flying to More Destinations on More Aircraft Every Day.' Accessed 14 July. http://www.emirates.com/

Etihad Rail. 2014a. 'Project Update.' Accessed 20 December. http://www.etihadrail.ae/

Etihad Rail. 2014b. 'Passenger Services.' Accessed 31 December. http://www.etihadrail.ae/

Fraport. 2014. 'Fraport Traffic Figures – December & Full Year 2013: Passenger Traffic Continues to Grow.' Accessed 1 August. http://www.fraport.com/

Frost & Sullivan. 2011. 'Frost & Sullivan Strategic Insight on the GCC Rail Sector.' Accessed 18 December 2014. http://www.frost.com/

Global Mass Transit. 2009. 'GCC Metro Plans: Ambitious Investment Plans for Metro Rail Sector.' Accessed 29 October 2014. http://www.globalmasstransit.net

Gulf News. 2004. 'Sharjah-Dubai Bus Service Makes Slight Impact on Traffic Woes.' 12 February.

Gulf News. 2013. 'Dubai-Sharjah Buses Get NOI Connectivity.' 25 June.

Gulf News. 2014. 'Dubai Metro Tops 12.4m Passengers in August.' 10 October.

Heathrow Airport Holdings. 2013. 'Heathrow Facts and Figures.' Accessed 20 December. http://mediacentre.heathrowairport.com/

Jaffe, E. 2013. 'Three Keys for Drawing Drivers to Mass Transit.' *The Atlantic Citylab*. Accessed 12 December 2014. http://www.citylab.com/

JHR. Jordan Hejaz Railway. 2014. 'Jordan Hejaz Railway: Establishment, Development and Features of Railway Transport.' Accessed 18 December. http://www.jhr.gov.jo/

Keilo, J., and C. Montagne. 2012. 'Dubai Metro and Dubai Bus: Local Efficiency and the City's Global Image.' Istanbul: *Megaron* 7 (EK 1), 113–121.

Kinninmont, Jane. 2010. *The GCC in 2020: Broadening the Economy*. London: The Economist Intelligence Unit.

Koenig, T. 2012. 'Oeffentlicher Nahverkehr – Verloren in der Tarif-Todeszone' (Public Transport: Lost in the Tariff Death Zone). Hamburg: *Der Spiegel*, 24 March.

Koolhaas, Rem. 2006a. *The Gulf*. Amsterdam: AMO.

Koolhaas, Rem. 2006b. 'Venice Biennale 2006: The Gulf, Italy, Venice.' Accessed 22 December 2014. http://oma.eu/

Molavi, Afshin. 2005. 'Dubai Rising.' *Brown Journal of World Affairs* 12(1), 103–110.

MOT. Bahrain Ministry of Transportation. 2014. 'GCC Railway.' Accessed 21 December. http://mot.gov.bh/

Muttoo, S. 2010. 'Full Speed Ahead: Transport System in the Middle East.' *Strategic Foresight Group*. Accessed 20 November 2014. http://www.strategicforesight.com/

Pinkerton, Stewart. 2005. 'Lawrence of Suburbia.' *Forbes*, 31 October. Accessed 31 December 2014. http://www.forbes.com/

Pirie, Gordon. 2009. 'Incidental Tourism: British Imperial Air Travel in the 1930s.' *Journal of Tourism History* 1(1), 49–66.

Railway Gazette. 2012. 'Gauge Convertible Sleeping Car Rolls Out.' Accessed 19 December 2014. http://www.railwaygazette.com/

Railway Technology. 2014. 'Stadler to Supply Passenger Cars to Azerbaijan Railways.' Accessed 16 December. http://www.railway-technology.com/

Reisz, T. 2010. 'On Al Manakh 2.' Transcript of Presentation at Columbia University. New York, 24 September. Accessed 4 July 2011. http://oma.eu/

RTA. Dubai Road and Transport Authority. 2014. 'Annual Statistical Report 2013.' Accessed 8 December. http://www.rta.ae/

Siddiqui, S. 2014. 'Al-Baker Sees Need for Unified Air Traffic Control in the Gulf.' *Gulf Times*, 16 January.

Skytrax. 2014. 'Skytrax Airline Product and Quality Ranking.' Accessed 2 August. http://www.airlinequality.com/

The Economist. 2008. 'The New Oases.' 10 April. Accessed 31 December. http://www.economist.com/

The Economist. 2010. 'Aviation in the Gulf – Rulers of the New Silk Road.' 3 June. Accessed 22 December 2014. http://www.economist.com/

The National. 2014. 'Warning Sounded on Gridlock in Arabian Gulf Skies.' 8 April.

Toshens, Nick. 2006. 'Dubai's the Limit.' *Vanity Fair*, June.

UITP. International Association of Public Transport. 2012. *A Vision for Integrated Urban Mobility: Setting up your Transport Authority*. Brussels.

UITP. 2014. 'Integration: Combined Mobility is Key to Citizens' Lifestyles.' Accessed 21 December 2014. http://www.uitp.org/

Part IV

Cross-cutting issues: labour, law and international cooperation

9 Workers and the green economy in the Gulf Cooperation Council countries

Amit A. Pandya and Kristin Sparding[1]

Introduction

In this chapter, we examine the labour-related questions that should be considered in the context of the green economy in the Gulf Cooperation Council (GCC, or 'Gulf') countries. We address economic activity directed at mitigation of damaging environmental change, economic activity directed at adaptation to the effects of environmental change, and the development of cleaner processes of production and distribution for either of the above purposes.

There occurs in the discourse and literature on such economic activity reference variously to 'green economy' and 'green growth'. We recognise that there is a debate about whether these are synonymous, and that the distinction is fraught, because growth is itself a provocative notion in much environmental discourse. Declining to address the issue, we instead use the term 'green economy' as broader in scope, and the term 'green growth' only where it is part of the title of a publication or a formal statement or strategy by national or international institutions, and only to quote such publications or summarise the content of such publications.

We also recognise that the working definition of green economy that we use does not incorporate the social dimension, as some definitions have.[2] This does not reflect our position on the value of social justice in a green economy, but rather logic and plain language. We believe that a green economy is not *in itself and necessarily* one that is beneficial to workers. It is possible to conceive of an economy that addresses issues of environmental sustainability without addressing social justice or welfare, however undesirable that might be. The thrust of this chapter is to argue for consideration of the social dimension as central to the *desirable* practice of a green economy. We believe that conscious and distinct commitment to skills development, employment policies, enlightened industrial relations and protection of workers' rights and interests is necessary if these are to be effectively and practically vindicated in a green economy, rather than simply taken for granted as part of a definition.

The core labour issues that arise in the labour markets of the states of the Gulf are those of workforce qualifications and skills, labour migration, worker safety and health, and international labour standards. The chapter seeks to elucidate both the particular ways in which the requirements of a green economy should shape our understanding of these, and the ways in which requirements from the world of work should shape our understanding of the green economy in the Gulf.[3]

In the chapter, we examine: the likely composition of the Gulf's green economy and labour markets, and workforce development and labour market strategies there; private sector actions as reflected in investment trends and patterns; likely impacts of these on labour markets and workers' interests; and the policy-making challenges these pose. We place these in the context of policy-making and institutions in the Gulf that will constrain or facilitate the development of appropriate labour policies. We also place these in the larger context of the global discourse on sustainable development, decent work[4] and green jobs,[5] examining the policy-making and institutions that frame that discourse. We examine models and lessons learned. We seek to offer a view of the green economy from the perspective of institutions and players from the world of work, such as labour ministries, workers and their organisations, employers and their organisations and the International Labour Organization (ILO).

The issues arising from the world of work fall into two categories. One relates to the availability, skills and training of an appropriate workforce. The other relates to the well-being of individual workers, including their rights under international standards, and workplace safety and health.

Environmental change and economic opportunity

Between October 2003 and April 2014 there were held under the aegis of the United Nations Economic and Social Commission for Western Asia (UNESCWA), according to its website, 150 meetings on economics of the environment. They encompassed topics as wide-ranging as finance, economics, science, engineering, institutions, trade, agriculture, food, water and energy. The only significant omission was labour (UNESCWA 2014).

Among the environment-related challenges that the Gulf countries face are desertification, droughts, soil degradation, management of watershed and water resources, management of invasive species, marine and coastal management, management of other natural resources, crop and livestock management, early warning of and response to rapidly developing environmental change or natural disasters, public health challenges such as coping with the effects of extreme heat or air pollution, and management of oasis ecosystems.[6]

The region is marked by significant amounts of pollution and emissions of all types. Its marine ecosystems are affected not only by the rapid development of urban populations and infrastructure and industry, but also by the Gulf's emergence as a significant centre of global maritime commerce (Pandya and Herbert-Burns 2011, 64). Some instances demonstrate the convergence of these factors, such as shipping related to the petroleum trade, where ballast from tankers, dredging and filling of waterways, offshore extraction infrastructure and emissions from ships converge to pose a challenge (Michel *et al.* 2010, 5).

Any and all of these are potential occasions for the development of green industries, as well as the greening of traditional brown industries such as the development of green buildings or the introduction of greener processes (such as less emission or water intensity) in the practice of agriculture.

Whereas not strictly an element of a green economy, some attempts at adaptation to the effects of environmental change will lead to increases in emissions or other pollution, and should also be noted as a related element that will affect the world of work. Water stress resulting from declines in rainfall and evaporation of surface water will continue to prompt reliance on energy-intensive methods such as desalination and pumping of groundwater. As soil and water changes take place, and as traditional methods of water management are tested or overcome by changes in the quantum of water, agriculture will inevitably become more dependent on energy-intensive irrigation processes and on increased external inputs such as fertilisers which in themselves are energy intensive and require polluting production processes. Increased urban populations will lead to greater demands for water and electricity. These processes can become part of a discussion of green economy where they may give rise to green innovation and the search for green alternatives (Klawitter *et al.* 2011).

The example of water scarcity is perhaps the one best understood for the GCC and indeed the entire Middle East and North Africa (MENA) region, which is among the most freshwater-scarce regions in the world (Michel *et al.* 2012). The average annual available water per capita was even in 2001 well below the United Nations (UN) definition of water scarcity. From a 2001 figure of 977 cubic meters, it is expected to decline to 460 in 2023. Only Egypt, Sudan, Iraq, Syria and Lebanon are expected to escape serious water stress. The International Finance Corporation (IFC) projected most government investment to address this to be in the three GCC states of Saudi Arabia, the United Arab Emirates (UAE) and Qatar (IFC 2009, 19).

Whereas environmental change offers opportunities for private investment in mitigation and adaptation efforts, it may also depress investment (and therefore job creation) that would otherwise have taken place, as water intensity, dependency and scarcity could be a risk factor for particular industries. This drag factor could compound the trend also seen among the community of institutional environmental investors to avoid the MENA region as a whole owing to the high prevalence of 'dirty' industry associated with the petrochemical sectors.

There are numerous ways in which these environmental threats may present opportunities or challenges related to employment creation or labour standards. Technologies addressed to the prevention or reversal of environmental damage, and the construction of infrastructure for the same purposes, such as watercourse restoration or defences against coastal inundation, will require production and installation, and could create new types of employment opportunities as well as new types of occupational hazards for the workers involved. So will production and installation of cleaner processes and equipment for water resource quality improvement or enhancement of the quantum of water resources, or the manufacture and installation of photovoltaic (PV) equipment.

Other examples include manufacture and installation of technologies for emissions mitigation and for environmentally responsible methods for cooling indoor spaces, and installation of infrastructure for prevention of or protection against environmental disasters. Efforts to address the environmental effects of the shipping, ports and docks, and hydrocarbon extraction sectors might also generate employment and require monitoring and regulation of working conditions. The specialised skills required for the production, installation and maintenance of these processes, technologies and infrastructure will require to be developed, and the awareness of the need to protect labour standards in such occupations and industries will need to be propagated among employers and workers.

It is clear that some of these types of economic activity will be capital intensive – particularly those requiring a high degree of technical sophistication – and others will be labour intensive. Some of the employment-creation effects of green economic developments will be direct, whereas others will be indirect, as in the provision to those working in green economic activity of ancillary services or goods not in themselves green.

Below we discuss briefly, by way of setting the framework and context for the discussion of labour issues, the various courses that a green economy might take in the GCC countries, as well as identify some of the inhibiting or facilitating factors for this. The course of green economy development in the Gulf will in turn determine the likely development of the labour picture. Given the current emphasis in the Gulf on alternative sources of energy, on addressing issues of water quantum and quality, and on reduction of carbon emissions, we can reliably surmise that the labour issues that arise in the first instance will be related to those.

The global context

Multilateral organisations including the ILO, the UN Environment Programme (UNEP), the G20 and the Organisation for Economic Co-operation and Development (OECD) have increasingly devoted resources to examining opportunities and challenges for linking employment generation with environmental protection and preservation. The ILO has pointed to its 1990 International Labour Conference (ILC) on the theme of Environment and the World of Work and to the brief mention of labour issues in the 2002 Declaration of the World Summit on Sustainable Development in Johannesburg. The ILO considers 2007 a turning point for global discourse on sustainable development, decent work and green jobs when the ILC's Committee on Sustainable Enterprises concluded that the three pillars of sustainable development – economic, social and environmental – coalesce in the workplace, and the ILO Director General launched the organisation's Green Jobs Initiative (International Labour Office 2013). The following year, the Japanese G8 presidency placed the employment aspect of global sustainability as one of three top issues on the agenda of the labour and employment ministerial meeting. At the meeting in Niigata, ministers declared their 'intent to contribute to addressing employment and social challenges arising from environmental concerns and issues in order to realise a resilient and sustainable society' (Ministry of Health, Labour and Welfare of Japan 2008).

In subsequent years, numerous international policy-making bodies have taken up the issue during conferences, in outcome declarations, and through research. Experts have addressed the skills needed, worker rights considerations and labour market data. In 2011, the OECD launched its Green Growth Strategy, as called for by its 2009 Ministerial Council Meeting. The Strategy includes discussion of labour market implications of green growth such as potential for job creation, long-term impact on employment, and skills policies, in an effort to provide guidance to governments from developed and developing countries (OECD 2011). The ILO's Green Jobs Program has expanded its efforts to provide training, research and advocacy, and technical assistance on green jobs.

In 2012, the international community solidified its recognition of the interlinkages between decent work and sustainable development. The outcome document of the UN Conference on Sustainable Development (Rio+20), entitled 'The Future We Want', addressed labour and employment issues significantly more than did the 1992 Rio Earth Summit or the 2002 Johannesburg Summit. An entire section of the document was devoted to 'promoting full and productive employment, decent work for all, and social protections', highlighting the importance of these areas to achieving sustainable development. Today, experts and international organisations have generated a wealth of detailed research on job growth in emerging green sectors, skills for green jobs, and the quality of jobs in the green economy, among other topics. For example, the ILO has published a paper on addressing the labour and employment-related challenges of e-waste (Lundgren 2012), and released a publication on green jobs potential in India's dairy sector (Harsdorff 2014). The OECD, in partnership with the European Centre for the Development of Vocational Training, has also released a report on greener skills and jobs, which articulates the skills needed for a low-carbon economy, and the role for education and training institutions and government coordination in helping develop a skilled workforce in green sectors (OECD/Cedefop 2014).

Perspectives of institutions and players from the world of work

According to the ILO, 'jobs are green when they help reduce negative environmental impact ultimately leading to environmentally, economically and socially sustainable enterprises and economies'. The ILO goes on to elaborate that:

> Green jobs are decent jobs that contribute to preserve or restore a sustainable environment, be they in traditional sectors such as manufacturing and construction, or in new, emerging green sectors such as renewable energy and energy efficiency. Green jobs help: improve energy and raw materials

efficiency; limit greenhouse gas emissions; minimise waste and pollution; protect and restore ecosystems; [and] support adaptation to the effects of climate change.

(ILO 2013a)

The Chair's summary and conclusions from the 1st Global Conference on the Partnership for Action on Green Economy (PAGE) held in Dubai in March 2014 offer a distinct but complementary and consistent definition:

All jobs can be green. Greening the economy refers to the broad category of work to be done in a range of productive activities across sectors, whether formal or informal. It refers to creation of new jobs but also to the upgrading of existing jobs. Furthermore, green jobs need to include decent working conditions for them to be beneficial for the environment and contribute to social inclusion. This calls for more attention to be paid to informal work, which represents 60 to 80 percent of jobs in developing countries, in addition to low income farming.

(UNEP PAGE 2014a, 4)

Labour ministries and trade unions focus on workforce development for the green economy and fundamental worker rights and occupational safety and health therein. Employer organisations also concern themselves with these areas, but often focus on innovation and investments in the green economy, as well as greening supply chains. At the 2013 ILC, the ILO's tripartite constituents – governments, trade unions and employer groups – discussed the labour and employment aspects of the green economy and agreed on common priorities. The conclusions recommended actions for governments, employers, worker organisations and the ILO respectively.[7]

The extent to which labour ministries around the world are involved in domestic green economy policy-making depends on a particular government's priorities. Labour ministries generate labour market information, identify demand for workers with particular skills or in certain sectors, and project future demand. Many also protect the fundamental rights of workers and their health and safety. Some have undertaken initiatives to spur worker training for green jobs in their countries. The Republic of Korea is a notable example of a country investing heavily in the green economy. According to the OECD's website, the Korean government articulated a long-term National Strategy for Green Growth for the years 2009–2050, and green growth featured prominently in its Five-Year Plan for 2009–2013. In 2012 the Ministry of Employment and Labor announced its Second Basic Plan for Vocational Skills Development for 2012–2017. One of the Plan's goals is 'to cultivate 200,000 skilled workers who can meet the needs of businesses in green, high-tech and root industries', and it is accompanied by a number of skills training and retention measures (Ministry of Employment and Labor of the Republic of Korea 2012).

Some labour ministries have also examined the impact of greening economies on worker health and safety. For example, the European Agency for Safety and Health at Work has published a study that attempts to understand and anticipate challenges for worker health and safety in emerging green technologies and sectors, such as green construction and waste processing, in order to tackle them in advance (EASHW 2013). The US Department of Labor's Occupational Safety and Health Administration has created a website on the risks to worker health and safety in certain green sectors and preventive solutions. The website includes a section on potential occupational risks in solar energy, such as falls, shocks and burns, as well as methods for preventing them such as installing guardrail or safety net systems in the case of falls (US Department of Labor 2014).

International trade union groups have strongly advocated for workers to benefit from the transition to green economies in terms of workforce development and labour rights. The International Trade Union Confederation and its affiliates have actively participated in major international meetings addressing the green economy, sustainable development and climate change such as Rio+20 and the UN Framework Convention on Climate Change (UNFCCC). They have promoted in these fora a 'just transition' for workers as countries seek to green their economies. The workers group in the ILO strongly advocated for what ultimately became a common understanding of this concept during the 2013 ILC. In addition to the aforementioned guidance for governments, trade unions and employers, the conclusions identify a number of key policy areas that comprise a 'basic framework to address the challenges of a just transition for all'. These include macroeconomic and growth policies, industrial and sectoral policies, enterprise policies, skills development, occupational safety and health, social protection, rights, and social dialogue and tripartism (ILO 2013b).

The International Organisation of Employers is active in UN and other international processes addressing green economy and related issues. Employers have advocated for the 'greening' of all jobs in order to advance the environmental efficiency of economies as a whole (ibid.). According to its website, the organisation recognises that government efforts to promote greener economies will affect businesses and supply chains, and will also present new enterprise and employment opportunities (IOE 2014). At the 2013 ILC, the employers group, *inter alia*, emphasised that the green economy can generate jobs by spurring innovation in products, processes and services. They also underscored the importance of skills and of sound and predictable regulatory environments (ILO 2013b).

As members of the ILO, the GCC countries may request technical assistance or policy advice from the ILO in developing and implementing green jobs policies. The ILO's Green Jobs Program provides technical assistance throughout the world, as demonstrated on its map on its website (ILO 2014b). In Mexico, the ILO conducted a green jobs assessment, including by sector, to help understand the potential for green jobs in the country (ILO 2013c; 2014c). In Zambia, the ILO is working with other UN agencies to support green jobs in the country's building and construction sector, with an emphasis on promoting the competitiveness of micro, small and medium-sized enterprises (ILO 2014d). As a UN agency the ILO can leverage expertise on green economy issues beyond labour standards and employment. It has established partnerships with the UNEP, the UN Institute for Training and Research, and the UN Development Programme (UNDP). This has manifested itself most recently through these organisations' joint launch in 2014 of the PAGE programme which 'will support 30 countries over the next seven years in building national green economy strategies that will generate new jobs and skills, promote clean technologies, and reduce environmental risks and poverty' (ILO 2014e).

The work of the PAGE suggests that the recognition of the labour issues transcends the world of work and the organisations that are primarily concerned with it. The very first of the objectives of the conference in Dubai referred to earlier, according to its website, was 'to take stock of best practices and lessons learned in advancing an inclusive green economy through policy reforms and shifting investment into key areas of the economy that produce jobs, social equity and income' (UNEP PAGE 2014b).

Existing models and lessons learned

Countries and regions throughout the world are researching and adopting measures in an effort to green their economies. The European Union (EU), for example, has studied and implemented a range of green economy and green jobs policy approaches. In 2013, the European Commission's Directorate-General for Employment, Social Affairs and Inclusion convened a multi-stakeholder conference on 'Sustainable Job-rich Recovery', during which experts identified a number of challenges, including lack of consistent political commitments across member states and policy coordination among actors, insufficient finances or incentives to stimulate demand for green jobs, skills gaps that lead to slower growth in green sectors, and a population unconvinced of the benefits of the green economy. A clear message emerged, and one that is applicable elsewhere: governments and their partners can play a critical role in the success of green economies by demonstrating political commitment to it. This commitment can manifest itself through a comprehensive policy mix of building consensus on common commitments and priorities, investing in capacity and network building across different authorities and implementing financial mechanisms (European Commission 2013).

'Green Growth Best Practice' is an initiative supported by the Global Green Growth Initiative, the European Climate Foundation, the Climate and Development Knowledge Network and the governments of the United Kingdom and the Netherlands, and guided by, among others, the World Bank, the OECD, UNEP and UNDP. While its publication on 'Green Growth in Practice' has almost no discussion of the experience of GCC countries,[8] it provides an instructive overview of global experience (Green Growth Best Practice 2014, 139). Six out of the nine 'effective practices for green growth' (7) that it identifies have bearing on and implicate labour considerations. Some have bearing at the level of planning, such as the call for coordination, clarity of vision and targets, and robust analysis and communication. These implicate labour considerations as essential elements in a total approach toward planning for growth of green economies. Others more explicitly address labour considerations, such as the impact on poverty reduction and the impact of particular measures and technology on the poor (11), or labour and skill development programmes to improve competitiveness and avoid bottlenecks to investment, increase employment opportunities, smooth workers' transition from declining sectors and reduce social inequalities especially for marginalised or lower skilled workers (13). The analysis also devotes dedicated attention to labour and skills development policy, which is discussed in detail later in this chapter (136).

Green economy – prospects and possibilities

In a report from 2012, the ILO and OECD stressed that 'the relationship between sustainable development, decent work, and good labour market performance can be mutually reinforcing' (International Labour Office and OECD 2012, 1). They recognised that though environmental policies will be the main drivers of green growth, labour market policies can help with the implementation of broader green growth strategies, and focused on four policy areas in particular: first, policymakers should emphasise skills training because a gap exists between the skills workers in declining sectors possess and the skills needed in emerging green sectors. More significant will be workers' capacity to green existing jobs, though the authors suggest this should not be particularly challenging since 'there appear to be few fully green skills' (11). Second, workers displaced from declining sectors should be helped to make the transition to new opportunities, with particular emphasis on strong social protection[9] systems being in place for workers in weathering the transition. Third, protecting fundamental worker rights in green sectors is important. Though acknowledging that efforts to protect worker rights in green sectors do not appear to differ from efforts to protect worker rights in all sectors, they suggest a need to be vigilant during periods of structural change. Moreover, in developing and emerging economies jobs that may benefit the environment, such as waste picking, tend to be found in the informal sector where workers lack protections. Finally, SMEs play a critical role in shifting to more sustainable production and consumption patterns (ibid., passim).

Enablers and inhibitors of green economy in the Gulf

The recent history of the Gulf region demonstrates several trends that can be expected to be sources of strength for the development of coherent green economy strategies and coherent labour strategies to accompany those. The hydrocarbon wealth of most of the states of the region provides the means to undertake the necessary initiatives – technical innovation, investment, and education and training. Moreover, the close control exercised by interlocking political and economic elites suggests favourable prospects of coherent policy-making and prompt implementation of those policies. The substantial inward and outward investment flows between the region and the global economy, and the accompanying corporate networks, offer a platform for integration with global innovation in green economy initiatives.

The GCC as a regional institution offers a functioning and functional institutional framework for sharing of lessons learned and coordination of effort. It also comprises states with broadly similar types of environmental and workforce challenges, and broadly similar political aspirations.

Natural and cultural endowments offer a solid foundation for the development of substantial green enterprise in the region. The frequency and duration of sunlight, coupled with the availability of extensive stretches of land, offer a promising environment for the development of substantial solar power generation. If potential synergies were realised between such power generation, and investment in research and development and manufacturing, there is a realistic prospect of the region emerging as a manufacturing centre for solar power equipment.

Indigenous water management techniques in the region, particularly *aflaj*[10] in Oman, can be the basis for the development of modern water management techniques that benefit from modern technology and investment of capital to form the basis for innovation research and offer a model for other societies. Because the success of *aflaj* relies on integration of local governance, low-tech engineering and hydrology, it can be a relatively labour-intensive activity for modelling to other societies. Unlike other labour-intensive green technologies and systems that have been criticised as 'de-skilling' and lowering productivity and therefore wages (Morriss et al. 2009), the relative sophistication of *aflaj* and similar initiatives based on updating it would offer occasion for 'up-skilling'.

GCC states have in recent years undertaken policy initiatives and investments in technology and research and development, and established a profile in the global conversation about green economy. All GCC states are parties to the UNFCCC and Kyoto Protocol. The government of Saudi Arabia has established the Saudi Energy Efficiency Centre, is developing a mandatory national energy efficiency plan, and established an Energy Conservation and Awareness Department in its Ministry of Water and Electricity. The government of the UAE launched a National Energy Efficiency and Conservation Program in 2011 (Meltzer et al. 2014, 33). Under the auspices of, and with the assistance of, the Global Green Growth Institute, the Government of the UAE has now adopted a National Strategy for Green Growth, under which Abu Dhabi has set a target of 30 per cent low carbon emission power generation by 2020, and Dubai has set targets of 30 per cent improvements in energy efficiency and 20 per cent of energy from clean sources by 2030 (Al-Abdooli n.d., 7). The UAE is also host to the global headquarters of the International Renewable Energy Agency and the World Future Energy Summit. The 1st Global Conference on PAGE recognised the UAE as 'playing a leading role in promoting the transition to a green economy' (UNEP PAGE 2014a, 1). Arguably the single most prominent example of both a policy initiative and investments in sustainable energy technology research and development in the region is Masdar, an initiative of the government of Abu Dhabi consisting of capital, clean energy, research and geographical location components.

Qatar has the dubious distinction of being the global leader in carbon emissions per capita. Nonetheless (or perhaps because of that), it too has made significant efforts in green economy activities. In 2012, it hosted the 18th session of the Conference of Parties to the UNFCCC, and has acted as host of the Doha Carbon and Energy Forum. The Qatar National Vision 2030 and the Qatar National Development Strategy 2011–2016 reflect recognition of environmental challenges, all of which naturally lead to green economy initiatives, though it should be noted that the emphasis in the discussion of environment is on the knowledge necessary rather than on production processes. Qatar has delineated no quantitative targets in its Vision 2030, though it has in its National Strategy for 2011–2016, and a number of announcements have been made by various government agencies in recent years (Meltzer *et al.* 2014, 12–13).[11]

The weaknesses in the GCC countries that might inhibit development of green economies and of appropriate accompanying labour policies include a shallow manufacturing base, lack of historical experience with a manufacturing economy, the lack of a fully integrated market within the region, poor relative investment in scientific and technical research and training, failure to value and reward scientific work, failure to adopt employment and training policies that are precisely calibrated with reliable and detailed labour market information, and above all the relatively shallow dissemination in elites and in the general population of a culture of sustainable development (IFC 2009, 9).

As the IFC describes the MENA region as a whole,

> sustainability understanding and action of government levels currently is fragmentary. While sustainable development is now being incorporated into some national strategic plans, it is at even earlier stages of being put into practice, as measured by country ESG [environmental, social, governance] performance.

The IFC also notes that

> MENA countries have made important strides, although many are still in the very early stages of development. Securities markets have initiated significant governance reforms and established new requirements, but this has not yet extended to the environmental and social components of ESG. The research also suggests that country level ESG performance is lagging what is mandated under existing ESG regulations.
>
> (Ibid.)

In the absence of a collective will among the GCC governments to avail themselves of the opportunity for policy-making to drive green economy initiatives, there are few countervailing forces to drive their governments to collective action across the GCC as a whole. Trade unions and other civil society institutions are relatively weak, and as yet not organised for transnational cooperation among themselves.

Investment

Environmental challenges in the GCC have prompted responses from the private sector (Beetz 2012). Many of the largest and most capital-intensive projects that may be described as 'green' have relied on a close nexus with governments or government entities.

In 2011, Phoenix Solar and Naizak Global Engineering Systems developed a small, 3–4 MW PV power plant in Saudi Arabia for the Saudi Arabian Oil Company (Aramco) (Phoenix Solar 2011). Other examples of close public-private interdependence include the following: the Mohamed bin Rashid Al Maktoum Solar Park in Dubai (Supreme Council of Energy) (Gifford 2012), the Dubai Electricity and Water Authority's collaboration with First Solar (Clover 2013), the Solar Roof Program of Abu Dhabi (and the collaboration with the Renewable Academy in Germany) (Stuart 2010a), and Masdar's partnership with Total and Abengoa Solar on the 100 MW Shams1 (Stuart 2010b).[12]

Such official involvement in economic activity in this sector reflects not only the usual commercial and financial imperatives but also the official commitment to certain green goals that require green economic activity, as described in the previous section.

The strong government and parastatal involvement in these types of innovative, technologically sophisticated and capital-intensive initiatives is relevant to labour policy. We argue later that the prospects of green economy development in the GCC will be constrained by labour market limitations, which will require active labour market policies and significant government commitment to these and to investment in workforce development. Therefore, the dominant role of state institutions in the economy might facilitate adoption of the necessary labour market and workforce development policies. Given the current pattern in the GCC of activist governments determining economic strategies and disposing of very significant sovereign resources, albeit with a substantial role for the truly private sector, there should be little difficulty in principle with addressing the need identified for the MENA region as a whole for sustainable development – that 'active development strategies must be put in place to drive this' (George 2011, 12). However, this will also require clear policy commitment to active labour market policies.

In the absence of government commitment the prospect is unpromising. The predominance of state-owned enterprises, family-owned enterprises and private small- and medium-sized businesses in the GCC economies results in substantial portions of the economy not being listed on exchanges. Foreign investors interested in green investments consequently have fewer opportunities to use environmental governance indicators in their investment decisions and strategies. Moreover, whereas many securities markets in the region have achieved improvements in corporate governance and disclosure regimes, and there is growing awareness among listed companies that the next phase of transparency will encompass environmental and social performance (including workers' interests), there has hitherto been little activism or interest on the part of investors (IFC 2009, 28).

Promising signs for environmentally sensitive investment might be found in the stringency and enforcement of environmental regulations in particular countries. The IFC's Advisory Services in the MENA, in the report 'Sustainable Investment in the Middle East and North Africa Region Report' (2009) provide a ranking of MENA countries for stringency and enforcement of environmental regulations. Oman and Qatar are rated the best performers among all MENA countries, followed by Tunisia and the UAE, with Saudi Arabia and Bahrain above the global mean and only Kuwait languishing at the bottom (ibid., 47). However, this is a controversial analysis and ranking, and has been disputed by first-hand observers and experts who have questioned whether Qatar's accomplishments in this respect merit its ranking.

Labour

The optimistic scenario for the effects of green economy on the labour market is that described by UNESCWA as follows:

> The global transition to a green economy could create huge opportunities of green jobs in the different economic sectors, such as employment in the fields of renewable energy generation, energy efficiency, ecosystem rehabilitation and protection, ecotourism, waste management, etc. Such transition brings solutions to eradicate unemployment in the Arab region. According to the latest studies of the [ILO] many green sectors require a more sizeable workforce than the less environment-friendly alternatives (for instance, organic farming versus traditional farming).
>
> (UNESCWA, LAS and UNEP 2011, 8)

When discussing the green economy in the Gulf, we are in large part speaking of prospective developments, and thus projecting on the basis of available information. One of the tasks identified in the recommendations at the end of the chapter is the need for more precise labour market analysis to establish what the prospects are for provision of adequately skilled workers for the tasks and occupations required in green economy sectors. One aspect of this is identifying what skills are available in the present workforce in any given economy, and what skills may realistically be expected to be produced in the future, or the degree of official or private sector commitment to and capacity for the development of those skills.

We have noted a high degree of government involvement in the development of green economic activity. Along with the green economic policy frameworks or 'visions' that have also been adopted by some GCC member governments, this might lead to expansion of employment opportunities in public sector green economic activity.

As illustrated by the identification of the occupational safety and health risks in some green economy occupations, and the identification of some occupations as being at the very least skilled end of the spectrum, some aspects of the green economy are not necessarily the most desirable, skilled or remunerative of occupations. In the case of some other occupations in the green economy, the types of skills in demand may require only modest upgrading from the skills already in evidence in equivalent occupations in the conventional economy. One should therefore be mindful of the variegated nature of the labour market, and the need to have a differentiated understanding and discussion of the skills and training required for employment in the green economy.

The conditions that prevail in the Arab region more broadly are also mostly found in the GCC countries. Unemployment, underemployment and precarious employment are found, as is low labour force participation of women and of youth, even among the better educated. Productivity in industry is sub-optimal and industrialisation is low relative to the gross domestic product (GDP), owing to the prevalence of primary resource extraction. Manufacturing and agriculture have declined, and employment has tilted more toward lower-skilled services. Where there is job growth, wages have stagnated, and there have been minimal or no improvements in efficiency or technology (ILO and UNDP 2012, 110). A comparison by the ILO of proportions of national economic activity that constitute manufacturing value added in selected Arab states finds the GCC states of Kuwait, Oman and Qatar to compare unfavourably with Syria, Tunisia, Palestine, Jordan, Morocco and Egypt. Oman and Qatar demonstrate better performance in medium-tech and high-tech manufacturing value added, but still lag behind Egypt, Jordan, Morocco and Syria (ibid., 111).

The development of green economies depends upon increasing sophistication in economies in general, and this in turn translates into labour markets characterised by progressive improvement in workforce skills, compensation and rights. The economic development of Gulf societies will depend upon diversification, higher value added and technology-intensive products and processes, and increases in the range of capabilities and knowledge. The extent to which these also result in the establishment of healthy green economies within the larger Gulf economies will depend on coherent industrial policy devoted to these ends. However, the recent economic history of the Gulf demonstrates governments that favour cronies and quick return through finance, resource extraction and real estate. Such industrial policy as exists appears to be shaped as much by foreign direct investment patterns and expectations, rather than shaping such investments (ibid., 112).

The recent and projected trends in numbers of workers employed in industry in the GCC countries suggest only modest likely future growth of industry (as distinct from agriculture and services). Sluggish industrial growth generally is likely to be reflected in limits to growth of green industries. Some green economy occupations will be found in services, both at the low-skilled (and most likely hazardous) end of the scale and in financial or information technology service occupations, but these must by their nature have a significant green economy to support, and are likely to be a relatively small proportion of the whole.

Projections for proportion of industrial employment relative to total workforce in the GCC countries suggest that the proportion of workforce in industry will not grow in the period through 2018. This compares with significant increases

Table 9.1 Employment in industry

	2004	2014	2018
Bahrain	15%	42%	41%
Kuwait	19%	18%	18%
Oman	17%	43%	44%
Qatar	41%	50%	50%
Saudi Arabia	21%	27%	27%
UAE	40%	22%	22%

Source: ILO (2014f)

over the past decade in all GCC countries except Kuwait which saw a negligible decrease and the UAE which saw a substantial decrease owing to the rapid development of financial services, information technology-related occupations and tourism (see Table 9.1).

Gulf labour markets mirror certain general trends identified by the ILO, and these are likely to be replicated in green economy occupations. Alongside global increases in unemployment, the ILO's 'Global Employment Trends 2014' identifies the following salient accompanying trends: reversal of previous improvements in labour force participation for women and young people; an increase in the proportion of vulnerable employment; a stalling of previous improvements in the incidence of working poverty; and significant persistence of informal employment (ILO 2014f, 4).

Modest signs may be identified of recognition in the GCC countries of the specific labour dimensions of green economy. The Chair's Summary and Conclusions from the 1st Global Conference on PAGE identifies 'green and decent jobs, ... social inclusion and poverty eradication' as overarching '[i]nsights and good practices' (UNEP PAGE 2014a, 3). As noted earlier, it also recognises that 'green jobs need to include decent working conditions for them to be beneficial for the environment and contribute to social inclusion' and that '[t]his calls for more attention to be paid to informal work' (4). More specific to the GCC, the UAE's National Strategy on Green Growth evinces recognition of the importance of the labour dimension by referring to creation of jobs and specifically green jobs (Al-Abdooli n.d., 2, 4). However, in identifying the components of the UAE's green growth plan (5) and 'key insights' (11) it makes no reference to labour considerations.

Whereas social inclusion has now become a standard feature of the international discourse on environmental protection, green economy and green growth, the specifically labour dimensions of social inclusion will face significant obstacles in many of the GCC countries. Trade unions and other workers' organisations are weak or non-existent in Qatar, Saudi Arabia and the UAE, beleaguered even in Bahrain where they previously enjoyed some influence with policymakers, and nascent in Oman. In the absence of strong labour voices, the capacity and willingness of policymakers to attend to workforce considerations from the perspective of workers' interests will thus be slight. We argue later that the totality of the work environment, including the rights and remuneration of workers – what distinguishes decent work – is itself necessary to the creation of labour markets which will sustain the skills levels necessary to growth of green economies. The poor industrial relations regime and the weakness of the workers' voice constitute significant challenges.

Skills and training

The percentage of executives reporting an inadequately educated workforce is significantly higher in the GCC (14.4 per cent) than for all Arab states (10.4 per cent), non-oil Arab states (6.6 per cent), other oil producers (8.6 per cent) or the OECD (6.2 per cent). Since the GCC countries appear to have active labour market policies in the form of highly regulated and targeted recruitment from and dependence on migrant labour from outside the GCC, substantially from outside the Arab region, this is highly noteworthy as an indicator of a serious workforce constraint on green economy development in the GCC. Within the GCC, the percentage of employers reporting inadequately educated workforces ranges from 7.1 per cent in Kuwait to 21.8 per cent in Oman. Qatar, Saudi Arabia and the UAE register percentages in excess of 15 per cent, whereas Bahrain and Kuwait register half that (ILO and UNDP 2012, 76).

Egypt, Jordan, Lebanon, Syria and Tunisia all demonstrate higher mathematics and science scores on internationally comparable tests than Oman, Kuwait, Saudi Arabia and Qatar (ibid., 75). Where employment is more or less guaranteed, the individual or family incentive to invest in education declines, even where education is free or on scholarship. And decent conditions of employment, such as those found in government employment for nationals of GCC countries, act as an additional disincentive for education and training for upward mobility in the labour market (82).

The GCC countries face real challenges in generating the trained workforce necessary for green occupations. The ILO has noted that employers in the region cannot rely on training centres, which have trainers teaching based on their past (and therefore likely obsolete) experience, but will instead have to do on-the-job or employer-sponsored training to meet specific skill requirements (ibid., 79). The question that arises in all such cases is that of who pays for the costs of training. Can we anticipate that governments will bear some of these costs? If not, will the default position of most GCC employers (and governments for that matter) of importing workers *ad hoc* to meet immediate needs from surplus labour markets discourage serious systematic efforts at national or regional labour market planning and workforce development?

The answer provided by one authoritative observer, the ILO Regional Office for the Arab States, is discouraging in this respect. The practice of recruiting expatriates, whatever the original justification for it in terms of meeting labour shortages, has now rendered employers in the GCC unwilling to offer training.

Moreover, the take-up by GCC nationals is poor of technical and vocational education and training that is available through publicly provided and financed means, and the drop-out rates are high. The small percentage of secondary education that accounts for technical and vocational education and training in the GCC – 2 per cent – suggests the scale of the problem of preparing GCC nationals for employment in a future green economy (ibid., 82).

Among the effects of reliance on expatriate workers for the range of workforce needs from unskilled manual labour to the highest technical occupations is the missed opportunity to create a national culture of innovation and upgrading of technical skills. Although some expatriate workers have made their homes in the GCC countries for periods of time, they maintain a sojourner mentality. Their sense of belonging and enthusiasm for social contributions belongs to their countries of origin. The longer-term the tenure of a particular worker, the greater will be that worker's contribution to the upgrading of skills in any given company or national economy.

The other significant determinant of innovation and training is the status of science, technical occupations and innovation in the broader GCC society and culture. Science and technology suffer from a lack of national policies and strategies, insufficient funding well below global levels, the absence of widely disseminated information and communication on scientific and technical matters, and most significantly for the present discussion the lack of strong professional associations and the lack of coordination between industry and research and development (AlMudhaf 2008, 37). The lack of public and elite awareness of science and technology issues and the lack of adequate support for these are mutually reinforcing.

This is not to suggest that sophisticated and advanced institutions are lacking. Indeed one of the many benefits of the national wealth and surpluses of GCC states has been the establishment of institutions such as the UAE and Zayed Universities, the King Abdulaziz City for Science and Technology and the Kuwait Institute for Scientific Research.

The predominance of expatriate workers in technical occupations, the culture relating to science and technology and the future course of the green economy come together in the following. More skilled jobs in the future could lead to innovation by the occupants of those jobs, and the extent to which those workers embody high value added and high investment in their current skills levels will act as an incentive to invest more in training and upgrading those human resources in order to maximise the economic benefit they provide. The higher the proportion of national workers in those jobs (rather than in public employment or sinecures) the higher will be the inducement for governments and businesses to make such investments as not likely to be lost upon repatriation, and the higher the level of dissemination of awareness of scientific and technical values in the national population.

Women's labour force participation rates in the GCC countries are also a significant factor. UNESCWA (2013 47, 62) notes, as a principal challenge among all challenges to development of a green economy in Kuwait and Saudi Arabia, the poor labour participation rates of women there. Compared to the global average of in excess of 55 per cent, women's participation in the GCC is in the range of 30–35 per cent. This is relevant to the discussion of skills and its relationship to participation of GCC nationals in skilled occupations because of the high rates of education and training of women. More women than men are registered for higher education in GCC institutions, and throughout the Arab world women outnumber men among science graduates (AlMudhaf 2008, 37). More equitable labour force participation by women could be a significant factor in bringing locally available skills to job requirements, and in providing national workers equipped with a basic foundation for specialised technical training. This relates to the issue of reliance on expatriate labour addressed below. Because non-national workers in GCC states are disproportionately male, excessive reliance on expatriate labour to respond to the labour market's demand for skills will subvert the promise presented by women's over-representation in science and technology education. Thus the simultaneous benefit of meeting labour market needs from national technically and scientifically trained workers and expanding women's labour force participation will be lost.

While fertility has declined in the GCC countries over the last four decades (Dyer 2008, 64), between natural growth and migration the GCC has experienced steady growth in population in recent years. Moreover, between 17 per cent (Qatar) and 38 per cent (Saudi Arabia) of the populations of the GCC member states are below the age of 15 (PRB 2009). Even these high proportions understate the extent of the challenge with respect to GCC-national populations. Because most GCC countries have very high proportions of non-nationals in their populations (most of whom are adults), the shares of nationals under 15 years of age requiring vocational training and employment opportunity are even greater than the figures above would suggest.

There is a wide consensus that the increased working age population throughout the MENA region, and including the GCC countries, has also experienced significant improvements in education and skills, owing to the substantial investments throughout the Arab world in human capital development. By 2000 the Arab region as a whole was ahead of South Asia in educational attainment, and barely behind Latin America and East Asia (Dyer 2008, 75). However, the same commentators also note the rise in labour supply relative to demand, from indigenous sources and from migration, as well as poor labour market outcomes (76, 78). Moreover, surely it must remain a source of concern – if not alarm – that youth unemployment in Arab states generally, and even in the GCC, remains too high (ILO 2014g, 30).[13]

UNESCWA, the League of Arab States (LAS) and UNEP (2011, 12) note that the high number of youth in the populations of the UNESCWA countries 'represents a new opportunity for development provided that youth receive enlightened education and are provided with sustainable production capacities…' Despite the improved educational outcomes for GCC youth, and despite the increasing focus on technical skills relevant to green economy occupations, matching of labour supply and labour demand will continue to be imperfect. Uncertainty remains about whether the skills and education possessed by workers and job-seekers fit the types of skills required.

It is noteworthy that at least one of the national development strategies of the GCC countries, that of Qatar, explicitly and intelligently recognises the drag posed on development of a technically skilled workforce by a labour market that has a built-in bias to demand low-skilled labour. In making a commitment to review policies with a view to addressing this problem it notes that:

> The presence of a pool of cheap labour creates a bias towards labour-intensive technologies that provide few opportunities for discovery or productivity advances. Only when cost structures change will businesses want to invest in new, less labour-intensive production methods and will job-seekers alter their expectations.
>
> (GSDP 2011, 98)

The Qatar strategy further notes that:

> Breaking out of the current low-wage configuration may raise costs in the short run and will require adjustments that may be difficult. But the accelerated productivity growth that follows will more than compensate for any rise in costs and will create incentives for innovation and the acquisition of knowledge.
>
> (ibid.)

The strategy also evinces a keen awareness of the relationship between labour market and workforce development policies when it notes that:

> Through modern education and training, citizens might qualify for successful careers in a knowledge-oriented economy. But possessing those skills does not guarantee that there will be jobs – particularly if employers can still orient their recruitment and production strategies around the availability of a large pool of cheap, unskilled immigrant workers.
>
> (ibid.)

It is clear that the extent to which GCC governments can address some of these challenges will depend upon the adoption of labour market reforms broadly defined. The desirable agenda for workforce development is suggested by the discussion above. The GCC governments are also engaged in reforms of the regime governing the immigration and terms of employment of expatriate workers, including attempts to indigenise the workforce, though with varying degrees of seriousness or effectiveness. The success of reforms that might be undertaken is likely to depend upon the extent to which they address the relationship between conditions of work, incentives and quality of workforce skills.

Migration

Complicating the labour market picture is the reliance – some would call it an 'addiction' – of GCC economies on expatriate workers at labour costs significantly below those commanded by nationals of the GCC countries. The IFC notes that while many countries have responded to concerns about expatriate workers' work conditions, pay, living conditions and freedom of mobility with significant regulatory and performance improvements, this nonetheless remains 'a sensitive and serious issue that will continue to feature prominently as a highly visible ESG consideration…' (IFC 2009, 21).

In 1975 there were fewer expatriate workers (1.1 million) than nationals (1.7 million) in the GCC countries. In 2010 the ratio had reversed substantially, with 14 million expatriates and approximately 6 million nationals. One does not have to follow events in the region closely to be aware of the ubiquitous presence of foreign workers in the GCC countries. Any casual observer or visitor becomes aware of this as one of the most distinctive features of these societies. As the ILO observes, 'it is no exaggeration that migration policy is the single most important issue in the GCC countries' (ILO and UNDP 2012, 38).

The ILO concludes that immigration policies that allow payment of lower wages to migrant workers than to national workers encourage the use of labour-intensive techniques in the private sector. These in turn lead to low labour productivity, which in turn leads to low wages, which in due course results in depressing wages and working conditions of nationals in the private sector. This, the ILO goes on to note, increases the incentives for nationals to seek employment in the public sector, and thus leaves few incentives to invest in human capital beyond the obtaining of formal credentials. These interlocking processes for low skills in the public and private sectors lead to economies locked into low productivity equilibrium, which in turn is an incentive for continued reliance on immigration (ibid., 38).

Large-scale migration dependency of entire economies or sectors of economies has a deleterious effect on labour standards. This is so both of wages and safety and health conditions in workplaces and of other labour standards such as the freedom of association in trade unions or other workers' associations and the right to collective bargaining. Indeed, even in those GCC countries that have relatively autonomous trade unions and relatively enlightened industrial relations regimes, such as Bahrain and Oman,[14] expatriate workers do not participate significantly in either the activities or the benefits of such organisations.

Labour standards are certainly of interest to labour practitioners from the perspective of the welfare and interests of workers. They should also be of interest to green economy analysts and practitioners because they provide the enabling conditions for training, upgrading of skills and innovation. This is because a workforce relatively unprotected by labour standards is likelier to be temporary, and therefore to possess few incentives or resources to innovate or upgrade its skills, or to offer employers few incentives to invest in training or upgrading of skills. A workforce protected by standards and able to secure improved remuneration will contribute to building enterprises of superior productivity and to stable industrial relations, and thus offer the stable and solid foundation for the types of innovative and high value added enterprises that will build a green economy activity.

A UNESCWA Bahrain country factsheet from 2013 recognises the negative relationship between type of work characteristic of a migrant labour dependent economy and the higher end production processes necessary to a green economy. Among the principal challenges to development of a green economy this notes

> a high reliance on foreign labour, most of which is often unskilled and engaged in low productivity trades in such sectors as construction and services. In general, such low skills level provides no motivation for increased productivity. This low productivity and depressed wage cannot attract higher-educated national labour. This persistence of low-wage, low productivity economy thus hinders the transition towards more knowledge based work and thus Green Economy.
>
> (UNESCWA 2013, 39)

The same report's country factsheets for all the other GCC members make almost the identical observation about the deleterious effects of reliance on foreign labour (47, 57, 60, 62, 68).

On the positive side, labour migration could address shortages of the relevant specific skills in the GCC countries as a short-term expedient. The effectiveness of this will depend on accurate skills matching. That in turn will depend on the accuracy and adequacy of labour market information in countries of origin and destination. Many Gulf countries of destination, despite enjoying the resources to gather labour market information, are still in the process of developing such systems, whereas many countries of origin of skilled and technically trained workers lack good systems and the resources to develop them. Bilateral technical assistance could help develop such systems, and regional systems could be developed of labour market information gathering and sharing, for purposes of skills matching.

There will remain difficulties because, whereas skills matching for the short term is relatively manageable, planning for supply of personnel with appropriate skills for the long term is fraught with difficulty. Long-term skills requirements are harder to predict and sufficient training in the appropriate skills is harder for more remote needs. In any case, greater attention must be paid, even in the best of national labour market information systems, to greater articulation of detail by sectors and occupations. It is also important to distinguish the distinct and varied requirements of skills matching for high-skilled occupations, for skilled occupations, for low-skilled occupations and for unskilled occupations. Moreover, prediction of labour market requirements is likely to be highly unreliable in view of what is by its very nature a dynamic picture of rapid technological change in green processes. Finally, even were these difficulties to be addressed adequately they would inevitably be frustrated by the fact that private calculations will occur regardless of public planning, as employers seek out satisfaction of their immediate workforce needs while individual migrant workers make decisions based on immediate incentives and imperatives.

If the countries of the GCC are to continue to rely on migrant labour for any significant part of the workforce of a green economy, at any point on the skill spectrum, certain considerations will have to be borne in mind. Wage differentials between foreign and domestic workers may be particularly problematical, even leaving aside issues of equity or justice, because the absence of merit-based advancement and remuneration will interfere with optimal labour productivity and upgrading of production processes. Evidence of drags on the overall labour market from the restrictive labour market that immigrant workers face is found in recent data from the OECD (ILO 2014h, 190).

The need for protection of the rights of migrant workers (ILO 2013d) arises in the context of green economy occupations quite as much as in other contexts. Lower skilled green economy occupations will pose a higher risk of poor workplace health and safety. This risk is likely to be heightened for migrant workers, and thus the international movement to introduce transparency and accountability in transnational labour recruitment will have much to offer. OECD data to be published soon indicates significant incidence of over-qualification among technically skilled workers. Therefore poor or unethical recruitment practices could also pose a danger to such relatively well-qualified workers.[15]

The states party to the Abu Dhabi Dialogue,[16] which consists of sending and receiving countries in the Gulf labour market, have taken initiatives such as ethical conduct pledges by recruiters and collaboration between governments such as those of the UAE and the Philippines. Most important in mitigating the risks of labour migration will be more effective enforcement of legal protections by destination country governments and greater monitoring of employers by civil society. The ILO's discussion of labour migration management has introduced an important new element in the form of a role for trade unions. ('Cooperation between these non-state actors across borders can also enhance the protection of migrant workers and their access to trade union rights in particular, most notably in destination countries where protection structures are relatively weak or underdeveloped' (ILO 2013b, 4).) Among the many bilateral and regional agreements to involve trade unions in monitoring such risks are actions taken by trade unions in Bahrain, Kuwait and Oman to protect migrant workers through interregional trade union cooperation. In 2009, three agreements were signed in Colombo, Sri Lanka between three national trade union centres in Sri Lanka and their counterparts in Bahrain, Kuwait and Jordan. In 2012, agreements were signed between the General Federation of Nepalese Trade Unions and unions in Bahrain and Kuwait (ibid., 7 fn. 8).

The ultimate goal in the field of transnational labour migration of the tripartite community which speaks from the perspective of the world of work is 'to ensure that the promotion of effectively operating labour markets offering decent work becomes a central element in discussions on migration and development' (ibid., 1). Among the ways that it proposes to do so is by focusing on a sectoral approach

(5), which would fit such an initiative well to address some of the challenges described in the specific context of the green economy.

Conclusions and recommendations

A green economy in large part requires a sophisticated economy. Increased labour demand is the key to breaking the cycle of low productivity and low-skill economies in the Gulf, and that requires public action (ILO and UNDP 2012, 20). The elements necessary are macroeconomic policy coherence, promotion of social dialogue, expanded social protection (26), improved migration management, active labour market programmes (27), more precisely focused education and training, and better data for policy-making (28).

Industrial policy and investment policy should more consciously emphasise measures to advance decent work, to improve workforce skills and to generate higher value added processes. Incorporation of international labour standards into planning will protect individual workers and yield productivity improvements.[17]

National plans for environment, education and economic development should be closely coordinated. Good policy requires improved data and its more systematic use for planning. The improvement of labour market information systems and environmental information systems should also be a priority.

As recent discourse on green growth and green economy has recognised, the complicated technical and economic transitions necessary require detailed and painstaking attention to all aspects of workforce development and labour market planning (Green Growth Best Practice 2014, 136). If governments are to

> [w]ork with the private sector to anticipate and address the effects of green growth policies on employment, using labour market and skills development policies to enable the reallocation of workers from declining to growing sectors and help prevent bottlenecks to growth
>
> (ibid.)

then social dialogue and consensus building between governments, employers and workers can facilitate transitions through such social and economic dislocations.

That in turn suggests the value of strong and representative workers' organisations and a solid culture of industrial relations. Governments and employers should accept the need to move beyond the highly restrictive trade union and industrial relations laws and practices that characterise the GCC. Governments should take steps to develop legal, regulatory and practical means for embodying international standards of freedom of association for workers and collective bargaining. In view of the prevalence of expatriate workers in most GCC labour markets, their organisation and rights should be incorporated into trade union priorities (ILO 2014g, 33). In all of the above, GCC member governments would benefit substantially from the technical assistance of the ILO.

Active measures are necessary for matching labour market demand and supply of proficiencies, including development of planning frameworks for aligning vocational training and education with labour market requirements. Where national plans, visions or frameworks call for systematic attention to policy-making and planning for skills development,[18] these should be consistently implemented and provided assurance of resources over a substantial period of time.

The education sector is essential in providing the training and knowledge necessary (UNESCWA 2013, 18). The figures for education spending as a percentage of GDP show uneven commitment of GCC members relative to other Arab countries, with Saudi Arabia doing the best, Oman performing relatively well, and the UAE least well of all the countries compared (36). Heightened commitment to education spending is necessary, with particular emphasis on green economy-related scientific, technical, engineering *and social science* disciplines.

Strategies for meeting demand for particular skills in the Gulf rely excessively on expatriate labour. This prompts excessive reliance on measures such as pre-departure certification systems, common occupational standards, and mutual recognition of technical and professional qualifications. These are short-term expedients. A more durable basis for a next-generation economy is the upgrading of national workforces, and training and education directed to that end. That will require increased government investment and active consultation and involvement of scientific and technical professional communities.

Improved women's workforce participation will enhance the skills base in the Gulf. Youth employment and training initiatives will maximise returns on investment over a longer working life.

Because of the huge significance of maritime industry and transportation in all GCC economies, particular attention should be paid to the development of a green maritime economy, and to training for that purpose. Active participation in the International Maritime Organization will offer a good return on investment, as both maritime environment and the fast-evolving nature of maritime labour in response to technological innovation are priority areas for the organisation. Although the International Civil Aviation Organization does not have as substantial an emphasis on labour in the aviation industry, the inclusion of environmental protection as one of five strategic objectives for the period 2014–2016 suggests further attention to it, in view of the significance of civil aviation in the GCC economies.

Cooperation on development and matching of skills and on training under the Abu Dhabi Dialogue – between the UAE and Kuwait as receiving countries, and India, Pakistan and the Philippines as sending countries – should be strengthened and expanded. A parallel effort to address labour standards and protection of workers' rights should be undertaken, in partnership with trade unions and employers.

Notes

1 The author writes in her personal capacity only, and the views expressed do not necessarily reflect the views of the United States Department of Labor or the International Labor Affairs Bureau.

2 The United Nations Environment Programme (UNEP 2014) has developed a working definition of

> a green economy as one that results in improved human well-being and social equity, while significantly reducing environmental risks and ecological scarcities. In its simplest expression, a green economy can be thought of as one which is low carbon, resource efficient and socially inclusive.

3 Owing to limitations of space, we do not here address social protection, but it should be noted as one of the central issues considered in discussions of the world of work.

4 'Decent work' is a term of art within the ILO that means employment with access to social protection, respect for fundamental worker rights and social dialogue – the four strategic objectives of the organization's work (ILO 2014a).

5 According to the ILO (2013a), 'jobs are green when they help reduce negative environmental impact ultimately leading to environmentally, economically and socially sustainable enterprises and economies'. The ILO goes on to elaborate that 'Green jobs are decent jobs that contribute to preserve or restore a sustainable environment, be they in traditional sectors such as manufacturing and construction, or in new, emerging green sectors such as renewable energy and energy efficiency' (ibid.).

6 The Arab Human Development Report for 2009 focused on the environment, and remains the most authoritative overview of the range of environmental challenges in the GCC. It thus provides a useful indication of the types of green economy opportunity that are presented in the GCC (UNDP 2009).

7 For governments, the recommendations included those pertaining to applying appropriate policy and regulatory frameworks, promoting coherence across institutions, and developing monitoring and data tools where possible. For trade unions and employers, the recommendations called on them to raise awareness, play a role in policy-making, and to promote social dialogue from the national level to the enterprise level. Finally, the recommendations requested the ILO to, *inter alia*, strengthen its research and knowledge base and dissemination in this area, continue to engage with other international organisations, and provide country-level capacity-building assistance to member states (ILO 2013b).

8 It does however identify Masdar City in the UAE in a highly selective list of 'examples of sector-based and provincial programs and initiatives that create green jobs and involve skills development'.

9 There is no universal definition of 'social protection'. However, in the labour sphere and within the ILO in particular, it generally refers to programmes and policies that provide access to income security and health care. Such programmes may include unemployment insurance schemes, conditional cash transfers and universal health care programmes.

10 *Aflaj* are traditional water channels taking advantage of gravity and elevation to deliver water from underground sources (Patterson 2008).

11 At least one authoritative study has without attribution identified Qatar as adopting a goal of 20 per cent renewable energy by 2024 (Meltzer *et al.* 2014).

12 Abu Dhabi has a 7 per cent target for renewables from total electricity generation capacity by 2020. The Dubai Energy Strategy 2030 aims at 1 per cent renewables by

2020 and 5 per cent by 2030. Bahrain's Energy Efficient Lighting Initiative depends on collaboration with the World Bank (World Bank 2013).

13 Youth unemployment in the Arab states as a whole is 23.2 per cent, the highest of any region in the world, and compares with a global average of 13.9 per cent (ibid.).

14 It is notable that these GCC states are also those that have free-trade agreements with the United States.

15 Notably, a delegate of one of the GCC countries very candidly publicly said to the recent Global Forum on Migration and Development (Stockholm, Sweden, 14–16 April 2014) that notwithstanding matching of qualifications and skills, malpractice and lack of transparency in recruitment remains a concern. Recollection of author Amit A. Pandya.

16 Notably for our purposes Bangladesh, India, Indonesia, Nepal, Pakistan, the Philippines, Sri Lanka and Thailand as sending states, and all GCC member states as destination countries.

17 The Qatar National Development Strategy 2011–2016 commits the government to prepare a Human Resources Master Plan 'to coordinate the needs of the economy, government strategy and the labour market' (GSDP 2011, 155). This will 'identify bottlenecks and define required labour force skills and capacities by sector, the type of higher education and training needed and the appropriate mix of expatriate workers for each sector' (ibid.).

References

Al-Abdooli, Eng. Aisha. Undated. *Introduction to Green Growth in the UAE: National Strategy for Green Growth.* (Unpublished PowerPoint presentation).

AlMudhaf, Hayfaa. 2008. 'Science, Technology and Transnational Security in the Middle East.' In *Transnational Trends: Middle Eastern and Asian Views,* edited by Amit Pandya and Ellen Laipson, 23–40. Washington, D.C.: Stimson.

Beetz, Becky. 2012. 'Q.Cells and CCC Realize PV Plant in Abu Dhabi.' *PV Magazine,* 24 May. http://www.pv-magazine.com/

Clover, Ian. 2013. 'Dubai Switches on Its First Solar Plant, with Promise of More to Come.' *PV Magazine,* 24 October. http://www.pv-magazine.com/

Dyer, Paul. 2008. 'Demography in the Middle East: Implications and Risks.' In *Transnational Trends: Middle Eastern and Asian Views,* edited by Amit Pandya and Ellen Laipson, 62–90. Washington, D.C.: Stimson.

EASHW. European Agency for Safety and Health at Work. 2013. *Green Jobs and Occupational Safety and Health: Foresight on New and Emerging Risks Associated with New Technologies by 2020.* Report. Bilbao: EASHW, April.

European Commission. 2013. *Pathways to Green Jobs: Strategies and Policy Options for a Sustainable Job-rich Recovery.* Thematic Event Report. Brussels: ICF GHK, June.

George, Clive. 2011. *Regional Review of Institutions for Sustainable Development in the Arab Region.* Presentation at the Regional Preparatory Meeting Series for Rio+20: Economic Policies Supporting the Transition to a Green Economy in the Arab Region. Beirut, 20–21 July. http://css.escwa.org.lb/sdpd/1610/S24.pdf

Gifford, Jonathan. 2012. 'UAE: 1 GW Solar Project Launched.' *PV Magazine,* 10 January. http://www.pv-magazine.com/

Green Growth Best Practice. 2014. *Green Growth in Practice: Lessons from Country Experiences.* June.

GSDP. General Secretariat for Development Planning of Qatar. 2011. *Qatar National Development Strategy 2011–2016: Towards Qatar National Vision 2030.* Doha: GSDP.

Harsdorff, Marek. 2014. *The Economics of Biogas: Creating Green Jobs in the Dairy Industry of India.* Geneva: International Labour Organization, May.

IFC. International Finance Corporation. 2009. *Sustainable Investment in the Middle East and North Africa Region Report.*

International Labour Office. 2013. *Sustainable Development, Decent Work, and Green Jobs.* Report V. International Labour Conference, 102nd Session. Geneva: International Labour Office.

International Labour Office and OECD. International Labour Office and the Organisation for Economic Co-operation and Development. 2012. *Sustainable Development, Green Growth and Quality Employment: Realizing The Potential for Mutually Reinforcing Policies.* Geneva and Paris: May.

ILO. International Labour Organization. 2013a. 'What is a Green Job?' 26 August. www.ilo.org/global/topics/green-jobs/

ILO. 2013b. *Fifth Item on the Agenda: Sustainable Development, Decent Work, and Green Jobs.* Report of the Committee on Sustainable Development, Decent Work and Green Jobs. Record of Proceedings. ILC102-PR12-[RELCO-130617-4]-En. 19 June.

ILO. 2013c. *Evaluation of the Potential of Green Jobs in Mexico.* Green Jobs Program of the ILO in Mexico. Geneva: September.

ILO. 2013d. *Tripartite Technical Meeting on Labour Migration.* ILO – TTMLM/2013/14. Geneva, 4–8 November.

ILO. 2014a. 'Decent Work Agenda.' Accessed October. http://www.ilo.org/

ILO. 2014b. 'Projects on Green Jobs.' Accessed October. www.ilo.org/global/topics/green-jobs/

ILO. 2014c. 'Mexico: Green Jobs Assessment.' Accessed October. http://www.ilo.org/global/topics/green-jobs/

ILO. 2014d. 'Zambia: Green Jobs in the Building Construction Sector.' Accessed 18 May. http://www.ilo.org/global/topics/green-jobs/

ILO. 2014e. 'New UN-led Global Partnership to Help Green 30 National Economies by 2020.' Press release, 4 May. http://www.ilo.org/

ILO. 2014f. *Global Employment Trends 2014: The Risk of a Jobless Recovery.* Geneva: January.

ILO. 2014g. *The ILO at Work: Development Results 2012–2013.* Geneva: May.

ILO. 2014h. *World of Work Report 2014: Developing with Jobs.* Revised edition. Geneva: ILO Research Department.

ILO and UNDP. ILO and the United Nations Development Programme. 2012. *Rethinking Economic Growth: Towards Productive and Inclusive Arab Societies.* Beirut: ILO.

IOE. International Organisation of Employers. 2014. 'Environment and Climate Change.' Accessed October. www.ioe-emp.org/

Klawitter, Jens, Christine Oarthermore, Katrina Uherova Hasbani, Adriana Valencia, Marcel Vietor and Ahmed Zahran. 2011. 'Implications of Climate Change on Energy and Security in the MENA Region.' In *The Environment in the Middle East: Pathways to Sustainability, Volume 1.* Middle East Institute Viewpoints. Washington, D.C.: Middle East Institute, February.

Lundgren, Karen. 2012. *The Global Impact of E-waste: Addressing the Challenge.* Geneva: ILO.

Meltzer, Joshua, Nathan Hultman and Claire Langley. 2014. *Low Carbon Energy Transitions in Qatar and the Gulf Cooperation Council Region*. Global Economy and Development Program. Washington D.C.: Brookings.

Michel, David, Amit Pandya and David Sobel. 2010. *Scientific, Intellectual and Governance Cooperation on Emerging Environmental Challenges in the Muslim World*. Washington D.C.: Brookings.

Michel, David, Amit Pandya, Syed Iqbal Hasnian, Russell Sticklor and Sreya Panuganti. 2012. *Water Challenges and Cooperative Response in the Middle East and North Africa*. Washington D.C.: Brookings.

Ministry of Employment and Labor of the Republic of Korea. 2012. 'Government Announces Its 2nd Basic Plan for Vocational Skills Development.' Press Release, 25 September. http://www.moel.go.kr/english/

Ministry of Health, Labour and Welfare of Japan. 2008. 'G8 Labour and Employment Ministers' Meeting, Chair's Conclusions.' 11–13 May, Niigata. http://www.mhlw.go.jp/english/

Morriss, Andrew P., William T. Bogart, Andrew Dorchak and Roger E. Meiners. 2009. *7 Myths About Green Jobs*. University of Illinois Law and Economics Research Paper No. LE09-007 and Case Western Reserve University Research Paper Series No. 09-14.

OECD. Organisation for Economic Co-operation and Development. 2011. *Towards Green Growth*. Paris: OECD, May.

OECD/Cedefop. 2014. *Greener Skills and Jobs*. OECD Green Growth Studies. Paris, OECD, February.

Pandya, Amit, and Rupert Herbert-Burns. 2011. *Maritime Commerce and Security: The Indian Ocean*. Washington D.C.: Stimson.

Patterson, Kendra. 2008. 'Water Management and Conflict: The Case of the Middle East.' In *Transnational Trends: Middle Eastern and Asian Views*, edited by Amit Pandya and Ellen Laipson, 213–227. Washington D.C.: Stimson.

Phoenix Solar. 2011. 'Phoenix Solar Builds Solar Power Plant for the Saudi Arabian Oil Company in Riyadh.' Press release, 17 February. http://www.phoenixsolar-group.com/en/press/

PRB. Population Reference Bureau. 2009. *2009 World Population Datasheet*. Washington D.C.: PRB.

Stuart, Becky. 2010a. 'UAE: Abu Dhabi Gears up for New Solar Incentive Regime.' *PV Magazine*, 22 June. http://www.pv-magazine.com/

Stuart, Becky. 2010b. 'UAE: Plans Underway to Build World's Biggest Solar Power Plant.' *PV Magazine*, 14 June. http://www.pv-magazine.com/

UNEP. United Nations Environment Programme. 2014. 'What is the "Green Economy"?' Accessed October. http://www.unep.org/greeneconomy/

UNEP PAGE. UNEP Partnership for Action on Green Economy. 2014a. '1st Global Conference on Partnership for Action on Green Economy, Dubai 4–5 March, 2014: Chair's Summary and Conclusions.' http://www.unep.org/greeneconomy/Portals/88/PAGE/ChairSummaryPAGE.pdf

UNEP PAGE. 2014b. 'First Global PAGE Conference.' Accessed October. http://www.unep.org/greeneconomy/PAGE/tabid/105854/

UNESCWA. United Nations Economic and Social Commission for Western Asia. 2013. *Mapping Green Economy in the ESCWA Region*. Version 1. June.

UNESCWA. 2014. 'Meetings and Events: SPDP: (Past Events).' Accessed October. http://www.escwa.un.org/information/meetings.asp?division=SDPD&condition=old OK

UNESCWA, LAS and UNEP. UNESCWA, the League of Arab States and the United Nations Environment Programme. 2011. *Green Economy in the Arab Region: Overall Concept and Available Options*. Reference Paper. May.

UNDP. United Nations Development Programme. 2009. *Challenges for Human Security in the Arab Region*.

US (United States) Department of Labor. 2014. 'Green Job Hazards.' Accessed October. https://www.osha.gov/dep/greenjobs/index.html

World Bank. 2013. MENA *Knowledge and Learning*, No. 96, July.

10 Agricultural sustainability and intellectual property rights in the era of a green economy: a case study of the United Arab Emirates[1]

Nihaya Khalaf

Introduction

As one of the most developed countries in the Gulf region that maintains a free-market economy with modest biological and agricultural diversity, the United Arab Emirates (UAE) may not seem the ideal case study country to consider the potential impact of the transition to a green economy on agricultural diversity. However, the UAE is one of the world's leading countries in implementing green economy policies. It seeks to become a global hub and a successful model of the green economy. In the same context, the UAE hosted the Global Partnership for Action on Green Economy (PAGE) Conference (in March 2014) in response to the United Nations (UN) Rio+20 Declaration call to support interested countries in developing greener and more inclusive economies. The goal of the 2012 UAE initiative on the green economy is to build an economy that protects the environment and an environment that supports the growth of the economy (WAM 2012). Central to that is the need to build a diversified economy that is based on knowledge and innovation through which natural and environmental resources can be protected.

Thus, one of the strategic areas of the national initiative is the conservation of biodiversity, including agrodiversity. In protecting the Emirate's natural assets, a variety of measures which require effective policies, strategies and regulations have been adopted to particularly limit the impact of development and growth on biological diversity (EAD 2014). According to the UAE's fifth national report to the Convention on Biological Diversity (CBD), the number of natural reserves had increased to 22 and the wetlands of international importance to 5, in 2013 (MEW UAE 2014).

Importantly, the UAE adopted Federal Law No. 9 on Plant Genetic Resources for Food and Agriculture, thereafter Federal Law (9/2013) on Plant Genetic Resources, in November 2013, which entered into force in March 2014. The Law aims at the conservation and sustainable use of plant genetic resources for food and agriculture (PGRFA), and the fair and equitable sharing of benefits arising out of their utilisation. As one of the first agrodiversity protection laws in the region, it can be considered a model law for other Arab countries to develop law and policy framework that conserves the region's unique biological diversity.

However, Federal Law (9/2013) on Plant Genetic Resources is likely to have a limited effect on the conservation of agrodiversity. One of the potential reasons is the patentability of PGRFA under the Federal Law (44/1992) for Organizing and Protection of Industrial Property for Patents, Designs and Industrial Models. Patenting of plants and animals and their genetic parts means granting exclusive rights of intellectual property over these essential resources for food and agriculture.

Historically, seeds and plants, the first link in the food chain, were held as common goods not only in the UAE, but also in the Arab region. This change in the legal status of PGRFA could have serious environmental and developmental implications, particularly in countries with limited technological capacities. However, the UAE adopted the above mentioned laws to bring its national legal system into harmony with the World Trade Organization (WTO) Agreement on Trade-Related Aspects of Intellectual Property Rights (TRIPs) on the one hand, and the International Treaty on PGRFA and the CBD, which is one of the conventions of the 1992 Rio Summit, on the other.

The Rio Summit adopted the principle of sustainable development to achieve economic and social development along with environmental protection in a way that ensures meeting the needs of present generations without comprising the ability of future generations to meet their own needs. Twenty years later, the Rio+20 UN Conference on Sustainable Development recognised that the green economy is the central driver of sustainable development (UNGA 2012a, para 56). To achieve this purpose, it reaffirmed its commitment to the three objectives of the CBD and recognised that the current severity of the global loss of biodiversity undermines sustainable development and food security (ibid., para 197). However, the Rio+20 definition of the green economy is constructively ambiguous. In the same context, Rio+20 failed to adopt a commitment that clearly explains how the green economy will take place. This raises concerns in respect of the two main aspects of any biodiversity and agrodiversity law. These are the conservation of plant genetic resources and the transfer of their conservation technologies.

This case study tests the proposition that the transition to a green economy of Rio+20, as part of the global institutional reform agenda that governs the allocation of rights over plant genetic resources for food and agriculture, is improper to chart the way towards agricultural sustainability. The main criticism is that green language is used by rich countries as a cover for 'lobbying for new markets to be created in biodiversity and ecosystems [which are] common goods that we all need and enjoy' (WDM 2012, 1–4). After setting the research framework in this section, the second section examines whether the transition to a green economy would lead to the 'financialisation' of biodiversity, including agricultural diversity. The third section analyses to what extent the missing common ground about the role of intellectual property rights (IPRs) on the transition to a green economy could lead to further commodification of plant genetic resources. The fourth section discusses what impact the absence of a global commitment on technology transfer in Rio+20 may have on the transfer of conservation technologies. Finally, the fifth presents a case study of crop biodiversity regulations in the UAE.

The study is based on the analysis of primary and secondary sources. Desk-based research has also been used, and is important, to evaluate the rapid legislative development at international level and in the UAE. This chapter argues that greening the economy through market-based mechanisms would increase the complexities countries face in implementing national laws that balance the special nature of plant genetic resources and plant-related innovations with national needs. Without adopting a true green economy that respects the limited capacity of the planet, the CBD and the International Treaty on Plant Genetic Resources for Food and Agriculture (ITPGR) may be degenerated into mere legal tools for the transfer of plant genetic resources and associated traditional knowledge.

Commodification of plant genetic resources for food and agriculture and the transition to a green economy

Typically, the evaluations of ecosystem services and goods – the very stuff of biodiversity, agriculture and food security – are in isolation from one another, even though links among them are many and significant (Hussain and Miller 2014, 2). Agricultural diversity in the broader sense is defined as 'the variety and variability of animals, plants and microorganisms that are used directly or indirectly for food and agriculture, including crops, livestock, forestry and fisheries' (FAO 2005, 2–3). In its narrow sense, agrodiversity refers to genetic resources of plant origin which are capable of self-reproducing or of being reproduced in certain biological conditions (Leskien and Flinter 1997, 8). This study focuses on the protection of agrodiversity in its narrow sense as addressed under the ITPGR, which as a whole applies to plant genetic resources. This is due to the importance of plant genetic resources (Moore and Tymowski 2005, 57). The ITPGR's Preamble acknowledges that PGRFA 'are the raw material indispensable for crop genetic improvement, whether by means of farmers' selection, classical plant breeding or modern biotechnologies, and are essential in adapting to unpredictable environmental changes and future human needs' (ibid.). Both managed agrobiodiversity and less managed biodiversity comprise natural resources that are crucial for development and their loss would ultimately have a serious impact on human wellbeing. In 1979, the UN Conference on Human Environment acknowledged for the first time the conflict between environment and development, recognising the urgent need to respond to the problem of environment. The 1980 World Conservation Strategy of the International Union for the Conservation of Nature emphasised the importance of biodiversity conservation for human development, especially sustainable development.

In addressing this complex relationship between ecological sustainability and human development, the World Commission on Environment and Development Report from 1987 coined the concept of sustainable development based on the unity of environment and development. This approach was later adopted by the 1992 Rio Summit, which placed the environment together with development in a single context through the principle of sustainable development. Sustainable development can be understood as a tool that permits continued improvements in the quality of life with less intense consumption of natural resources, while ensuring that future generations will be able to meet their needs (Munasinghe 2000, 2–6). It, thus, entails, in addition to ecological practices that ensure future generations' needs, a change in patterns of production and consumption in a way that ensure currently wasted resources are saved and redirected to meet the needs of the world's population equitably.

As one of the Rio conventions, the objectives of the CBD are the conservation of biological diversity, the sustainable use of its components, and the fair and equitable sharing of benefits arising from their utilisation (CBD 1992, Article 1). To achieve its objectives, the CBD obliges parties to facilitate access to genetic resources after recognising states' sovereign rights over biological resources within their territories. In harmony with the CBD, the ITPGR was adopted to deal specifically with the conservation and sustainable use of plant genetic resources for food and agriculture. However, the development of entitlements over genetic resources, including plant genetic resources, was continued within other international fora. The TRIPs Agreement for instance sets up the first intellectual property system in biological resources, including plant genetic resources. Preceding this, there was the International Union for the Protection of New Varieties of Plants (UPOV) Convention, adopted in 1961, which provides an effective intellectual property protection for plant varieties.

Appropriation of genetic resources through intellectual property, which has led to the concentration of proprietary biotechnologies in a number of transnational life-sciences corporations, could have a negative impact on food security, particularly in developing countries (QMIPRI 2004, 56–57). Moreover, in many countries local varieties have been replaced with commercial improved varieties. This could lead to the spread of monoculture, which is prejudicial to biodiversity and under which farmers and breeders have a narrow food genetic base with the susceptibility of improved varieties to disease and pesticides. An obvious example of the danger of genetic uniformity is the Irish potato famine of the 1840s (FAO OCC 1993). In contrast, the CBD, in addressing the relationship between biodiversity and development, recognises that patents and other IPRs 'may have an influence on the implementation of this Convention' calling parties to cooperate to prevent these rights from creating obstacles to the attainment of CBD objectives. Moreover, the ITPGR prevents claiming IPRs or other rights that limit access to plant genetic resources or their genetic parts or components, in the form received (ITPGR, Article 13). How does Rio+20, in defining the future of sustainable development, address the relationship between the environment and IPRs?

To answer this question, the analysis in the following subsection focuses on how the Rio principle of sustainable development is being implemented in the CBD and ITPGR. The subsequent subsection provides an in-depth analysis of how Rio+20 defines greening the economy with agriculture.

Sustainable development of the Rio Summit and its implementation in the CBD

The relationship between ecological sustainability and development is of a broad nature requiring a holistic approach conceived as the principle of sustainable development. As a 'model case of sustainable development' (Stoll 2009, 3), the CBD is the first environmental agreement that links environment to development adopting conservation and sustainable use of genetic resources along with fair sharing of benefit arising from the utilisation of these resources. However, it codifies that biological diversity is a 'common concern of humankind' after being a common heritage of mankind freely accessible around the world (CBD 1992, Preamble).

Historically, plant genetic resources were openly shared and moved between countries (Biber-Klemm and Cottier 2005, 58). The common heritage principle refers 'to collective resources which are co-managed and around which social institutions … are created for allocating access to the resources and benefits thereof' (Stewart 2010, 30). However, the commons principle is criticised for leading to what property law scholars term the 'tragedy of the commons'. In other words, plant genetic resources, as un-owned and unmanaged like other global commons, are available to all, which has led to overuse of these resources and underinvestment in their maintenance (Baslar 1998, 307).

Indeed, the 'common concern' principle presents a paradigm shift from the principle of 'common heritage' of mankind of the 1983 International Undertaking on Plant Genetic Resources. Common concern implies that while states retain control over their biological resources, they in turn have a commitment to cooperate with other states in the sustainable management of these essential resources for the benefit of the international community (Biber-Klemm and Cottier 2005, 58).[2] As such, the CBD obliges parties to create conditions that facilitate access to these resources establishing an Access and Benefit Sharing regime. This regime aims to enable providers of genetic resources to obtain fair and equitable benefits in exchange for their genetic resources, which thereby contributes to the conservation cost (Stoll 2009, 57).

In harmony with the CBD, the ITPGR provides for the conservation and sustainable use of PGRFA, and the fair and equitable sharing of benefits arising from their utilisation as the basis for sustainable agriculture and food security (Moore and Tymowski 2005, 57). The Treaty recognises that PGRFA is a common concern of the international community. Due to the importance of the continued flow of PGRFA, the ITPGR established a multilateral system on access to plant genetic resources of major food crops and forage species (ITPGR, Article 11). The pooled resources of the multilateral system include 35 crops and 29 genera of forage listed in Annex 1 to the Treaty, in accordance with criteria of food security and interdependence. Facilitated access under the multilateral system is only for the purpose of conservation and utilisation for research, breeding and training for food and agriculture.

However, two decades after of the adoption of the CBD, the world is facing unprecedented challenges relating to biodiversity loss, climate change and the economic crisis. Within agrodiversity, approximately a third of the world's PGRFA have been lost since the beginning of the twentieth century (FAO OCC 1993). This is despite the fact that, at the Rio Summit the international community agreed that states must pursue development that is socially, economically and environmentally sustainable. The failure of the international community to implement sustainable development is attributed to the absence of practical tools to effectively address the three dimensions of sustainable development (FAO 2012, 3). Therefore, a key objective of the summit held in Rio de Janeiro in June 2012 was to define the future of sustainable development.

Green agriculture to transition to green economy

In marking the 20th anniversary of the Rio Summit, the Rio+20 outcome document recognises that green economy is one of the main available tools to achieve sustainable development (UNGA 2012a, para 12). In this context, it recognises that green economy does not substitute sustainable development (ibid., para 15). It must, thus, be a tool to achieve ecological, economic and social sustainability. As the green economy implies reconciling the conflicted requirements for development and environment through the efficient use of the planet's limited resources (ibid., para 60),[3] greening the economy with agriculture is crucial. Agriculture provides the world's population with food, fibre and fuel. It is also the single biggest sector that provides livelihoods for 40 per cent of the world's population, or approximately 2.6 billion people (FAO 2012). Thus, agriculture provides a genuine transition to the green economy.

However, the question is how to green the economy with agriculture. The first problem is that the cost of greening the economy with agriculture is likely to be higher than in other sectors. Agriculture occupies 60 per cent of the world's ecosystems, and about one-third of the greenhouse gas (GHG) emissions are attributed to agriculture. In addressing the issue, the Rio+20 outcome document reaffirms the necessity to promote more sustainable agriculture that not only improves food security, eradicates hunger and is economically viable, but also conserves land, water and genetic resources of plants and animals, and biodiversity and ecosystems, and enhances resilience to climate change and natural disasters. It also recognises 'the need to maintain natural ecological processes that support food production systems' (UNGA 2012a, para 111).

Accordingly, greening the economy with agriculture should eradicate hunger, improve public health, and reduce adverse environmental impacts and GHG emissions. Another question is how this definition of greening the economy with agriculture could be achieved in the transition to a green economy. The Rio+20 outcome document neither defines the concept of green economy, nor provides a mechanism through which green economy could be achieved. There has been also no agreed definition between environmentalists and economists. The most cited definition of the green economy, by the UN Environment Programme (UNEP), as 'one that results in improved human well-being and social equity, while significantly reducing environmental risks and ecological scarcities', provides limited value for the interpretation and implementation of the concept (UNDESA *et al.* 2011, 4).

The green economy is perceived as moving from an economic system that has partly caused the current food, economic and climate crises to a system that would proactively address these (ibid.). This is because under this economic system the environmental cost of economic activities is not priced into the market. Thus, biodiversity or ecosystem services need to be defined, quantified and certified as natural capital or services (European Civil Society Groups 2012). It is important to mention that under the original Rio Summit outcome, plant genetic resources became a 'common concern of humankind' after they had been 'common heritage' of mankind. However, to what extent would the transition to a green economy lead to the financialisation of biodiversity? This question will be focused on in the following section.

Financialisation of biodiversity

The World Development Movement, which campaigns against the root causes of poverty and inequality, argues that creating financial markets in biodiversity and ecosystem services would be the next step in the commodification of nature, attributing this to The Economics of Ecosystems and Biodiversity (TEEB) initiative (WDM 2012, 3). The notion of the TEEB focuses on making the economic values of nature visible through calculating the value of ecosystem services and goods and, contrarily, measuring the economic consequences of their loss. The 2008 TEEB Report criticises considering ecosystem goods and services as common goods, and suggests a number of approaches to solve this problem (Sukhdey 2008, 9). It, thus, suggests 'payments for ecosystem services' as a solution to the imbalances that harm biodiversity and impede development.

TEEB, or in other words commodification of biodiversity, is confirmed in the UN Secretary-General's High-Level Panel on Global Sustainability, which was a critical input for Rio+20 that sets guidance on the characteristics of the green economy (UNGA 2012b, 47–55).[4] The Panel Report states that the green economy should set an accurate pricing system by including social and environmental costs in a pricing mechanism, and also ensures using finance to set the foundations for higher performance of sustainable development (ibid.).

'Turning the planet into profit'

Schemes to create payments for biodiversity are already implemented in some countries, such as 'wetland banks' in the United States (US) and a biodiversity banking and offsets scheme in Australia. Bio-banking is defined as 'a market-based scheme that provides a streamlined biodiversity assessment process for development, a rigorous and creditable offsetting scheme as well as an opportunity for rural landowners to generate income by managing land for conservation' (NSW Government 2012). It is alleged that bio-banking schemes aim to create a market in biodiversity credits in order to give landowners incentive to commit to biodiversity values and to offset impacts on other areas (DECC NSW 2007, 3). These credits can be sold to create income through which landowners can manage their lands in a more sustainable way. The credits can be sold to developers to offset impacts from their development.

However, placing monetary value on biodiversity implies that social and environmental obligations will be assignable, that is, one can 'buy one's way out' (WDM 2012, 4). In addition, biodiversity banking goes beyond commodification of biodiversity to creating financial instruments derived from the artificial values assigned to these commons. It is argued that such schemes might lead to betting on the common good of biodiversity on futures markets and speculators trading in them (Gaia Foundation 2011). Biodiversity banking contradicts the CBD and ITPGR, as its normative approach reflects the existence of a 'new global commons' (Halewood 2012, 1–11). The following section presents another problem linked to biodiversity commodification, but of a completely different nature.

Intellectual property rights and commodification of agrodiversity

The transition to a green economy increases concerns related to the commodification of plant genetic resources.[5] The Rio+20 outcome document recognises 'the right to use, to the full, the provisions contained in the Agreement on Trade Related Aspects of Intellectual Property'. This recognition ignores the review of Article 27.3(b) of the TRIPs Agreement, which is at the heart of the debate on TRIPs and development (UNGA 2012a, para 142). Although global trade law, of which the TRIPs Agreement is part, recognises sustainable development along with its primary objective on trade liberalisation (WTO Marrakesh Agreement), IPRs expansion in plant genetic resources has raised concerns of potential environmental and developmental implications, particularly in developing countries.

Article 27 obliges members of the WTO to make patents available for all inventions, both product and process, in all fields of technology, including agriculture. Although Article 27.3(b) allows the exclusion of plants and animals and biological processes for their production from the patentability, it mandates TRIPs signatories to protect plant varieties. This commitment implies that members, including developing countries, have to extend intellectual property protection to their agricultural sectors. The issue is of a recent origin even in industrial countries (Dhar 2002, 4).

Plant variety protection

Article 27.3(b) obliges parties to the WTO to protect plant variety either by patents, an effective *sui generis* system, or any combination thereof. It provides no details of which *sui generis* system will meet protection requirements. This holds true for the word 'effective'. It is argued that Article 27.3(b) does not necessarily mean that members have to adopt a plant variety act that is identical to, or even consistent with, the UPOV, nor become members of its convention (Leskien and

Flinter 1997, 27). However, many countries have met the plant variety protection requirements through the adoption of the UPOV Convention.

The UPOV Convention sets distinctness, stability and uniformity as protection criteria (Le Buanec 2006, 50).[6] The amendment of the UPOV in 1991 considerably strengthens plant breeders' rights (ibid.). First, the breeders' exemption to use protected plant varieties to breed new varieties is restricted under the 1991 UPOV Convention, which requires the new variety to be registered to not be essentially derived from the protected variety. The breeders' exemption was adopted to ensure that germplasm materials remain accessible to all breeders which enables them to optimise plants' improvement (UPOV, Article 16). Also, the amendment restricts farmers' privilege to use protected varieties. It only permits farmers to save seed for propagating purposes from the harvest they obtained from protected varieties on their own holding (ibid., Article 15.2).

In practice, plant variety protection and the growing orientation of patenting plant varieties no doubt deter agricultural research and erode farmers' rights to save, use and exchange seeds. In the case 'Monsanto Co. v McFarling Nos. 05-1570–1598', the defendant McFarling, a farmer in Mississippi, US, argued that the contractual prohibition against producing seeds for his own use the following season by using a patented plant constituted a violation of the seed saving provision of the Plant Variety Protection Act. However, the Federal Circuit rejected McFarling's argument and upheld the jury's verdict of a reasonable royalty of USD40 per bag of genetically modified soybean seeds (ibid.). The next section discusses patent protection of plant genetic resources related inventions.

Plant patents

The TRIPs Agreement (Article 27.3(b)) provides that patents shall be provided to inventions in all fields of technology including agriculture. For an invention to be patentable, it sets certain criteria. The invention must be new. In biotechnological inventions, the novelty issue has brought new challenges to the patent system because some of the subject matter that is claimed to be invented is already available in nature (Rudolph 1996, 62).

The TRIPs Agreement also requires an invention to involve an inventive step to be patentable. An inventive step means that an invention must not be obvious to a person skilled in the particular field of the invention. In the case 'National Research Development Corporation v Commissioner of Patents (NRDC) (1959) 102 CLR 252', the Australian High Court decided that a new use of a known chemical is patentable because it takes 'advantage of a hitherto unknown or unsuspected property of the material' to achieve a useful result.[7] The third requirement for patentability is industrial application.[8] Industrial applicability requires that the claimed product can be produced. An invention in the area of agricultural biotechnology demonstrates an inventive step if it forms a significant technical application of a defined function of biological material (QMIPRI 2004, 58). In the NRDC case, the High Court ruled that the weedkilling process constitutes a manner of manufacture in agriculture (ibid.). However, Article 27.3(b) of TRIPs allows members to exclude from patentability, *inter alia*, plants and animals and essentially biological processes for their production. The underlying reason for this exclusion is to prevent claiming of exclusive rights over plants and animals and processes for their production for public policy considerations (Correa 2013, 12). The question is what the value of this exclusion is if the patenting of a cell or a gene within a plant could prevent the rest of the plant from being used.

Patenting of plant cells and genes

Historically, human intervention has played a major role in maintaining plant genetic resources and the emergence of new characteristics that do not exist in nature, but without claiming exclusive rights over these resources until recent decades (Rudolph 1996, 62). Two recent cases illustrate that plant cells and genes cannot be considered plants, and therefore they could not be excluded from the patentability. In 'Monsanto Canada Inc. v Schmeiser [2004] 1 S.C.R. 902, 2004 SCC 34', the Federal Court of Canada considered the question of whether the intentional growing of a genetically modified plant by Percy Schmeiser, a farmer, constituted 'use' of the patented gene within the meaning of the Patent Act S.42. It unanimously ruled that the cultivation of the canola was an infringing use holding that Monsanto's right to the patented gene extends to the plant containing it (ibid.). Given that the source of the patented canola in Schmeiser's farm was unclear, the court recognised that the wind could blow the seeds into his farm from neighbouring farms.

In 'Bowman v Monsanto Co.', Hugh Bowman, a farmer from Indiana, US, grew commodity soybeans that he had purchased from a local grain elevator. The commodity soybeans were contaminated with the Monsanto's Roundup Ready soybean as more than 90 per cent of the lands were planted with it. The Federal Circuit upheld the district Court's decision that patent exhaustion did not protect Bowman, because patent exhaustion does not permit farmers to replicate patented seeds through planting them without the permission of the patent holder (ibid.). The US Obama Administration, in its Amicus Curiae brief, states that the Congress is well equipped to address such public policy concerns, ignoring that such rigid protectionism of patents might undermine traditional agricultural practices of using parts of the last harvest to produce the next (US Department of Justice 2007, 11). The following subsection continues the discussion of the exclusion of Article 27.3(b), but in relation to essentially biological processes for the production of plants and conventionally bred plants.

Patenting of essentially biological processes for the production of plants

Although the exclusion of essentially biological processes for the production of plants is optional, it is of significance in determining patentable processes, as well as products that are directly obtained by a patented process. In other words,

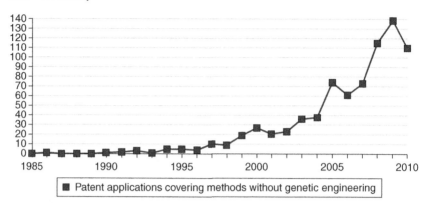

Figure 10.1 Patent applications in the sphere of plant breeding without genetic engineering, 1985–2010

patenting of plants or plant parts depends on the interpretation of this exclusion (Leskien and Flinter 1997, 22). The TRIPs Agreement does not define the concept of essentially biological processes nor the European Patent Convention.

In the last few years, there has been a dramatic increase in the number of plant patents, inclusive of conventional breeding processes and conventionally bred plants (see Figure 10.1). The number of pending plant patent applications to the Patent Cooperation Treaty was 8,226, and applications registered within the European Patent Office totalled 3,978, of which nearly 1,000 patent applications were on conventional plant breeding in 2011 (Then and Tippe 2012, 7).

In the same year, about 2,000 patents on plants with using or not using genetic engineering were granted by the European Patent Office (Then and Tippe 2011, 9). More than 30 per cent of 350 applications in 2010 claimed patent over traditional plant breeding methods and their products, that is, traditional plants and seeds (see Figure 10.2).

Recently, the European Patent Office has given a binding interpretation of the exclusion of 'essentially biological processes' in consolidated cases G2/07 'Broccoli' and G1/08 'Tomatoes'. The Broccoli case concerned a patent application filed by Plant Bioscience Ltd of the United Kingdom, in 2002. The patent application claimed methods to produce *Brassica oleracea* with high levels of specific glucosinolates, as well as product that directed to certain Brassica and broccoli plants, and to parts of edible portion of Brassica, seed, inflorescence and plant cell. However, the patent was opposed by Syngenta and Limagrain claiming, *inter alia*, the non-patentability of the method claimed in view of Article 53.b of the European Patent Convention.

The 'Tomatoes G1/08' case concerned a patent application filed by the Israeli Ministry of Agriculture in 2000. The application claimed a breeding method for tomatoes that had reduced water content and products of the method. In 2003, the patent was granted. An opposition was filed by Unilever in 2004, on the grounds that the patent related to essentially biological processes and

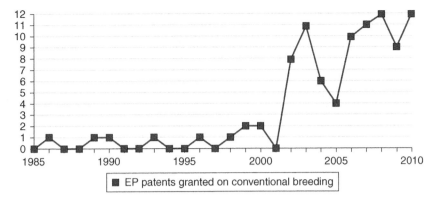

Figure 10.2 Patents granted on conventional breeding without genetic engineering, 1985–2010

these processes were not patentable under the European Patent Convention. The Opposition Division revoked the patent for the breeding method, deciding to maintain the patent in an amended form that does not cover the breeding method. The decision was appealed by the patent proprietor in 2006.

In 2007, the Technical Board of Appeal referred two questions of law to the Enlarged Board of Appeal, the highest judicial instance, seeking clarification on the concept of 'essentially biological processes'. The questions related to the interpretation of the exclusion of essentially biological processes under Article 53(b), specifically under which circumstances processes for plant production have to be considered as 'essentially biological'.[9] A binding interpretation of the prohibition of essentially biological processes for the production of plants and animals was given by the Enlarged Board of Appeal in December 2010. Decision G1/08 of the Enlarged Board of Appeal ruled that biological processes are not patentable and these processes do not escape the exclusion of Article 53(b) of the European Patent Office merely because of containing, as a further step or as part of any of the steps of crossing and selection, a step of a technical nature.[10]

Nonetheless, questions were left unresolved relating to the patentability of plants derived from biological processes, that is, seeds and harvest material (Then and Tippe 2012). It is argued that patenting of these products will render the prohibition of patenting of essentially biological processes for the production of plants meaningless (ibid., 5). In 2012, the Technical Board of Appeal for the first time referred the same case twice to the Enlarged Board of Appeal to decide on the potentiality of conventionally bred plants (ibid.).

Technology transfer, IPRs and agrodiversity from Rio to Rio+20

This section attempts to analyse Rio+20 provisions relevant to the transfer of biodiversity and agrodiversity conservation technologies. Different concepts have been used to refer to environmentally sound technologies (ESTs), such as climate change technologies, environmentally friendly technologies and green technologies.[11] Generally, these interchangeably used concepts refer to technologies employed to safeguard the environment and natural resources, and reduce human impact on the Earth.

In contrast to the Rio Summit, countries at the Rio+20 were not able to reach a global commitment on the transfer of ESTs, despite their indispensable importance to the transition to a green economy, particularly to developing countries (Abdel Latif 2012, 4). Similarly, there was no global consensus on the role of IPRs in technology transfer. The evolution of international debate on technology transfer in Rio+20 has been characterised as 'a step backwards' by developing countries.

Abdel Latif examines why countries, in identifying a path to accelerate sustainable development and transition to a green economy, were unable to reach an agreement on the role of IPRs (ibid.). He attributes it, on the one hand, to the increasing importance of IPRs and innovations, which have become fundamental to economic growth and to address global environmental challenges. On the other hand, he identifies the rise of technological capabilities of emerging economies countries such as China as a factor (ibid.). The WTO Secretariat's contribution to the debate in Rio+20 questions whether the current debate at Rio+20 '... is "just another" [intellectual property and] technology transfer debate, or whether environmentally friendly technologies present distinctive challenges for [intellectual property] law, policy and administration, calling for distinctive solutions' (WTO Secretariat 2012, 3). In the following, this section first discusses technology transfer within the Rio Summit and relevant multilateral environmental agreements. Then, it provides an analysis of the fragmented international policy and law in light of the relevant technology transfer provisions of the Rio+20 outcome.

Are there any strong moves towards transfer of ESTs at the Rio Summit?

At the 1992 Rio Summit, technology transfer was a key issue. The Rio Declaration underscores the fundamental importance of technology transfer, especially innovative and new technologies, in achieving sustainable development (UNCED, Principle 9). Chapter 34 of Agenda 21 (the Agenda 21 being one of the principal outcomes of the summit) was devoted to address transfer of ESTs (Abdel Latif 2012, 5). It emphasises the importance of facilitating access to and transfer of technologies and corresponding know-how, especially to developing countries. One of its goals is to promote ESTs in order to rebuild their capacities in adapting to climate change (Agenda 21, para 14). It stipulates that technology transfer must be in favourable terms for developing countries, but it also must be on mutually agreed terms taking into account intellectual property protection.

Thus, Agenda 21 invites developing countries to benefit from useful technological knowledge that lies in the public domain (ibid., para 9). Other options include purchasing patents and licences on commercial terms to transfer them to developing countries on non-commercial terms, or to adopt legislative measures such as compulsory licensing in compliance with the TRIPs Agreement (ibid., para 18). In a similar vein, Chapter 34 calls on governments and international organisations to address barriers to the transfer of ESTs, and to take possible measures to reduce the impact of such barriers in a framework that fully integrates the environment and development (ibid., para 18(d)). Paragraph 10 states that 'consideration must be given to the role of patent protection and intellectual property rights along with an examination of their impact on the transfer of EST' (ibid., para 10). The following section explains how these guiding principles have been interpreted in the CBD, as one of the Rio conventions.

Transfer of conservation technologies

This section attempts to explain the legal provisions and policy concerns that lie behind the adoption of the CBD and ITPGR provisions on technology transfer. Access to, and transfer of, conservation technology is recognised as essential in the attainment of the CBD objectives (CBD, Article 16.1). It also constitutes an integral component of the ITPGR, due to its importance to sustain agriculture.

Article 16 of the CBD establishes a commitment to technology transfer. It calls parties to provide or to facilitate access to and transfer of 'technologies that are relevant to the conservation and sustainable use of biological diversity or make use of genetic resources and do not cause significant damage to the environment'. The obligation to technology transfer under the CBD is broad and includes, in addition to hard technology, corresponding know-how and soft technology. It also includes *ex situ* conservation technologies, for example technologies used in gene banks, as well as *in situ* conservation technologies, which include technologies related to sustainable management of biological resources, and biodiversity monitoring technologies to enable developing effective conservation strategies and action plans. Transfer of biotechnology is also recognised in Article 16.1 as an important technology relevant to biodiversity conservation.

Technology transfer is conceived as a tool to acknowledge and recompense the contribution of countries and communities with rights over these genetic resources (Greiber *et al.* 2012, 216). Article 16.3 mandates member states to take legislative, administrative and policy measures to facilitate access to conservation technologies, particularly for developing countries that provide genetic resources. Article 16.2 requires technology transfer to be facilitated to developing countries on fair and most favourable terms, including on concessional and preferential, and on mutually agreed terms. However, it provides that transfer of technologies that are protected by patent or other IPRs must be on terms that recognise and are consistent with adequate and effective protection for these rights. These provisions are the most contested because they place the burden of biodiversity conservation on developing countries which are often biologically rich (Bernasconi-Osterwalder *et al.* 2012, 307). A recent technical study on the role of IPRs in technology transfer under the CBD concludes that both intellectual property laws and mechanisms 'do not constitute a single, stand-alone form of knowledge management, necessarily to be adopted or rejected in their entirety, or to be used to the exclusion of other forms of knowledge management, innovation promotion and technology diffusion' (UNEP 2008, 46).

In parallel, the ITPGR calls for the transfer of technologies as a form of non-monetary benefit sharing of the multilateral system. Article 13(b)i, using wording and structure drawn from Article 16 of the CBD, obliges parties to provide or facilitate access to technologies for the conservation and sustainable management of PGRFA. However, transfer of these technologies must be provided on terms that recognise and are consistent with effective protection to IPRs (ITPGR, Article 13(b)iii). Less than one decade later, Resolution 4/2011 of the Governing Body called for innovative approaches to realise effective technology transfer in order to enhance the capacity to use plant genetic resources (ibid., 2). The Rio Six-point Action Plan for the ITPGR, launched at Rio+20, recommends, as a priority, establishing a platform for the co-development and transfer of technologies as part of non-monetary benefit sharing. However, at a recent workshop, the ITPGR noted the difficulty of finding an effective approach to technology transfer which has created uncertainty about non-monetary benefit sharing (ITPGR 2012).

The transition to a green economy: technology transfer and IPRs

At Rio+20, transfer of green technologies witnessed a polarised discussion (Chatterjee 2012). Developing countries maintained that access to ESTs on terms that are favourable is essential to accelerate sustainable development and to the transition to a green economy. Their arguments to facilitate green technology transfer in Rio+20 included the use of TRIPs flexibility or establishing patents pools (ibid.). They, however, were not able to get a global commitment to access to green technologies, nor to develop modalities on their transfer. In turn, key industrialised countries strongly resisted technology transfer, claiming that attempts to transfer technologies without adequate protection to IPRs would be likely to have negative impacts on the development of green technologies.[12]

In the course of the Rio+20 negotiations, industrialised countries insisted that technology transfer needed to be on mutually agreed terms. The phrase 'voluntary transfer on mutually agreed terms and conditions' was suggested by the US to be applied to all references to technology transfer. This phrase was added to the outcome document after dropping the word 'voluntary' (TWN 2012). Additionally, the title of the chapter pertinent to the role of technology in the transition to a green economy simply reads 'Technology' (ibid.).

Drawing a parallel to access to medicine indirectly influenced the negotiations in Rio+20 (Abdel Latif 2012, 4). This is because TRIPs provisions, particularly on patents, have far-reaching implications on other public policy areas, in other words environment, agriculture and food security, and health care.[13] For instance, reference was made to TRIPs flexibilities in a completion text put by Brazil, which called for 'making use of existing flexibilities and addressing the issue of access to technologies with particular attention to the needs of developing countries'. Key industrial countries refused to accept the proposal (TWN 2012).

The result was the Rio+20 outcome document, a compromise text of 53 pages, introduced by the Brazilian presidency and entitled 'The Future We Want'. The Rio+20 outcome document comes with general reference to technology transfer in the transition to a green economy. This is combined with the absence of any committal language on IPRs' role in this context.[14] The outcome document recalls the Johannesburg Plan of Implementation provisions on technology transfer, finance, access to information and IPRs.[15] The recall on the Plan's provisions has been considered a step backward by developing countries (TWN 2012). Abdel Latif asserts that this recall would have no effect in practice, despite, in theory, extending to Agenda 21 provisions on IPRs (Abdel Latif 2012, 6).

In incentivising green innovation in developing countries, the Rio+20 outcome document calls governments, in accordance with their national capacities, 'to create enabling frameworks that foster environmentally sound technology, research and development, and innovation, including in support of green economy...' (UNGA 2012a, para 72). It can be asked that, if this can be deemed as a call to explore an alternative to IPRs in promoting and protecting innovation, what legal value would it have while IPRs are still recognised as key requirements for technology transfer at the international level, and even at the national level and in developed and developing countries in compliance with their obligations under the TRIPs Agreement? Finally, the Rio+20 outcome document refers to exploring modalities to enhance developing countries' access to ESTs to other relevant forums (ibid., para 270).

Fragmented international policy and law

The Rio+20 outcome document reaffirms its commitment to the objectives of the CBD and recognises the severity of the global loss of biodiversity and how it undermines sustainable development and affects food security (ibid., para 197). In contrast to Agenda 21, which required parties to facilitate the transfer of conservation technologies without prejudice to the CBD provisions, the Rio+20 outcome document includes no reference to technology transfer and its importance in attaining the CBD objectives (ibid., para 198).

It is early to look at the implications of such evolution of international debate on technology transfer on biodiversity. Even so, the transfer of conservation technologies has to be considered in light of two facts: conservation technologies, particularly those related to agrodiversity, are proprietary technologies, which sometimes involve the coverage of more than one IPR (WTO Secretariat 2012); and most of these privately owned technologies have developed through the propertisation or at least use of plant genetic resources.

Thus, the impact of IPRs, especially patents and plant variety protection, is significant in the transfer of conservation technologies. At the time of the adoption of the CBD, IPRs were an obscure issue, and remained so until the adoption of the TRIPs Agreement (Abdel Latif 2012, 7). The CBD and ITPGR, in addressing the issue of technology transfer, use words such as 'as appropriate', and 'mutually agreed terms' requiring technology transfer to be consistent with intellectual property protection. By doing that, they place the burden of biodiversity and agrodiversity conservation on developing countries where most of the world biological diversity exists (Bernasconi-Osterwalder *et al.* 2012, 307). The debate in Rio in 2012 delved into the heart of the balance between incentivising innovation, protecting inventor rights and public interest that define the patent system (WTO Secretariat 2012). However, its outcome does not provide the breakthrough needed to solve the environmental challenges that the world faces.

Case study: the regulation of crop biodiversity and plant-related innovation in the UAE and the transition to a green economy

The UAE is one of the world-leading countries in implementing green economy policies. In 2012, it launched a long-term national initiative to build a green economy. The aim is to create an economy that protects the environment and foster an environment that supports the growth of the economy (WAM 2012). Central to this is the need to build a diversified economy that is based on knowledge and innovation through which natural and environmental resources can be protected (ibid.). The UAE's Prime Minister Sheikh Mohammed bin Rashid Al Maktoum has asserted that the Government is 'serious about the transformation of our development process to reach the first position on the global level' up to 2021 (ibid.).

One of the strategic areas of the national initiative is the protection of biodiversity and agrodiversity. In protecting the Emirate's natural assets, a variety of measures which require effective policies, strategies and regulations, have been adopted to particularly limit the impact of development and growth on biological diversity (EAD 2014). While according to the UAE's fifth national report to the CBD, the number of reserves increased to 22 and the wetlands of international importance to 5 in 2013 (MEW UAE 2014, 2–3), the country's third national report identifies the problem of unsustainable agricultural activities, emphasising the importance of adopting a programme to promote and develop institutions' and farmers' capacities to preserve and sustainably use agricultural resources (MEW UAE 2005). Part of this effort has been the adoption of Federal Law No. 9 on Plant Genetic Resources for Food and Agriculture in 2013. The law aims at the conservation and sustainable use of PGRFA, and the fair and equitable sharing of benefits arising out of their utilisation. In practice, however, it seems to have a limited role in agrodiversity conservation. One of the potential reasons is the Federal Law (44/1992) for Organizing and Protection of Industrial Property for Patents, Designs and Industrial Models, which allows the patentability of plants and animals (UAE Federal Law No. 44 of 1992, Article 6.1).

In relation to the transition to a green economy, the constructively ambiguous definition of the green economy, along with the failure of Rio+20 to adopt a commitment that clearly explains how to green the economy, raise concerns of agrodiversity commodification. Thus, this study tests the proposition that Rio+20, as part of the global institutional reform agenda that governs allocation of rights over plant genetic resources, is inappropriate for charting the way towards agricultural sustainability. In order to test this proposition, it is important to analyse how the UAE implemented its obligations under the international law of agrodiversity and intellectual property law, particularly the TRIPs Agreement.

This study highlights that the green economy, as part of the global institutional reform agenda, would increase the complexities countries face in implementing national laws that balance the special nature of plant genetic resources and plant related innovations with national needs.

The regulation of crop biodiversity in the UAE

The UAE joined the ITPGR in 2004. It is also party to the CBD since 2000, and has adopted a number of national biodiversity strategies and action plans. The 2011–2013 National Biodiversity Strategy and Action Plan aims to understand the underlying reasons for the country's environmental problems, biodiversity loss, desertification and human economic activities' impacts on the environment (MEW UAE 2011). It attributes special importance to the conservation of agricultural diversity due to its linkage to food security. In addition to the development of a policy framework, Article 5 of Federal Law (9/2013) establishes a national gene bank to preserve the country's genetic diversity and cultural heritage. It also recognises farmers' rights in respect of their contribution to the creation and conservation of genetic resources and food security. Article 16 further provides for the protection of farmers' varieties. Importantly, the Law addresses issues related to access to PGRFA and associated traditional and cultural knowledge.

In terms of coverage, Federal Law (9/2013) applies to PGRFA that are conserved in *ex situ* collections as well as in *in situ* conditions. It applies to traditional and cultural knowledge associated with PGRFA. Article 1, using language corresponding to the ITPGR, defines PGRFA as any genetic material of plant origin of actual or potential value for food and agriculture. Given that the UAE ratified the CBD, the UAE should provide the scope for its implementation particularly. Moreover, PGRFA could be accessed for other non-food and agriculture purposes. In relation to access provisions, Federal Law (9/2013) requires the permission of the national gene bank as the designated national authority for granting the prior informed consent. Article 7.2 allows the use of the Standard Material Transfer Agreement to transfer non-Annex 1 material. Article 1 defines material transfer agreement as an agreement between the Ministry of Environment and a user to transfer accessed plant genetic resources out of the country.

Article 14.1, on benefit sharing, establishes that the Ministry of Environment and Water and the designated authority have the right to share benefits arising out of the utilisation of PGRFA and associated traditional and cultural knowledge. These benefits shall be agreed upon by the Ministry, designated authority and user of plant genetic resources. According to the Law, benefits to be shared are information exchange, capacity building and monetary benefits. It is important to note that technology transfer has been overlooked in Article 14 despite its importance in agrodiversity conservation. While Federal Law (9/2013) confines the obligation to benefit sharing to access for commercial exploitation and how it differs from commercial research of PGRFA, it does not define what is meant by commercial exploration. Article 10 states that access permission will define the purpose of access as: (a) permission for academic research; (b) permission for commercial research; or (c) permission for commercial exploitation.

In practice, differentiation between the above-mentioned access purposes constitutes another challenge in the implementation of the Law, because all these access forms are characterised by the intent of doing the research and not by its form. In particular, the same methods and facilities can be used in both academic research and commercial research, which may be pursued even by public institutes (Greiber *et al.* 2012, 119–121).

In the context of agricultural innovation, the Law defines innovations as creating a new product or process or improvement of existing knowledge and process related to plant genetic resources either through accumulation, collection, using the characteristics or value, or breeding of PGRFA. Plant related innovations are mainly protected in the UAE by the Federal Law (44/1992) on the protection of Industrial Property and the Federal Law (17/2009) on Plant Variety Protection. The Law does not explain what is meant by the term 'innovation'. Most Arabic laws related to the protection of plant genetic resources refer to agricultural innovations by directly using IPRs, especially patents and plant variety protection. Simultaneously establishing a system of multiple rights, plant breeders' rights, patent rights and farmers' rights, raises question about its potential impacts on PGRFA.

Plant intellectual property protection in the UAE

Federal Law (44/1992) provides for the protection of patents. Article 4 stipulates that patents shall be available for any inventions, processes or products, in all fields of technology, including agriculture. This is confirmed in the definition of industrial application of Article 4 of Federal Law (44/1992), which recognises that 'industry' 'shall be understood in its broadest senses, which includes agriculture...'. Article 6 excludes from the scope of patentability biological processes for the production of plants and animals. It also excludes plant and animal research. However, it is not clear what is meant by 'plant and animal research' which is different from plants and animals that can be excluded from the scope of the patentability under Article 27.3(b) of the TRIPs Agreement. In this case, biological processes for the production of plants and animals are excluded from patentability, but it is not clear whether plants and animals themselves are excluded or not.

Moreover, Federal Law (44/1992) does not exclude from patentability diagnostic, therapeutic and surgical methods for the treatment of humans, plants or animals, as stated in Article 27.3(a) of the TRIPs Agreement. This implies that genetically modified plants can be patented. This also opens the flood gates for the patentability of native traits if the claimed invention contains an additional step of a technical nature. Despite Article 6.iii excluding discoveries, this exclusion could have limited value in practice without clear reference to plants and animals. This also entails providing dual protection to plant variety under both patents and Federal Law (19/2009) on the protection of plant varieties.

The UAE adopted Federal Law (19/2009) in compliance with its obligations under the TRIPs Agreement. To qualify for protection, Article 5 stipulates that a variety must be new, distinct, stable and uniform. It requires the new variety to not be harmful to the environment and public health. Finally, it must not be contrary to *Sharia* or any law in the UAE. Registration of a crop variety confers legal ownership over the developed variety and grants the plant breeder exclusive commercial right for a limited period of 20–25 years.

Even though providing effective intellectual property protection enables the UAE to be regarded as a reliable partner in international fora, the country provides protection that exceeds the standards of protection required in the TRIPs Agreement. Indeed, the UAE does not benefit from the flexibility provided in the TRIPs Agreement. The problem is that the main area affected by providing such high standards of intellectual property protection is seeds and plants, the first link in the food chain. As methods of agriculture, seeds and plants were not formerly patentable in the UAE, but were held as common goods, not only in the UAE, but in the whole Arab region.

Although PGRFA are carriers of development, they cannot be considered a commodity to be commercialised. In the transition to a green economy, Federal Law (44/1992) needs to be amended to exclude plants and plant varieties from the scope of patentable subject matter. Equally, the green economy, with the generality of the Rio+20 outcome document, should be interpreted in a way that prevents the financialisation of biodiversity, including agrodiversity. With all the critiques of the commons approach, the market cannot be the primary mechanism in the transition to a green economy (Stewart 2010, 35). Biodiversity and ecosystem services should be treated as something we all share rights to and a responsibility for (WDM 2012, 5).

Conclusion

The case study of the UAE provides an important contribution to this chapter's subject matter, which focuses on the study of international law relevant to agricultural diversity and the impacts the transition to a green economy may have on food security. Despite its modest genetic diversity, the UAE is one of the leading countries in the region in striving to build an economy that is based on knowledge and innovation, and through which it can protect natural and environmental resources. However, in building an inclusive green economy, a market-centred approach – in other words, the commodification of agricultural diversity and turning the planet into profits – cannot be the primary instrument. This chapter has focused on available options to improve the applicable legal framework with a view to making the law a genuine tool to promote equity, development and ecological sustainability.

Building upon the analysis of international intellectual property law relevant to plants, which provided insights on the flexibilities and constraints on national implementation of the TRIPs Agreement, it is argued that it is important for the UAE to amend its Federal Law (44/1992) to exclude plants and animals from the scope of patentability. This exclusion is also important with regard to preventing the patentability of plant varieties because this growing trend has raised concerns on access to breeding material, an issue that affects plant breeders and farmers. In addition, it is important to exclude diagnostic, therapeutic and surgical methods for the treatment of humans, animals and plants because, for instance, the method of producing a date palm that is resistant to inflorescence rot by introducing genes can now be covered by the exclusive rights of patents even if the patent covers only the invented genes and not the plant itself.

In this context, the UAE Federal Law (9/2013) in addressing farmers' rights in respect to their role in the development and conservation of agrodiversity includes no reference to their rights to save, use and exchange farm-saved seeds. It also does not address farmers' rights to participate in national-level decision making on issues related to the conservation and sustainable use of PGRFA (see Article 15). Finally, Federal Law (9/2013), in addressing sharing of benefits arising from access to PGRFA, does not recognise technology transfer as one of the benefits to be shared in accordance with Article 13.2(b)(i) of the ITPGR.

Notes

1 The author is heartily thankful to her PhD supervisor, Dr Wei Shi, whose encouragement and support enabled her to write this chapter, which is based on her doctoral thesis research. The author would also like to make a special reference to Dr David Keeble, without the help of whom it would have not been possible to write this chapter, and to Wedad Elmaalul, the one the author tends to turn to first when she has something to discuss.
2 Common concern is considered as tempering the principle of states' sovereign rights over their biological resources (Biber-Klemm et al. 2005, 58).
3 'The future we want' (UNGA 2012a, para. 60) emphasises that the green economy will enhance and promote, among others, the ability to manage natural resources sustainably with lower negative environmental impacts and increase resource efficiency.
4 The Report devoted to address the issue is entitled 'Incorporating Social and Environmental Costs: Regulation and Pricing to reflect Externalities' (UNGA 2012b, 47, 55).
5 The Rio+20 outcome document includes three references to IPRs: two in the context of their role in technology transfer, and the third in relation to the TRIPs Agreement and the Doha Declaration on the TRIPs Agreement and Public Health. Also, it indirectly refers to the TRIPs Agreement, specifically the TRIPs review, and developments

within the World Intellectual Property Organization/Intergovernmental Committee on Intellectual Property and Genetic Resources, Traditional Knowledge and Folklores.

6 A variety eligible for protection must be new. In other words, it has not been exploited in the territory of the country in which the application has been filed for more than a year. Concerning distinctness, a plant variety is deemed to be distinct if it differs from all other varieties that are known by important botanical characteristics. The UPOV also requires a variety to be 'sufficiently uniform in its relevant characteristics'. Due to the direct link between uniformity and stability, a variety is stable if the plant characteristics remain the same after repeated propagation (Le Buanec 2006).

7 The NRDC case concerned a new method developed by NRDC to kill weeds, leaving the useful crop unharmed by applying a known chemical. The Commissioner rejected NRDC patent application on the grounds that the invention lacked novelty since agricultural process could not be a method of manufacture. NRDC brought an appeal under the Patent Act 1952–1955. The court had to determine if the new process of weedkilling is a 'manner of manufacture' according to s. 6 of the Statute of Monopolies.

8 Industrial application implies that through the application of the claimed invention a product can be produced or an industrially useful result can be achieved. NRDC v Commissioner of Patents (1959) 102 CLR 252.

9 The questions referred to the Enlarged Board of Appeal were: (i) Does a non-microbiological process for the production of plants which contains the steps of crossing and selecting plants escape the exclusion of Article 53(b) of the European Patent Convention merely because it contains, as a further step or as part of any of the steps of crossing and selection, an additional feature of a technical nature? (ii) If question 1 is answered in the negative, what are the relevant criteria for distinguishing non-microbiological plant production processes excluded from patent protection under Article 53(b) of the European Patent Convention from non-excluded ones? In particular, is it relevant where the essence of the claimed invention lies and/or whether the additional feature of a technical nature contributes something to the claimed invention beyond a trivial level (EPO 2013)?

10 The Enlarged Board of Appeal decided to answer the referred questions in case T 83/5(G2/7) and case T 1242/06(G 1/08) in consolidated proceedings. The Enlarged Board of Appeal ruled that: (1) A non-microbiological process for the production of plants which contains or consists of the steps of sexually crossing the whole genomes of plants and of subsequently selecting plants is in principle excluded from patentability as being 'essentially biological' within the meaning of Article 53(b) of the European Patent Convention. (2) Such a process does not escape the exclusion of Article 53(b) of the European Patent Convention merely because it contains, as a further step or as part of any of the steps of crossing and selection, a step of a technical nature which serves to enable or assist the performance of the steps of sexually crossing the whole genomes of plants or of subsequently selecting plants. (3) If, however, such a process contains within the steps of sexually crossing and selecting an additional step of a technical nature, which step by itself introduces a trait into the genome or modifies a trait in the genome of the plant produced, so that the introduction or modification of that trait is not the result of the mixing of the genes of the plants chosen for sexual crossing, then the process is not excluded from patentability under Article 53(b) of the European Patent Convention. (4) In the context of examining whether such a process is excluded from patentability as being 'essentially biological' within the meaning of Article 53(b) of the European Patent Convention, it is not relevant whether a step of a technical nature is a new or known measure, whether it is a trivial or fundamental alteration of a known process, whether it does or could occur in nature or whether the essence of the invention lies in it.

11 Each concept has a specific meaning and is addressed under different international fora. Green technologies refer to a constantly evolving group of methods that vary from techniques for generating energy, like solar or wind power, to non-toxic cleaning products. Climate change technologies encompass technologies to adapt to climate change, such as seeds with increased tolerance to drought or high temperature.

12 Two letters were addressed to officials in key industrialised countries to not include IPRs in Rio+20 discussions. One was addressed to the US officials from the President of the Intellectual Property Owners' Association. The letter states that the Rio+20 Conference 'has become the latest forum with the potential of undermining IPR in the name of sustainable development and climate change'. The second was addressed by the IP Federation, as the representative of a wide range of UK industries, to Liz Coleman of the Intellectual Property Office of the UK. The letter expresses the industry's concerns and requires UK and EU delegates to be 'well-prepared' and with a very clear technology-related policy: (a) Any Rio+20 outcome must take into account and be fully consistent with prior (and future) UNFCCC outcomes, and the negotiating positions that were taken and agreed. (b) Language on IP rights has no place in a final Rio+20 outcome and must be rejected. (c) Any references to technology transfer should be clearly qualified and conditioned to include only voluntary transfer on mutually agreed terms. (They are not consistently conditioned and qualified as such in the current draft.) (d) Any efforts to include non-voluntary technology transfer obligations should be firmly rejected and any such language unconditionally removed. (e) Broad and often very vague requirements for 'access to (environmental) information' effectively provide governments and government-related entities flexibility to access business confidential and proprietary business and commercial information, including the IP that we are trying to protect. Any such provisions must be firmly rejected.

13 Concerns on access to medicines, whether they would be available and affordable in developing countries, led to the adoption of the 2001 Doha declaration on TRIPs Agreement and public health. The Declaration states that the implementation of TRIPs 'does not and should not prevent members from taking measures to protect public health'. Paragraph 6 of the Declaration recognises difficulties facing member states with insufficient or no manufacturing capacities in the pharmaceutical sector to benefit from compulsory licensing, and it therefore instructed the TRIPs Council to find an expeditious solution to this problem. The legal means to implement paragraph 6 was agreed in 2003 when the WTO decided to waive Article 31(f)'s provision on 'domestic market restriction' permitting generic medicine copies being exported to countries that lack manufacturing capacity.

14 This is illustrated in paragraph 73 of the Rio+20 outcome document which states:

> We emphasize the importance of technology transfer to developing countries and recall the provisions on technology transfer, finance, access to information, and intellectual property rights as agreed in the Johannesburg Plan of Implementation, in particular its call to promote, facilitate and finance, as appropriate, access to and the development, transfer and diffusion of environmentally sound technologies and corresponding know-how, in particular to developing countries, on favorable terms, including on concessional and preferential terms, as mutually agreed.

This is also illustrated in paragraph 269 of the Rio+20 outcome document (UNGA 2012a).

15 The Johannesburg Plan of Implementation reinforced the consensus of international community in the Rio Summit by recalling states to promote, facilitate and finance technology development, transfer and diffusion, especially to developing countries and countries with economy in transition.

References

Abdel Latif, Ahmed. 2012. *Intellectual Property Rights and Green Technologies from Rio to Rio: An Impossible Dialogue?* Policy Brief No. 14. International Centre for Trade and Sustainable Development (ICTSD), July.

Baslar, Kamal. 1998. *The Concept of the Common Heritage of Mankind in International Law.* The Netherlands: Kluwer Law International.

Bernasconi-Osterwalder, Nathalie, Daniel Magraw, Maria Julia Oliva *et al.*, eds. 2012. *Environment and Trade: A Guide to WTO Jurisprudence.* London and Sterling, VA: Earthscan.

Biber-Klemm, Susette, and Thomas Cottier, eds. 2005. *Rights to Plant Genetic Resources and Traditional Knowledge: Basic Issues and Perspective.* Oxfordshire: CABI International.

Biber-Klemm, Susette, Thomas Cottier, Philippe Cullet and Danuta Szymura Berglas. 2005. 'The Current Law of Plant Genetic Resources and Traditional Knowledge.' In *Rights to Plant Genetic Resources and Traditional Knowledge: Basic Issues and Perspective,* edited by Susette Biber-Klemm and Thomas Cottier. Oxfordshire: CABI International.

Chatterjee, Patralekha. 2012. 'Rio Climate Talks Finish with Little IP: Flexibility under Fire.' *Intellectual Property Watch*, 25 June. http://www.ip-watch.org/

Correa, Carlos. 2013. 'TRIPs Flexibility for Patents and Food Security: Options for Developing Countries.' *Bridges Africa* Vol. 2, No. 3. ITCSD.

DECC NSW. Department of Environment and Climate Change of New South Wales, Australia. 2007. 'Bio-banking, Biodiversity Banking and Offsets Scheme – Scheme Overview.' Sydney South.

Dhar, Biswajiat. 2002. *Sui Generis Systems for Plant Variety Protection, Options under TRIPs.* Discussion Paper. Geneva: Quaker United Nations Office.

EAD. Environment Agency – Abu Dhabi. 2014. *Environmental Atlas of Abu Dhabi Emirate.* Accessed 23 July. https://www.environmentalatlas.ae/

EPO. European Patent Office. 2013. 'Communication from the Enlarged Board of Appeal Concerning Case G2/13.' *Official Journal of the EPO* Vol. 36: 8–9.

European Civil Society Groups. 2012. 'Financialization of Nature: Why Green Economy?' Video. *Attac TV*, June. http://whygreeneconomy.org/

FAO. Food and Agriculture Organization of the UN. 2005. *Building on Gender, Agrodiversity and Local Knowledge: A Training Manual.* Rome.

FAO. 2012. *Greening the Economy with Agriculture: Taking Stock of Potential Options and Prospective Challenges.* Rome.

FAO OCC. Office for Corporate Communication of the Food and Agriculture Organization of the UN. 1993. 'Harvesting Nature's Diversity.' Accessed October. http://www.fao.org/3/a-v1430e/V1430E01.htm

[The] Gaia Foundation. 2011. 'The Financialisation of Nature: Linking Food, Land Grabs, Climate & Mining.' http://www.gaiafoundation.org/blog/

Greiber, Thomas, Sonia Pena Moreno, Mattias Åhrén *et al.* 2012. *An Explanatory Guide to the Nagoya Protocol on Access and Benefit-Sharing.* Gland: International Union for Conservation of Nature (IUCN).

Halewood, Michael. 2012. *What Kind of Goods are Plant Genetic Resources for Food and Agriculture? Towards the Identification and Development of a New Global Common.* Discussion Draft developed for the 1st Thematic Conference on 'the Knowledge Commons' of the International Association for the Study of the Commons, 12–14 September, Louvain, Belgium.

Hussain, Salman, and Dustin Miller. 2014. *The Economics of Ecosystem and Biodiversity (TEEB) for Agriculture & Food – Concept Note*. The Economics of Ecosystems and Biodiversity (TEEB), February.

ITPGR. International Treaty on Plant Genetic Resources for Food and Agriculture. 2012. Report of a Workshop to Discuss a Platform for the Co-Development and Transfer of Technologies. 7–8 August, Brasília, Brazil.

Le Buanec, Bernard. 2006. 'Protection of Plant Related Innovation: Evolution and Current Discussion.' *World Patent Information* 28: 50–62.

Leskien, Dan, and Michael Flinter.1997. *Intellectual Property Rights and Plant Genetic Resources: Options for a Sui Generis System*. Issues in Genetic Resources No. 6. Rome: International Plant Genetic Resources Institute.

MEW UAE. Ministry of Environment and Water of the UAE. 2005. *Third National Report to the Convention on Biological Diversity of the UAE*.

MEW UAE. 2011. *National Biodiversity Strategy and Action Plan of the UAE 2011–2013*.

MEW UAE. 2014. *Fifth National Report to the Convention on Biological Diversity (National Biodiversity Strategy and Action Plan of the UAE 2014–2021)*.

Moore, Gerald, and Witlod Tymowski. 2005. 'Explanatory Guide to the International Treaty on Plant Genetic Resources for Food and Agriculture.' *Environmental Policy and Law Paper* No. 57. IUCN.

Munasinghe, Mohan. 2000. 'Development, Equity and Sustainability (DES) in the Context of Climate Change.' In *Development, Sustainability and Equity*, compiled by Ramon Pichs, 9–66. Geneva: IPCC.

NSW (New South Wales) Government. 2012. 'BioBanking.' Accessed 2012. http://www.environment.nsw.gov.au/biobanking/

QMIPRI. Queen Mary Intellectual Property Research Institute. 2004. *The Relationship between Intellectual Property Rights (TRIPs) and Food Security*. European Commission, DG Trade.

Rudolph, John. 1996. *A Study of Issues Relating to the Patentability of Biotechnological Subject Matter*. Gowling, Strathy and Henderson. Prepared for the Intellectual Property Policy Directorate of Industry Canada.

Stewart, Keith. 2010. *Avoiding the Tragedy of the Commons: Greening Governance through the Market or Public Domain?* Public Domain Project, York University.

Stoll, Peter-Tobias. 2009. 'Access to Genetic Resources and Benefit Sharing: Underlying Concepts and the Idea of Justice.' In *Genetic Resources, Traditional Knowledge and the Law: Solutions for Access and Benefit Sharing*, edited by Evanson C. Kamau, and Gerd Winter, 3–18. London: Earthscan.

Sukhdey, Pavan. 2008. *The Economics of Ecosystems and Biodiversity: An Interim Report*. TEEB, May.

Then, Christoph, and Ruth Tippe. 2011. 'Seed Monopolists Increasingly Gaining Market Control: Applications and Granting of Patents in the Sphere of Animal and Plant Breeding in 2010.' *No Patents on Seeds*, March.

Then, Christoph, and Ruth Tippe. 2012. 'European Patent Office at Crossroads: Patents on Plants and Animals Granted in 2011.' *No Patents on Seeds*, March.

TWN. Third World Network. 2012. 'Tough Fight over Means of Implementation.' *TWN Rio +20 News Update*, 22 June.

UNDESA, UNEP and UNCTAD. United Nations (UN) Division for Sustainable Development, UN Environment Programme and UN Conference on Trade and Development. 2011. *The Transition to a Green Economy: Benefits, Challenges and Risks from a Sustainable Development Perspective*. Report to the Second Preparatory Meeting for the UN Conference on Sustainable Development.

UNEP. UN Environment Programme. 2008. *The Role of Intellectual Property Rights in Technology Transfer in the Context of the Convention on Biological Diversity.* Technical Study. UNEP/CBD/COP/9/INF/7.

UNGA. UN General Assembly. 2012a. *The Future We Want.* A/RES/66/288. 11 September.

UNGA. 2012b. *UN Secretary-General's High-Level Panel on Global Sustainability: Resilient People, Resilient Planet: A Future Worth Choosing.* New York: UN.

US Department of Justice. 2007. *Brief for the US as Amicus Curiae Brief on Petition for Writ of Certiorari to the US Court of Appeals for the Federal Circuit.* No. 11–796. US Supreme Court.

WAM. Emirates News Agency. 2012. 'Mohammed Unveils UAE's Green Economy.' *Emirates 24/7*, 15 January. http://www.emirates247.com/news

WDM. World Development Movement. 2012. *Rio+20 Summit: Whose Green Economy?* Supporter Briefing. May.

WTO Secretariat. 2012. 'Rio+20 WTO Secretariat Contribution Regarding "A Facilitation Mechanism that Promotes the Development, Transfer and Dissemination of Clean and Environmentally Sound Technologies".' http://sustainabledevelopment.un.org/content/documents/1243wto.pdf

International Treaties and Instruments

Agenda 21. *Agenda 21 of the UN Conference on Environment and Development* (1992).

CBD. Convention on Biological Diversity (1992).

ITPGR. International Treaty on Plant Genetic Resources for Food and Agriculture (2001).

UNCED. UN Conference on Environment and Development. *Rio Declaration on Environment and Development* (1992).

UPOV. International Union for the Protection of New Varieties of Plants Convention (1961).

TRIPs. Trade Related Aspects of Intellectual Property Rights Agreement (1994).

WTO. World Trade Organization. *Marrakesh Agreement Establishing the World Trade Organization* (1994).

National Laws

UAE Federal Law No. 44 of 1992 for Organizing and Protection of Industrial Property for Patents, Designs and Industrial Models.

UAE Federal Law No. 17 of 2009 on Plant Variety Protection.

UAE Federal Law No. 9 of 2013 on Plant Genetic Resources for Food and Agriculture.

Cases

Bowman v Monsanto Co. 133 S. Ct. 1761–2013.

Monsanto Co. v McFarling Nos. 05-1570–1598.

Monsanto Canada Inc. v Schmeise [2004] 1 S.C.R. 902, 2004 SCC 34.

National Research Development Corporation v Commissioner of Patents (1959) 102 CLR 252.

Plant Bioscience Limited v Syngenta Participations AG and Groupe Limagrain Holding, T0083/05 (Broccoli/Plant BioScience). 22 May 2007.

State of Israel, Minister of Agriculture v Unilever NV, G0001/08 (Tomatoes/State of Israel) G0001/8. 9 December 2010.

11 Green economy pathways in the Arab Gulf: global perspectives and opportunities

Kishan Khoday, Leisa Perch and Tim Scott[1]

Introduction

A marked shift from the 1992 Rio Earth Summit to the recent 2012 Rio+20 Summit has been the role of emerging economies in terms of leading new solutions and global cooperation for achieving local goals of sustainable development and green economy in their own economies, and in leading cooperation with other countries across the South. As emerging economies, including the BRICS (Brazil, Russia, India, China and South Africa) as well as the countries of the Arab Gulf (Bahrain, Kuwait, Oman, Qatar, Saudi Arabia and the United Arab Emirates), come to the centre of the global economy, the interactions between production and consumption are also shifting, in turn shaping efforts to resolve sustainable development challenges and achieve green economy goals.

Debates about sustainable development have historically been characterised by the developed-developing country dichotomy that has defined world order in the post-colonial era. But trends in recent years make it clear that we are moving to a new multipolar era of global policymaking and cooperation, and this will have critical implications for our ability to achieve sustainable development and green economy goals in the decades to come. Emerging economies, like the BRICS and the Arab Gulf, are starting to show leadership in crafting new green economy policies and responses in their own countries, while important connections are also starting to be made to their growing and influential levels of South-South cooperation (SSC), official development assistance (ODA) and outward direct investment (ODI) to developing countries around the world.

Our ability to achieve global sustainable development and green economy goals in the future will increasingly hinge on sustainable energy, water conservation, climate change and other green economy-related policies and actions within emerging economies, and in turn, the way in which emerging economies translate these issues into their global cooperation strategies as well as local and foreign investments.

This chapter seeks to explore these two aspects of pursuing green economy goals in the Arab Gulf. The following section starts with a global overview of the green economy paradigm and its relevance to the development trajectories of developing and emerging economies. Then, narrowing the focus to the Arab

Gulf, the third section provides a contextual analysis of challenges of pursuing green economy goals in resource-rich countries (RRCs) around the world as an important comparative perspective of relevance for future challenges and opportunities in the Arab Gulf. The chapter then concludes in the fourth section with a view to the Arab Gulf's important role as a Southern provider of SSC, ODA and ODI to developing countries around the world, and how this could well support the global green economy agenda.

Green economy strategies and actions: an opportunity for the South

As noted at the 2012 Rio+20 Summit, without a paradigm shift in how natural resources and economies are managed, inequality and instability will continue to deepen, and human development in current and future generations will be threatened within and across the global North and South. Pushing to achieve the Millennium Development Goals (MDGs) and moving to the post-2015 development framework and Sustainable Development Goals (SDGs) requires deeper transitions to less polluting, resource-efficient and climate-resilient growth that reduces inequalities and brings multiple social, economic and environmental benefits for women and men over the medium and longer term.

As recognised by the Rio+20 Outcome Document (see Box 11.1), inclusive green economy policies can be key to broader efforts to eradicate poverty and advance sustainable development. Ultimately, such efforts are about influencing how public and private policy and investments are used to reduce inequalities and advance environmentally sustainable growth through integrated 'whole-of-government' approaches. This means helping countries better prioritise and incentivise sustainable development investments, while addressing trade-offs within and across sectors and groups, including for those living in poverty.[2]

Box 11.1 Inclusive green economy approaches in the Rio+20 Outcome Document

The Rio+20 Outcome Document affirms that green economy approaches should:

- serve as tools for reducing poverty and supporting more sustainable development;
- promote inclusive economic growth and create opportunities for employment and decent work for all;
- maintain the healthy functioning of Earth's ecosystems;
- contribute to the Millennium Development Goals;

- improve the livelihoods and empowerment of the poor and vulnerable groups;
- mobilise the full potential and ensure the equal contribution of both women and men;
- engage all stakeholders and major groups, including civil society and the private sector;
- respect human rights and national sovereignty;
- avoid unwarranted conditionalities on official development assistance and finance;
- not be used as arbitrary or unjustifiable discrimination or a disguised restriction on international trade;
- derive from integrated planning processes, enabling environments and effective institutions at all levels; and
- be supported by the UN and partners through capacity development and technical assistance.

Source: RIO+20 Outcome Document, paraphrased by authors.

While there are positive trends in the Arab Gulf in engaging on green economy-related issues as noted above, there are also many barriers to achieving more broad-based and in-depth transformational changes both within their own local economies and within their outward cooperation.

In the unique context of the oil-rich Arab Gulf, countries are under pressure to define green economy goals in their specific context. They share much in common with other RRCs and there are many lessons learned as to challenges and prospects for achieving green economy goals in such contexts, as explored further below.

RRCs have emerged with somewhat unique characteristics which makes green economy strategies and actions a challenge as well as an opportunity, thus requiring innovative analysis and tools – in other words, 'business un-usual'. Moreover, as this richness or wealth has been tied to the 'resource curse', also known as the 'paradox of plenty'[3] (Karl 1997) wherein countries and regions with an abundance of natural resources, specifically non-renewable resources like minerals and fuels, tend to have more skewed development outcomes than countries with fewer natural resources, it calls for special approaches to managing the transition to green economy solutions.

RRCs can be characterised as having closed operating systems which can make a green economy transformation a highly sensitive undertaking when confronting the political economy dynamics around the extractive sector, no less in the Arab Gulf as the world's capital for conventional oil supply. Structural change processes, even with slow and modest steps, can have significant implications and push-back effects from both government and industry.

Despite the uphill battle, some Arab Gulf countries have nonetheless expressed aspirations, or are already making progress to craft locally adapted strategies, for pursuing a green economy pathway. Some countries have initiated strategies for goals such as: improving resource efficiency; low-carbon technologies; energy efficiency and renewable energies; integrated water resource management; food security strategies; and sustainable transport and city design.

At the base of this there are rapidly growing pressures on energy, land and water resources within the Gulf. As the drive to diversify the economy away from oil exports gains traction, new industrial ventures are arising, which are often energy-intensive ones and place growing demands on energy and water resources. Meanwhile surging levels of urban expansion combine with some of the world's highest per capita levels of energy and water consumption and waste generation, creating resource security risks. The region is also seeing fast-growing levels of sea-water desalination capacity, a very energy-intensive exercise. As average temperatures continue to rise, air conditioning has become the single largest source of energy consumption, up to 70 per cent of electricity demand in Saudi Arabia, for example. With most electricity generation in the Gulf based on fossil-fuel-burning power facilities, growing demands from new industrial facilities, as well as growing urban demands for water and air conditioning, are creating a serious drain on energy reserves.

Inefficient use of resources is thus creating risks to the sustainability of the oil-export-based social welfare systems in Gulf countries. In Saudi Arabia, for example, while today 7 million barrels per day (mbpd) are exported and about 3 mbpd are used locally, some foresee this trend to reverse with 7 mbpd equivalent needed for local needs by as early as 2030. It has been estimated by some that the Gulf could forego about USD500 billion of oil export revenues by 2030 as energy is instead diverted to local needs (Khoday 2011). With the majority of public revenues and budgets based on oil exports, this creates challenges for the sustainability of health, education and other social welfare systems.

The United Arab Emirates (UAE), for example, while also benefiting strongly from oil exports, has made good progress in diversifying its economy, and seeks to engage green economy options as a means of generating a future high-tech knowledge economy, connecting to potential new global markets for green goods and services, and a way of overcoming local risks from waste and water insecurity, among others. This includes a decision to host the regional branch of the Global Green Growth Institute, development of a UAE Green Growth Strategy, hosting a regular World Green Economy Summit started in 2014, and publication of annual 'State of Green Economy' reports. This should serve as inspiration and instigation to other Gulf countries to likewise take a proactive stance on green economy goals as a means of addressing the above-noted constraints.

Country views on green economy continue to evolve and vary within and across regions, as well as within and across governance institutions and among different civil society and private sector stakeholder 'major groups'. Country contexts even within the Arab Gulf differ widely with respect to: development starting points and priorities; political will and stability; institutional capacities; technical, financial and natural resources; and economic structure and position within regional and global markets. As such, there are different pathways for inclusive green economies among the Gulf countries, and approaches should thus be adapted accordingly. As noted in paragraph 56 of the Rio+20 Outcome Document:

> We affirm that there are different approaches, visions, models and tools available to each country, in accordance with its national circumstances and priorities, to achieve sustainable development in its three dimensions ... In this regard, we consider green economy ... as one of the important tools available ... and that it could provide options for policymaking but should not be a rigid set of rules.

The South and the broader development community have already learned much about supporting transitions away from business-as-usual approaches to more inclusive green economy approaches over the past 20 years, including efforts to bring about 'triple wins' for environmental sustainability, social progress and inclusive growth. These experiences are very useful for the Arab Gulf as it pursues new green economy strategies, and are partially captured through a series of ongoing research available through such global forums as the Green Growth Knowledge Platform and the Best Practice Initiative. A range of United Nations (UN) and partner programmes are contributing to this diverse and growing set of demand-driven country-based evidence and knowledge for supporting inclusive green economy, poverty reduction and sustainable development planning.[4]

Through these and related fora, several key messages and priorities have emerged, including the need for:

(i) Strengthening institutional capacities and governance systems;
(ii) Identifying issues of political economy;
(iii) Operationalising inclusive green economy approaches through inclusive green economy toolkits;
(iv) Reinforcing links between the sustainable development agenda and multi-dimensional poverty;
(v) Meaningfully engaging stakeholders, including governments, civil society and the private sector;
(vi) Empowering of vulnerable groups; and
(vii) Measuring development progress in a way that looks across the three strands of sustainable development.

Achieving inclusive green economy goals in the resource-rich context of the GCC

The starting point for greening the local economy in RRCs, including the member states of the Gulf Cooperation Council (GCC), is a complex web of challenges shaped by internal, mixed internal-external and external factors (see Table 11.1). Most relevant to the GCC states are the following:

Table 11.1 Summary of factors defining resource-rich countries' (RRC) use of wealth, management and inclusion pathways

Internal factors	Internal/external mixed	External	Country/policy examples globally	Relevance for GCC
Few RRCs are just RRCs. They face other challenges such as political fragility. There are more than 30 post-conflict and more than 30 mineral-dependent economies.	Political fragility could lead to power being centred in the hands of a minority but also be a vulnerability exploited by external actors. Such a concentration of few actors makes for a balance of power favouring the private sector (MacLennan 2013).		The Democratic Republic of Congo is an LDC, a post-conflict state and mineral-dependent while Trinidad and Tobago is mineral-dependent while neither post-conflict nor seen as necessarily fragile (Ross 2007). In South Africa, the world's largest gold producer with a global share of 17% of new mined production (Infomine 2014), there are over 500 companies in operation. On the other hand, in Suriname and Angola there were two and one respectively (Infomine 2014).	GCC member states are generally stable but are surrounded by countries in varying states of conflict and fragility. Concentration of GDP and development in relatively few sectors. Highly export dependent for income.
In some cases, the economy itself may be relatively underdeveloped or with limited pre-existing diversification and/ or structures for diversification		This can then result in resource wealth combining with labour-importing which limits the gateway doors to inclusion that labour has usually provided	Angola's economy is dominated largely by oil. The oil sector accounts for more than 80% of exports and the majority of government receipts. In recent years, while dips in revenues have occurred, diversification and growth in new sectors remains limited. Revenues from taxes rely almost solely on one type of tax. Tunisia and Egypt (Ban 2011). This volatile mix is also seen in recent tensions in Southern Africa, particularly in the mining sector, where repeated protests have affected operations as well as profits (Kings 2013).	Can make it difficult to initiate and develop niche areas
The areas where such resource wealth is concentrated are usually poor, or even the poorest part of the country, creating an underlying spatial inclusivity gap and an inclusive growth deficit				Non-urban areas tend to lag behind more urbanised areas in GCC states

Table 11.1 (cont.)

Internal factors	Internal/external mixed	External	Country/policy examples globally	Relevance for GCC
Poor records of translating resource wealth into well-balanced resource management strategies linked to appropriate social investment which builds human capital (Sayeh 2011).	Yet even where there may be interest in investing differently, current international environmental finance instruments do little to enable social investment or connections between economic, social and environmental sectors	Resource wealth is and increasingly a trans-boundary issue. Analysis by the Economist Intelligence Unit (2011) speculated that the growth of China's urban expansion will continue for some years, influencing the availability and the cost of several commodities including copper and aluminium.	GCC member states also tend to rank highly in some areas. Generally, the outliers to this trend are Small Island Developing States which have traditionally invested heavily in health and education – often more so than other countries both resource-rich and non-resource-rich (Perch and Roy 2010).	The Small Island Developing States' reality is important for Bahrain. High human development is often built on highly resource-consumptive economic sectors and reliant on consistent demand from external markets. Most GCC states are in the high or very high human development bracket of the 2014 Human Development Report. This urban expansion in China is also likely to drive demand for oil which is linked to construction and in transport as well as the intensified use of plastics. Moreover, China is expected to become the main export and import partner of GCC countries by 2020 (EIU 2010).

Source: Authors based on various sources

- High dependence on hydrocarbon-based gross domestic product (GDP). Most GCC member states have less than a 50 per cent non-hydrocarbon GDP share (except for Bahrain and the UAE) (IMF 2011).
- Concentration of GDP in relatively few sectors.
- Spatial inclusivity gap in terms of where production is generated versus the state of development in those areas (uneven development).
- The transboundary nature of this kind of resource wealth, including a reliance on external demand and the influence of global trade patterns, which affect the fiscal space and the pace of green economy actions.

In the oil-rich Gulf, local industry and non-oil export revenue are often focused on industries that benefit from cheap energy, including: energy-intensive manufacturing, for example petrochemicals, plastics and aluminium; mining and mineral-based industries; trade and logistics; and tourism, hospitality and aviation (IMF 2011). All of these are amongst the most carbon-intensive sectors and the key target sectors for greening economies (UNEP 2011).

Furthermore, also a result of its energy wealth, the Arab Gulf now hosts some of the planet's fastest rates of energy intensity growth. Green economy and sustainability strategies and policies have arisen in this context, with all Arab Gulf countries now moving ahead with new policies and measures to reduce energy intensity of growth through energy efficiency and renewable energy measures, and to expand use of water conservation and water reuse, among others. Saudi Arabia, for example, has made public elements of a new national renewable energy action plan, with USD100 billion to be mobilised to rapidly expand solar energy, to 20 per cent of the energy mix by 2030, while in 2012, the UAE launched a new Green Economy Initiative meant to position the country in the future as a global pioneer in the green economy as well as a hub for new high-tech knowledge economy growth.

Using the relative share of non-hydrocarbon GDP to hydrocarbon GDP as an indicator of the extent of greening at a structural level and of diversification, one can say that GCC economies are still at relatively early stages. Non-hydrocarbon GDP still has a relatively low share in most countries, and the regionalisation of such efforts is also low (Cevik 2014), and has not consolidated into a regional strategic pillar for future development. Analysis of 2010 data and for the previous two decades suggests that:

- In 2010, the non-hydrocarbon GDP of the UAE, which has the most sweeping suite of renewable energy policies, was higher than it had been in 1990 but less than in 2000.
- Bahrain, which started out with a non-hydrocarbon GDP of 81 per cent, now has a 75 per cent share, while the other four countries (Kuwait, Oman, Qatar and Saudi Arabia) have less than 50 per cent of their GDP derived from non-hydrocarbon sources.

A more recent report by the Institute of International Finance (2014) provides further evidence of middling to low progress on expanding non-oil growth in the GCC countries, with generally low levels of revenues from non-oil sources observed. Qatar and the UAE appear to be performing better on non-hydrocarbon expansion than other GCC members. Hydrocarbon revenues represent, on average, 84 per cent of budget receipts for the GCC although the contribution of oil and gas to real GDP seems to be at about 33 per cent (ibid.). With a clear target for reducing the oil intensity of growth in its 2030 Vision, the Emirate of Abu Dhabi provides a possible model for other GCC countries to follow, in other words, taking the GCC countries towards the type of oil-based growth that Norway has managed to achieve.

Progress but insufficient progress

Some policy reforms are already under way or forthcoming in the Gulf, but are often seen as lacking results to date. For example, Dubai aims to rank as one of the world's top ten sustainable cities by 2020 (*The National* 2013). Qatar similarly aims to generate 2 per cent of its electricity from renewable energy by 2020 (MOEI 2012). Kuwait's targets cover solar PV, wind and concentrated solar power (CSP), with targets set for 2030, and those of Saudi Arabia include, among others, a major solar energy (PV and CSP) rollout, as well as deployment of geothermal and waste-to-energy conversion (REN21 2014). Overall, though the GCC countries, particularly in the UAE and Qatar, have made significant policy commitments to expanding energy options, the rate of implementation is still deemed by some as slow, including Burck *et al.* (2014), who have examined Saudi Arabia.

Moreover, there is some evidence of a policy shift in negotiating politically sensitive aspects of the shift to green economy pathways in RRCs. Particular indicators of ambition are shifts in the promotion of fossil fuel dependence within the economy. Traditionally, the oil sector has benefited greatly from state subsidies, which often create a GDP diversification burden for the GCC countries and disincentivise many green economy options. Recent policy shifts in Kuwait on the removal or reduction in fossil fuel subsidies to diesel suggest a willingness to tackle some of the tougher dimensions of greening, namely, disincentivising the use of fossil fuels (IMF 2014). At the same time in Kuwait, it has been estimated that there is continuing growth in non-hydrocarbon GDP, estimated by one source to have reached 2 per cent over the past few years (ibid.).

Limited progress in 'greening' in a RRC context is evident in three areas: (i) the mismatch between current approaches and the political economy realities of resource-rich economies; (ii) scarce and exceptional pockets of political innovation despite a body of knowledge that suggests this would be fundamental; and (iii) the challenge of sustaining action and keeping upward momentum on non-hydrocarbon-based sources of green growth. Green growth practices are often unsuited to the political realities of many RRCs. The green economy narrative is still largely 'economic' with real inclusion lingering at the edges, arising in exceptions rather than as a transformation into a new 'business as usual' (Saad and Perch 2014).

In a critical area for the GCC member states, the removal of fossil fuel subsidies, which have been one of the main forms of inclusion in oil wealth, the available guidance is limited in terms of the practical politics of such actions, and lessons from other countries provide evidence of the need for caution. This is evident in the reversals of plans for reductions or eliminations in other countries between 2008 and 2013, as noted by the International Monetary Fund (IMF 2013). It is also visible in some of the unintended consequences from fossil fuel subsidy reduction in Mexico, which may turn out effective on the low-carbon scale but could generate additional health issues due to the sulphur content of alternatives that poorer households are now using.

Furthermore, there is the prospect of and for green jobs. According to some estimates, 600 million productive jobs (ILO 2012, 9) will need to be created in the next decade. The ones generated from green economy strategies, including in the energy sector, according to an analysis by Burkolter and Perch (2014), are more likely to be generated indirectly rather than directly.

Limited political innovation: The lack of political innovation is potentially the most significant challenge to resource-rich economies. Giddens (2010) has made the point that there is a need not just for economic but also social and political innovation. He argues convincingly that 'there is too much focus on technology at present and that social, political and economic innovation is far more important'. This gap still remained at the time of writing in 2014. If compared with other RRCs such as the Democratic Republic of Congo, Mongolia, Morocco, Nigeria, Trinidad and Tobago and Norway, the GCC countries are pursuing relatively common approaches in greening their energy economy. The GCC member states have concentrated much of their renewable energy efforts in the area of public finance, according to analysis in the latest global renewables status report by REN21 (2014).[5] This bodes well for a public policy approach to inclusion as well as for maximising the opportunities for jobs through green growth efforts. Of the six countries in the GCC, however, the UAE has by far the most expansive and comprehensive approach – including financial incentives to promote both alternatives and make carbon intensity less profitable, as well as public financing and regulatory policies (see Table 11.2).

As in most RRCs, it is more common to find incentives for the generation of green solutions like renewable energy, and less common to find disincentives for more hydrocarbon-based or carbon-intensive activities, which is understandable given that the latter also provide the fiscal space for green economy innovation. This is an important lesson for the GCC countries, as are the political challenges that have arisen in several countries attempting to make such changes.

Sustaining action: Through the lens of the trends in the share of non-hydrocarbon GDP as a share of GDP between 1990 and 2010, some insights are available on this issue. This matter is a critical one given some of the collapses that have accompanied some large-scale, seemingly innovative and game-changing reforms in other resource-rich contexts, for example Ecuador. The issue of relevance is the foregoing of income from hydrocarbon sources and its replacement by other

Table 11.2 Renewable energy promotion policies in the GCC and other resource-rich countries

Countries		Financial incentives			Public financing		Regulatory policies				
		Capital subsidy, grant or rebate	Tax incentives	Energy production payment	Public investment, loans or financing	Public competitive bidding	Feed-in tariff	Utility quota obligation	Net metering	Obligation and mandate	Trade renewable energy certificate (REC)
GCC countries	Bahrain										
	Kuwait				×						
	Oman			×	×	×					
	Qatar					×					
	Saudi Arabia										
	UAE			×	×	×					
Other RRCs	Democratic Republic of the Congo	×						×		×	
	Mongolia										
	Morocco				×	×	×				
	Nigeria	×	×		×		×			×	
	Trinidad and Tobago	×	×		×						
	Norway	×	×		×	×		×		×	×

Source: REN21 (2014)

means, as well as the kind of political and other commitments needed to make this happen and sustain such action.

Until its cancellation in 2013 by the President of Ecuador, the Yasuni Ishpingo Tambococha Tiputini Trust Fund (Yasuni ITT Trust Fund), or the Yasuni ITT, was often touted as a good example of public-private sector partnership. It also had the potential to serve as a political innovation – gathering a cross-sectoral coalition at the national level (Wallace 2013) as well as at the international level – and potentially ushering in a unique way of greening that went beyond the sectoral approach. Its collapse in mid-2013 (*Record* 2013) underscores the complexity of sustaining policy action.

Not so dissimilarly, there are wavering trends in the GCC countries to sustain momentum in greening economies. Bahrain's non-hydrocarbon GDP has declined slightly, and neither Kuwait, Oman, Qatar nor Saudi Arabia have been able to take their non-hydrocarbon GDP to above 50 per cent, maintain that threshold and keep it growing. Achieving parity and advancing towards a declining share of hydrocarbon-based GDP is one of the immediate challenges facing green economy efforts in RRCs, as is doing so in a way that does not pass the burden directly on to the population.

Signposts for more green economy intensity

The preceding analysis highlights both opportunities and challenges for green transformations and new forms of innovation, particularly when the frame of analysis is extended to a global one. The GCC's efforts do not, and will not, occur in a vacuum, and they also need to be complementary with other efforts. Three issues are noteworthy in this context: (i) the renewed focus on resource-driven development in many parts of the world; (ii) complementary advances in corporate social responsibility, which creates an enabling environment for public-private sector partnership for green economy goals; and (iii) increasing momentum and innovative financing experiments linked to, and around, the post-2015 development and SDG agendas.

Growing social responsibility interest and action by the private sector

Movement from the private sector through the efforts of the Ethical Corporation, a sustainability business intelligence company, including its Responsible Extractives Summit (see Box 11.2), the 2 Degrees network and a number of other home-grown initiatives suggest that RRCs would have partners in the private sector and would not necessarily be working uphill or alone. Companies like Rio Tinto, Unilever and Hess have shown growing commitment to social performance and environmental risk management, which would help to ensure that green growth efforts would deliver for both people and nature, and for both communities and nations as a whole. The focus of the Responsible Extractives Summit in 2014 (Ethical Corporation 2014) potentially provided the kind of momentum needed to consolidate operational definitions for inclusive green growth in a resource extractive context and to operationalise it.

Box 11.2. Excerpt from the Responsible Extractives Summit 2014

- **Maximise shared value:** Achieve greater collaboration with host governments to aid development and secure political stability.
- **Mitigate human rights impacts:** Overcome the challenges to removing human rights risks from your security, supply chain and business practice.
- **Optimise your social risk management strategy:** Hear the latest approaches companies are using to build trust with communities and minimise risk of social disturbance to operations.
- **Mitigate water risk to operational continuity:** Learn the latest strategies to manage competing interests for water through best practice stakeholder engagement.
- **Ensure financial viability through sustainability:** Understand investor, lender and insurer needs to make your company a low-risk venture, long-term investment and viable business partner.

The SDGs design process and the post-2015 agenda

Once their design is finalised in 2015, the SDGs are expected to serve as internationally agreed objectives that will be underpinned by targets. Applicable to all countries unlike the MDGs, the SDGs should also reflect the realities and priorities at national levels and a three-pillar approach to sustainable development, serving as a tool for guiding public policies. Leveraging the SDG process during its design stages could ground the discourse politically and socially in ways not as yet seen, and furthermore could allow for emerging Gulf actors to leverage their green economy actions for broader results, and particularly their international elements. Clean energy and water resources would be key focus areas for such engagement, including the energy-water nexus, which is a major priority for green economy goals in the Gulf.

Looking forward

A number of recommendations start to emerge for resource-rich economies:

- a specific service line of support to green economy transitions in resource-rich economies that allows for adaptable, tailored interventions;
- enabling South-South multilateral cooperation and partnership between resource-rich economies; and
- twinning support programmes that support North-South and South-South bilateral partnership, for example between Norway and Arab and African states which are oil-dependent, cooperation between Arab states and SIDS on sustainable energy and water access, and between old and new oil

producing countries, for example Norway, other Arab states, Brazil, Chad, Ghana, Nigeria and others.

On balance, there is still a limited good practice canvas from which to shape 'inclusive' green economy lessons for the Arab Gulf or resource-rich economies in general. This does, however, provide a space for emergent Gulf actors to shape the global script and good practice in this area.

Overall, one significant question faces RRCs in the Arab Gulf. With limited choices and alternatives, particularly if alternatives mean having to out-compete pre-existing markets, should their green economy of necessity look like that of other countries, and even other RRCs, or do Gulf-specific or hybrid options exist?

The Arab Gulf and global partnerships for a green economy

One factor for success in the global drive to a green economy future will be the extent to which local uptake of green economy policies and actions will also translate into new global partnerships between emerging economies and developing countries around the world. As leaders in the South emerge as some of the largest new sources of SSC, ODA and ODI, their outward investments into developing countries of Africa, Asia and the Americas are starting to have important implications for issues of energy, land and water use, toxic pollution, climate change and other green economy-related issues. This has special relevance to emerging partners from the Arab Gulf.

A significant share of Arab Gulf outward ODA and ODI is related to natural assets like energy, minerals and agriculture, with their expanding footprint shaping not only trends of ecological change and social development in less developed countries, but also opportunities to advance global goals for an inclusive, green economy. Sustainable development issues are starting to be integrated into ODA and ODI strategies as it is increasingly recognised that new South-South processes linked to the Gulf could be leveraged for the benefit of developing countries across the South as the world enters a more multipolar era of sustainable development cooperation.

The power of South-South development cooperation is potentially significant, given its estimated value at about USD12–15 billion/year. According to the UN Secretary General report on 'Trends and Progress in International Development Cooperation', in recent years, the world has seen a 78 per cent rise in South-South development cooperation (UN 2012). In many cases, countries have now included SSC within overall foreign policy frameworks while some have established formal aid agencies, policies and programmes (UNDP 2011). Examples include the Turkish International Cooperation and Development Agency, the Indian Development Cooperation Agency with lines of credit now valued at USD8.5 billion for 58 developing countries, the Malaysian Technical Cooperation Programme with partnerships in 140 countries achieving over 9 per cent of gross national income (GNI) to SSC in 2010, and the Thai International Development Agency, with over 11 per cent of GNI to SSC (UN 2012). Joint approaches among countries of the South are also on the rise, such as the recent launch of the BRICS Development Bank, which has an important focus on sustainable development issues.

Arab development partners have growing importance as well. Saudi Arabia and the UAE are already among the world's largest Southern providers of development cooperation, and are also to some extent expanding their policy influence and financial support globally on issues of sustainable energy, land and water use, natural resource development, climate change and other green economy-related themes.

Kuwait, Qatar, Saudi Arabia, Oman and the UAE, while often under-examined, have been important players in global development for many years, and as the global development agenda shifts towards issues of sustainable development so too their outward cooperation strategies of Arab Gulf partners likewise are starting to move in this direction. The Arab Gulf has a strong history of SSC. From 1973 to 2008, Arab ODA stood at about 1.5 per cent of GNI on average, double the target of 0.7 per cent set by the UN for Organisation for Economic Co-operation and Development (OECD) members (Denney and Wild 2011). Saudi Arabia, Kuwait and the UAE all have dedicated international development agencies and, since the 1970s, have channelled ODA to developing countries across the Arab, African and Asian regions. Kuwait was the first among Gulf countries to establish a dedicated international development agency, the Kuwait Fund for Arab Economic Development, launched in 1961, followed by the Abu Dhabi Fund for Development in the UAE, in 1971, and the Saudi Fund for Development, in 1974. While the countries of the Arab Gulf have not often figured prominently in analyses of development cooperation trends, they are also playing an increasingly important role in global policy dialogues over the nature of global policy and cooperation for development, climate change, sustainable energy, water and other issues of importance for the shift to a green economy.

According to OECD statistics, Saudi Arabia is the largest Arab provider of ODA, with over USD3 billion in annual contributions in recent years, reaching the same levels as Italy, Denmark, Australia and Belgium (OECD 2011). The UAE records about USD1 billion each year per OECD statistics while Kuwait has reached over USD500 million annually. According to the OECD, in 2010 the UAE started reporting its ODA to the group for the first time and was the first non-DAC donor to report to the DAC Creditor Reporting System in a detailed manner, while Saudi Arabia and Kuwait have also started reporting to the OECD system as part of the non-Development Assistance Committee (DAC) donor group. ODA policies and strategies are also increasingly coordinated and harmonised among countries through the Arab Coordination Group (ibid.). In the group's recent meetings (Kuwait 2009, Vienna 2010 and London 2011), Gulf members expressed interest in learning from other ODA providers in the European Union and beyond, and in exploring collaborations in emerging global priority areas such as food security, sustainable energy for the poor and climate change.

Recent years have also seen the Gulf host a number of international platforms for moving forward the global sustainability agenda. These include the 2008 Riyadh Declaration on Energy for Development, the 2012 UN Climate Change Conference in Doha, the 2014 Arab States' South-South Development Expo, with a core focus on climate change, energy and water, in Doha, the 2014 World Green Economy Summit and 2014 Abu Dhabi Ascent on Climate Change, both in the UAE, and numerous annual gatherings, such as the World Future Energy Summit and the World Food Security Summit. Through these and many other processes the Gulf has sought to use its convening power as an increasingly influential player in global dialogues.

The Gulf is also starting to move from dialogue to action by investing in global solutions. The Saudi-based Islamic Development Bank (IsDB), the major multilateral channel of Arab Gulf ODA, is for the first time launching an energy strategy to guide its ODA, with an important focus on ways to achieve sustainable energy and low-carbon goals in recipient countries in Africa, Asia and the Arab region. IsDB also took an important step at the 20th Anniversary of UN Conference on Sustainable Development (Rio+20) by joining a new global endeavour to scale up low-carbon, sustainable transport options together with other international financial institutions. The Organization of the Petroleum Exporting Countries (OPEC) Fund for International Development (OFID) is also playing a role, having scaled up assistance to developing countries in recent years as part of a broad USD1 billion commitment to support sustainable energy access for the poor. In 2014, OFID committed to 139 million in funding to 35 developing countries with a focus on the 'water-food-energy nexus' (OFID 2014a), a nexus critical to inclusive green economy efforts. A significant number of these interventions directly target the agriculture sector and in particular smallholder farmers, for example in Lesotho. Ten grants at the same time also support non-governmental actors, including UN agencies, in linking renewable energy access to livelihoods, including in Gaza, Kenya, Tanzania and Zambia. A number of facilities have also been established to promote access to finance renewable energy proliferation and adaptation by specific vulnerable groups (OFID 2014b).

In parallel to Arab multilateral channels, progress is also evident at the level of bilateral ODA. For Saudi Arabia for example, in addition to being the largest stakeholder in Arab multilateral entities, with about 25 per cent of overall budgets for IsDB and OFID, scope is also arising for green measures within its bilateral assistance programmes. The Saudi Fund for Development (SFD), for example, is a large global provider of assistance to developing countries for infrastructure cooperation, with potential to integrate low-carbon sustainable energy and water conserving measures, with lessons to be had from the experiences emerging from China and elsewhere, as touched on above. Meanwhile, SFD is one of the world's largest providers of humanitarian assistance, with important scope to integrate issues like sustainable energy, water security and waste management into crisis response programming for vulnerable communities. These issues are often the most pressing ones for refugees and forced migrants for example,

254 K. Khoday et al.

with an important opportunity for partners like SFD, as well as Saudi Arabian foundations, to integrate green solutions to energy and water access, and waste management.

The UAE has gone a step further by formally integrating low-carbon sustainable energy goals into its outward ODA strategies. This now includes more than USD400 million of assistance from the Abu Dhabi Fund for Development to help expand renewable energy in developing countries, an initiative undertaken in concert with the International Renewable Energy Agency (IRENA), which is hosted by the UAE after the government successfully competed with other potential host countries around the world. As the first global multilateral agency to be hosted in the Arab region, IRENA also marks an important milestone as to the important role the region can play in the future in supporting global capacities and institutional systems for green economy-related goals. With the UAE having also succeeded recently in its bid to host the 2020 World Expo, partners are likewise keen on integrating green economy and sustainability measures to make the expo a green one to share the emerging vision of Arab Gulf partners to support global efforts in this regard.

Lastly, while most Arab ODA has traditionally operated through Arab multilateral platforms and Gulf countries' own bilateral development agencies, there are benefits to be had from increasing connectivity with other Southern providers of ODA, like China. The centre of gravity in the global economy is rapidly shifting East, and this also causes shifting in the lines of development cooperation. At the 2012 World Future Energy Summit in the UAE for example, Chinese Premier Wen Jiabao committed to strengthening not only conventional oil trade with the Gulf but also cooperation between China and the Arab Gulf on clean energy technology development and deployment, and such a new partnership could have dividends for broader global goals.

With Asia-Africa partnerships growing in importance for future development goals, and with the Arab region increasingly looking to cooperation with Asia for new growth and innovation potentials, including on sustainable energy, water and related initiatives, strategic linkages could be made in the future between Asian and Arab providers of ODA. This could be a powerful force for the common goal of supporting new development solutions in Africa for example, with Arab and Asian ODA providers both expected to scale up support to Africa in the post-2015 era. New partnerships among development partners of Asia, Africa and Arab regions could one day help reconnect age-old routes of trade, cooperation and innovation, and maybe even forge a 'new silk road' of development solutions.

Conclusion

With a focus on innovation for sustainable pathways, green economy solutions at their core address both opportunities and risks. They can help create new high-tech sectors in energy, water and smart city spheres, while also at the same time reducing the serious climate, food, water and energy risks facing the world.

Beyond being mere externalities to economic growth, in coming years such risks will bring serious challenges to the core of the world's economies, including those of the Gulf. Pursuing effective green economy responses is thus about more than technology and finance; it is also about rethinking the foundations of development and growth in the GCC. New long-term visions for a green economy pathway among some actors in the Gulf hold hope in this regard.

The set of challenges and opportunities highlighted in this chapter are a call to action for those institutions in the Gulf region, and indeed for like-minded countries across the South, aiming to emerge as global thought and action leaders and respected voices in a shifting and increasingly green world economy. The elaboration of local green economy strategies in the Gulf is also coupled with a growing commitment to becoming a global partner to other countries in the South.

A particular theme of relevance for the region is the tension between *evolution* and *revolution* in pursuing change. The Arab region has experienced great debates in recent years on how this applies to political and social change, but less so on the perhaps equally important topic of how countries and communities govern and manage their natural assets and future sustainability. As noted by some commentators, given the serious trends of energy, water and food insecurity across the Arab region, new green approaches to development and growth need to be factored into new thinking locally among policy makers and leaders in the economy, especially among the new generation of leadership. This should go well beyond the mere repackaging of standard paradigms of reform and progress from the past towards ambitious transitions at this critical turning point and crossroads for the region's environment, society and economy.

Pursuing a green economy future in the Arab Gulf likely needs both evolutionary and revolutionary dynamics in terms of a new era of development policy to engage issues of both sustainability and equity in resource governance. Innovation is key to the region's future. Entrepreneurship which brings together economic, social and environmental strands of development will need to accompany the standard forms of economic recovery and growth being pursued, and such entrepreneurship needs to be social and political as well as economic. As such, confident and proactive governments can play a pivotal role on a GCC green economy agenda.

Current economic drivers, such as the opportunity costs in the Arab Gulf from growing diversion of oil resources away from exports to surging local electricity and water generation, are both key drivers towards a green economy transition, but may be insufficient in and of themselves to advance a true and lasting transformation in development and growth policy. Though commitment to green economy-related approaches is steady and growing in the Arab Gulf, its pace and scale still lags behind those of ongoing investments in traditional sectors. Leveraging the public policy agenda for green economy approaches to development is one of the key areas where value-added lies in future international cooperation with the Arab Gulf. Learning from green economy movers in the Gulf will be key to doing so, including through linking aspiring leaders in the Gulf to global partnerships for green economy and SSC.

Notes

1 The opinions expressed are those solely of the authors and do not necessarily represent those of the UNDP, the RIO+ Centre, the UN or its Member States.
2 Based on initial findings from a series of UN-facilitated global and regional dialogues with national green economy stakeholders.
3 Other seminal pieces of the resource curse literature include Gelb and associates (1988), Sachs and Warner (1995), Ross (1999) and Auty (2001). Important pieces put forward by NGOs include Global Witness (1999), Christian Aid (2003) and Gary and Karl (2003). For the full names of the works see Bagattini (2011).
4 This evidence includes: (i) recommendations from a series of UNDP-DESA-UNEP inter-regional dialogues held in Dakar, Bangkok and Nairobi in 2012 and 2013 with over 200 government, civil society and resource experts from 50 countries on Rio+20 and follow-up; (ii) UNDP and UNDESA, Synthesis of national reports for Rio+20, published December 2012; (iii) results from the series of regional, national and thematic consultations on emerging post-2015 framework and SDGs, including the UNDG 'A Million Voices: The World We Want' and ES Consultation Report on 'Breaking Down the Silos'; (iv) an evaluation of integrated national policy work drawing on the UNDP-UNEP Poverty Environment Initiative experiences; and (v) experience gained through the MDG Achievement Fund, which supports over 130 UN joint programmes in 50 countries from five regions on various sustainable development themes through integrated policy work and stakeholder engagement at all levels.
5 It should be noted that data was not available for Saudi Arabia and Qatar in this report. However, this was felt to be best applicable in this case since comparability with other countries is implied in its methodology and relevant for the analysis in this section.

References

Bagattini, Gustavo Y. 2011. The Political Economy of Stabilisation Funds: Measuring Their Success in Resource-Dependent Countries. IDS Working Paper 356. Sussex: Institute for Development Studies.

Ban, Ki-Moon. 2011. Young People Vital to Sustainable Development. New York: UN.

Burck, Jan, Franziska Marten and Christoph Bals. 2014. The Climate Change Performance Index 2014. Bonn: Germanwatch.

Burkolter, Pablo, and Leisa Perch. 2014. 'Greening Growth in the South: Practices, Policies and New Frontiers.' South African Journal of International Affairs 09/2014, 21(2): 235–259. London.

Cevik, Serhan. 2014. 'Without Oil, How Do Gulf Countries Move? Non-hydrocarbon Business Cycles.' Journal of Economic Integration 29(2). Washington D.C.

Denney, Lisa, and Leni Wild. 2011. EDC 2020 Policy Brief – Arab Donors: Implications for Future Development Cooperation. London: Overseas Development Institute.

EIU. The Economist Intelligence Unit. 2010. The GCC in 2020: Broadening the Economy. London.

EIU. 2011. Building Rome in a Day: The Sustainability of China's Housing Boom. London: Access China Service.

Ethical Corporation. 2014. Responsible Extractives Summit: Maximise Shared Value and Social Licence Post 2014, London.

Giddens, Anthony. 2010. The Four Mistakes about Green Growth. Green Growth Leaders. Speech at the World Climate Solutions 2010 meeting. Copenhagen, September.

IIF. Institute of International Finance. 2014. GCC: Strong Diversified Growth, Limited Risks. Washington D.C.

ILO. International Labour Organization. 2012. *Global Employment Trends 2012*. Geneva.

IMF. International Monetary Fund. 2011. *Gulf Cooperation Council Countries (GCC): Enhancing Economic Outcomes in an Uncertain Global Economy*. Washington D.C.

IMF. 2013. *Energy Subsidy Reform: Lessons and Implications*. Washington D.C.

IMF. 2014. *Kuwait: Concluding Statement of the 2014 Article IV Consultation*. Washington D.C.

Infomine. 2014. 'Country Profile of South Africa.' Accessed September. http://www.infomine.com/

Karl, Terry Lynn. 1997. *Paradox of Plenty: Oil Booms and Petro States*. Los Angeles: Regents.

Khoday, Kishan. 2011. *Sustainable Development as Freedom*. Background Paper for the 2011 Arab Development Challenges Report, Cairo: UNDP Regional Center.

Kings, Sipho. 2013. 'AngloGold Mine Charged with Radioactive Contamination.' *Mail & Guardian*, South Africa, January.

MacLennan, Michael. 2013. *Locating the Policy Space for Inclusive Green Growth within the SADC Extractive Sector*. Brasília: International Policy Center for Inclusive Growth.

MOEI. Ministry of Energy and Industry of Qatar. 2012. 'Qatar Launches Project to Produce Electricity from Solar in Parallel with the COP18.' Accessed 31 October 2013. http://www.mei.gov.qa/

OECD. Organisation for Economic Co-operation and Development. 2011. *Development Cooperation Report – Notes on Non-OECD Providers of Development Co-operation*. Paris.

OFID. Organization of the Petroleum Exporting Countries Fund for International Development. 2014a. 'OFID's Governing Board Approves Fresh Funding to Boost Socio-economic Development in over 35 Partner Countries.' Press release, 23 September. http://www.ofid.org/

OFID. 2014b. *Profile: September 2014*. Austria.

Perch, Leisa, and Rathin Roy. 2010. 'Sustaining Development and Resilience in SIDS: Beyond Crisis Management.' *International Policy Centre for Inclusive Growth* 113. Brasilia.

Record. 2013. 'Conservation V Oil: Ecuador's Yasuni ITT Initiative.' 6 September. http://www.newsrecord.co/

REN21. Renewable Energy Policy Network for the 21st Century. 2014. *Renewables Global Status Report*.

Ross, Michael L. 2007. *Mineral Wealth, Conflict, and Equitable Development*. SSCNet. California.

Saad, Layla, and Leisa Perch. 2014. *Searching for the Social Engine of the Green Growth Locomotive: Green as Social in the New Growth Paradigm*. Working Paper N° 1. Rio de Janeiro: Rio+ World Centre for Sustainable Development, May.

Sayeh, Antoinette. 2011. 'Beyond Growth: The Importance of Inclusion.' *IMF Direct*, 11 July. http://blog-imfdirect.imf.org/

The National. 2013. 'Dubai Aims to Rank among the World's Top 10 Sustainable Cities by 2020.' 16 December. http://www.thenational.ae/

UN. United Nations. 2012. *UN Secretary General Report on Trends in South-South Cooperation*. New York.

UNDP. UN Development Programme. 2011. *Capacity Development for Southern Providers of ODA*. New York.

UNEP. UN Environment Programme. 2011. *Towards a Green Economy. Pathways to Sustainable Development and Poverty Eradication (A Synthesis for Policy Makers)*. Geneva.

Wallace, Scott. 2013. 'Rainforest for Sale.' *National Geographic Magazine*, January.

Index

Made in the USA
Las Vegas, NV
05 September 2021